Castles in the Sand

Castles in the Sand

A City Planner in Abu Dhabi

MICHAEL CAMERON DEMPSEY

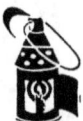

McFarland & Company, Inc., Publishers
Jefferson, North Carolina

LIBRARY OF CONGRESS CATALOGUING-IN-PUBLICATION DATA

Dempsey, Michael Cameron, 1980–2013
Castles in the sand : a city planner in Abu Dhabi / Michael Cameron Dempsey.
p.   cm.
Includes bibliographical references and index.

ISBN 978-0-7864-7760-9 (softcover : acid free paper) ∞
ISBN 978-1-4766-1319-2 (ebook)

1. City planning—Abu Zaby (United Arab Emirates : Emirate)
2. Cities and towns—Abu Zaby (United Arab Emirates : Emirate)
3. Abu Zaby (United Arab Emirates : Emirate)—History.
4. Cities and towns—Growth. I. Title.

HT169.U48D46 2014   307.1'216095357—dc23   2013048597

BRITISH LIBRARY CATALOGUING DATA ARE AVAILABLE

On the cover: Bulldozers lined up in front of Aldar's
"HQ" headquarters at Raha Beach (courtesy Curt Bidinger);
background image: Sand dunes along the edge of the
Empty Quarter near Liwa (Michael Dempsey)

Manufactured in the United States of America

*McFarland & Company, Inc., Publishers
Box 611, Jefferson, North Carolina 28640
www.mcfarlandpub.com*

To my family
for all of their love, encouragement, and support

Table of Contents

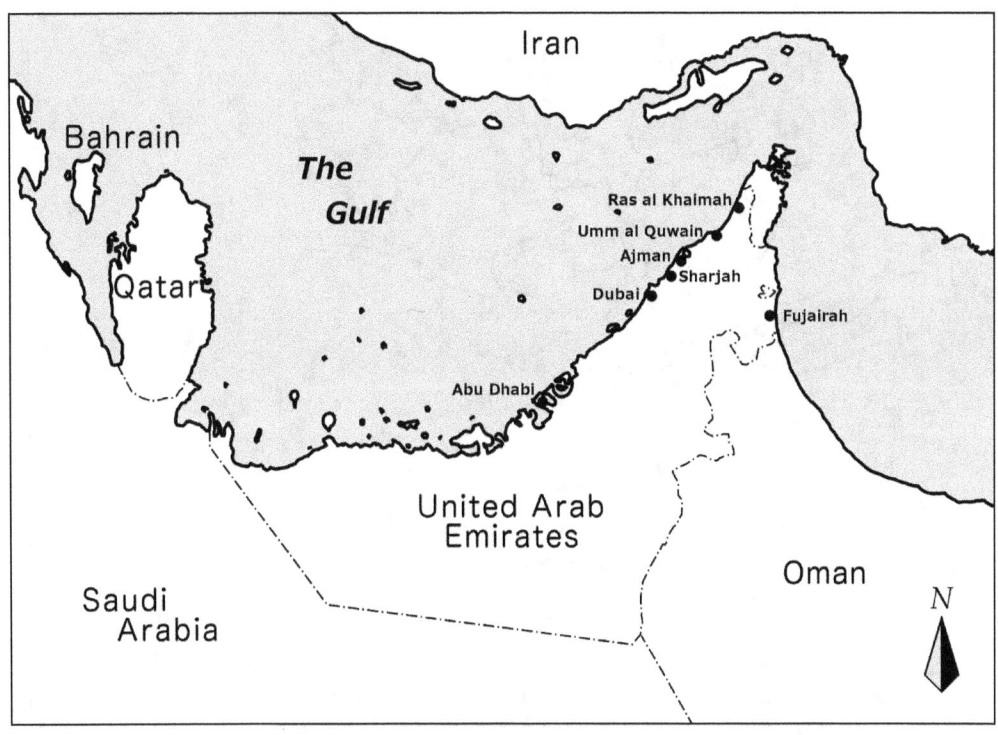

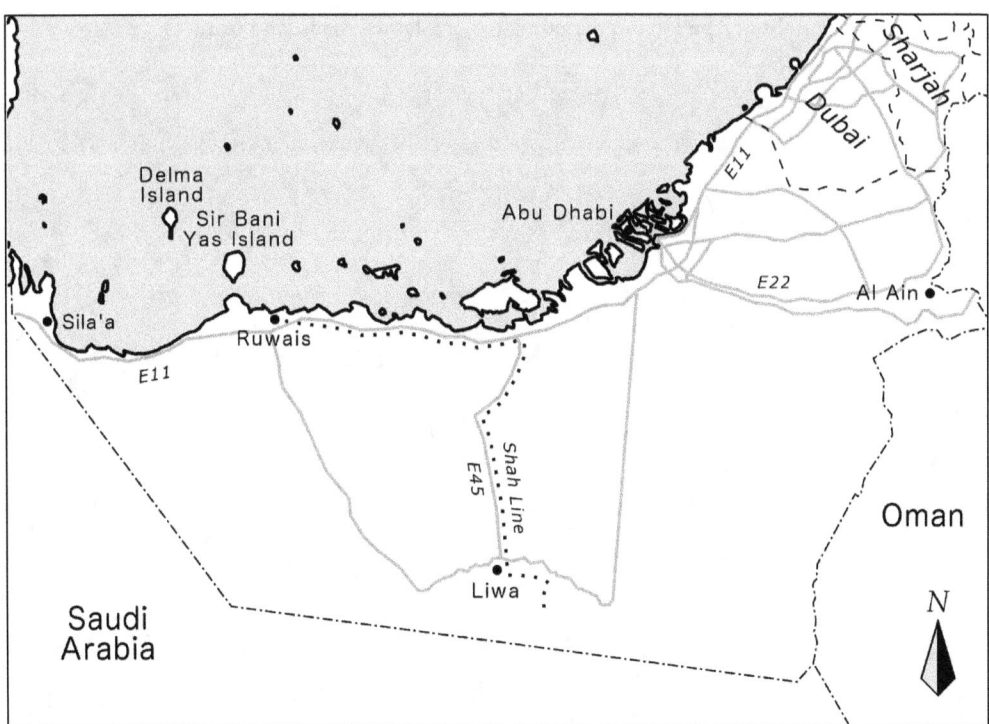

Top: The UAE and its constituent emirates. *Bottom:* The emirate of Abu Dhabi, including major settlements and roads.

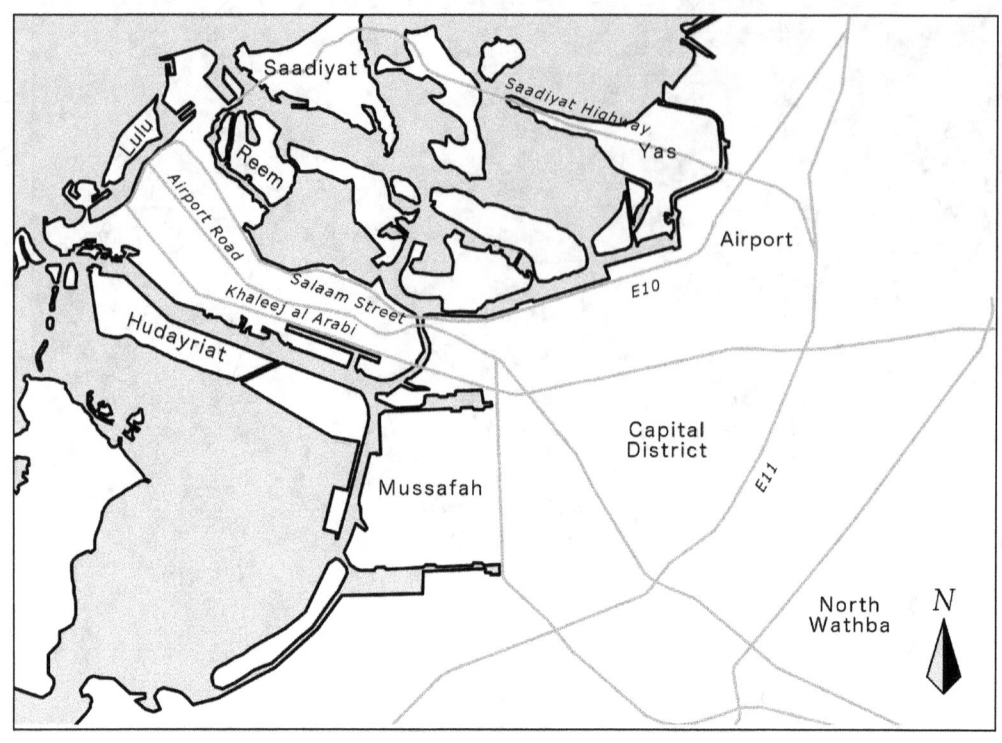

Metropolitan Abu Dhabi, including major islands, roads, and features.

Preface

This book is not, in the strictest sense, a work of nonfiction. Some of the characters in these pages are composites, and I have changed just about everyone's name for the sake of privacy. Though I have tried to recount conversations as best as I can recall them, I may have occasionally put words in others' mouths. I could very well be charged with having embellished or rearranged the order of certain events, to which my only defense is that the passage of time tends to make my memories more colorful.

No single book can claim to paint a comprehensive picture of a city and its people, and I have not attempted such a feat here. Rather, I have tried to give readers a snapshot of Abu Dhabi at a unique and critical juncture. I was privileged to spend just over two years in the city, two years that coincided with the frenzied peak of its transformative boom. I hope my faltering words convey a sense of that fascinating, tumultuous moment in Abu Dhabi's history. Although I have mused at length on Abu Dhabi's people, I am not an anthropologist, and this is not a formal study of their culture. All mistakes in its interpretation are mine alone.

In light of these disclaimers, why should you bother to read this book? For starters, Abu Dhabi is one of the most important places you've probably never been to. This obscure Middle Eastern principality controls one-tenth of the world's oil. It has been called the richest city on Earth, and for good reason: its citizens are worth about seventeen million dollars each.[1] Its stupendously wealthy state investment funds have spent the last decade quietly combing the globe, buying stakes in everything from international banking conglomerates to New York real estate to the Italian supercar manufacturer Ferrari. Abu Dhabi's ongoing experiment in city-building, in addition to being a captivating story in its own right, has profound implications for our increasingly urbanized planet. To my knowledge, no one else has yet attempted to tell that story in narrative form.

Although I intended this to be a contemporary account, I also wanted to let some time pass in order to see how things in Abu Dhabi panned out, so the events recorded herein are already a few years old as of publication. Nevertheless, I believe that the reader will find much that is still true of Abu Dhabi. I hope this modest work might thus serve as a sufficiently broad introduction for the visitor or new arrival to Abu Dhabi—the kind of introduction I wish had been available when I first landed in the emirate. For those readers who have not set foot in Abu Dhabi, I would be honored were this book to succeed in convincing you to pay the emirate a visit and witness for yourselves the remarkable changes taking place there.

Prologue

The desert of southern Iraq at midday was an oven. I sat beneath a canvas shade on the stoop of my trailer and watched the mercury in the thermometer climb skyward. The scenery around me was bleak. A row of trailers identical to mine stretched off to one side; a cluster of armored vehicles resembling ice cream trucks from a nightmare were on the other. A layer of thick gravel was strewn across the sand, and a palisade of concrete blast walls hemmed everything in. That was all—no grass, no plants, no colors besides the monotonous beige and gray.

For nearly a year I had called this austere military base home while working as a civilian advisor to a joint American-Iraqi reconstruction team. Now, in early 2009, I was contemplating leaving. I had just been offered a job in Abu Dhabi, an even more remote corner of the Middle East. The little-known principality at the foot of the Arabian Gulf had gone on a building spree, raising skyscrapers and laying down infrastructure in an effort to reinvent itself as an international hub of business and tourism. I had been asked to join the Urban Planning Council, the new government agency in charge of coordinating all the activity. For a city planner like me, it was the opportunity of a lifetime.

My brief career in city-building thus far had been a fluke. Nearly a decade before, I had studied computer science as an undergraduate in my home state of Michigan. By the time I realized I didn't care to toil away the rest of my evenings and weekends in monitor-filled dungeons, it was too late to change majors. So I followed the time-honored tradition of seeking a do-over in graduate school. The university happened to offer a master's program in the arcane field of urban planning, in which I enrolled. Cities had long fascinated me, with their energy, their intricacy, and their juxtaposition of order and chaos. I grew up in the suburbs of Detroit, and my interest was stoked by witnessing that city's postindustrial plight and learning the history of its rise, decline, and repeated attempts at renewal. A career devoted to the shaping of cities, arguably mankind's most complex creations, seemed promising. If nothing else, I figured it would beat a life spent hunting for syntax errors.

Upon finishing graduate school I absconded to Germany, where I began a yearlong postgraduate fellowship studying that nation's particular flavor of urbanism by working at a series of planning agencies. I discovered that the Germanic ardor for order has had a profound impact on the country's settlements, whose development is as tightly controlled as the operation of their ubiquitous public transport systems. German cities are tidy, predictable, seldom beautiful but seldom ugly, and essentially harmless. Much like the Germans themselves.

At the conclusion of my year overseas I returned home with hopes of applying my fledgling skills to Detroit's revitalization. I joined the city's leading development agency at a particularly auspicious time. It had just been charged with transforming a huge swath of the city's waterfront, encompassing more than three hundred acres of former industrial land along the Detroit River, into a new mixed-use district. For the next four years I partook in just about every activity on the redevelopment continuum, from creating a new master plan for the district, to demolishing dilapidated factories and pulling industrial sludge out of the ground, to supervising the design and construction of new infrastructure, and finally to negotiating with developers to fill the district with new real estate. After more than three decades of grand ideas and false starts, Detroit's riverfront was being reborn.

Unfortunately, all of this took place under the most corrupt mayoral administration in Detroit's already sordid history. Just as our agency's efforts were reaching fruition and a slew of new buildings were ready to break ground, a scandal broke that would eventually land the mayor in federal prison. The drama dominated local news for months on end, torpedoing political support for any initiative remotely associated with the mayor and his entourage—including the redevelopment of the riverfront. At the same time, the national housing market began to implode after years of speculative overheating, delivering the coup de grace to our labors by decimating the ranks of prospective buyers for the riverfront's new residential projects. By early 2008, Detroit's nascent riverfront renaissance had ground to a halt.

As the work slowed I decided to look for opportunities elsewhere, and pondered going abroad once more. I happened across a magazine article profiling the Arabian Gulf, where a development bonanza was just taking off—in stark contrast to the doldrums then descending upon the industrialized world. The Gulf's oil sheikhdoms were bankrolling grandiose urban expansions across the board. This was partly in response to having some of the fastest-growing populations in the world; by 2020 the inhabitants of the Gulf were predicted to increase by more than a third. The Gulf's monarchs had their work cut out for them just trying to stay ahead of this curve, but they also seemed to be competing with one another to see who could use his petrodollars to buy the fanciest makeover for his city-state.

At that stage my knowledge of the Gulf was limited to Dubai. I had read story after story about the extravagant desert fantasyland, where new skyscrapers rose from the sands every week and shorelines were remade with fanciful palm-shaped islands visible from space. In every city planner lurks a hint of megalomania; a place like Dubai embodied a tantalizing chance to set it free. Yet it was not Dubai that drew my attention now, but instead Abu Dhabi, a city further down the Gulf coast. All I had known about Abu Dhabi up to that point was that it was the mysterious destination to which Garfield the cat often mailed his counterpart Nermal in the eponymous comic strip.

Its anonymity notwithstanding, Abu Dhabi appeared to be pursuing the Gulf's most ambitious urban transformation by far. Its leaders had announced a plan to remake the city into one of the world's leading centers of commerce and leisure, tripling its size by 2030. They had enticed prominent institutions of culture (the Louvre and Guggenheim museums), education (New York University and the Sorbonne), medicine (the Cleveland Clinic), and media (CNN) to establish franchises in town. But Abu Dhabi was doing more than just raising buildings; it was charting a holistic strategy for growth. Its ruling sheikhs aimed to balance progress and change with tradition, preserving and showcasing Abu Dhabi's character as a traditional Arab city in the midst of rapid development. Abu Dhabi's citizens wanted to retain their proud identity and their cherished culture while embracing the best the modern world had to offer.

This city-scaled experiment would have huge ramifications for an increasingly urbanized world. Perhaps not coincidentally, it was during that same year, 2008, that the United Nations estimated that more than half the world's people would live in cities for the first time in history.[1] Societies around the globe were grappling with the tensions brought about by urbanization's rapid shifts in population—geographic shifts from countryside to city and from wilderness to ward, and also cultural shifts from tents to tenements and from tribesmen to townspeople. Abu Dhabi might be able to offer solutions to these challenges. The city's metamorphosis would be a test case for the "New Urban Order" of the 21st century.

Abu Dhabi was also making sustainability a cornerstone of its growth. In the midst of one of Earth's harshest climates, the city's new incarnation sought to strike a balance with nature. Electricity would come from solar farms and other renewable sources. Extensive mass transit systems and pedestrian networks would offer alternatives to the automobile. New buildings would be constructed with energy-efficient methods, materials, and designs. And instead of pursuing unconstrained, unplanned expansion, Abu Dhabi was taking a more measured and deliberate approach, one that would maximize the efficiency of the city's tens of billions of dollars of new real estate and infrastructure. To coordinate all of this, Abu Dhabi's leaders had established a new agency, the Urban Planning Council, and empowered it with a sweeping mandate to plan and oversee the city's transformation.

In short, for anyone working in the built environment—the fields of architecture, planning, civil engineering, and so forth—Abu Dhabi represented perhaps the most dynamic, innovative, and inspiring spot on Earth. Even China, for all its frenetic urban growth, didn't seem to be pushing the envelope quite as far. And the Urban Planning Council sounded like the place to be, in the very center of all the action. I didn't bother to check whether it was hiring. I simply sent my resume along with a cover letter requesting I be considered for any open position whatsoever. Not surprisingly, I didn't receive a response.

Several months later, as I sat in my office mulling over other ideas, the thought occurred to me that the ongoing conflict in Iraq had supposedly created plenty of reconstruction jobs—perhaps they were in need of planners? I googled *Iraq urban planning jobs* and telephoned the recruiter for the first result.

"Do you want to carry a gun?" she grilled me.

"Not particularly," I responded, unsure what that had to do with planning.

"Good. We get too many people wanting to go over there and play cowboy." She asked me to send in my resume. A few days later she called back to say that I'd been hired, and that I had two weeks to get to Jordan in order to catch my flight to Baghdad.

Admittedly, for someone who makes plans for a living, my course of action was perhaps not all that well thought-out. A local business paper quipped of my departure: "Only in Detroit would someone see a job in Baghdad as a step up."[2]

It wasn't. I spent a month in purgatory at my new employer's compound in Baghdad's Green Zone, waiting for the military to issue me an identification badge. Once it arrived I was shipped south to join a civilian-military reconstruction team on a forlorn base outside the city of Najaf. When I arrived in the spring of 2008, Najaf was relatively calm compared to hotbeds like Basra and Mosul. Fortunate as that was, it also meant the people of Najaf received little attention from either the Iraqi or the American authorities, who were busy spraying money and manpower at fires elsewhere. Our reconstruction team was left with a grab bag of projects ranging from the rehabilitation of a local park to the creation of a vocational training center. While we fussed with these trivialities, Najaf's bigger problems went unaddressed. The city's roads were a mess, its citizens suffered a pronounced housing shortage, and its sputtering grid delivered no more than four hours of electricity a day. Even if we'd had the resources to tackle these challenges, we were hampered by a dearth of reliable partners in the Iraqi government, and by an astonishing quagmire of bureaucracy, indifference, and incompetence in our own chain of command.

Then one day, quite unexpectedly, I received an e-mail from the Abu Dhabi Urban Planning Council, thanking me for my earlier inquiry and inviting me to a phone interview.

I spent the hour-long call running around the Najaf base, trying not to lose the erratic cellular signal while the annoyed interviewers kept cutting in and out. It was a disaster. By the time I hung up, I knew I'd blown my chance at possibly the most interesting job I'd ever come across. More weeks passed and I gave up hope. And then, nearly a year after I had first sent my letter, the Urban Planning Council offered me a job.

Now I sat outside my trailer with a copy of their offer. It quoted a jaw-dropping salary and not much else—no job description, no list of projects I'd work on, nothing about life in Abu Dhabi. Despite my earlier excitement, I was hesitant. I had read great things about Abu Dhabi's transformation, but the character of the place itself was still a mystery.

I also wasn't ready to leave Iraq just yet. My work up to that point had seemed mostly futile, but I'd finally found a project that could make it all worthwhile. The local representative of the Iraqi Ministry of Health had worked with me to identify a dozen critical medical clinics in some of Najaf's poorest areas. Like the rest of the city, the clinics faced recurrent power outages from the decrepit electric grid. I had learned that the U.S. military had funded the installation of solar-powered streetlights in other parts of the country. Though it had taken nearly a month, I'd tracked down the responsible parties at the central headquarters in Baghdad and had persuaded them to pay for solar-powered backup systems for the Najaf clinics, so that they could keep their vital life-support equipment running when the power cut out. It was a makeshift solution, but it would at least provide immediate benefits to some of the city's most vulnerable residents, and it relied on one thing Iraq had in abundance: sunlight. The military promised to give the initiative their full support.

I had sent in the final paperwork more than a month before. Now I was just waiting for headquarters to tell me when the equipment would be delivered. I didn't want to leave until I had at least seen the project get started. At the same time, the Abu Dhabi offer was too alluring to pass up. If I said no, the Urban Planning Council could surely find a dozen other planners more than willing to take my place. I sat on my front step, baking in the heat and weighing the chances that they might prolong their offer if I asked.

I heard the crunch of boots on gravel as a colleague rounded the corner.

"I just got off the phone with Baghdad about the solar panels," he said when he saw me.

"Do they have a delivery date?"

He scowled. "They don't even have a record of the project. There's nothing in the databases. As far as they're concerned, it doesn't exist."

I was stunned. "What? They've been telling us for weeks that it was on the way."

"Yeah, but it's Baghdad. That place is the abyss."

"Can we at least reapply?"

He shook his head. "I asked. This year's cutoff date has already passed. And they might not have funding next year."

I was crestfallen. As my colleague walked away, I wondered how I was going to explain this fiasco to my Iraqi counterpart, who'd been calling me every other day to eagerly inquire when the solar equipment would be delivered.

My hesitation evaporated. Whatever Abu Dhabi was like, it couldn't be more farcical than this. I stood up, went inside, and replied to the Urban Planning Council with a single question: How soon could I start?

One

Origins

Thirty years ago we had no buildings, and when we saw buildings in other countries we used to envy them and wonder how we could convince our people to be satisfied with what they had. —*Sheikh Zayed bin Sultan al Nahyan*[1]

My flight to Abu Dhabi touched down at one in the morning. It is common for long-haul flights in the Gulf to take off and land in the middle of the night. A pilot once told me that this is partly to enable travelers to make early-morning connections in Europe, and partly to save fuel.[2] The Gulf's daytime heat and humidity act as aerodynamic anchors, forcing planes to make longer takeoff runs as they lumber down the runway like overweight albatrosses struggling to get aloft.

The nighttime's relief was limited at best. Walking out of the airport, I felt as though I'd stepped into a sauna. I thought my time in Iraq had conditioned me to Middle Eastern climates, but I was wrong. The blistering temperatures of Iraq's desert were a dry heat. Here along the Gulf coast, the air was sodden and heavy.

It was not just in terms of the time of day that I had arrived in the dark. I knew almost nothing about Abu Dhabi apart from what I'd read of its development boom. I was aware that the city sat on a coastal island roughly a hundred miles from Dubai, that it was the capital of the United Arab Emirates, and that it had a lot of oil. As to Abu Dhabi's history and culture, I was utterly ignorant.

It wasn't for lack of trying. After accepting the Urban Planning Council's offer I had tried to get my hands on more information about Abu Dhabi and its history. I came up with almost nothing. There seemed to be practically no extant literature about the city, past or present, at least in English. This is, as I later came to learn, in no small part because Abu Dhabi's people have little use for written history, for two reasons. First, until about fifty years ago they didn't have much to record, as their way of life had changed little for centuries. And second, history is messy, overflowing with infamy and embarrassments. This is anathema to Abu Dhabi's citizens, who prize social harmony above all else, even if it means sweeping the past under the rug. Over the subsequent two years I spent in Abu Dhabi, I managed to form a sketchy picture of the emirate's history, gleaned from conversations with locals and long-time expatriate residents as well as the handful of written sources I eventually uncovered.[3]

The story of Abu Dhabi is intimately tied to its location on the margin where the Arabian Peninsula meets the Gulf. All cities are functions of their surroundings, and Abu Dhabi is no exception. The environment has shaped the city's form throughout its brief history and continues to influence its character. Few regions on Earth are as barren as Arabia. In the entire peninsular mass east of the Jordan River and south of the Euphrates, an area one-third the size of the continental United States, there flows not a single river—only dry wadi channels that flood during the infrequent rains. Dotted across the desert like afterthoughts are oases where aquifers percolate up through the sands, forming the only inland bodies of water between the Gulf and the Red Sea. At the southern end of the peninsula, igneous crags frame the expanse of trackless, towering dunes known in Arabic as the *Rub Al-Khali*, the Empty Quarter.

Arabia was not always so desolate. Its sands have yielded fossils hinting at the existence of a shallow freshwater sea that covered the peninsula in the Miocene era and teemed with prehistoric marine life. By the time the first humans arrived on the scene those waters had long since vanished, leaving behind a landscape that was hot, arid, and infertile. Even in such an austere setting, however, civilizations were born. In the peninsula's southwest reaches, what is today Yemen, the Sabaean culture grew rich by supplying the ancient world with frankincense and myrrh. Their kingdom built one of the world's first dams at Marib to capture the annual monsoon rains for irrigation,[4] and may have been the homeland of the legendary Queen of Sheba. A thousand years later the Nabateans of northern Arabia traded with the Roman Empire. The magnificent city they carved from solid rock at Petra was lost to the outside world for ages upon their decline, only to be rediscovered in 1812 by the Swiss explorer Burckhardt and later showcased in *Indiana Jones and the Last Crusade.*

No such civilizations arose on Arabia's northeastern shores. The coastal plains along the Arabian Gulf are forbidding, even by the peninsula's standards. Vegetation is scarce amid the featureless terrain of gravelly deserts and caked salt flats. The climate is brutally hot and humid with barely three inches of rain a year. It is one of the least suited places on the face of the earth for human habitation. Yet eastern Arabia has not been able to defy mankind entirely. For millennia the region was home to tribes of hardy desert nomads who called themselves *Bedu*[5] and waged a constant fight for survival in the unforgiving land. Some migrated between the coast and the interior, fishing and diving for pearls along the shores during the cooler months before the overwhelming summer humidity drove them to drier areas inland. Others cultivated dates in the oases along the edge of the Empty Quarter, while still others perpetually wandered the desert with their herds of camels.[6]

Life for the Bedu of eastern Arabia changed little over the ages. In the seventh century of the Common Era their brethren on the far side of the peninsula united under the leadership of a prophet from Mecca, captured his hometown from its idolatrous inhabitants, and fanned out to conquer lands beyond. Their empire at its zenith spanned from the Atlantic to the Indus and gave birth to such advances as algebra and distillation. But even the rise of the Caliphate had little impact on eastern Arabia. The Bedu adopted the new religion of Islam, but otherwise continued life as they had always known it.

Legend has it that one day in the eighteenth century a Bedu hunting party followed a gazelle out onto one of the myriad tidal islands that line the lower Gulf coast. They discovered a brackish but potable spring where the gazelle came to rest. The hunters pitched camp on the site and named it *Abu Dhabi*, Father of the Gazelle. In time the camp became a small settlement of thatched palm-frond *barasti* huts, its population ebbing and flowing with the migrations of the seasons. Even at its peak the hamlet counted no more than a few hundred families as year-round residents. The only permanent structure was the ruler's stone fort, which was called *Qasr al Hosn* and doubled as Abu Dhabi's only landmark.[7] Residents subsisted on fish and whatever else they could obtain by bartering pearls with the seagoing traders who plied the Gulf. Life in Abu Dhabi was difficult, and starvation was not uncommon.

Around the time of Abu Dhabi's founding, the colonial powers of Europe arrived in the Gulf. They jockeyed for position until the British gained the upper hand in the mid-nineteenth century by securing a series of treaties with the coastal sheikhdoms they dubbed the Trucial States.[8] Once the British had established their hegemony over the lower Gulf, they accomplished little with it, particularly in Abu Dhabi. The backwater had nothing to exploit, no natural riches to develop and plunder. The British cast themselves as the Trucial States' protectors while scarcely lifting a finger to improve the destitute living conditions of the locals. Abu Dhabi remained one of the poorest and most backward settlements along the coast, lacking a single school or hospital until the late 1960s.[9]

Two world wars came and went, other nations raced to launch a man into space, and still the people of Abu Dhabi lived just like their ancestors. If anything, Abu Dhabians saw their lives worsen in the first half of the twentieth century after the Japanese flooded international markets with artificially cultured pearls. The subsequent collapse of the pearling trade caused the population of Abu Dhabi to dwindle from 6,000 at the start of the century to one-third that number by the 1950s.[10]

Unbeknownst to the inhabitants of this remote, forgotten place, they were sitting atop a fortune. Abu Dhabi rests on one of the largest deposits of what would eventually become the world's most valuable resource. Nature, it seems, is not without a sense of irony. The prehistoric seas that once blanketed eastern Arabia left layer upon layer of rich biological accretions, which putrefied over eons to become mammoth basins of oil. Foreign prospectors first struck black gold on the Gulf island of Bahrain in 1932, and soon the rush was on.[11]

After several disappointing initial explorations, substantial oil deposits were discovered in Abu Dhabi's territorial waters in 1958, and on land in even greater quantities shortly thereafter.[12] Commercial drilling and export began in earnest in 1962, and soon the money started pouring in. By the end of the decade Abu Dhabi was awash in more wealth than its inhabitants could fathom.

The astute Sheikh Zayed bin Sultan al Nahyan, who became Abu Dhabi's ruler in 1966, used the newfound riches to transform the lives of his people. Under his guidance, Abu Dhabi embarked on a crash course of modernization. Over the next fifteen years the unassuming sandbar on which the settlement sat was the scene of one of the most rapid urbanizations in history. Buildings rose. Roads were paved. Water and electricity coursed through new utility lines. Schools and hospitals opened to the public. Abu Dhabians went from being desert wanderers to city dwellers almost overnight, a remarkable transformation given that countless generations before had lived with so little change to their way of life. Huts were swept aside and replaced with cement and cinderblocks. Formerly nomadic families settled in newly built villas, and more residents were drawn from the oases of the interior. The pace of change was unmatched by anything in history. In comparison, when Great Britain was undergoing its fastest urbanization at the height of the Industrial Revolution, the share of its population living in cities increased from one-half in 1850 to two-thirds in 1881.[13] One hundred years later, Abu Dhabi's urbanized population went from zero to almost 99 percent in half that time.

The meager local population couldn't hope to supply all the labor needed for Abu Dhabi's upgrading. To make up the difference, Sheikh Zayed invited foreign workers to help provide the necessary skills and manpower, drawing professionals, merchants, and laborers from the West, the other nations of the Middle East, and South Asia. By 1972 Abu Dhabi was a small but established city with an increasingly diverse population that numbered more than seventy thousand, nearly five times the figure of a decade before.[14] But Abu Dhabi's people could not escape the desert entirely. The dearth of rain and groundwater forced the city to build numerous desalination plants to quench its thirst, a resource-intensive approach that would have dire implications in the future.

While Sheikh Zayed was busy leading this modernization, he also employed the state's oil revenues and his own considerable charisma to convince the rulers of other coastal sheikhdoms to join Abu Dhabi in forming a modern nation. When the British withdrew the last vestiges of their colonial presence from the Trucial States in 1971, Zayed and his fellow sheikhs formed the United Arab Emirates (UAE), a confederation of six emerging city-states along the lower Gulf coast: Abu Dhabi, Dubai, Sharjah, Ajman, Umm al Quwain, and Fujairah. A seventh, Ras al Khaimah, joined the following year. Zayed was instrumental in securing international recognition for the fledgling nation, ensuring that its larger Saudi and Iranian neighbors didn't gobble it up. Zayed's clout made him the natural choice to become the UAE's first president, and Abu Dhabi was designated as the federal capital.

Within the federation, the UAE's seven constituent emirates were politically analogous to American states or Canadian provinces. Each emirate consisted of a principal coastal city and the sparsely populated hinterlands to which its Bedu tribes laid historic claim. The emirates derived their names from their respective primary cities, so that Abu Dhabi, for example, could refer to either the city or the emirate, not unlike the arrangement in New York. While each *emir* or ruler retained considerable control over the internal affairs of his emirate, all seven had an equal say on matters affecting the entire country.

Or so went the theory. In practice, Abu Dhabi dominated the other emirates geographically, economically, and politically from the federation's inception. Abu Dhabi claimed nearly nine-tenths of the new country's land, which in turn contained 94 percent of the UAE's proven oil reserves. Control of the oil stayed firmly at the emirate level, leaving Abu Dhabi in sole command of roughly one-tenth of the world's proven petroleum reserves—no fewer than ninety-eight *billion* barrels, the fourth largest among the members of the Organization of Petroleum Exporting Countries (OPEC).[15] It thus fell to Abu Dhabi to bankroll most of the UAE's federal budget. Zayed did not want the rest of the country to lag behind, so Abu Dhabi contributed to the development of infrastructure and services in the six other emirates as well.

Although Zayed served as a dynamic and engaging leader of the country, Abu Dhabi retained a special place in his heart. As emir he played an active role in the emirate's development, often meeting with those in charge of planning and building major projects. Zayed was determined that his people should not lack anything, but he also did not want their traditions obliterated in the name of progress. In 1977 Zayed put a moratorium on the construction of new residential and commercial buildings, seeking to safeguard his people's traditions and culture in the face of continued modernization.[16] Though development continued under the auspices of governmental agencies, the '80s and '90s were comparatively calm after the tumult of the preceding two decades.

Despite its newfound persona as a modern city, Abu Dhabi retained much of the feel of a provincial town. Abu Dhabi's citizens, now called *Emiratis* like the rest of their countrymen, struggled to come to grips with their urban surroundings and new identity. The emirate's oil wealth had catapulted the Emiratis from abject penury to a percapita wealth near the top of international rankings. Still, much of the evidence was superficial. The Emiratis drove luxury cars and enjoyed air conditioning in their new, expansive villas, but their city was short on substance. It was missing the cultural institutions, public spaces, and the sense of place and character that give a city soul.

More important, the citizens of Abu Dhabi lacked validation. Their people had been ignored for the duration of recorded human history. Now they had the means to gain the world's attention and respect, but still their city remained a nonentity for the rest of mankind, an unknown spot with a curious name. Most people outside the Middle East couldn't even locate Abu Dhabi on a map. It would take the arrival of a new millennium and a second, even grander, program of modernization for Abu Dhabi to take its rightful place on the international stage.

* * *

I walked out the front door of my hotel and the world exploded in blinding white: white buildings, white cars, white sky. The stark Arabian sun bathed everything in albescence, its rays reflected and magnified by rows of glass buildings. The city was a colossal prism.

I was still disoriented from my arrival the night before. It was nearly two-thirty in the morning by the time I had reached the hotel. After checking in, I collapsed in my room and slept until noon. I had come to Abu Dhabi on a Friday, the first day of the local weekend, so I had time to recover before reporting for work on Sunday. When I woke I wolfed down a late breakfast and headed out for a leisurely walk, both to orient myself to the city and to shake off the jet lag.

There is no substitute for getting to know a city on foot. The pedestrian gains an intimate feel for the scale and pattern of a city's streets and the rhythms of the people who inhabit them. Such understanding cannot be had from an automobile's cocoon. As the philosopher Henry David Thoreau opined, "The swiftest traveler is he that goes by foot."[17] His French counterpart Charles Baudelaire went a step further, coining the term *Flâneur* to describe a "botanist of the sidewalk," someone who strolls the city simply to observe its street life. Whenever I traveled to a new city, I took their advice by spending my first few days wandering around without purpose or goal.

I stood for a moment as my eyes adjusted to the glare, and consulted my map of the city. Abu Dhabi occupies a low coastal island jutting into the shallow waters of the Gulf, roughly the same length as Manhattan but up to twice as wide in places. The island starts at a rounded taper next to the mainland, broadens gradually along its length, kinks slightly at its midpoint, and terminates on the Gulf side in a flat top with an appendage on either end, one of which houses the landmark Emirates Palace hotel and the other the Mina Zayed industrial port. The island's ungainly shape can be likened to a scorpion missing its stinger or even to a uterus with the hotel and port. Although the scorpion's head (or cervical wall) is oriented more to the west than the north, residents invariably refer to the Gulf end of the island as north and the landward end as south.

My hotel was situated on the main thoroughfare that runs like a spine through the middle of the island for its ten-mile length. As with many of Abu Dhabi's main roads, this one is named for a sheikh—in this case, Sheikh Rashid bin Saeed al Maktoum, the former ruler of Dubai. But residents just call it Airport Road, so named because it continues onto the mainland and terminates at the city's international airport.

Namesakes aside, I felt that "road" was something of an understatement for the bituminous ten-lane expanse in front of me, which coursed with unceasing traffic. It was more like a freeway with stoplights. As though the road weren't wide enough on its own, service lanes doubling as parking lots lined either side of the main drag. In between were strips of sidewalk chopped into pieces every fifty feet or so by access slips between the road and the service lanes. Everything was oddly out of scale, from the eighteen-inch-tall curbs to the three-hundred-foot span between the buildings on either side of the outsized road. The Brobdingnagian dimensions reminded me of Saddam Hussein's infamous Hands of Victory parade ground in Baghdad—although Airport Road's right-of-way was twice as wide.

Framing each side of this urban chasm was a row of buildings forming an almost seamless wall of concrete and glass stretching to infinity in either direction. Unlike the setbacks typical of North American skyscrapers, most of these structures were wider on top than on bottom.

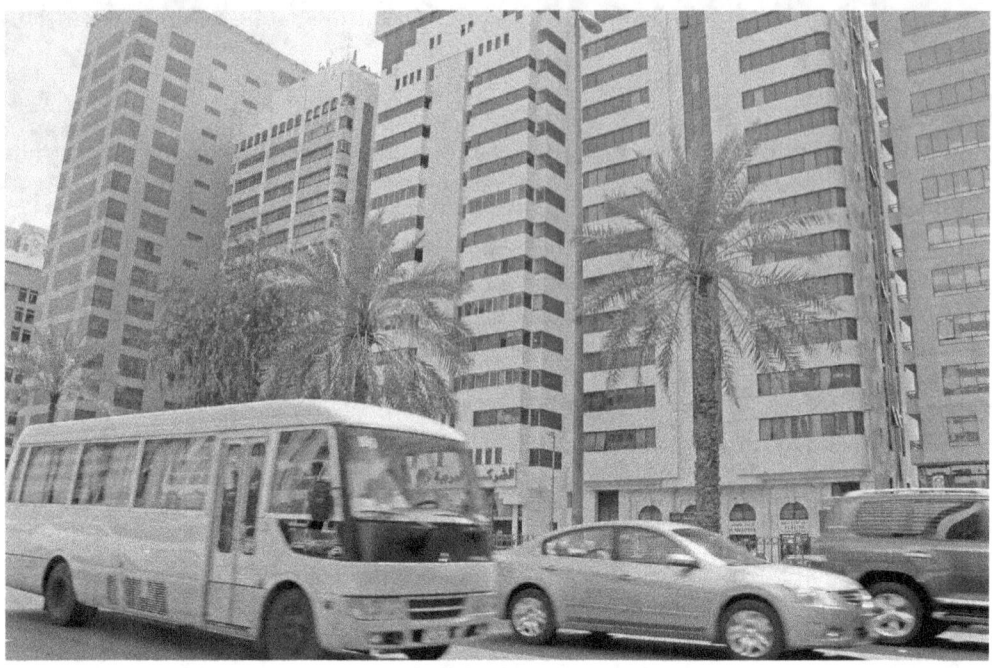

Airport Road.

They rose straight out of the ground for two or three stories, jutted out diagonally, and then continued straight up again. They looked, in effect, like overturned milk cartons. The buildings topped out at fifteen stories in roofs so uniformly flat they looked to have been pruned with a monstrous hedge trimmer.

The edifices themselves were a mixture of old and new. The concrete façades looked dated, crumbling at the edges from years of corrosion in the saline air. The newer, look-alike metallic boxes were covered in aluminum paneling and opaque plateglass windows, a giant hall of mirrors that amplified the glare. The buildings were stacked side by side with just a few feet between them, barely enough room for a claustrophobic footpath at ground level. A resident on the fifteenth floor could reach out his window and shake hands with his neighbor in the adjoining building. It was a disorienting scene, one with many familiar elements, but in shapes and arrangements I'd never seen.

I began walking along the road in the direction of the Gulf. Light poles, signs, and other fixture debris cluttered the footpath, sometimes placed as though intended to trip up unwary pedestrians. Every fifty paces or so I had to hop up or down the tall curbs where the sidewalk was interrupted by an access slip for cars. It was clear that the pedestrian realm wasn't an intentional creation; it had merely been cobbled together from the leftover right-of-way not already devoted to the automobile. I felt like I was negotiating an obstacle course. The experience of walking was degraded even further by the roaring traffic just a few feet away. If Airport Road was any clue, Abu Dhabi appeared to be a city built for cars rather than for people.

That assumption actually wasn't far from the truth, as I later discovered while researching the history of the city's planning and development. When Abu Dhabi commenced its oil-fueled modernization in the 1960s, Sheikh Zayed envisioned a modern city on par with any of its counterparts in the West. It was a tall order, as Abu Dhabi had to start from scratch in terms of its buildings and infrastructure, as well as the know-how to assemble them. Zayed was obliged to turn to a string of foreign sources for the necessary expertise. A British architect named John Harris developed the first master plan for the new city in 1962 which tried to marry new roads and buildings with the organic pattern of the existing settlement.[18] Preserving the old, raggedy Abu Dhabi was the last thing on its inhabitants' minds, and the plan was dumped. The international consultancy Halcrow subsequently produced another plan that called for the erasure of the existing settlement in favor of a new rectilinear street grid. This plan was augmented by the input of a Japanese consultant, Dr. Katsukiko Takahashi,[19] and then passed to the firm Arabicon in 1968 for further refinement under the guidance of an Egyptian named Abdel-Rahman Makhlouf, who would later become the city's principal planner.[20]

At the time, urbanism was dominated by an obsessive rationalism that viewed cities as diseases in need of a cure. The prescription was engineering, systematization, and the eradication of all that came before, in favor of superhighways and high-rise towers. In keeping with this philosophy, Abu Dhabi's planners blueprinted the new city as a grid of superblocks, each roughly a kilometer long (the length of eleven football fields) and half as wide. Although automobiles had just arrived in Abu Dhabi, the planners assumed that everyone would employ them to get around. It was a self-fulfilling prophecy, as the sheer size of the superblocks necessitated driving. Wide arterial roads were laid out between the superblocks to channel traffic. The planners omitted smaller cross streets, eliminating the need for additional intersections along the arterials and allowing traffic to flow more freely. Land uses were strictly segregated, with commercial and residential buildings lining the periphery of the superblocks and lower-scale neighborhoods located in the interiors. In principle, the plan would facilitate a logical, measured expansion of the city. As the population grew, more superblocks could be added to its ever-expanding quilt. The concept was calculated, hierarchical, and foolproof, a poster child for the rationalist urbanism of the 1960s, which is to say it was all wrong.

The rationalist school of thought, led by deluded pundits like the Swiss architect Le Corbusier, ignored the inconvenient considerations of how people actually behave in and perceive their cities. As the new Abu Dhabi rose from the sands, its shortcomings soon became evident. The gargantuan superblocks were absurdly oversized and cut off from one another by the gaping rights-of-way between them. The bewildering networks of internal streets varied from one superblock to another, requiring anyone who managed to decipher one labyrinthine interior to begin anew the next superblock over. The superblock system funneled all cross-town traffic onto the arterials, increasing their congestion all the more. The lack of connecting side streets turned the average trip into a series of oscillating zigzags often twice as long as the actual distance between origin and destination.

Cars took priority over humans at almost every juncture. Parking lots far outnumbered parks. In most areas, the only public spaces were landscaped strips of leftover right-of-way next to the main roads. The lookalike streets and buildings made orientation difficult, and the eradication of the old settlement left the city without a historic core or any real center to speak of. A cluster of slightly taller buildings near the northeast corner of the island was the closest thing to a downtown, but it lacked the requisite city-center elements of public plazas, monuments, regal government buildings, and so forth. This omission was more than just a superficial concern; as noted urbanist William Whyte observed, the yearning for a center is one of the most powerful of all human impulses.[21]

After the initial modernizing frenzy of the '60s, subsequent waves of development seemed to wash over Abu Dhabi from the Gulf, layering higher buildings on the northern part of the island and pushing the city further south until it sprawled onto the mainland.

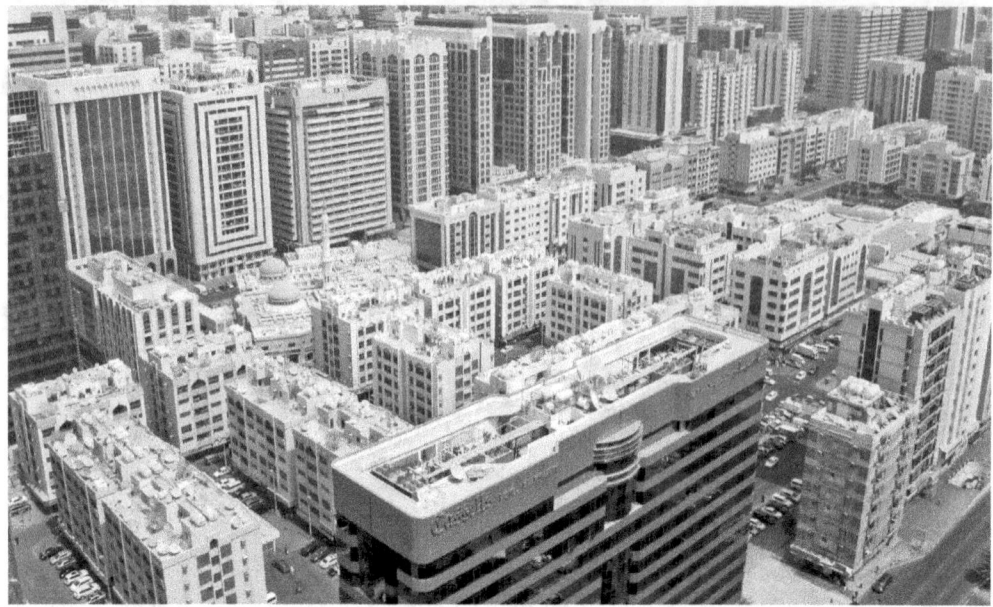

A typical downtown Abu Dhabi superblock, with low-rise residential buildings in the interior and high-rises around the edges.

As the city grew, so did the ambitions of its landlords. The sky-high oil prices brought about by the Arab oil embargo of the late 1970s left Abu Dhabi even more flooded with cash than before. Owners were eager to invest in their properties, and buyers were ready to snap them up. The Abu Dhabi Municipality, which had been given responsibility for the city's planning, was pressured into lifting the height restrictions along the periphery of the city's superblocks from six floors to anywhere between thirteen and twenty. Despite Sheikh Zayed's 1977 moratorium on new construction, the city continued to grow at a modest pace, adding around two hundred buildings per year in the '80s and '90s.[22]

Abu Dhabi's rationalist plan didn't deal well with these departures from its rigidly prescribed ratios. Whereas the plan had anticipated a maximum population of 350,000, residents already numbered 415,000 by 1985.[23] Even with its emphasis on the automobile as the main mode of transportation, the plan utterly failed to handle the concurrent increase in the city's traffic. As the population swelled from the continued influx of foreign workers, the number of cars on the road grew at an astounding rate of nearly 20 percent a year. The superblock interiors became constipated with parked cars—on sidewalks, in empty lots, and even down the middle of streets. The arterial roads between the superblocks were expanded up to six lanes in each direction. Roundabouts were gridlocked with traffic volumes they were never designed to handle; most were eventually converted to four-way signals. The master plan was repeatedly updated to cope with the growth, most recently in 1988 with the help of the United Nations Development Program.[24] Yet, even all these measures couldn't address the more fundamental flaws in the city's structure.

The Abu Dhabi plan's lasting deleterious effects—the inhuman scale of the streets, the crowded high-rises lining the superblocks, the unrelenting traffic—were all visible as I walked along Airport Road. Seeking refuge from the noise and exhaust, I ducked between a pair of high-rises and into the superblock's interior. The instant calm was almost bucolic compared with the cacophony of the road. The internal buildings were lower, between two and five

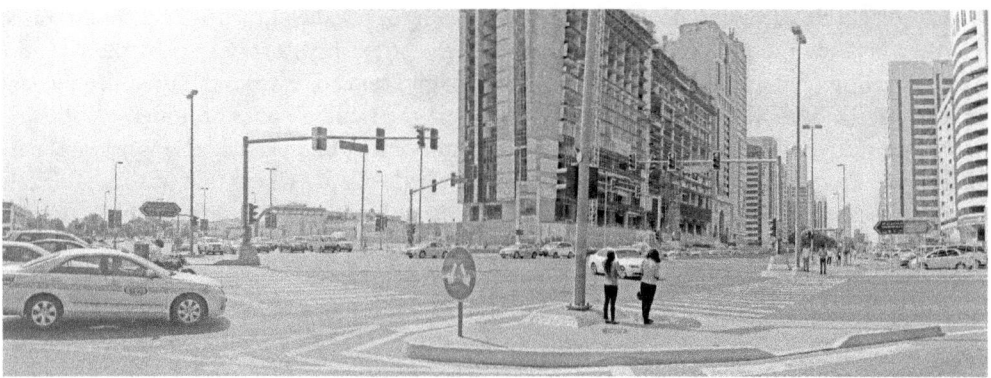

The welcoming environs of a normal Abu Dhabi intersection. This one is at Airport Road and 11th Street.

stories at most. Vehicles were parked all over, but the congestion at least forced passing drivers to slow.

Here was actually a semblance of urban life. A gaggle of kids played pick-up soccer between rows of cars. Residents and patrons milled around the storefronts that lined the ground floors of the buildings. It intrigued me that most of the people I saw were South Asian; my ears caught far more Urdu and Hindi than Arabic. An intoxicating panoply of aromas wafted across my nostrils: burnt tobacco from a cafe where patrons smoked the *shisha* water pipe, fresh fruit from a grocery, shaving cream from a barber, starch from a laundry. The city had a pulse after all. I slowed my pace to enjoy the ambience. I emerged back onto the periphery at the far end of the block. By now I'd become acutely aware of the temperature. It was two in the afternoon in the middle of March, and already I was drenched in sweat. If this was early spring, what would summer be like?

The four-way intersection that faced me at the corner was a monster. Zebra-striped pedestrian crossings stretched across yawning spans of asphalt, linking together a string of concrete pedestrian refuges that resembled landing obstacles on a Normandy beach. The prospect of crossing brought to mind the video game *Frogger*. The first stage was a curved slip lane that allowed drivers to turn right without stopping at the light. I stepped forward into the crossing and was nearly flattened by a Land Cruiser whose driver didn't even slow. In most cities, white stripes on pavement are a signal for motorists to yield to pedestrians (or in Italy, to at least swerve around them). In Abu Dhabi, apparently they denoted a target gallery.

On the first island, I joined a huddle of brave souls waiting to cross the main road. We waited and waited. Finally the walk signal lit up and we shuffled across to the narrow refuge in the median, where we waited again. The split-phased traffic signal only allowed one of the four directions of cars to proceed at any time. I soon saw why. When the light turned green in any direction, many of the drivers in all but the rightmost of the five lanes surged forward into arcing left-hand turns or U-turns. Permitting two directions of traffic to do this simultaneously would have been calamitous. All of this was necessitated by the grid's lack of cross streets and the medians that prevented drivers from making left-hand turns mid-block.

When I finally reached the far side of the intersection I made for the interior of the next superblock. I repeated this hopscotch pattern all the way to the Corniche, the waterfront promenade along the island's northern edge, where I caught my breath on a bench after one last death-defying crossing. Having explored enough for one day, I turned back and retraced my path to the hotel. I fought the climate and the streetscape every step of the way and arrived feeling (and undoubtedly smelling) as though I had come from the urban equivalent of a safari. To cover just four miles it had taken me the same number of hours.

As I recovered in the hotel's blissful air conditioning, one particular observation perplexed me. From my initial foray there seemed to be little of Abu Dhabi that was recognizably Middle Eastern. The architecture was generic, particularly the newer repetitious glass façades. The mosques on every block were about the only reminders that this was Arabia, yet even these were indistinguishable from their counterparts in Casablanca or Kuala Lumpur. An amnesiac waking up in Abu Dhabi could be forgiven for thinking he was somewhere in South Asia, judging by the people he saw and the voices he heard. For a city that had placed so much emphasis on the preservation of its identity, at first glance it was hard to tell just what that identity was.

Two

Ready, Fire, Aim

Abu Dhabi has all the vigor and likeability of an experimental society. Never in history had so much money, so much technical expertise, or so powerful a social and religious vision been at anyone's disposal to build a civilization from scratch as was occurring here and now. At the same time, it exuded an anxiety.... All its energy seemed to be in danger of being sapped by the sense that everything and everybody were only temporarily here. —*Jonathan Raban, Arabia: A Journey through the Labyrinth*

For the life of me, I couldn't figure out why someone would sing opera at half past four in the morning. I buried my head in the pillows, but still the tenor voice assaulted my eardrums. It sounded like a protégée of Pavarotti was performing right outside my window. With a bullhorn.

My grogginess cleared and I remembered where I was. The singing was the early morning *adhan*, the Muslim call to prayer, emanating from the mosque next to my hotel. As part of its blending of the traditional and the modern, Abu Dhabi has put a contemporary spin on this ancient custom. Most of the city's mosques are linked to a central public address system from which a lone male voice serenades residents five times a day—a stark contrast to the cacophony one hears in other Middle Eastern cities, where each mosque issues its own call to prayer. I took to calling Abu Dhabi's adhan the Giant Voice, the term that inhabitants of Baghdad's Green Zone employed for the bellowing civil defense system that warned them of incoming mortars and rockets.

Abu Dhabi's Giant Voice happens to belong to the *muezzin*, or prayer caller, at the city's Sheikh Zayed Mosque. This immense white structure sits at the southern end of the island and dominates the mainland entrance to the city, although the lack of nearby buildings makes it difficult for the onlooker to appreciate its true size. The mosque is by far the largest in Abu Dhabi and the third largest in the world, capable of accommodating more than forty thousand worshippers in its prayer halls and courtyards. Its chandeliers are plated in twenty-four-karat gold, and the hand-woven Persian carpet that covers the main prayer hall is the world's most expansive. The mosque is especially breathtaking at night, when watery blue and purple lights ripple across its eighty egg-shaped domes. Although the Sheikh Zayed Mosque has become Abu Dhabi's most recognizable symbol, its architecture is actually more Indian than Arabian, taking most of its cues from the Mughal style of the Taj Mahal. Sheikh Zayed started construction on the mosque in 1996, yet when I arrived more than thirteen years later, workers were still putting the finishing touches on its façade.

The Giant Voice is a fitting complement to such a regal structure. During my first few days in Abu Dhabi I had already been amazed by the muezzin maestro's talent for stretching a single word of the prayer call across a dozen notes or more. Most days his song was bold and haunting, ending on a minor key as if more were to come. Sometimes he would switch

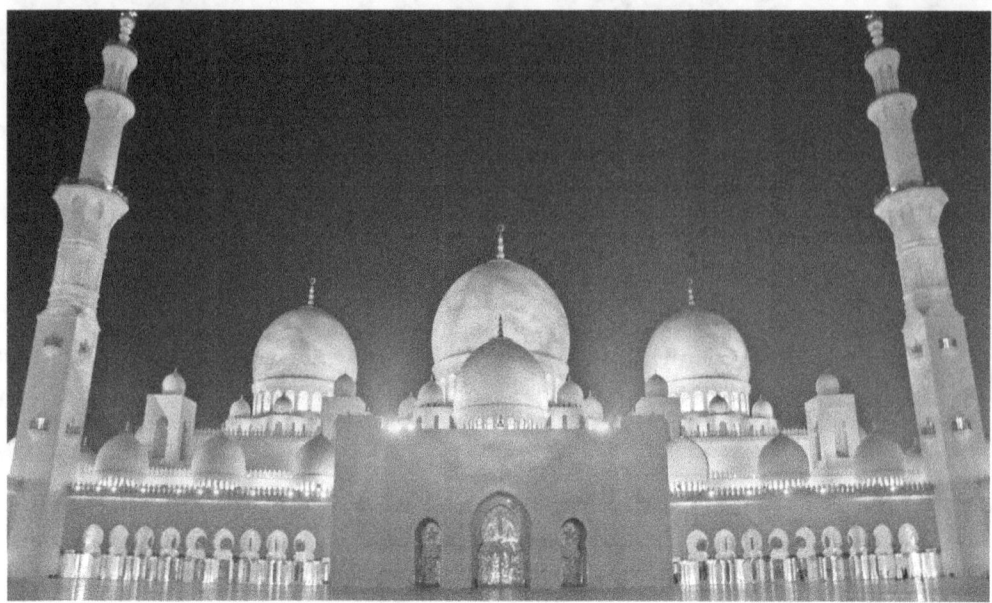

The Sheikh Zayed Mosque at night.

things up in the late afternoon, calling out to the setting sun with a soaring paean that was equal parts celebration and mourning for the passage of another day. Even for a non-Muslim, it stirred the soul. On this day, however, the earliest of the calls to prayer was an alarm clock I could have done without.

After another hour of fitful slumber I awoke again, stumbled over to the window, and opened the curtains. Sunlight poured into the room. From my twelfth-floor vantage point I would have had a commanding view of the eastern side of the city—if it weren't for the towering eyesore standing in the way.

Rising outside my window was a thirty-story concrete partition as wide as it was tall. Gaping voids pockmarked the unfinished façade like squares on a checkerboard, with scarcely a detail or ornament to break the repetition. Semi-circular turrets bulged out at either end of the building, rising above the height of the façade and topping out in the shape of upside-down fedoras. Clumps of uncut rebar jutted out from every edge and corner like flagella. A half-dozen tower cranes soared above the structure, keeping watch over the hundreds of laborers swarming about like worker bees.

This was the western side of Wahda City, one of dozens of new real estate projects that had sprouted like weeds in Abu Dhabi's ongoing development boom. Architecturally, it left much to be desired. Wahda City was far too big for the piece of land on which it sat, a modest plot barely four hundred feet square. On the opposite side of the elongated building visible from my window, the development also included a pair of equally tall towers with narrow elliptical floorplates. The three buildings were wedged onto the plot at odd angles to one another, like strangers trying to avoid contact in a crowded elevator. The entire cluster loomed twice as tall as the surrounding buildings, a dissonant chord among the otherwise uniform harmony of the skyline. When finished, the development would overflow with more than a million square feet of offices, apartments, retail space, a movie theatre, and an 850-room luxury hotel.

In addition to its bulk, Wahda City also occupied a singularly poor location. It was surrounded on three sides by a mall, a stadium, and the city's main bus station, each of which already generated huge amounts of traffic. The streets of the unfortunate superblock that housed this cluster were choked at all hours of the day, and the single arterial to which Wahda City had access was already a free-for-all due to the cars entering and exiting the mall. It was anyone's guess as to what would happen with the additional traffic Wahda City would beget; the nearby roads simply had no more room.

Developers are fond of the phrase "highest and best use" to describe how they maximize the utility of real estate. Wahda City certainly fulfilled the "highest" part; "best" was another story. Any of its flaws—the amateurish aesthetics, the disproportionate scale, and the awkward location—should have been a show-stopper for whoever was in charge of reviewing development proposals when Wahda City was first put forth. Yet here it was, rising before me in all its elephantine inelegance. Hadn't anyone tried to stop this?

* * *

"We keep the shades closed for a reason." Alex nodded at the obscured window. "Normally I enjoy a room with a view, but when the sun comes up, we roast in here." His darkened office was like the cave of a hermitic bibliophile. Reports, papers, and engineering drawings in various stages of unrolling covered every surface and spilled from the bookshelves. Alex's office mate, Ethan, sat in front of his computer in the far corner, surrounded by piles of paper. Alex was perhaps a half-foot shorter than Ethan, but his spiked hair nearly made up the difference. Both were Canadians from Toronto in their late thirties.

Alex was my new supervisor. He had been at the Urban Planning Council all of nine months, which made him an old-timer at the fledgling agency. I had met him briefly when I first arrived at the office for my orientation, but he was so busy that I barely saw him during the following days. Only now, at the end of the week, had he finally found time to brief me on the Urban Planning Council's role in Abu Dhabi's development and the part I was to play. He cleared a space for me to sit and launched into an overview of the agency's history.

In the later years of his reign, Sheikh Zayed had become ever more protective of Abu Dhabi. His 1977 moratorium on private construction left development in the hands of government agencies that peppered the city with bland apartment towers and commercial buildings. This moderate pace of development slowed to a crawl in the late 1990s and early 2000s, even as the neighboring emirate of Dubai embarked on a building spree.

Zayed's death in late 2004 changed everything. The mantle of leadership passed to his nineteen sons. The eldest, Khalifa, inherited Zayed's dual positions as president of the UAE and ruler of Abu Dhabi, while the third-eldest, Mohammed, became the emirate's crown prince. Khalifa concentrated on federal issues, while Mohammed took charge of administering Abu Dhabi.

The sons of Zayed soon unveiled an ambitious vision to transform Abu Dhabi into one of the grandest cities in the world. Underlying it was a desire to diversify Abu Dhabi's economy beyond its virtually exclusive dependence on oil. Like the leaders of the Gulf's other oil-rich states, Abu Dhabi's sheikhs were realizing that their petroleum-funded windfall wouldn't last forever. They began looking for ways to broaden their economic bases so that when the crude ran out, their people wouldn't suffer a dramatic decline in the comfortable standard of living to which they had become accustomed.

Here Ethan chimed in. "The Saudis have a joke about it. 'My father drove a camel, I drive a Benz, my son will drive a Gulfstream ... and his son will drive a camel.'"

"They're all a bit paranoid about going back to the Stone Age," Alex agreed. "Rightfully so, I guess."

The attempts at diversification were not novel. When author Jonathan Raban visited the Gulf in the late 1970s, he observed that some of the region's city-states were already setting up basic local industries like steel smelters. Although these were helpful for replacing imports, Raban pointed out the illogic of their competitive position in global markets: "Why ship alumina from the Pacific to be smelted in Bahrain and then shipped back to the Pacific as aluminum?"[1]

The emirate of Dubai was one of the first places in the Gulf to pursue diversification on a large scale. In the 1980s Dubai began using the revenues from its own modest oil discoveries to jump-start an economic expansion centered on real estate, tourism, and entertainment. The endeavor paid off. By the early years of the new millennium, Dubai had captured international attention with its meteoric growth and its ever more outlandish projects, including the creation of artificial islands and the construction of the world's tallest building.

I interrupted to ask whether there was a rivalry between Dubai and Abu Dhabi.

Alex laughed. "It's more than that. Ask any of the Emiratis whose families have been in Abu Dhabi for generations, and they'll tell you that Dubai is just an upstart. Abu Dhabi is the real UAE. The power and culture are here. They think that their cousins in Dubai sold out."

Ethan added, "All the same, you can imagine how watching your neighbors get the glory for all those years could give you something of an inferiority complex."[2]

Dubai's expansion also attracted plenty of foreign critics who disparaged the emirate as an Arabian Disneyland, lacking substance and authenticity. The frenzied activity and construction eventually surpassed the realm of realistic growth and became a speculative bubble in danger of bursting. At its peak, Dubai had more real estate under development than Shanghai, a city with thirteen times Dubai's population.[3]

In their post-Zayed vision for diversification, Abu Dhabi's sheikhs elected to cast a wider economic net than had Dubai. They wanted to develop local industries in a broad range of sectors, including manufacturing, defense, renewable energy, media, and more. The emirate's state-owned sovereign wealth funds started targeting companies around the globe for acquisition and investment, looking for opportunities to transfer those enterprises' knowledge and facilities to Abu Dhabi. They also started buying stakes in everything from global financial corporations like Barclays and Citibank to New York City office towers and London's Gatwick Airport. In 2008 one of the sheikhs spearheaded the purchase of Manchester City, the English Premiere League football (i.e., soccer) club, subsequently investing more than a billion pounds in new players and facilities.[4] The state dumped billions of dirhams, the UAE's currency, into a raft of new Abu Dhabi-based enterprises like the flagship Etihad Airlines.

In order to create a suitable skyline for the new and improved Abu Dhabi, the sheikhs lifted the emirate's development restrictions. Within a year and a half of Zayed's death, untested development companies like Aldar and Sorouh had broken ground on dozens of projects across the city, projects like Wahda City. The initial results of this new wave of development were disappointing, to put it mildly. "The developers built a lot of junk," Alex said. "Awful designs, cheap materials, poorly chosen locations. And there was no one to stop them. The Abu Dhabi Municipality rubber-stamped everything the developers handed them."

This didn't escape the crown prince's notice. He realized that without a comprehensive plan for the transformation of Abu Dhabi's built environment, the emirate risked repeating Dubai's speculative excesses and incoherent urban form. Dubai's frenzied development had been poorly planned, with projects and buildings scattered across the desert seemingly at random. Most of Dubai barely felt like a city at all; it was instead a mishmash of skyscrapers and housing estates strung together by highways that resembled a plate of tangled spaghetti.

The crown prince wanted no such fate for Abu Dhabi. If anything, he had in mind the example of Vancouver, whose reputation as one of the world's most livable cities had caught his eye. "The Vancouver obsession is one of three things you need to know to understand Abu Dhabi," Alex said. "Actually, it's a dual obsession with Vancouver and Singapore. Abu Dhabi's leaders look to Singapore as the model of success for a small city-state—trade and transportation hub, advanced knowledge economy, Singapore Airlines, global importance and identity, that sort of stuff. And they want it to look postcard-perfect like Vancouver.

"The sheikhs," Alex continued, "are the second thing you need to know about. They control everything here. I keep saying that we should have a 'know your sheikhs' chart that describes what each of them owns and controls. But if our Emirati staff have that knowledge, they aren't telling. Our general manager ultimately answers to the crown prince, but we deal with the other sheikhs all the time, or at least with the companies they control. And what a sheikh wants, he tends to get. And third, the notion of the private sector is far different here. The state owns the oil industry and big chunks of most major companies across the rest of the economy." Alex explained how the sheikhs' personal holdings confused the concept of the private sector even further, as the boundaries between their bank accounts and the state's were often blurred.[5]

In 2007 Sheikh Mohammed invited Vancouver's former principal city planner to bring a team to Abu Dhabi and map out the emirate's transformation. "What they came up with was this," Alex said as he rummaged through the piles on his desk. He pulled out a thick volume with the label *Plan Abu Dhabi 2030: Urban Structure Framework Plan* on the cover.[6] "It's a framework for the broad expansion of metropolitan Abu Dhabi over the next twenty years. The population today is about a million. *Plan 2030* foresees it tripling. The plan channels that growth into specific areas, including some of the nearby islands."

Alex turned to a map on the wall and pointed out several of the larger islands in the archipelago surrounding Abu Dhabi, each of which would be developed with its own distinct character under *Plan 2030*: Suwwah Island would be the new financial district, Reem Island would house nearly two hundred thousand people in a forest of high-rises, Saadiyat Island was envisioned as a cultural district with branches of the Louvre and Guggenheim museums, and Yas Island would be a smorgasbord with an F1 race track, an IKEA, a Ferrari-branded theme park, gigantic marinas, and another hundred thousand residents. Alex also indicated a large empty triangle on the mainland between Abu Dhabi Island and the airport and explained that it would be the home of the new Capital District, containing all the organs of the federal government and another three hundred fifty thousand people.

Plan 2030 may not have had the benefit of starting from a blank slate like the original urban plan of forty years before, but if anything, its directives were even more sweeping and its aspirations grander. Tripling the population of a city in twenty years would be no mean feat—and that was merely the plan's moderate scenario; its most aggressive projections pegged the 2030 population as high as five million.[7] By way of comparison, it took New York City more than twice that length of time to grow from one million to three million inhabitants.

As I leafed through the plan, I saw that it called for "setting an international example of cutting-edge sustainable growth—that which filters all decisions through environmental, social, and economic criteria."[8] The plan repeatedly emphasized taking a measured approach to development as a means of both protecting the emirate's fragile natural environment and preserving Abu Dhabi's identity as a traditional Arab city. "Abu Dhabi has the rare oppor-

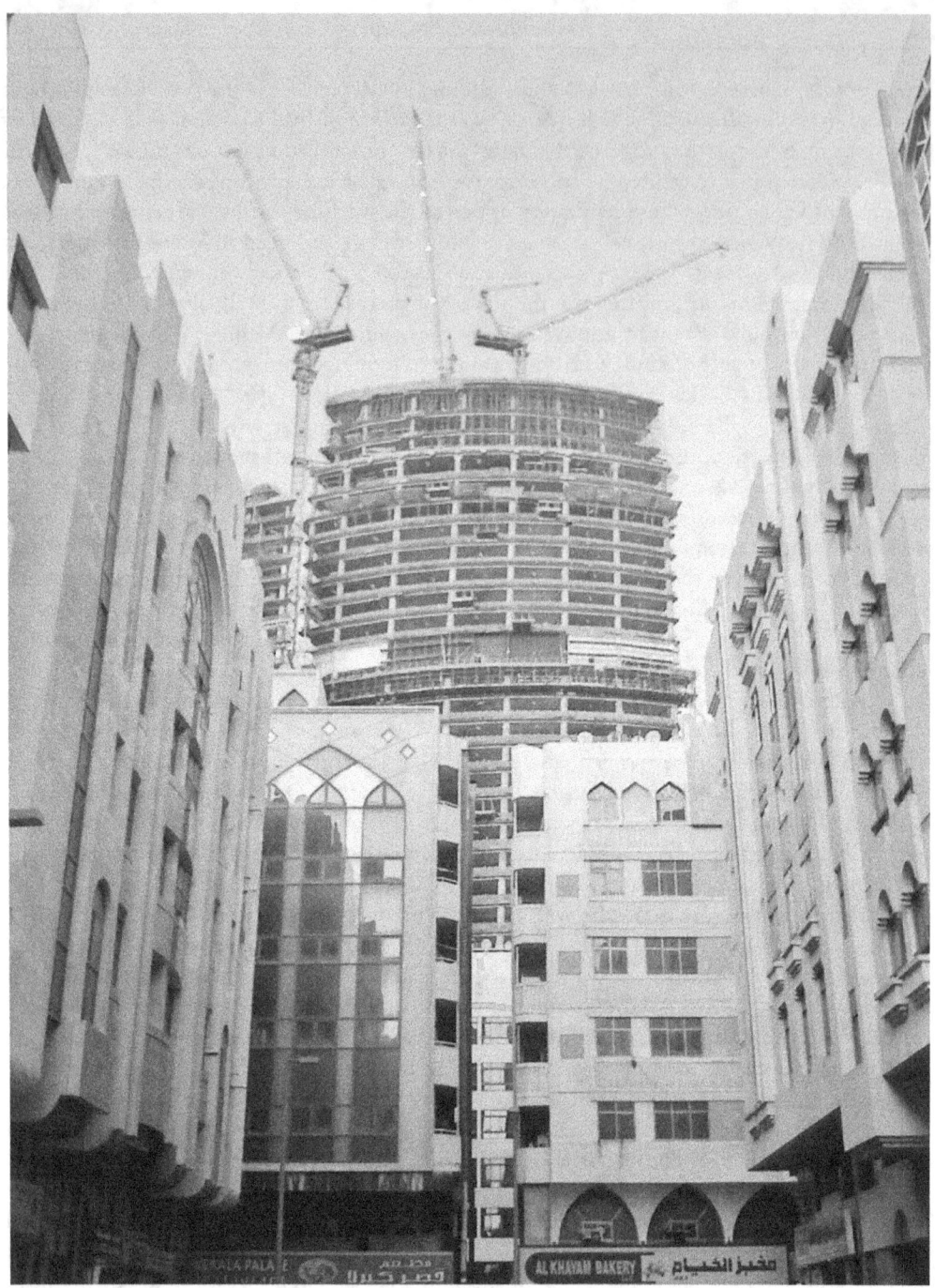

Old versus new in downtown Abu Dhabi. Pictured are closely packed 1970s–era buildings and one of their newer counterparts.

tunity to offer a special combination of features in its urban identity: an authentic and safe but also progressive and open Arab city; a personality garnered from the desert and the sea; a traditional way of life but with the latest 21st century options,"[9] the plan confidently boasted.

Alex explained that the Vancouver contingent had also helped set up a new agency to oversee the implementation of the plan—the Urban Planning Council, or UPC.[10] The crown prince gave the agency a threefold mandate: first, guide the emirate's growth by producing development policies and master plans ranging from the regional level all the way down to individual neighborhoods; second, review developers' proposals to ensure they complied with those plans and policies; and third, coordinate among the various government agencies and developers to make sure everyone was working in sync.[11] Those three functions were reflected in the UPC's three main departments: Planning Policy, Development Review, and the catchall TIES, which stood for Transport, Infrastructure, Environment, and Spatial Systems.

Within the TIES department, Alex supervised the UPC's transport team, who numbered just four when I arrived. This tiny squad was in charge of the big-picture planning for Abu Dhabi's transport infrastructure, in essence making sure that all the developers' new projects fit together with the mammoth transport investments planned for the city. *Plan 2030* called for the creation of a new subway system, the Metro, along with a network of trams and dedicated bus lanes, and noted, "Abu Dhabi cannot rely solely on the auto when the population reaches three million."[12] It also proposed a new national railway that would span the width of the UAE from Saudi Arabia to Oman. These projects were augmented by more mundane elements such as hundreds of kilometers of new roads and highways. "All of this stuff will be built in the next ten to twenty years. The total price is estimated at something like a hundred and twenty billion," Alex said.

"Dirhams?" I asked. At the fixed exchange rate of 3.67 dirhams to one U.S. dollar, the figure was impressive.

"Dollars." (Correction: the figure was staggering.) "And in case you haven't noticed, the existing roads could use some help. The public realm is a mess, and the traffic keeps getting worse. So we're trying to fix that, too."

I asked what that involved on a day-to-day basis.

"A little bit of everything. We provide transport input to Planning Policy's master plans. We do the same for Development Review when they review developer proposals. And we manage our own projects and initiatives. But we probably spend more time running interference between the various agencies and developers than on anything else. It mostly just takes getting the right people together in one room and trying to make them talk to each other." He smiled. "Like herding porcupines."

I'd battled a growing sense of worry during this part of the conversation. The truth was going to be obvious sooner or later, so I figured I might as well get it out now, even if it meant I would be shipped back home the next day. "Look, I'm not really sure why I was picked for your team, but ... well, I'm not a transport planner."

Alex frowned. "Have you done any transport work in your other jobs?"

"A little, but nothing like what you're talking about."

"What about your academic background?"

I shook my head. "I didn't take a single transport class for my planning degree."

Alex thought for a moment, then shrugged. "To tell you the truth, neither did I. I was supposed to be an urban designer, but somehow all my jobs wound up being transport-related. Don't worry. Most of what we do is at the strategic level anyway. We leave a lot of the technical details to others. Besides, even if you had decades of experience, it wouldn't help you much. Abu Dhabi has a way of turning experts into fools."

He extended his hand. "We're all novices here. Welcome aboard."

I left Alex's office and walked back towards my own. The UPC occupied the former headquarters of the Abu Dhabi Department of Public Works at the corner of Airport Road and Delma Street, near the midpoint of the island. From above, the building's floorplan resembled a stylized falcon, the UAE's national bird, which the Emiratis' Bedu ancestors prized for its hunting prowess.[13] The whitewashed stucco structure looked to have been built during the initial boom of the early 1970s. The UPC's offices had been remodeled in a contemporary style, complete with sleek new furniture and smoked-glass windows, but they retained a patina of age, from the squat toilets in the bathrooms to the faint aroma of *oud* incense that lingered in the hallways. I liked the feel of the place, with its hints of a bygone era.

As I entered my office I nearly ran head-on into a figure clad in black from head to toe. I recoiled at the sight of the *abayya*, the ink-hued gown that Emirati women wear over their clothes. It wasn't the garment that repelled me, but the prospect of touching an Emirati woman, even accidentally. I had come to Abu Dhabi with an irrational fear of Emirati females, thanks to a friend from graduate school who had worked for years in the UAE. "Emirati women are ice queens," she had warned me. "The only time you'll see them is when they're shopping at the mall, and then they'll act like you and everybody else don't exist. Whatever you do, don't try to shake hands with one unless she offers first, which will probably never happen." Physical contact between an Emirati woman and any male who wasn't a family member was evidently a huge taboo.

I relaxed when I recognized the Emirati in front of me as Mahra, a young woman from the UPC's public relations team. I had met her earlier in the week during my orientation, and she had been kind enough to show me around the office. In between introductions to the other staff, she interrogated me about my background, interests, and family, while proudly discoursing on the traditions and culture of her own society. True to form, she hadn't shaken my hand, and had actually asked me not to try. But apart from that, she proved exactly the opposite of what I was conditioned to expect. Mahra was smart, friendly, and genuinely pleasant to talk to.

"Sorry, I didn't realize you were coming through the door," Mahra said. Beneath the black wrap of her *shayla* headscarf, her face was flushed from our near miss. She had a winsome smile and dark, beguiling eyes, and didn't look a day older than twenty-five. "I just came by to give you this." She handed me a bag. "Remember when you asked me the other day about books on Abu Dhabi's history, and I said there was a very famous one that I couldn't remember? This is it. I hope you enjoy." I reached in and pulled out a copy of Wilfred Thesiger's *Arabian Sands*.

I forced what I hoped was a suitably appreciative smile. Thesiger was the last of the legendary English explorers, a Luddite famed for his vocal disdain of modern advances as well as for his remarkable adventures. During my time in Iraq I had begun reading *The Marsh Arabs*, Thesiger's account of his travels through the riverine labyrinth of southern Mesopotamia in the 1950s. The narrative was as boggy as the marshes and the Englishman's self-importance was excruciating. Thesiger revered tribal societies, such as the Arabs who inhabited the marshes, as the last bastions of mankind not corrupted by modern inventions. He deplored human settlements as scourges on the land, engines of decay filled with weak, slothful people. As one making a career in the development of cities, I did not exactly share Thesiger's point of view.

I was also put off by his seeming hypocrisy. Although Thesiger ranted against the evils of "the motor-car and the wireless," he apparently saw nothing wrong with gallivanting around by plane and spending much of his time back in decidedly non-primitive England, sipping tea and lecturing in the plush drawing rooms of the Royal Geographic Society. Even while traveling, Thesiger enjoyed the comfort of a thermal sleeping bag and dispensed modern pharmaceuticals wherever he went. At times he seemed more a poseur than someone serious about rejecting modernity and adopting the way of life of his precious tribes. I quit reading *The Marsh Arabs* halfway through the book.

My brain hurt at the mere thought of having to endure another of Thesiger's jeremiads. *Arabian Sands* is his account of his journeys with the Bedu of southern Arabia during the late 1940s, during which he made two perilous treks across the unforgiving sands of the Empty Quarter. The book has become synonymous with old Abu Dhabi; no article on the emirate's history is complete without an obligatory nod to Thesiger's magnum opus. This misconception proves that few people bother to read it. *Arabian Sands* covers Abu Dhabi in barely a dozen pages. Thesiger made only a brief stop at the village and did not particularly care for it: "A large castle dominated the small dilapidated town which stretched along the shore. There were a few palms, and near them was a well where we watered our camels while some Arabs eyed us curiously.... Near us some small cannon were half buried in the sand. The ground around was dirty, covered with the refuse of sedentary humanity.... In the evening, a young Arab came out from a postern gate, walked a little way across the sand, squatted down, and urinated."[14]

Thesiger liked Abu Dhabi even less when he returned in 1977. The high rises and oil refineries of the modern city were for him a nightmare, leaving him "disillusioned and resentful ... as this symbolized all that I had rejected in Western civilization."[15] I felt sure I was in for more of this sunny disposition throughout *Arabian Sands*, but I resolved to skim the first few chapters in case Mahra later asked whether I'd read it.

The book turned out to be spellbinding. Thesiger painted a compelling portrait of the Bedu and their way of life, rendered all the more bittersweet by his knowledge of the inevitable and irrevocable changes that oil, wealth, and modernization would bring. He sometimes slipped into hyperbole when describing the stark beauty of the Empty Quarter, but it was impossible to question his respect for both the harsh terrain and the Bedu companions who kept him alive in it. I would return to the book time and again throughout my own sojourn in Abu Dhabi to seek clues into the mystifying psyches of my Emirati hosts from among Thesiger's observations of their forebears.

Despite my initial reservations about Mahra's gift, her thoughtfulness touched me and I offered my thanks. "No, it should be me thanking you for asking in the first place," she said. "Most foreigners don't show much interest in our history or culture. If you're going to come here, I feel that it's the least you can do to find out about our people. We're very proud of our traditions, you know. I like to think of myself as a daughter of the pearl fishers." Mahra straightened with visible satisfaction at this last thought. In reality, she had told me that her father was in the military, but I didn't begrudge her the poetic license.

Mahra at least seemed to practice what she preached regarding her society's customs. Whereas many foreigners saw the coverings of the shayla and abayya as symbols of female oppression, Mahra wore them with pride. Some of the other young Emirati women at the UPC favored abayyas embroidered with all sorts of sequins and bling, rather defeating their intended purpose as garments of modesty, but Mahra's was a pure, unadorned black. That didn't stop her from shifting as she stood in front of me so that her abayya parted slightly, betraying the sleek dress and designer shoes that she wore underneath. She smiled when she saw that the flare of color had caught my eye. "You like my shoes?" she asked.

Lights flashed and sirens blared as my friend's earlier words of warning came back to mind. Was this a test? I was doomed either way. If I said yes, the Culture Police would jump out and arrest me for having the nerve to set my eyes upon an Emirati woman's footwear. And if I said no, Mahra would obliterate me where I stood. I froze like a deer caught in headlights.

Thankfully she changed the subject. "How have you been enjoying our city so far? I hope you've seen something besides the office and your hotel." I told her that I was still getting to know Abu Dhabi. When I mentioned my walk the previous weekend, she blanched. "You *walked* to the Corniche?!"

"Um ... yes?" Had I committed some strange pedestrian faux pas?

Mahra shook her head. "Nobody walks here. Not unless you have to. I mean, I've walked *along* the Corniche, but never *to* it. I have my driver take me there."

"You don't drive yourself?" I blurted out the question before I realized how rude it was.

She didn't seem offended. "Actually I don't know how. My family has always had a driver, so I never needed to learn." Her tone was matter-of-fact. Mahra's comment hinted at the kind of privileged lifestyle modern Emiratis enjoy, a more luxuriant standard of living than most people can imagine.

Mahra smiled again. "Anyway, enjoy your reading. I'll be sure to quiz you next time we talk." She left, her flowing abayya seeming to glide down the hallway.

The diversity at the UPC was nothing short of extraordinary. In its short eighteen months of existence the agency had hired more than a hundred staff, half of them Emiratis and the others a miniature League of Nations of expatriates. The foreigners included plenty of westerners—North Americans, Europeans, Australians and so forth—but also several from more exotic places like Brazil, Japan, Russia, and even Fiji. There was also considerable representation from other Arab countries and the Indian subcontinent.

Like the UPC itself, the staffers were generally quite young. Few of the department heads were much over forty; the general manager, an Emirati, was only thirty-six. The locals in particular were a wellspring of youth. They had been handpicked from other agencies or scooped up right out of college to become the first cadre of Abu Dhabi's indigenous urban planners. Working alongside their expat colleagues, they would gain the skills and experience that would eventually enable Abu Dhabi to look inward for the expertise to build its future. One day the UPC's eager young Emiratis would run the place.

That day was still a long way off. Planning was a new field for Abu Dhabi. Even *Plan 2030* admitted that it was merely "an interim tool for evaluating development and growth propositions prior to full induction of a planning culture within the city."[16] The Emiratis who joined the UPC faced a steep learning curve. They had all come from different fields and had to be retrained. The general manager himself had to start from scratch when the crown prince picked him to head the agency; his first year or so on the job had been a crash course in the basic principles of what makes a city work. The emirate's first academic planning program at the Sorbonne's new Abu Dhabi branch, then under construction, was still a few years away from graduating its first students. The UPC was thus finding it a challenge to recruit Emirati staff that fit the agency's unique mission. As a result, some sections of the agency were made up almost entirely of expats.

Alex's little transport team was one of them. Our only Emirati was a young civil engineer named Khalid. Clancy, our transit specialist, was a gifted young Australian just a few years out of university. Lakshmi, a serene young Indian woman, was a technology virtuoso who managed the digital maps and population databases we used for our transport plans. Shortly after I joined, the team increased to six with the addition of Carlo, a dapper Italian who possessed his country's fashion sense in spades, as evidenced by his monogrammed shirts and colorful ties. Though he looked to have come straight from a Milan catwalk, in reality he had more in common with Fermi and Marconi than with Gucci and Versace; his analytic mind could rapidly decipher traffic models that looked like hieroglyphics to anyone else.

The UPC's rapid growth made for cramped quarters at the office. I was put in an overflow room with several other recent arrivals. Liz hailed from Leeds and had joined the environment team. Her diminutive frame packed outsized opinions, which she dispensed with oh-so-proper English. Chris was a Kiwi architect who rarely talked except to complain; he had come to Abu Dhabi thinking he would be designing paradigm-shattering buildings, but he had instead been relegated to the role of a glorified draftsman. Lastly there was Sultan, a young Emirati graduate who worked for Development Review. He seemed like a fish out of water, struggling to adjust to a regular work schedule and learn the planning principles that were required of him.

One afternoon Liz walked into the office, dumped a ream of papers on her desk, and collapsed into her chair with a sigh. When I asked what was wrong, she muttered a single word: "Estidama."

The Estidama project was the UPC's initiative to develop a set of codes for designing and building energy-efficient structures and communities. In essence, Estidama was intended to produce something similar to the internationally accepted Leadership in Energy and Environmental Design (LEED) guidelines, but ones adapted to Abu Dhabi's exacting climate. Although Estidama had begun with the best of intentions, it had quickly gone astray. The UPC in its embryonic state had hired an untested consultancy to develop the codes. Its performance had been lackluster. Estidama became a byword around the office, playing on the dual meaning of the term itself: in Arabic, *estidama* translates as "sustainable," but with a slightly different pronunciation it can also mean "mishap." When Liz arrived, she was given the unenviable task of sorting the troubled project out.

"What's the latest?" I asked.

"The consultants won't make any more changes to the drafts. I've gone back to them with the same edits three times. At first they just ignored me, but now they flat-out refuse to do what I tell them." She nodded at the pile of papers. "This thing's rubbish. Worse than useless."

I leafed through the pages. The quality was amateurish, with elementary spelling errors, grammatical mistakes, illegible diagrams, and entire sections that looked like they had been lifted straight from LEED. "You're not kidding," I said.

"I finally told them just to send me the originals so I can make the changes myself. And you know what? They said they won't give us anything until we pay off the rest of their contract." Her rancor caught the attention of Sultan, who came over from his desk to inspect the documents.

I tried to make light of the situation. "That's what we get for hiring the lowest bidder, right?"

Liz glared at me. "Hardly. Their contract is twelve million dirhams."

I let fly a rather indelicate response before I could censor myself. I glanced at Sultan, concerned he might be offended, but he didn't seem to mind. Because of the cultural stress placed on social harmony, Emiratis rarely criticize anyone directly, and harsh invectives are frowned upon. Still, three million dollars for the garbage in front of us was highway robbery. "I'd call this a waste of taxpayer money if we were in the States," I said, trying to atone for my faux pas, "but I guess that doesn't apply here." Abu Dhabi is a tax-free locale; the government derives its revenue almost solely from oil.

Sultan laid the papers back on Liz's desk. "No, it's not your money they're wasting. It's ours." I could detect no concern in his voice.

Three

The Mean Streets

To me the sun-blistered skeleton of a car seemed infinitely more horrible than the carcass of a camel. — *Wilfred Thesiger, Arabian Sands*

Abu Dhabi's streets are designed to kill." The presenter's blunt statement shocked his audience awake. We were in the second day of a workshop convened to help create a new design manual for Abu Dhabi's streets, one of the UPC's foremost initiatives. The workshop's momentum had begun to drag, prompting the presenter to try and shake things up.

The dapper man at the podium was Dr. Adam, one of the UPC's senior managers some of the staff had nicknamed the Professor. He oversaw the TIES department, including Alex's transport team, and had an air of genius about him. The Professor was in his fifties, a shade over five feet tall, with a Cheshire-cat grin and a shock of hair reminiscent of Einstein. He had left his native England when he was a teenager, hitchhiked through Asia on the Hippie Trail, and eventually landed in Australia. Within a few short years he had picked up a PhD in planning and Australian citizenship. He had that rarest of intellectual combinations: the scholarly mind that was also organized. Finding the life of an academic to involve too much pondering and not enough doing, he had gone into practice, bringing to his work a cerebral touch that had earned him his soubriquet. Although the Professor was Alex's supervisor and thus my uber-boss, he was friendly and approachable, with a witty retort always at hand.

Creating a design manual for Abu Dhabi's streets was the Professor's labor of love. The brutality of the roads had appalled the Professor when he came to the emirate in late 2007 as one of the UPC's first hires. He had proposed creating a manual to guide both the design of all new streets and the retrofit of existing ones. Among its interventions, the manual would reduce the width of Abu Dhabi's gaping rights-of-way by moving certain utility lines beneath the road surfaces. Although such a configuration is standard practice in just about every other city, Abu Dhabi's utility companies had resisted it since the early days of the emirate's urbanization, instead demanding wide underground corridors on either side of main thoroughfares.[1] It had taken months of painstaking negotiations, but the Professor and the members of the UPC's infrastructure team had persuaded some of the utilities to permit their lines to run beneath the streets.

In addition to making better use of space and giving the streets a more human scale, the manual's reduced rights-of-way would also facilitate tightening lane widths to reduce speeds, drawing on recent research demonstrating that driver speeds are more influenced by road design than by posted limits or the velocity of other cars.[2] Slower speeds would in turn render unnecessary the ubiquitous (and ubiquitously annoying) speed bumps that littered Abu Dhabi's smaller streets. The manual would also prescribe how Abu Dhabi's new tram and bus transit systems were to integrate into the street network. It would improve the harsh pedestrian realm with landscaping, bike lines, furniture, and shading. In keeping with *Plan*

2030's recommendation to break the city's existing superblocks into smaller and more navigable clusters, the manual outlined how to accomplish this with the addition of more frequent cross-streets.

At the time, street design manuals were an emerging fashion in the transport field. Agencies such as the United Kingdom's Department for Transport and New York City's Department of Transportation had paved the way with design guidebooks that had significantly improved the safety and aesthetics of their jurisdictions' thoroughfares. The UPC's manual would draw heavily on these precedents. It had taken the Professor more than a year to line up funding and hire consultants to do the legwork, but the development of the manual was now underway.

The street design manual was intended to do more than just prettify Abu Dhabi's streets; it would also make them safer and encourage a better balance between pedestrians and cars. Following *Plan 2030*'s mantra of "all trips begin and end with a walk,"[3] the manual aspired to make walking as comfortable as possible all year round, thereby encouraging residents to walk—especially for short trips. If Abu Dhabi ever hoped to become a leading world city, the manual was absolutely necessary for rehabilitating the city's public realm and image. On a more practical level, the manual would also save lives. The Professor's frank statement to the workshop attendees was no hyperbole: Abu Dhabi's streets were deathtraps, especially for pedestrians.

Having captured everyone's attention, the Professor proceeded to outline some of the more fatal elements of the city's current street designs. He pulled up a slide showing a cross-section of one of Abu Dhabi's ten-lane arterials. "Pedestrian crossings on the arterials, as you're all aware, are spaced too far apart. A pedestrian must walk to either the nearest intersection or the mid-block underpass, if one is present. In this climate, it's unrealistic to expect people to go half a kilometer out of their way. And so we see this." His next slide showed a photo of a group of laborers darting through heavy traffic. "The medians have knee-high curbs and fences to discourage this sort of behavior, but people do it anyway, of course. By slowing them down, the obstructions in the medians merely make them easier targets.

"Now let's consider junctions." The Professor advanced to an isometric view of a typical four-way intersection. "Your average Abu Dhabi junction is an accident waiting to happen. The dedicated slip lanes for right-hand turns are angled so that drivers must crane their necks to look over their left shoulder while turning, rendering them oblivious to any pedestrians in front. The island refuges are concrete blocks with divots for footpaths, barely wide enough to hold one person, and heaven forbid she be pushing a stroller. The split-phase signal timing is confusing and encourages people to jaywalk. Even drivers aren't safe." He switched to a picture of one of the traffic signal poles that protruded from the medians at every intersection. "The signal poles are encased in concrete that comes up to waist height and is half a meter thick. If an oncoming car hits one of those, I assure you, the pole will survive but the driver will not."

The Professor continued lecturing for a solid fifteen minutes, his crisp speech a mix of King's English and Crocodile Hunter. He inventoried all the incongruities of the street environment I had observed while walking the city, as well as many I had missed. Although he was a doctor of philosophy rather than of medicine, his dissection of Abu Dhabi's streets mimicked the clinical precision of a surgeon. By the time he was done, I was halfway convinced that the engineers who had originally designed Abu Dhabi's streets should be charged with manslaughter.

"If any of you wonder why this matters, I'd like to quote from a recent article," the Professor said. He held up a copy of the *National*, a local English-language newspaper, the Abu

Dhabi government had founded in 2008 to experiment with an open press. The UAE's other Arabic and English dailies were little more than government mouthpieces, like much of the press throughout the region. Their front pages favored breathless accounts of Sheikh So-and-So entertaining some foreign dignitary. Not so the *National*, which was given considerable leeway to report on topics that were normally off limits.

"'A French tourist was run down and killed yesterday on a pedestrian crossing in Abu Dhabi," the Professor read, "just ninety minutes after he had disembarked from his cruise ship. The victim's wife and a friend managed to jump out of the way as the driver, an Emirati, sped off in his BMW."[4] The Professor rested the newspaper on his lectern. "So far this year, thirty percent of road accidents have involved pedestrians, up considerably from just two years ago. Our surveys indicate that two-thirds of pedestrians don't use crossings because they're too far out of the way. There were nearly six hundred pedestrian accidents last year—one every fourteen hours, many of them fatal. That, ladies and gentlemen," the Professor paused for emphasis, "is why the street design manual matters."

At the lunch break later in the day, the Professor waved me over to his table. "Let me introduce you to Larry, the UPC's distinguished founder," he said. Beside him sat a genial-looking man in his early fifties. I had heard plenty about Larry from my UPC colleagues and was delighted to finally meet him.

Larry had spent most of his planning career with the City of Vancouver, rising through the ranks to become codirector of planning in the 1990s. During his tenure he presided over a huge residential expansion in the form of dozens of condominium towers that rose all over the downtown. International affairs magazines fawned over Vancouver's aesthetics and high-class lifestyle, portraying it as a sort of city-sized Club Med with mountains instead of sunshine. Vancouver's cultural amenities, modern infrastructure, and low levels of crime and congestion earned it a reputation as one of the world's most livable cities.[5] There was some debate over the extent to which Larry and his policies drove this wave of success, with critics claiming he was merely an accessory to Vancouver's rise. Nevertheless, Larry was awarded the Order of Canada for his role in shaping the city.

When Larry left the Vancouver government, the crown prince's people made him an offer he couldn't refuse: a blank check to develop a blueprint for Abu Dhabi's future and also help set up a new agency to implement it. Larry brought along nearly a dozen of his former underlings to serve as the UPC's first staffers. Around the office, they lightheartedly referred to themselves as the Vancouver Mafia and to their kingpin as Legendary Larry. In the year and a half since then, Larry and his acolytes had finished *Plan 2030* and gotten the UPC up and running, after which he had switched roles and become more of a mentor to the agency's senior staff. That, at least, was what I had gathered from my colleagues; after two weeks at the UPC I still hadn't met Larry or even seen him in our offices.

Larry greeted me with a smile. "Welcome to the UPC. What section are you in?"

"The transport team," I replied.

"Transport, great. You know, we have a saying in Vancouver: 'The best transportation plan is a good land use plan.'"[6] I thought I saw the Professor roll his eyes.

I had a dozen burning questions for Larry about his experience and his theories on urbanism, but all that came out was inanity: "So ... how do you like living here? I imagine it's quite a change from Vancouver."

"I don't live here," Larry replied. Responding to my confused look, he clarified. "I come out from Vancouver every other month to help the UPC with strategic direction."

"Oh, I'm sorry. No one told me you had moved back to Canada."

"I didn't. I never moved here to begin with."

This came as a surprise. It struck me as odd that someone charged with planning a city's future wouldn't want to live there while doing so, for the sake of understanding the context if not for simple expediency. One must inhabit a city in order to know it.

Redirecting the conversation, the Professor asked, "So, Michael, what's your take on the street design manual?"

I told him how my own experiences with Abu Dhabi's streets underscored the manual's importance. The Professor's eyes flashed and he muttered, "Mmm ... quite right ... mmm." In our previous conversations he had displayed a tendency to slip into this mad scientist mode, acknowledging whomever was speaking with while his mind chewed furiously on something else. Had I told him his hair was on fire, undoubtedly he would have murmured his assent.

Even though the Professor's thoughts were elsewhere, I measured my words. I said that the street design manual was a good start to the desperately needed overhaul of Abu Dhabi's public realm. In reality, while I fully believed this, I also felt something was still lacking. The workshop's discussions and the draft sections of the manual I had read were thorough, but they largely ignored informal or unstructured activity on the part of the people in the street. Indeed, they lacked any mention of honest-to-goodness public spaces, the areas for urban ingenuity that give a city vitality. The manual aimed to regiment every inch of Abu Dhabi's rights-of-way, making them nice and neat and pretty. That was certainly preferable to the current state of affairs, but it was also possible to swing the pendulum too far in the other direction.

The street design manual was not alone in this regard. An obsession with control permeated the documents that were shaping the new Abu Dhabi. The government had produced an ensemble of visions, plans, and policies covering every aspect of the emirate's transformation—including the UPC's own *Plan 2030*, the Council for Economic Development's Economic Vision 2030, the Environment Agency's Environment Vision 2030, and so forth. The government had even gone so far as to create a stand-alone entity, the Office of the Brand of Abu Dhabi (referred to by its amusing acronym, OBAD), to act as the "guardian and patron of the city's brand identity,"[7] largely by making sure that all of the other government agencies adhered to the proper logos, typesetting, and buoyant party-line messages in their public communications.

It was all very slick, but I also felt it was too rigid and utopic, particularly the parts that dealt with the city's built environment. The great irony of urban planning is that disorder and chaos are just as necessary to the health and growth of a city as are organization and command. As Jane Jacobs explained in her seminal *The Death and Life of Great American Cities*, healthy cities are "spontaneous and untidy," and their apparent disarray often masks a complex and elegant organic order.[8] The planner's role is not to squash the chaos but to guide it. While traveling in nearby Qatar in the 1970s, Jonathan Raban met a planner who put it eloquently: "The planner's job is just to make the skeleton, and then wait and see what kind of flesh the people grow on it."[9]

The Orwellian undercurrent of Abu Dhabi's transformational plans reminded me of Alex's statement regarding the leadership's fascination with Singapore. For decades Singapore has enjoyed a reputation as a tightly run ship. The island nation is a police state where chewing gum is outlawed and graffiti is punishable by caning. William Gibson called it "Disneyland with the death penalty, a relentlessly G-rated experience."[10] That was one aspect of the Singapore model Abu Dhabi's leaders might have been better off trying *not* to mimic.

But of course I said none of this to the Professor. I had all of a few weeks in Abu Dhabi under my belt; surely my worries were exaggerated. Besides, he was obviously occupied with weightier matters. No sooner had I finished praising the street design manual's merits than he said, "Right, well, let's hope our friends at the Department of Transport agree. The way they talk, you'd think they want to make another bloody Dubai."

The UPC's transport team faced an uphill battle. It was our mission to remake not only Abu Dhabi's streets, but also the emirate's entire transport paradigm. Life in Abu Dhabi revolved around the automobile—fitting for a place that owed its modern existence to oil. But the automotive addiction was also one of the emirate's greatest shortcomings and a detriment to its residents' lives.

Visitors to Abu Dhabi and the UAE as a whole are often bewildered at the contradiction of the country's roads, where the first and third worlds collide. In terms of the quality of their design and the extent to which they cover the country's major population centers, the UAE's highways are comparable to in any the West. Their shortcomings are relatively minor. On-ramps and off-ramps, for example, have an annoying tendency to change course mid-turn, so that a driver proceeding down an off-ramp at a reasonable speed can suddenly find himself pointed directly at the concrete barrier lining the ramp's outer edge. Lanes also have a habit of disappearing without warning, resulting in confused scrums as drivers are forced to merge. Setting such annoyances aside, however, the UAE's highways are on a par with North America's great "high-speed slashes of concrete and tar," as John Steinbeck called them.[11] I can vouch that the UAE highways certainly put Michigan's potholed interstates to shame.

Yet these advanced highways are full of drivers who cannot grasp the concept that a motor vehicle can injure or even kill. The result is a road circus that would be hilarious if it did not so often end in tragedy. The U.S. Department of State includes these sobering words in its official advice to travelers: "Traffic accidents are a leading cause of death in the UAE.... The UAE has the highest rate of road fatalities in the Middle East and one of the highest rates in the world. Drivers often drive at high speeds. Unsafe driving practices are common, especially on inter-city highways."[12]

This is a monumental understatement. Unsafe driving practices are legion, and the country's road safety record is appalling. In 2009 the UAE averaged 37.1 road deaths for every one hundred thousand people, the ninth-highest rate in the world, and more than double the global average of 18.8.[13] Traffic accidents are the country's second leading cause of death after cardiovascular disease, ranking ahead of contagions such as AIDS and tuberculosis.[14] In Abu Dhabi, the renewed influx of foreign workers in the post-Zayed years has caused the numbers of registered cars to skyrocket, further exacerbating the chaos. There were a total of 116,487 road accidents in Abu Dhabi in 2009—one wreck every four and a half minutes, an astounding 149 percent increase from just four years before. The chaos is compounded by the policy of leaving accidents in place even if they are blocking traffic. If the drivers involved in a collision attempt to move their cars out of the way, the police will not file a report and the insurance companies won't pay out. Driving the death-defying roads is one of the worst aspects of life in the emirate.

Although Abu Dhabi's Western expats are wont to complain about the dangerous driving of the city's South Asian cabbies and truckers in particular, who presumably honed their skills amidst the chaos of Dhaka or Kabul, all of the emirate's myriad ethnic groups share the blame. The native Emiratis are certainly no exception. They are the driving force behind Abu Dhabi's car craze, piloting the biggest SUVs, the poshest sedans, and the sleekest sports cars. The UAE, and Abu Dhabi in particular, is one of the most lucrative automotive markets in the world, home to fully one-sixth of the three hundred Bugatti Veyrons in existence, each of which costs a cool $1.5 million. The UAE is Porsche's fourth-largest market after Germany, China, and Russia, countries with anywhere from ten to 137 times its population. Sales of

Rolls-Royces in Abu Dhabi tripled between 2006 and 2007.[15] Cars I used to glimpse only at Detroit's annual auto show are commonplace on Abu Dhabi's roads. After my first few weeks in the emirate, Ferraris, Bentleys, and Maseratis no longer turned my head.

Unfortunately the Emiratis steer their fancy rides as though they have a collective death wish. One popular travel Web site drolly states, "Emiratis are a proud but welcoming people and, *when not in their cars*, are generally extremely civil and friendly."[16] It is standard procedure for an Emirati to cut across six lanes of highway to make a last-minute exit, or to pull out in front of oncoming traffic without looking. Young Emirati men are the worst offenders. A 2011 study by the Emirates Foundation for Philanthropy found that young locals perceive tailgating as a respected behavior, whereas obeying the speed limit, keeping a safe distance, and pulling over to make phone calls are considered "unmanly." Half of Emirati males between the ages of 18 and 33 admitted to not wearing a seat belt or driving on the wrong side of the road. A quarter boasted of reckless speeding, passing in the wrong lane, and bullying, the infamous Emirati habit of bearing down from behind with high-beams flashing, regardless of whether the driver in front can even change lanes. One in six Emiratis said they drive more aggressively in the presence of a foreign driver or even a local with a license plate from another emirate—the tribal Bedu mentality in modern form.[17]

Deplorable as these statistics are, they don't do justice to the horrific human tragedies that Abu Dhabi's road psychosis produces. Shortly after I arrived in the emirate, the *National* reported on three Emirati girls between the ages of four and seven who were killed attempting to cross Airport Road in front of the Carrefour supermarket. Their three Indonesian nannies were also injured, one sustaining such severe brain damage that she died more than a year later after being moved back to her home country. The driver who ran them down, a twenty-year-old Emirati, was jailed for six months, fined five thousand dirhams, and made to pay another three hundred thousand in "blood money" restitution to the parents.[18] With such derisory penalties for the locals, it is perhaps no wonder they drive like mad.

In short, Abu Dhabi's roads in early 2009 were a hot mess. The UPC's *Plan 2030* hoped to change that, primarily by outfitting the city with an extensive multimodal transit system. Transit was an entirely new concept in Abu Dhabi; the city hadn't even had buses until a trial fleet was introduced in late 2008. Those first buses were soon packed to capacity at all hours of the day, confirming what everyone instinctively knew: the pent-up demand for transit was huge. The subway system, trams, and additional bus lines prescribed in *Plan 2030* would give residents an alternative to driving and relieve pressure on the beleaguered roads. Without the transit systems, the emirate's car dependency would simply continue to grow unabated, turning the new Abu Dhabi into a giant parking lot.

The UPC wasn't alone in its quixotic effort to reinvent Abu Dhabi's transport ethos. Among the emirate's other newly formed government agencies was the DOT, the Abu Dhabi Department of Transport. In theory, the UPC and DOT had complementary roles in the transport sphere, the former being responsible for integrating the transport networks within Abu Dhabi's broader strategic planning, and the latter being in charge of policy and implementation.

In practice, the relationship was already bumpy. The DOT's staff tended to see their UPC counterparts as hopeless idealists, whereas we often thought them myopic. The DOT had poached many of its staff from Dubai's Roads and Transport Authority (RTA) in the wake of the downturn that hit the neighboring emirate in late 2008. The RTA exiles brought with them the belief that Dubai's disjointed, unintelligible system of roads was the model to follow. Their canon was the infamous *Policy on the Geometric Design of Highways and Streets* propagated by the American Association of State Highway and Transportation Officials, which had helped eviscerate many a North American city.[19] For the DOT's traffic engineers, mass transit meant widening highways from four lanes to six.

The differences of opinion between staffs of the UPC and DOT were more than just philosophical: they had significant implications for the city's future form. For example, when I mentioned my reservations about the Wahda City project beside my hotel to Alex, he showed me a study that the DOT had undertaken to estimate the effects of the traffic volumes that the development would generate when finished. Not surprisingly, the results showed seven of the nearest arterial intersections degrading to Level-of-Service F, the lowest grade, meaning that drivers would face waits of ninety seconds or more. In response, the DOT had proposed converting each of those intersections into a grade-separated flyover—in essence, a highway overpass—a move that would have further chopped up the already disjointed urban fabric. The Professor and Alex had managed to kill that idea, at least for now, by arguing that any new transport infrastructure should make the city more connected and not cut it to ribbons. But the incident showed that even within the government there were conflicting views as to how the new Abu Dhabi should take shape.

* * *

"You all understand why this initiative is so important." The Emirati leaned forward and rested his hands on the immense boardroom table. He was dressed in a snow-white *kandora* robe and matching *gutra* headcloth, the national habiliment of Emirati males. The kandora is a striking garment, but not terribly practical for any kind of physical activity. As noted in the film *Syriana*, the kandora's primary purpose is to convey on behalf of its wearer the message "It's hot, and I don't have to work."

This particular Emirati's garb was even whiter than most, accented by a sundial-sized Rolex watch and a Mont Blanc pen clipped below his collar. These accessories are the other unofficial but ubiquitous elements of the male Emirati uniform, the only means for locals to personalize their monochrome chrysalis while dropping not-so-subtle hints regarding their wealth. In the present case, the accessories were redundant. Even without the trappings of his position, the chairman of the Abu Dhabi National Exhibition Centre (ADNEC) dominated the room. I had come to the Exhibition Centre for a meeting with representatives of Abu Dhabi's major government agencies, which the staff of ADNEC (the term used interchangeably for the centre and the state-owned company that ran it) had convened in order to introduce a new transport-related proposal. Alex had tasked me to join Khalid, the transport team's sole Emirati, in representing the UPC. In addition to Khalid and me there were attendees from half a dozen government departments, the police force, and all of the utility companies. Even the army had a seat at the table. For a private development company to summon such a gathering was certainly unusual in my experience. ADNEC obviously had some importance beyond just serving as a giant showroom.

In fact, ADNEC was one of the most visible showpieces of Abu Dhabi's strategy of economic diversification, designed to lure conferences and exhibits from around the region. When it opened in 2007, the centre was the largest of its kind in the entire Middle East, with no fewer than twelve exhibit halls and 730,000 square feet of floor space. In just its second full year of operation, ADNEC was already hosting over a hundred annual events, including the World Future Energy Summit, the International Petroleum Exhibition, and the Cityscape real estate conference. The most important event on ADNEC's calendar was the International Defense Exposition (IDEX for short), a biennial weapons bazaar that drew dignitaries, defense ministers, and arms dealers from all over the world. Abu Dhabi's sheikhs loved their military toys, and IDEX was a huge source of pride for them.

At the beginning of the meeting the ADNEC staff had proposed a project that would allow them to expand IDEX's footprint and take the show to the next level. They wanted to drop the highway that ran alongside the exhibition centre into a tunnel over which they would construct a concrete plaza fifteen hundred feet long and four hundred feet wide. The plaza would enable IDEX to host its spectacular outdoor demonstrations—tanks bouncing over obstacle courses and commandos jumping from helicopters—without having to shut down the highway, which had caused huge traffic headaches the last time around.

Though the project sounded straightforward, it would be far from easy. The highway in question, named after the Khaleej al Arabi (Arabian Gulf), was one of only three arteries that connected the populous northern half of Abu Dhabi Island with the southern end and the mainland beyond. Khaleej al Arabi ran along the island's western edge, Airport Road went down the middle, and the third arterial, the Shar'a al Salaam (Street of Peace), curved along the eastern edge. The Municipality had already torn up Salaam Street, as the latter was commonly called, in late 2008. In an attempt to stave off the gridlock that all of the city's new developments would produce, the Municipality's engineers had elected to redesign Salaam Street as a free-flowing, grade-separated freeway to channel traffic from one end of the island to the other. Abu Dhabi had thus lost one-third of its cross-town traffic capacity for at least half a decade while Salaam Street was being rebuilt. When I arrived in 2009, the entire northeast quadrant of the city had been chopped into a maze of dead-ends and detours where the freeway's new three-mile tunnel was burrowing its way beneath the downtown. For being the Street of Peace, Salaam had created plenty of strife.

Now ADNEC proposed to do the same thing with another of Abu Dhabi's main arteries, albeit on a smaller scale. While unveiling the concept for the Khaleej al Arabi tunnel, the ADNEC staff had tried to preempt our concerns by promising that they would keep the road open during the tunnel's construction. They would lay a temporary asphalt detour to reroute the highway between the area for the tunnel box and the shoreline roughly two hundred feet away. Even if they managed to squeeze the realigned road into such a tight space, I was skeptical that everything would go so smoothly. During my career I had managed enough construction projects to know that nothing ever went as planned. The representatives of the other agencies evidently shared my concerns. As soon as the ADNEC staff finished their presentation, they faced a barrage of questions and concerns from around the room.

That prompted ADNEC's chairman, who had sat silent while his staff presented the project proposal, to stand up and take charge. His tone was patronizing, as if he were instructing children. He explained to us in no uncertain terms that he expected our various agencies to spare no effort to make his project happen. "This initiative has the full support of top leadership. I trust you all know what that means." I had no idea what it meant.

"We'll need the utmost cooperation from all of you to make sure the project is completed by the next IDEX in 2011," the chairman continued. "That gives us twenty-three months." There were murmurs of disbelief around the room. Two years was an improbable timeframe for such a project, especially considering that all ADNEC had to show so far was a couple of abstract renderings—no design drawings, no engineering studies, nothing substantive. Before anyone could object or even pose a question, the chairman glanced at the enormous horologe on his wrist. "Now if you'll excuse me, I have another appointment. Thank you all for your cooperation." With that, he rose and walked out.

The room devolved into bedlam. What had been a single meeting became ten as factions formed around the table, arguing heatedly amongst themselves. An ear-splitting ringtone jangled from the mobile phone of one of the utility company representatives. He pushed back from the table and cupped a hand over his mouth, evidently thinking this placed him in some sort of cone of silence, and proceeded to hold a conversation at the top of his lungs. The Indian tea staff entered the room to deliver the drinks we had ordered at the start of the meeting, which compounded the confusion since everyone had since shifted seats. At the time, I thought that this uproar was all just the attendees' flustered reaction to the impossible task with which we had been saddled. Eventually, however, I came to realize that such chaos was typical of every Abu Dhabi meeting.

I slid several chairs down next to Khalid, my colleague from the UPC's transport team. In some regards Khalid and I were like alter egos: same age, same height, even the same olive skin tone. He kept his beard trimmed in the five o'clock shadow favored by Emirati men and wore squarish glasses similar to my own. Like all Emiratis his age (but unlike me), he was married, and had two kids, with a third on the way.

When Alex had first introduced me to Khalid, he mentioned that we would be working closely together on a number of projects. Although Khalid was only in his early thirties, he was one of the UPC's more experienced Emiratis, having worked previously with the Municipality as a civil engineer. I was delighted to be partnered up with someone so knowledgeable. That he happened to be an Emirati was an added bonus. Though I enjoyed being surrounded by the UPC's diverse expat tableaux, I also wanted to actually get to know some locals during my time in Abu Dhabi.

The first few conversations between Khalid and me had been cordial enough, but I didn't feel we were quite on the same wavelength. He spoke fluent English, albeit with an Arabic-inflected grammar and pronunciation all his own that took some effort to decipher. Though I could tell what he was saying, I never felt I knew what he was thinking. There always seemed to be something more going on behind the curtain of his glasses. Khalid's inscrutable demeanor brought to mind Thesiger's description of Sheikh Zayed's older brother Shakhbut: "He was courteous, even friendly, but aloof, and seemed to impose a rigid restraint on a naturally excitable temper. I suspected that he mistrusted all men."[20]

I pulled Khalid aside so we could hear each other over the din. "Is this thing for real?"

He seemed puzzled that I would ask. "Yes, of course. But I dunno if they can do it in time. Twenty-three month for design *and* build? Come on, you kidding me."

"I'm more concerned about the cost," I replied. "Did you hear their estimate—three billion dirhams? For something that gets used only a few days every other year?" Even taking into account Abu Dhabi's bottomless coffers, I couldn't help thinking that the project was excessive. I flipped through the renderings that the ADNEC staff had handed out. They showed a sparsely landscaped slab atop the tunnel, with tiny people milling around on it like ants. The presenters had assured us that the plaza would be a lovely public space for the 96 percent of the time that it wasn't a make-believe war zone. However, they conveniently failed to mention who would use that public space, or why. ADNEC was the only major generator of activity in the area. In Abu Dhabi's climate, there was little chance that the centre's patrons, or anyone else for that matter, would want to wander around outside on a concrete frying pan.

"Well, that's why we here," Khalid replied. "We supposed to keep them honest. If you think we need to do something, we can discuss it with Alex."

"What about that 'senior leadership' bit? What does that mean?"

"It mean sheikh or Executive Council." The Executive Council was the body of high-ranking Emiratis who helped the crown prince run Abu Dhabi. They made the decisions on many of the emirate's administrative affairs and were second in power only to the sheikhs themselves. The UPC's general manager reported to them.

"So if the sheikhs or the Executive Council have already approved this, what can we do about it?" I asked. Khalid flashed a smile worthy of a politician. "The developers say this about every project, umkak?" I had previously ascertained that his "umkak" meant "okay." "They show their sheikh nice pictures, and he say, go study it some more. Then they turn around and say to everybody, sheikh loves it and wants it tomorrow. Don't worry, these guys not as far as they make it sound."

I wasn't convinced, but I had to trust Khalid's judgment. The inner workings of Abu Dhabi's development arena were still a mystery to me.

After the chaotic remnants of the meeting eventually petered out, I made my way back through the exhibition center's cavernous interior towards the parking lot. From inside, ADNEC had the look and scale of a space-going cruise ship. The partitioned exhibit hall curved around in the shape of a squared-off horseshoe, the inside of which was lined by an airy two-story atrium with floor-to-ceiling windows, stylized elliptical skylights, sliding doors shaped like airlocks, and a host of other futuristic touches. Every surface was white and impossibly shiny.

I detoured into one of the restrooms. Inside, handmade "Out of Order" signs covered two of the three urinals. While I answered nature's call at the third, I noticed that its companions had been installed in clumsy fashion, which explained their malfunction. The porcelain bowls hung on the wall at odd angles and appeared to be held in place by wads of caulk. At the sink, the soap dispenser nearly came off in my hand. On closer inspection, just about everything in the restroom displayed shoddy workmanship. Even the expensive marble tiles on the floor and walls were smudged with dried glue. It was a curious contrast to the flawless sparkle of the rest of the exhibition centre.

I walked back out onto the atrium balcony, but stopped in my tracks after a few short paces. I could feel a slight vibration through the balcony floor. As I stood motionless, the vibration grew more pronounced, then subsided, and then picked up again. Ordinarily such a tremor wouldn't be surprising if there were a subway or some other below-ground source of vibration nearby. But I knew very well that Abu Dhabi had no subways as of yet, and the city was in a seismic zone with minimal earthquake risk.

The only other thing I could surmise was that one of the nearby construction sites was transmitting vibrations through the building's foundations. ADNEC (the company) was building a cluster of more than a dozen high-rise towers—a miniature downtown in its own right—next door. Judging by the quivering of the floor, the vibrations seemed alarmingly close to the exhibition centre's resonant frequency. Although I wasn't a structural engineer, I knew that unchecked resonance could have catastrophic consequences. A structure that absorbs vibrations matching one of its resonant frequencies will oscillate with increasing ferocity until it literally shakes itself apart. The driving forces of these vibrations can come from unexpected sources. For example, when London's Millennium Bridge opened in 2000, its designers were chagrined to discover that the bridge's swaying caused pedestrians to sway along with it, further exacerbating the swing. The issue was so severe that the bridge was closed for two years and retrofitted with dampers to offset the wobble.[21]

As I felt the balcony trembling beneath my feet, I wondered whether ADNEC's designers had taken any countermeasures in light of the construction nearby. I quickly shrugged this off. The architects shaping Abu Dhabi's new skyline were supposed to be some of the best in the world. The emirate was shelling out a fortune on its metamorphosis. Surely the folks in charge had covered all their bases.

Four

Nanny State

It is my duty as the leader of the people of this country to encourage them to work and to exert themselves in order to raise their own standards and to be of service to the country. The individual who is healthy and of a sound mind and body but who does not work commits a crime against himself and society.—*Sheikh Zayed bin Sultan al Nahyan*

S alim stood in the corner, looking lost. He was the only Emirati among the expats scurrying about the room, a lone kandora in a herd of sport coats and pantsuits. Given that the occasion concerned the provision of housing for his people, Salim's solitude was all the more ironic.

We were gathered in the conference room for a presentation on North Wathba, a new community that the UPC was master planning. At present North Wathba was ten thousand acres of windswept sand on the mainland, just south of the equally large and empty expanse that would soon be the new Capital District. *Plan 2030* called for North Wathba to become one of the Capital District's supporting neighborhoods, with housing for one hundred twenty thousand people. Officially, most of those residents were supposed to be Emiratis, the functionaries who would staff the Capital District's government offices, along with their families.

The new Abu Dhabi envisioned in *Plan 2030* had an almost uniformly Emirati face. The plan's renderings and pictures showed groups of smiling Emirati men, women, and children wandering contentedly through their shiny new city. Many of the new developments would consist almost entirely of housing built specifically for locals. Yet, at the time, Emiratis constituted an anemic portion of Abu Dhabi's population, less than 15 percent. From where their additional numbers would come was anyone's guess.

Managing the North Wathba plan was Elise, an energetic young Belgian woman from the UPC's Planning Policy Department. She had set foot in more countries than most people could name, having done everything from humanitarian work in West Africa to a half-year float down the Mekong. She had first come to Abu Dhabi to work for one of the emirate's newly formed real estate development companies, a stint that she referred to as her time with the Dark Side. On joining the UPC she had been put in charge of the agency's various Emirati housing projects, of which North Wathba was the largest. It was an impressive position for someone who had just turned thirty. I met her when Alex tasked me with the role of the transport representative on the team that would support Elise and Salim, her Emirati apprentice, in creating the North Wathba plan.

As with most of our projects, the UPC had contracted out the heavy lifting for North Wathba to one of Abu Dhabi's numerous consultancies. The city was a veritable Klondike, overrun by professionals instead of prospectors. The siren call of Abu Dhabi's boom had been answered by a host of expatriate consultants, advisors, and "experts" of every stripe who filled the ranks at government agencies, state-owned enterprises, and the myriad international consultancies that had set up a local office. Just as the French army had once staffed its Saharan outposts with criminals and ruffians from all corners of the globe, Abu Dhabi had assembled its own white-collar Foreign Legion, all drawn to the emirate by the money, or the adventure, or even just the chance to escape their bourgeois lives back home.

For North Wathba, the UPC had elected to work with an obscure consultancy from the Pacific Northwest. I had never heard of them before coming to the emirate, so I was surprised to learn that, in addition to North Wathba, they were working on a half-dozen other projects for the UPC. Evidently they had established a foothold in Abu Dhabi early in the post-Zayed years, had cultivated the right relationships, and were now raking in the cash.

The team of consultants had recently finished a set of preliminary concepts for the North Wathba plan, which they were now preparing to present to the UPC's general manager. It would be a key meeting that would influence the direction of all that would follow, and the consultants had flown in reinforcements from Portland to augment their Abu Dhabi staff for the occasion. They all rushed around the conference room making last-minute preparations, tacking diagrams to the walls and fine-tuning their slides.

The general manager entered the room and everyone stood in respect. It was the first time I had seen him in person. The general manager was shorter than I expected, but that didn't make him any less intimidating. His mouth was locked in a frown, and his chin jutted out as though daring anyone to defy him. As he took his seat at the head of the table, I could feel the tension in the room. He adjusted his *gutra* headcloth and said, "I have another meeting in half an hour, so please start."

The consultants, who had been told they would have two hours for the briefing, did a good job adjusting their presentation on the fly. They breezed through their slides and hit the major points, foregoing the technical details. Their three concepts for North Wathba all focused on transit-oriented development, clustering population and amenities around the stations for the Metro and tram lines that would connect the neighborhood to the Capital District and the wider transit network. With the incorporation of this density, North Wathba would avoid becoming just another suburban tract of monotonous single-family houses.

Density is an epithet across much of North America, conjuring up images of teeming, fetid slums.[1] Although nobody likes overcrowding, a certain degree of density is not only beneficial but also necessary to the creation of vibrant, efficient communities. Amenities such as transit, retail, cultural venues, and public spaces all require a certain concentration of population in order to be viable. A low-density neighborhood will by its nature be incapable of supporting these amenities, obliging residents to go elsewhere even to buy a loaf of bread, and forcing them to drive to get there. The consultants' incorporation of denser, transit-oriented clusters in North Wathba endeavored to avoid these pitfalls.

Fifteen minutes into the presentation, the general manager interrupted. "How many villas are you planning?" Unfortunately, the concept of Emirati housing was synonymous with the villa, that great architectural blight of the modern Gulf. In the 1950s American oil companies began building California-style villas in Saudi Arabia, filling entire expat housing compounds with the clone-like single-family houses. Villa fever caught on among the locals and spread like an epidemic from Kuwait to Oman. Thesiger saw some of the first examples and bemoaned them: "Now the spoiling hand of progress was on the land. Already some of the richer and more ostentatious sheikhs had built themselves houses which were as hideous as they were incongruous. These houses were much admired and would, I knew, be assiduously copied. Soon this new style would oust the local architecture, which, although harmonious and beautiful, was suddenly no longer fashionable, simply because it had lasted unchanged for centuries."[2]

The villa is the antithesis of the traditional Arabian house, which wraps around one or more courtyards offering privacy and shade. From outside, a traditional house reveals few hints as to its contents or the wealth of its owner.[3] A villa, on the other hand, typically sits alone in the middle of a large, sandy lot, its size and adornment apparent to all. The widespread embrace of villas by Gulf nationals over the decades was more than just a change in tastes; it marked a shift in fundamental cultural values, a departure from the Bedu aversion to any appearance of greed.[4]

The villa had become ubiquitous across Abu Dhabi. Within ten years of the discovery of oil, villas had crowded out the native architecture like an invasive species; they were an omnipresent scourge on the landscape. At first the desire for more living space was understandable. It was common for three or four generations to live together under one roof, and Emiratis had large families, averaging 9.8 persons per household. By 2009, however, that statistic had become questionable in light of the falling birthrates among locals, brought about by their advanced standard of living. None of my Emirati colleagues had more than four children. Nevertheless, the 9.8-persons-per-household figure was what the UPC continued to use, which in turn made spacious villas seem necessary. But even if a family felt they needed ten thousand square feet of home, there was no reason that home couldn't take a non-villa form that still offered the space and privacy locals cherished. A villa offered only isolation, exorbitant consumption of utilities, and a sandbox yard that rarely saw use.

North Wathba was going to be the UPC's first attempt to wean Abu Dhabians from their villa addiction by introducing alternate forms of housing designed for Emiratis, which would offer the requisite space but take a shape more suited to the climate and historical precedents. Responding to the general manager's inquiry as to how many villas North Wathba would provide, Elise explained: "The three concepts vary between three thousand and thirty-five hundred Emirati housing units. We've spread them among villas, townhouses, and multi-family buildings."

The general manager's frown deepened. "I need ten thousand Emirati houses. Villas, not apartments."

The lead consultant took this as hyperbole. "We might be able to get forty-five hundred units if we adjust the ratios. But there's no way they could all be villas."

The general manager was unmoved. "Was what I said unclear? I need ten thousand *villas*. I have a list of thousands of Emirati families waiting for houses."

Ah, The List. My colleagues spoke of it as the bane of their existence. The List was the nebulous register of Emirati families awaiting public housing assistance, which in Abu Dhabi meant a free plot of land with either a villa already in place on it or a no-interest loan to build one. A hardscrabble life in the projects, it certainly was not. The List supposedly numbered in the tens of thousands, but that was simply improbable. Abu Dhabi had fewer than twenty-five thousand Emirati households to begin with, and it wasn't as though one saw many homeless locals on the streets. None of the UPC's expats had ever laid eyes on The List, and most thought it nothing more than a ploy to buttress the official rhetoric of an Emirati-heavy future for Abu Dhabi.

Whether or not the general manager really needed them, he was adamant that there would be ten thousand villas in North Wathba. It looked as though this wouldn't be the project to loosen the villa's stranglehold on the emirate. Elise didn't mince her words. "If we include ten thousand villas, there won't be room for anything else. We'd have to reduce the community clusters to almost nothing, and the transit most likely won't work."

The general manager was equally blunt. "That's your problem, not mine," he said, rising from his chair. "Don't come back to me until you have those villas." With that, he left the room.

* * *

Housing handouts are merely one dish on the buffet of benefits that the Abu Dhabi government extends to its citizens. Emiratis enjoy one of the most bountiful and comprehensive welfare systems in the world. In addition to free land and housing finance, the state pays for nationals' healthcare, education, startup business capital, and even weddings, and heavily subsidizes their utilities, food, and fuel.

This largesse traces back to the patronal role of the sheikh within the tribal society of the Emiratis' Bedu forebears. The sheikh mediated disputes and ensured harmony among his tribe or clan, often by distributing scarce resources. Even if a sheikh gained respect as a competent leader, his position was far from guaranteed. On the contrary, sheikhs gained and retained power only through their ability to dispense patronage among their camps. A sheikh had to compete for the loyalty of his own tribesmen by the lavishness of his hospitality and gifts.[5] Bedu poets praised the ideal of the sheikh who gave so freely that he retained nothing but his people's esteem. This was no exaggeration; Thesiger recorded a companion's eulogy for a sheikh who gifted himself into penury: "His generosity ruined him. No one ever came to his tents but he killed a camel to feed them. By God, he is generous!' I could hear the envy in his voice."[6]

Abu Dhabi's recent history offers a case study of the consequences for a stingy sheikh. At the time oil was discovered in 1958, Abu Dhabi was ruled by Sheikh Zayed's older brother, Sheikh Shakhbut bin Sultan al Nahyan. Shakhbut expected the oil windfall to be short-lived and hoarded the revenues instead of using them to better the harsh lives of his people. For example, Shakhbut refused to allow the generation of electricity—with the notable exception of his own Al Hosn Palace, which he illuminated using portable generators, giving it the appearance of Disneyland among the otherwise unlit settlement. Half a decade later, Abu Dhabi still had not a single doctor or nurse, much less a clinic in which to practice; as late as 1965 it was still common for local women to die during childbirth.[7]

As the years passed and Shakhbut's subjects saw no benefits from the oil money they knew to be pouring in, they began to grumble against him. The relationship between Shakhbut and his people became so strained that senior members of the Al Nahyan clan and other prominent Abu Dhabi families enlisted the help of the British to quietly depose the ruler in 1966 and replace him with the dynamic Zayed. This transition of power was actually one of the least blood-stained in the history of Abu Dhabi's rulers, a history peppered with patricide, fratricide, and plenty of other intrigue. Zayed's own father, Sultan, was killed by his half-brother Saqr, but only after the two of them had already conspired to murder their older brother Hamdan and seize leadership in 1922.[8] Saqr in turn was killed by a family bodyguard avenging the death of Sultan, which paved the way for Shakhbut as Sultan's eldest son to take the reins in 1928.[9] Fearing more bloodshed, the mother of Shakhbut and Zayed made her sons swear an oath never to kill one another, which eventually assisted the smooth transfer of power from Shakhbut to his younger brother in 1966. Abu Dhabi's tapestry of taboos ensures that Shakhbut's ouster is rarely mentioned. Official histories give the impression that Abu Dhabians simply woke up one morning to find Zayed at the helm.

Once his plan for the modernization of Abu Dhabi began to take form, Zayed instituted a policy of giving each male Abu Dhabian three plots of land: one for a home, another for a commercial building along a main street, and another for an industrial site or workshop, thus providing both housing and sustainable sources of income.[10] Some locals who received plots on main roads or in central areas complained that they would have preferred more secluded locations, reflecting the cultural stress on privacy. Eventually, however, those prime landholdings would make their owners fabulously wealthy.[11]

As Abu Dhabi and its fortunes grew, so did the scope of the state's welfare. At Zayed's direction, the government paid for Emiratis to receive free health care in the city's new clinics. If treatment wasn't available locally, the state paid for its citizens to go to Europe. Government-run schools offered free enrollment to every Emirati student, as did the universities that later followed, although ambitious locals also had the option of obtaining degrees in North America or Europe at the government's expense. The public utilities sold water and electricity at rates far below cost, and the state-owned oil monopoly, the Abu Dhabi National Oil Company (ADNOC), did the same with fuel. The government established price controls on staples like bread, milk, produce, and soft drinks. Investment funds were created to offer Emiratis low-cost financing to start businesses. And as though all these benefits weren't enough, it also became evident that the state would take no action against Emiratis who delayed or defaulted on their low-to-no-interest housing loans. There was hardly an expense category in which the government did not underwrite its citizens' lifestyles.

After Zayed died, the welfare state continued to grow under the leadership of his sons. By 2009 the government's giveaways, subsidies, and other wealth transfers had reached a cumulative value of nearly two hundred thousand dirhams—that's fifty-five thousand dollars—per Emirati per year.[12] This figure might seem insignificant in light of the theoretical seventeen-million-dollar net worth of each of Abu Dhabi's citizens, but that inflated sum is derived from dividing the state's total wealth by the number of Emiratis. When one considers only the personal assets of Emirati households, the average citizen's net worth is probably no more than a paltry one or two million dollars. In any case, being given fifty-five thousand dollars a year with no strings attached is not a bad deal.

The benefits are doled out among citizens with rigid equality. Emirati society prizes consensus and harmony, so the government takes pains to avoid appearing to favor any individual or family over another. This approach would come back to haunt us at the UPC, as the Emirati housing plots we were obligated to create had to all be the same thirty-meter by thirty-meter square size, with an identical villa plunked down on each, a recipe for suburban sprawl in the extreme.

In both official publications and everyday talk, Emiratis are fond of using the term "tribal capitalism" to describe Abu Dhabi's unique blend of modern-day enterprise and traditional values.[13] Viewed from a different angle, the breadth, magnitude, and egalitarianism of the government's handouts to its citizens make Abu Dhabi seem more communist than the Soviet Union ever was, especially when one factors in the state-owned conglomerates that dominate the economy.

The effects of the welfare state make Abu Dhabi resemble the USSR in another regard, namely, its authoritarian politics. This has not always been the case. Over the last half-century the emirate has become significantly less democratic. Prior to the discovery of oil, Bedu society scorned the concept of hereditary leadership. Writing in the fourteenth century, Arab scholar Ibn Khaldun noted that "the Bedouins are the least willing of all nations to subordinate themselves to each other, as they are rude, proud, ambitious, and eager to be leaders. Their individual aspirations rarely coincide."[14] Within the open and fluid Bedu political structure, a leader was effective only when he mustered consensus to support the actions he proposed.[15] Thesiger likened the sheikh's position to that of the chairman at a committee meeting.[16] For generations, the sheikhs of the Al Nahyan clan had maintained their rule over Abu Dhabi not because of their lineage, but only because each successive ruler obtained the support of the tribe. A ruler who lost credibility, such as Shakhbut, was summarily removed.

The advent of the welfare state profoundly altered this political equation. The bounty that Zayed showered upon his people won him their hearts and cemented their support for his rule. It also transformed Abu Dhabi and the UAE as a whole from a fluid rule-by-acclaim regime into an autocracy. Zayed was the incarnation of the ideal benevolent sheikh, so his people didn't question his consolidation of power. Demonstrations and political parties were banned,[17] as was criticizing the government or the ruling family or saying anything deemed "harmful to society." A substantial state security apparatus was also erected as a safety measure against unrest. As the decades passed and the UAE's standard of living improved, the country slid lower on international lists of political freedom. In 2010 the Economist Intelligence Unit ranked the UAE 148th of 167 countries on its Democracy Index, below Belarus and Zimbabwe.[18]

The Emiratis also did not object as the Al Nahyan clan leveraged Abu Dhabi's oil wealth to amass a fortune worthy of Midas. The magnitude of the royal family's riches is difficult to gauge because of the fuzzy boundaries between state and royal bank accounts. Most observers estimate their collective wealth at around a trillion dollars[19]—that's trillion with a T—equal to the total annual economic output of Mexico or South Korea.

In essence, Abu Dhabi's welfare system is a two-way street. Observers refer to it as the "ruling bargain," a social contract under which the ruling family via the state provides free healthcare, education, housing, and other services in exchange for its subjects' acquiescence. In a way, the regime of Zayed & Sons is merely the latest in a long string of urban political machines stretching from Tammany Hall back to the Medicis of Renaissance Florence, all of which thrived at their respective cities' apogees by distributing largesse among their inner circle and, to a lesser extent, the population at large.[20]

Although Abu Dhabians were initially the sole beneficiaries of the new emirate's welfare, it was not long before Zayed extended the benefits to nationals from the other emirates as well, as a means of solidifying the identity and cohesion of the new United Arab Emirates. Since these benefits, along with the entire federal budget, were funded almost entirely by oil revenues, they also helped establish Abu Dhabi's primacy among the emirates. At first Abu Dhabi was intended only as a temporary seat of federal power; the UAE's 1971 constitution stipulated that within seven years of its ratification, a permanent capital was to be established in a new federal district along the border between Abu Dhabi and Dubai.[21] In addition, the rulers of the seven emirates were to elect a new president from among their number by secret ballot every five years. But with Abu Dhabi holding the purse strings, these provisions were never enforced. The other rulers dutifully reelected Zayed twice every decade until his death. The idea of a new federal district was finally dropped in 1996 when the constitution was amended to acknowledge Abu Dhabi as the permanent capital.[22] When Zayed's eldest son, Khalifa, succeeded him as president in 2004, the legacy of Zayed & Sons as unquestioned masters of a nation-leading Abu Dhabi was confirmed.[23]

All this talk of autocracy and welfare is not meant as criticism. For nearly five decades both the leadership of the Al Nahyan clan and Abu Dhabi's primacy among the emirates have benefited the UAE tremendously. Emiratis rightfully point out that their country boasts a level of security and stability sorely lacking across most of the Middle East. The UAE enjoys the greatest political stability of all six Gulf monarchies, despite offering the fewest political freedoms; even Saudi Arabia holds token elections. Friendly relations with neighboring countries and the absence of internal dissent have created a favorable climate for the UAE's economy to bloom. The country has become a magnet for both people and capital fleeing kleptocracies and unstable political powder kegs from Algeria to Afghanistan. Some political scientists laud the regime as a rare real-world example of a benevolent dictatorship.

The government's generosity comes at a steep cost, however. In order to fund its handouts, the state must divert nearly three-fourths of the price it receives for each barrel of oil it exports.[24] The state in turn exacts a toll from its citizens in the form of increasingly tighter controls on their private lives. Dress codes are one example. In the 1970s the government adopted the kandora and abayya as the obligatory national dress, with the aim of standardizing and cleaning up its citizens' shabby looks. Locals' clothing was much more varied and personalized prior to 1971; old photos show Bedu men naked from the waist up or clad in a simple waistcoat.[25] The government also began to take a firmer stance on whom its citizens, particularly its female citizens, could marry. Whereas it was common for Emirati women to marry husbands from other Arab countries well into the 1970s, any woman who does so today will be stripped of her citizenship and most likely disowned by her family.[26] A male Emirati, on the other hand, can marry whomever he wants, so long as he doesn't exceed the four contemporaneous wives permitted by Islam. Emiratis are also not exempt from Big Brother's watchful eye. As with everyone else, the state security services monitor nationals for any hints of antigovernment sentiment.[27]

This culture of control is so completely opposite from Abu Dhabians' pre-oil way of life that it is difficult to fathom. During Thesiger's five years in Arabia, he remarked time and again on the independence of the Bedu, which they prized far more than comfort; indeed, their suffering and hardship were a source of tremendous pride.[28] The Emiratis' Bedu forebears would no doubt have difficulty understanding the extent to which their descendants have traded freedom for lives of wealth and ease.

Nevertheless, today's Emiratis are much like their ancestors in at least one regard: they see no disgrace in soaking up the largesse their leaders dispense. "No Bedu thinks it shameful to beg," Thesiger observed. "Often he will look at the gift which he has received and say, 'Is this all that you are going to give me?'"[29] Modern Abu Dhabians are no different. And just as the Emiratis have come to take the state's bounty for granted, the state is powerless to wean them from its teat. It is widely accepted that the normally pliant Emiratis would not hesitate to jettison any sheikh who tried to roll back their benefits. The ruling bargain is a set of golden handcuffs joining the rulers to the ruled.

Perhaps the most troublesome aspect of this welfare state is the entitlement mentality it breeds. Emiratis are conditioned from birth to expect that the world, or at least their government, will give them everything on a silver platter. The effects are evident in locals' low rates of workforce participation. The official unemployment rate among Emiratis stood at 20 percent as of 2009, but owing to the sensitivity of the topic, the real rate is assuredly higher. When locals do choose to work, they gravitate almost exclusively to positions reserved for locals in government agencies and state-owned companies. Across the UAE, fewer than 10 percent of Emiratis work in the private sector, where foreigners make up a staggering 99 percent of the labor force.[30] The government has set aggressive "Emiratisation" targets to support its goal of nationals comprising half the labor force by 2015, but this is a pipe dream.

The self-perception of the Emiratis as an entitled elite is also evident in their behavior. One does not have to stay in Abu Dhabi for long to become accustomed to Emiratis cutting to the front of queues in stores, movie theaters, and government offices. Locals frequently drive without regard for traffic laws or anyone else on the road, knowing that if they are pulled over, they can talk their way out of ticket or call a relative in the police to get it dismissed. The elitism also expresses itself in more sinister ways; journalists have occasionally slipped news stories past the censors about Emirati families caught abusing their domestic helpers. If anything, Abu Dhabi's welfare benefits have only reinforced their recipients' inherited Bedu ethnocentrism.

The Arabic language has a term for this money-fueled hauteur: *Muhdath al-Na'ema,* which has roughly the same connotation as the French *nouveaux riche*. Abu Dhabi's English-speaking expats have derived their own label, a play on both the meaning of the emirate's name and the speed and ease with which locals have come by their wealth. To them, the Emiratis are all gazellionaires.

* * *

Unfortunately for me, the state's munificence didn't extend to foreigners, at least not when it came to housing. The UPC was generous enough to put me up in a hotel for my first month, but after that I was on my own. Apartment hunting in a new city is rarely easy, but in Abu Dhabi it was a nightmare. When I arrived in early 2009 the city faced a dire housing shortage. The influx of foreigners from the post-Zayed boom had overwhelmed the existing housing supply, and the first new developments were still a year or two from completion. Apartment prices skyrocketed to levels on par with Manhattan and central London, but those cities had far more to offer for the money.

When I began looking for housing, my colleagues warned me to keep my expectations low and my budget high. More than a few of the UPC's expats felt baited-and-switched. They had been lured to Abu Dhabi at least in part by the promise of lucrative tax-free salaries, only to discover after arriving that up to half of those sums could be lost to housing costs. "Welcome to Rob-You Dhabi," one colleague groused.

Thankfully I had help. A young Syrian woman named Noor, who was an acquaintance of mine from university, had been living in Abu Dhabi for several years at that point. She generously offered to take me apartment hunting with her estate agent.

After work one evening Noor pulled up to my hotel in one of the battered gold-and-white Toyota Corollas that made up the city's cab fleet. The Taliban Taxis, as they were called, had acquired their pejorative name not just from their dismal states of repair, but also because most of their drivers hailed from Pashtunistan and probably either had cousins in the eponymous militant movement or were themselves alumni. The taxis were notoriously unsafe; they received little maintenance, and their drivers followed rules of the road more appropriate to a demolition derby. In 2009 the DOT stopped renewing the Taliban Taxis' licenses and began phasing in a new fleet of silver Nissans with better-trained drivers in an effort to improve Abu Dhabi's image. For the next few years, however, the two-toned jalopies would still be a fixture of the emirate's roads.

We drove to the residential neighborhood of Khalidiya on the west side of the city, which was popular with upscale expats and Emiratis alike. There we met Noor's agent, a portly Egyptian with a baseball cap perched backwards on his head. "Hello, mister, I am Sharif with you." Later on I would reflect that this was a fitting introduction. He wasn't forthcoming with me about the legality of the places we viewed, and he certainly wasn't honest with me when it came to my deposit, so being Sharif with me would have to do.

Sharif took us inside an apartment building to look at a studio on the second floor. It was appalling. The main room was small and looked like it hadn't been cleaned in decades. The only illumination came from blue mood lights recessed into the ceiling. The kitchen consisted of a broken hot plate on the floor; there was no sink or stove in sight. The bathroom was even more claustrophobic. The toilet wobbled precariously, and the tub looked like it had been used to brew moonshine. Sharif surveyed this shambles and grinned. "For you my friend, I make special price: dirhams ninety-five thousand." Almost $26,000. I decided to keep looking.

Over the following hours we visited another half-dozen units, all similarly decrepit. None of them would have passed the most basic safety code. Were I a municipal inspector,

I would have condemned on the spot not only all of the units in which I set foot, but the buildings that housed them as well. I began to despair of finding anything remotely habitable and seriously considered staying in the hotel, though it would cost nearly two-thirds of my salary.

Finally Sharif took us to Mushrif, a quiet villa neighborhood near the south end of the island. We pulled up in front of a new villa that was in the final stages of construction. Sharif showed me studios on each of the three floors. All were cramped, bare, and strewn with construction dust, but at least there was no filth oozing from the walls. It was clear that the "studios" hadn't been designed as separate residences; they were just rooms in a big house, with closet-sized bathrooms and doors that opened onto a central stairwell. Sharif didn't think it odd that none of the units had so much as a sink for a kitchenette.

It was rank profiteering. At the office I had heard that Emiratis were cashing in on the housing crisis by getting free land from the government, building villas with upwards of fifty rooms apiece, and renting them out by the room in contravention of the law. Left unchecked, this illegal subdividing could lead to widespread overcrowding, with concurrent public health and safety risks. The authorities, however, seemed unable or unwilling to crack down.

I didn't relish the prospect of living in such confinement, but Noor advised me that I was unlikely to find anything better: "Believe me, I've looked." I asked Sharif what it would cost.

He did some mental math and replied, "Dirhams seventeen thousand," about $4,600. Well, at least the price was right. Noor spoke with him in Arabic, then clarified that he actually meant *seventy* thousand dirhams. I would shell out $19,000 for the honor of spending a year in this hovel. My college dorm room had been larger.

I resigned myself to my fate. "Fine, I'll take the studio on the top floor."

Noor translated and Sharif produced a one-page contract in Arabic. "What are the conditions?" I asked.

"You'll pay all the rent up front, you agree not to cohabit with anyone you're not married to, you agree not to house more than eight people in one room," Noor read. I certainly had no objections to the latter two conditions. I didn't see how the studio could fit more than one person as it was.

"Does it say anything about tenant's rights?"

Noor laughed. "You're in Abu Dhabi. You have no rights. By the way, I told Sharif you wanted the studio on the middle floor." Before I could protest she added, "You don't want anything on the top or bottom. You'll thank me later."

On our way out, Noor examined the landing outside my new apartment and the wide entrance hall on the ground floor. With a cryptic smile she said, "Enjoy it while it lasts."

Five

Into the Desert

In the deserts of southern Arabia there is no rhythm of the seasons, no rise and fall of sap, nothing but empty wastes.... No man can live this life and emerge unchanged. He will carry, however faint, the imprint of the desert, the brand which marks the nomad; and he will have within him the yearning to return, weak or insistent according to his nature. For this cruel land can cast a spell which no temperate clime can match.—*Wilfred Thesiger, Arabian Sands*

Seriously, does this ever end?" Liz said from the back seat of the Jeep.

"I know," replied Austin, the driver. "Feels like the backside of beyond, right?"

The highway stretched before us like an endless asphalt ribbon. On either side, reaching unbroken to the horizon was a tapioca-hued desolation of sand and scree. As far as the eye could see there was no terrain to speak of other than the occasional low ridge rising in the distance. The scattered smudges of scrub blurring past outside the window could very well have been mirages. This was desert in every sense of the word; it had none of the chromatic beauty or spectacular topography of the southwestern United States. It was as though this corner of the world had been passed over during the creation.

We had been driving for hours on the E11 highway, which runs from Abu Dhabi to the Saudi border almost two hundred miles to the west. The scenery at first had not been so bleak. For fifty or so miles beyond the city, both sides of the highway were lined with palm trees several rows deep, another of the late Sheikh Zayed's legacies. The date palm, *Phoenix dactylifera*, is one of the few plants that can tolerate the high salinity and intense heat of the Arabian desert; the Bedu had cultivated palm groves in the Liwa oases for generations.[1] In 1973 Zayed ordered the planting of millions more of the palm trees across the emirate in a herculean effort to green the desert. The four million palms that had been planted in Abu Dhabi by 1981 have since grown to more than eight times that number, making the emirate home to fully one-third of all the date palms in the world.[2] The trees give Abu Dhabi's major roads and highways a pleasantly leafy appearance and help keep the blowing sands at bay, in addition to yielding more than four hundred thousand metric tons of dates per year. Yet, despite the date palm's hardiness, it still needs regular watering; each of those thirty-three million trees requires at least three gallons of water every day to keep it alive in the desert, at a cost of roughly fifty-five dirhams.[3] Pumping millions of gallons of water through thousands of miles of irrigation lines costs the government billions of dirhams every year. The desert blooms at a steep price.

After an hour of driving down the long green hallway, the palms suddenly ended and we shot out across a howling emptiness. Although I had been in Abu Dhabi nearly three months, this was the first time I had been out of the city to see the legendary Arabian desert over which Thesiger and other writers had waxed poetic. My first thought was that they all must have been sun-struck. The only spell such a wasteland could possibly cast upon its victims was that of tedium-induced hypnosis.

Despite being set amongst a terrain so devoid of distractions, the E11 bears the ignominy of being one of the world's deadliest roads. For much of its length the highway is unlit and consists of only two lanes in each direction, separated by a narrow sandy median. The ruler straightness of the road, the dullness of the landscape, and the shimmering heat all conspire to tranquilize drivers, particularly the pilots of the lorries that lumber along the highway like herds of mechanical cattle. The overloaded lorries have gouged such ruts in the highway's asphalt surface that certain stretches resemble an old wagon trail. The highway has few flyovers, so that drivers wishing to turn around or exit to the far side of the road are forced to execute the death-defying maneuver of pulling into one of the U-turns in the median, waiting for a break in traffic, and then darting across to the opposite shoulder to merge from there. With cars and SUVs barreling down the highway at blistering speeds far above the posted limit of one hundred twenty kilometers per hour, accidents are legion and often fatal.

In the course of our drive we passed several charred, mangled hulks left on the side of the road as a gruesome warning to other motorists. Just a few weeks before, Khalid had told me how his cousin had been killed on this very highway. He had been cruising at more than 120 miles per hour in his Mercedes when he slammed into the side of a lorry that was halfway across the highway trying to make a U-turn. Khalid recounted the story with an almost clinical detachment. When I offered my condolences, he shrugged and said, "*Ma'shallah*, it was the will of God." Such determinism, according to Thesiger, was a defining characteristic of the Bedu: "Their way of life naturally made them fatalists; so much was beyond their control.... They did what they could, and no people were more self-reliant, but if things went wrong they accepted their fate without bitterness, and with dignity as the will of God."[4]

As the number of cars on Abu Dhabi's roads soared in the post-Zayed years, so did the E11's number of victims. In response, the DOT undertook a study of the improvements needed to make the highway safer. In early 2009 the department began canvassing banks and investment funds to take on the upgrading and maintenance of the highway for a performance-based fee. Expressions of interest poured in; the initiative would potentially be one of the largest public-private infrastructure partnerships in the world, in terms of both the monetary value of the contract and the size of the asset it concerned.

Still, as we drove the highway we were reminded that road improvements were only half the equation. Improving the safety of the E11—and for that matter, all of Abu Dhabi's roads—would require a fundamental shift in the emirate's driving culture, particularly among locals. Even with Austin barreling along at nearly one hundred miles per hour, every few minutes a luxury sedan or hulking Land Cruiser would hurtle past. Most had the blackened windows characteristic of Emirati drivers, the only ones who can get around the 25 percent tint, limited by law. Speed cameras were placed roughly every dozen miles along the highway, but they were pointed in the direction of travel and were visible far ahead. The Emiratis simply ignored them.

Austin, the driver, worked in the UPC's Planning Policy department. A Texan in his early thirties, he was fond of cowboy boots and Elton John-like sunglasses, and was unabashedly flamboyant. Unlike most of the UPC's expats, he actually had the cultural qualifications to work in Abu Dhabi. He had written his graduate planning thesis on the historic urbanism of Arab cities, and in between various stateside jobs he had learned to speak passable Arabic in North Africa. In view of these unique skills, the UPC's management sentenced him to toil in near solitude on the planning for the remote western hinterlands through which we were driving, the region known as *Al Gharbia.*

The emirate of Abu Dhabi is divided into three regions: metropolitan Abu Dhabi, comprising the city proper, the neighboring islands, and the adjoining urban areas on the mainland; the Eastern Region, which includes the inland city of Al Ain and its surrounding territory; and Al Gharbia, the Western Region, which consists of everything else. At twenty-three thousand square miles, Al Gharbia is the largest of the three regions by far, enclosing four-fifths of the emirate's territory and 71 percent of the landmass of the entire UAE. It spans from the edge of Abu Dhabi city in the east to the Saudi border in the west, and from the Gulf coast on the north to the dunes of the Empty Quarter in the south. Al Gharbia is Abu Dhabi's most sparsely settled region, with a 2009 population of barely one hundred thousand scattered among a half-dozen settlements. Much of it is a barren coastal plain of gravel desert and *sabkha* salt flats, which gives way further inland to shifting dunes that eventually become the towering sand ridges of the Empty Quarter south of the Liwa Crescent.

Forlorn though Al Gharbia may be, modern Abu Dhabi would not exist without it. Abu Dhabi's Bedu founders, the Bani Yas tribe, hailed from Al Gharbia's Liwa Crescent, a string of oasis settlements tucked along the edge of the Empty Quarter that is so remote it was not discovered by Europeans until 1906.[5] The region is also the source of modern Abu Dhabi's oil wealth. Nearly all of the emirate's proven oil reserves lie beneath Al Gharbia's sands and the waters off its coast. The region is home to the vast majority of the emirate's wells, pipelines, refineries, tanker terminals, and other oil infrastructure. If oil is the lifeblood of modern Abu Dhabi, Al Gharbia is the heart that pumps it.

Despite its obvious significance as the emirate's primary source of wealth, until recently Al Gharbia has had little to show for its contributions. As part of Abu Dhabi's modernization in the 1960s and 1970s, the settlements in Liwa and a few fishing villages along the coast were upgraded into legitimate towns with streets, buildings, and utilities. A new administrative center, the *Madinat Zayed* or "City of Zayed," was built from scratch at the region's geographic midpoint, and a community for oil workers was built near the new coastal refinery complex at Ruwais. After this initial spurt of development, however, Al Gharbia was essentially left to fend for itself. The dusty towns changed little over the next three decades, and their populations plateaued.

Along with the 2007 reorganization that resulted in the creation of the UPC, the government decided to breathe new life into Al Gharbia. The ruling sheikhs appointed one of their younger brothers, Sheikh Hamdan, as their special representative for the region's reinvigoration. TDIC, the state-owned Tourism Development and Investment Corporation, unveiled plans to turn the austere desert into an eco-tourism destination by building a series of resorts in the dunes near Liwa and on islands off the coast. As part of the new focus, the UPC was charged with creating a strategic plan for the region's future—Al Gharbia's own *Plan 2030.*

And that plan was why Austin, Liz, and I were headed west this particular day. We were driving to Sila'a, the westernmost of Al Gharbia's towns, where we were to meet with local officials to solicit their help. The UPC was creating detailed settlement plans for Sila'a and six other Al Gharbia towns, all of which Austin was managing simultaneously with Al Gharbia's *Plan 2030.* Although Liz and I had been assigned to help with our respective sectors, planning Al Gharbia was mostly Austin's one-man show. He was hopelessly overworked, but by his own admission, he relished being singularly responsible for planning an area the size of Switzerland.

Halfway to Sila'a we pulled into one of the ADNOC service stations that were the
E11's only features. Austin had topped off his tank before we left that morning, but his Jeep
had the aerodynamics of a refrigerator, and the steady desert headwind probably reduced
our fuel economy to single digits. Back home Austin had been something of a tree-hugger,
so it seemed a bit incongruous that one of his first acts upon arriving in Abu Dhabi was to
buy a brand new fully-loaded Wrangler. But he was hardly alone; the emirate's automotive
obsession and cheap gas made it a rite of passage for expats to splurge on vehicles they could
never afford in their countries of origin. Liz, for example, drove a sleek Mercedes roadster
that she named Felicia.[6] I, for one, certainly didn't second-guess Austin's choice of vehicles.
It was reassuring to be wrapped in a big steel cage while negotiating Abu Dhabi's perilous
roads.

It was well after noon when we finally reached Sila'a. As we pulled into the parking lot
of the municipal offices, Austin spotted the unmistakable cream-colored tint-windowed
Lexus belonging to Hammad, his Emirati manager. Hammad had driven separately and,
despite having departed Abu Dhabi considerably later, had still somehow managed to arrive
before us. "Must be nice to not have to worry about getting a ticket," Liz quipped.

Hammad was already meeting with the town's municipal manager, a sort of unelected
Emirati mayor, when we came in. They continued chatting in Arabic for several minutes
before deigning to notice us. "Oh, you're here," Hammad said flatly. "I do not think you
need to stay. I am taking care of this." Out of the corner of my eye I saw Austin trying to
mask his ire. We had come all this way for nothing.

On our way out to the Jeep we nearly ran into Colin, Liz's colleague on the UPC's environment team, who had ridden with Hammad. Having found himself similarly redundant,
he had made a detour to the cafeteria. "Well then," he said, holding up a large pizza box,
"can I interest anyone in a luncheon?"

Back in the Jeep, Austin's exasperation was audible between bites of pizza. "For an
agency whose job is to plan things, you'd think we could coordinate amongst ourselves."

I asked Colin how the drive had been.

"Rotten," he said in his thick Irish accent. "He played Emirati music the whole time."

Austin burst into laughter, his head tilting back at the jaw like one of Jim Henson's
Muppets. Liz said, "You poor thing."

Colin nodded. "It all sounds like the same song, doesn't it, then?"

We decided to make good our journey by touring the settlement. Sila'a felt like the
Town at the End of the World, in both geographic and chronological senses. Its dusty streets
were lined with rundown workshops and peculiar bunker-like houses that looked like they
belonged on the planet Tatooine. Other than the irrigated greenery in the median of the
main road through town, there was barely any vegetation to speak of. Ostensibly these barrens
were home to eight thousand hardy souls, but the residents were nowhere to be seen. All
that was missing were tumbleweeds rolling down the eerily empty thoroughfares.

Austin followed the road to the pavement's end at the north edge of town, then continued into the desert along a sandy track for several more miles. He halted the Jeep on a
rise that spilled down to the coastline below, where the sands melted into the Gulf. The
scenery mirrored the words of the English scholar William Palgrave, one of the first Europeans to explore this part of Arabia in the 1860s: "My readers must figure to themselves
miles on miles of low barren hills, bleak and sun-scorched, with hardly a single tree to vary
their dry monotonous outline: below these a muddy beach extends for a quarter of a mile
seawards in slimy quicksands, bordered by a rim of sludge and seaweeds. If we look landwards
beyond the hills, we see what at extreme courtesy may be called pasture lands, dreary downs

with twenty pebbles for every blade of grass."[7] If Limbo were a place, this would be it. Austin turned off the engine and said, "Perfect spot for the next Chernobyl, don't you think?" So this was to be the site of Abu Dhabi's first nuclear power plant.

The UAE was a nation with a looming electricity problem. After the turn of the millennium, the rapid growth of the emirates of Dubai, Abu Dhabi, and Sharjah had outstripped the country's electricity generating capacity. The UAE's electricity consumption nearly doubled between 2002 and 2007,[8] causing rolling blackouts that began in the summer months of 2008. The blackouts were an embarrassing paradox for the oil-rich UAE. The government found itself obliged to turn to imports to slake the growing thirst of its dozen or so power plants, 85 percent of which ran on natural gas.[9] That such imports were necessary despite Abu Dhabi's own gas reserves, which at 200 trillion cubic feet were not insubstantial, underscored the magnitude of the problem.[10] The UAE's natural gas consumption topped 1.7 trillion cubic feet per year in 2007, surpassing domestic production for the first time. The government rushed to finish the Dolphin Pipeline, an undersea conduit that upon its completion in 2009 began pumping two billion cubic feet of natural gas per day from nearby Qatar. Even so, with the UAE's electricity demand predicted to grow by a blistering 12 percent per year, far greater than the rate at which new conventional power plants could be built, the blackouts were guaranteed to worsen.

As usual, it fell to Abu Dhabi as the preeminent emirate to come up with a solution. The sheikhs and their advisors concluded that going nuclear was the only way to meet the country's electricity needs. In 2008 the government issued a white paper announcing its intent to embark on a civilian nuclear energy program. A federal nuclear regulatory body, the Emirates National Energy Corporation (ENEC), was inaugurated shortly thereafter in keeping with the recommendations of the International Atomic Energy Association. Since Abu Dhabi was funding the program, ENEC's headquarters and the first reactors would be located in the emirate. Five days before leaving office in January 2009, the administration of President George W. Bush signed an agreement with the UAE to provide U.S. assistance to the program's development.[11] Both countries intended the deal as a strong rebuke to Iran, whose murkier nuclear ambitions were a perennial annoyance to the Americans and an existential threat to the Emiratis. The UAE was determined to set an example as the first Middle Eastern country to pursue nuclear power for exclusively peaceful purposes.

The site near Sila'a had been chosen to host the UAE's first nuclear facility for two reasons. First, it had access to an ample supply of water for cooling the reactors. And second, if anything did go wrong, it was as far away within the country's borders as one could get from the major population centers—although they were still downwind. ENEC expected to start construction on the first reactor in December 2009.

We left the Jeep and walked down to the muddy shoreline, where we had to pick our way through a minefield of igneous rocks uncovered by the low tide. The water lapped feebly at the sand, and it was difficult to tell where the land ended and the Gulf began.

Austin tried to put a positive spin on the pitiful scene. "I love Al Gharbia. It's so serene."

Liz demurred. "This beach is minging."

We mucked around in the shallows for a few minutes while the sun beat down overhead, until finally deciding we had had enough for the day. We followed a secondary road on the west side of town back towards the E11. Ahead of us I noticed a blurry black line on the horizon. As we neared the highway, the line coalesced into a queue of lorries parked bumper to bumper on the shoulder of the highway, stretching out of sight in either direction.

"How far does this go?" Liz asked incredulously.

"All the way to the border," I replied. I had read the previous weekend's edition of the

National, which had reported that the lorry queue was the unfortunate by-product of a diplomatic spat between the UAE and Saudi Arabia. The Gulf Cooperation Council (GCC), an international body set up to promote cooperation among the oil-rich states of Bahrain, Kuwait, Oman, Qatar, Saudi Arabia, and the UAE, had recently chosen to locate its new central bank in the Saudi capital of Riyadh—over the vocal protests of the UAE, which had lobbied hard to put the bank in Abu Dhabi. As a result, the UAE quietly bowed out of the GCC's plans to create a unified currency for its member states, a sort of Arabian version of the euro. A few days thereafter, the Saudis announced heightened inspections for all traffic entering their country from the UAE—a pure coincidence, the Saudis claimed.

The border choke point created a line of trucks on the UAE side that grew longer by the day. The real victims of the international pissing match were the hundreds of hapless lorry drivers stranded in the desert without water, food, or toilets in the withering 120-degree heat of the early Arabian summer. Their dire situation risked becoming a humanitarian catastrophe. Few drivers were willing to leave the queue to walk to Sila'a for provisions, not only due to the prospect of crossing miles of scorching sand, but also because they had to be ready at a moment's notice to fire up their engines every time the line lurched forward a few meters or risk losing their spot in the queue. After three weeks, the line numbered eight thousand trucks and stretched for twenty-five solid kilometers along the highway.[12]

Austin squeezed the Jeep between two of the lorries and drove alongside the queue for several minutes. We passed drivers huddled around portable stoves or sleeping on blankets in the shade of their trucks. I saw one man stripped to his waist, scrubbing himself with sand. That the authorities on both sides of the border could treat the drivers so callously was appalling. For all their modern veneer, the nations of the Gulf were still bickering tribes at heart, and woe to the unfortunates who got caught in their disputes.

We reached a U-turn and headed back towards Abu Dhabi. The sight of the stranded drivers had left us all in a heavy silence, which didn't sit well with Austin. "Come *onnn*, it's like a funeral in here," he whined. He turned on the digital stereo and cycled through his extensive collection of stored songs before settling on one.

I looked at him askance. "Dancing Queen?"

By that point all four of us were slightly delirious, whether from the sun or the mind-numbing landscape or the unreal sight of the lorry queue. Soon we were all singing along. Accompanied by a soundtrack of Swedish disco and bad karaoke, the Jeep lashed across the desert and into the looming twilight.

* * *

My firsthand look at Al Gharbia's terrain proved useful shortly thereafter when Alex assigned Khalid and me to help manage the initiative to build a new national railway system from scratch. The railway would span the UAE when finished, with conventional rail tracks for freight trains and high-speed tracks for bullet trains. It would also be the UAE's contribution to a wider rail network that would eventually link all six countries of the GCC. Although the GCC network concept had been bandied about for decades, the UAE was the first country to start work on its part. Indeed, apart from Aramco's freight line from Riyadh to Dammam and the defunct Ottoman-era Hejaz Railway, the UAE's national railway would be the first of its kind on the Arabian Peninsula. Although the project was nationwide in scope, Abu Dhabi was once again running the show. Most of the network would fall within the emirate's territory anyway.

The project was still very much embryonic in mid–2009. The government had set up an agency called Etihad Rail (*Etihad* being Arabic for "union") and had hired a consultancy

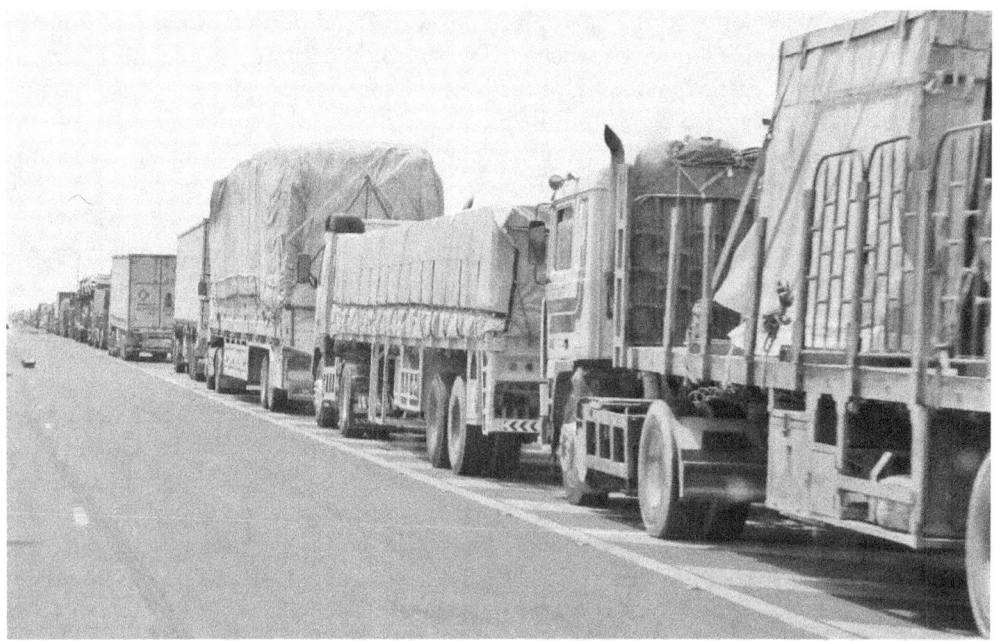

Lorries lined up bumper-to-bumper for twenty-five kilometers along the E11 highway near the Saudi border, summer 2009.

to design and engineer the network.[13] The UPC had been brought in to help manage the design work and ensure that the railway meshed with the strategic plans for Abu Dhabi's population growth and wider transport infrastructure. The consultants had already established "limits of deviation," broad corridors through which the rail lines would eventually run. Now they were moving into the more exacting work of defining the precise alignment for the first phase of the railway, a 120-mile segment running north from the Liwa Crescent to the coast and then west to the industrial complex and port at Ruwais. The second phase would extend the coastal line west to the Saudi border and east to metropolitan Abu Dhabi, and subsequent phases would continue along the coast to the Northern Emirates and east to Al Ain and the Oman border.

At first I thought it strange that the government had prioritized the Al Gharbia sections of the railway, as the population was sparsest there. Surely it made more sense to start off with the proposed high-speed passenger line between Abu Dhabi and Dubai. Already many of Abu Dhabi's employees were moving to Dubai, where housing prices had plunged following the late 2008 bursting of its own real estate bubble. I had briefly considered making the move myself, until I considered the prospect of spending four hours every day among the hordes of harried long-distance commuters on Sheikh Zayed Road, as the portion of the E11 between Abu Dhabi and Dubai was known. Since this commuting trend was expected to grow as Abu Dhabi's economy boomed and Dubai's continued to wane, there was a strong case for prioritizing a bullet train to provide an alternate means of travel between the two emirates.

The government saw things differently. The railway's Liwa-Ruwais segment had been given top billing to coincide with the construction of a new natural gas extraction plant at Shah, in the dunes just south of Liwa. The Shah Line, as it was called, would run freight trains from the plant up to the port at Ruwais, where their cargoes of sulfur pellets would be loaded onto ships for export. The extension of the coastal portion of the line from the Saudi border to Abu Dhabi, which would follow shortly thereafter, would absorb some of the freight currently carried by the E11, benefiting the highway by taking exhaust-belching lorries and their beleaguered drivers off the road.

Despite my reservations about the railway's phasing, I was thrilled to finally have a project into which I could sink my teeth. Trains were the one form of transport I actually knew something about, having studied European railways during my time in Germany. My expertise on the subject was admittedly still that of a greenhorn, but I could at least bluff my way through meetings without sounding like the village idiot. The project's scope ranged from broad strategic-level planning down to tiny details, such as how to thread the tracks between individual dunes. The Shah Line in particular would need to navigate some formidable terrain, from the hazardous salt flats of the coastal plain to the shifting sand massifs in Liwa. Along with the small cadre of Etihad Rail staff and their consultants, Khalid and I faced plenty of headaches trying to find the path of least resistance and cost. But complaining was the last thing on my mind. I was getting to play a part in the wholesale creation of a country's rail system. Back in planning school I had entertained delusions of such grandiose schemes, but never seriously thought I'd be part of one, much less at this early stage of my career.

The intense activity on the national railway was typical of the UPC's general atmosphere throughout the summer of 2009. The entire agency maintained a blistering tempo, matched only by the rising temperatures and humidity outside. Abu Dhabi's developers barraged us with proposals for new projects; we received at least a dozen every week. The UPC also continued to push forward its own initiatives, such as the North Wathba and Al Gharbia plans. The work was stimulating and challenging, and the sheer magnitude and breathless pace of the city's transformation left me awestruck. It was impossible not to catch the excitement of being at the center of all the action.

Work was my life during those summer months, as it was for just about everyone else at the UPC. My social circle was limited to my colleagues, who were kind enough to invite me, the newbie, to dinners and other after-hours gatherings. Unlike many, if not most, sets of coworkers, they were actually a delight to spend time with, equally as brilliant in their free time as they were during office hours. I often felt humbled to be allowed among such a gathering of personalities from around the globe. Even so, the demanding workload made it all too easy for me to spend evenings and weekends toiling in the office.

I certainly wasn't tempted to while away my free time at my lowly apartment, which I had furnished with the barest of essentials: bed, wardrobe, small refrigerator, stove, and collapsible camping chair. This was one area where Thesiger and I saw eye to eye: "I wondered why people ever cluttered up their rooms with furniture, for bare simplicity seemed to me infinitely preferable."[14] Besides, I couldn't have crammed much else inside the tiny room had I so desired.

I had barely finished moving in before the annoyances began. The wall-mounted air conditioner developed a habit of sucking the moisture from the room during the day and spewing it back out onto the floor at night. The lack of circulation gave the air a stale, enervating flavor, particularly when the afternoon sun cast the room in sepia tones and reflected off the floating motes of dust. I discovered only after moving in that the room's sole window refused to open, compelling me to keep a hammer beside it in case there were ever a fire. Seemingly every other day brought a new color of water from the bathroom faucet. I soon took to visiting my apartment only to bathe and sleep.

On the few occasions when I didn't stay late at the office, Abu Dhabi unfortunately didn't offer many distractions. The punishing summer climate obviated any thoughts of out-

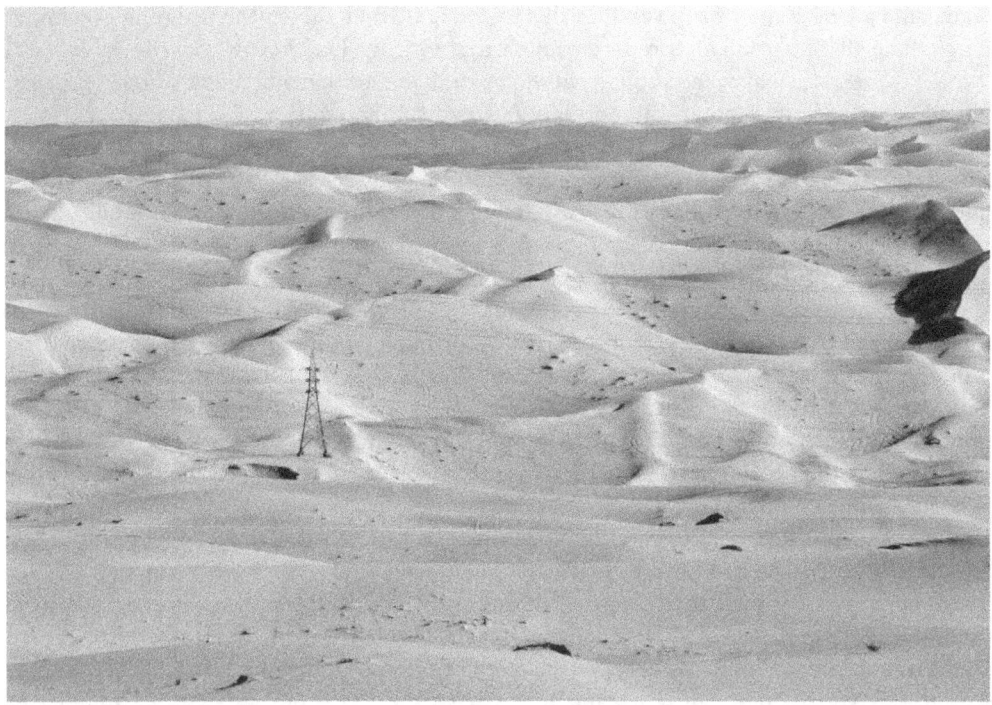

Sand dunes along the edge of the Empty Quarter near Liwa. The national railway would need to traverse this challenging terrain in order to reach its terminus at Shah.

door activity. Abu Dhabi's mid-year humidity is so thick that the air becomes an intermediate state of matter between liquid and gas. Super-heated and sopping, the daytime atmosphere singes the nostrils and pools in the lungs, bringing to mind the words of Ibn Khaldun: "When the moisture with its evil vapors ascends to the brain, the mind and the ability to think are dulled. The result is stupidity, carelessness, and a general intemperance."[15] This description fits just about everyone in Abu Dhabi at some point or another. Even after dusk the ground exhales the heat it absorbed during the day, making it feel as though the sun's rays are penetrating from the far side of the earth.

Summers in Abu Dhabi are so miserable that even the locals don't want to stay. Back in the Bedu era, much of the settlement's population migrated to the drier inland desert during the summer months. Nowadays Abu Dhabi sees a similar mass exodus every June as Emiratis decamp to their summer homes in Europe. The UPC's Emiratis disappeared for months at a time (while still getting paid); Mahra and her family went to southern Germany for eight straight weeks. The Foreign Legion was left behind to guard the fort, trying their sweaty best to maintain the pace of work while scuttling from one air-conditioned bubble to another.

From April to September I did not see a single cloud. Every day the robin's-egg blue of the morning sky would change to a steam-colored haze by noon, as though the atmosphere itself were boiling off in the heat. Late in the afternoon the descending sun would bathe the skyline bronze, giving Abu Dhabi the likeness of the fabled City of Brass from the collection of Near Eastern folk tales known as *The Thousand and One Nights*.[16]

When it came to the indoors, the barrenness of the desert mirrored Abu Dhabi's cultural aridity. The city had no galleries, no theaters, not even any decent cafes. Though Abu Dhabi had come a long way in forty years, in this regard it still resembled the fledgling boomtown of the late 1960s, in which a reporter noted that visiting Europeans "must learn to waste time."[17] I found the only centers of activity to be the half-dozen major malls, which performed double duty as both shopping emporiums and as the only public spaces to speak of.

Abu Dhabi's malls are, if anything, even more all-encompassing destinations than their counterparts in the West, bringing together everything under one roof: banking, grooming, bill paying, child care, and even real estate sales, in addition to the normal retail outlets. Many of Abu Dhabi's malls include big-box grocery stores in their basements, a feature that even the Mall of America, the largest shopping center in the United States, cannot boast.

No other place so embodies the contradictions of modern Abu Dhabi as the mall. On the one hand, it caters to the Emiratis' tastes for modern toys and conveniences. On the other, it epitomizes much of what the Emiratis dread about the outside world. Abu Dhabi's citizens define themselves by their traditions and their culture, and they resent outside influences that threaten that identity. Although the Emiratis follow a less stringent version of Islam than their Saudi neighbors, they are still quite conservative compared to many other Muslim countries. To varying degrees the Emiratis view Western culture as decadent, corrupt, and inferior. But that doesn't stop them from shelling out their dirhams for Western commodities and media. Abu Dhabi's malls are filled seven days a week with Emiratis basking in the superiority of their society while tapping away on Blackberries and sipping Starbucks lattes.

As a planner, I despised malls for the role they played in cannibalizing the commercial vitality of North American cities and towns from the 1950s onwards. And I found Abu Dhabi's malls to have all the shortcomings of their American cousins in spades: banal architecture, mediocre food, artificial lighting, stuffy atmospheres laced with muzak and ennui. But I patronized Abu Dhabi's malls just like everyone else. There were simply no alternatives.

When the weekend came and I wasn't at the office, I would head to the mall to start the day with a leisurely brunch, after which I would move to a coffee shop and read the weekend edition of the *National* from cover to cover. In the afternoon I would often catch a movie, which was invariably an exercise in patience. The theater floors were always sticky, the seats stained with sweat and who-knows-what-else, the films often missing critical plot points thanks to government censors, and the Emirati audience members seeing nothing wrong with talking on their phones or shouting advice to the characters on the screen. After the movie I'd get an early dinner; if nothing else, the mall meals helped me get used to the appalling service that features in all of Abu Dhabi's restaurants. Finally, I'd round out the evening with a walk through the hypermarket, the grocery store in the basement.

Abu Dhabi's hypermarkets wear this name for good reason. Friday night at the hypermarket was always a scene of outright pandemonium. It was shopping as a combat sport, not unlike the mosh pit at a heavy metal concert. Hundreds of wild-eyed shoppers thronged the aisles and besieged the cashiers. Carts collided. Elbows flew. Children scampered underfoot. A disembodied voice rose occasionally over the cacophony to call for cleanup on aisle so-and-so. Stock boys tried frantically to buttress the inventory flying off the shelves. It always looked as though the city's residents were stockpiling goods for some imminent disaster. And as if to throw fuel on the fire, the hypermarket where I shopped was fond of playing bellicose classical numbers such as the overture from *Carmen* over its public address system, subliminally whipping the crowds into even greater frenzy.

The shoppers mirrored the ethnic makeup of the city as a whole. There were plenty of Indians in colorful saris and Nehru collars, as well as Pakistanis in their characteristic baggy-pajama *shalwar khamees*. Filipinos staffed the cash registers and the deli. Occasionally I would spot the black and white wardrobe duo of an Emirati couple, usually trailed by their Indonesian domestic helpers. Westerners were scattered throughout, castaways adrift on a sea of pan-Asian humanity. The items that the shoppers piled in their carts were, like the shoppers themselves, almost entirely sourced from overseas—European and Australian produce, Pakistani textiles, Indian rice, Chinese appliances. It was in the hypermarket that I first realized the extent to which nearly everything in the emirate is imported. From the people to the goods to the materials that make up the city itself, Abu Dhabi is all places and no place at once.

Six

Proletarians, Unite!

I cannot understand how physically fit young men can sit idle and accept the humiliation of depending on others for their livelihood. — *Sheikh Zayed bin Sultan al Nahyan*

Toward the end of summer 2009 the Executive Council issued a decree: the hundreds of thousands of laborers who manned Abu Dhabi's construction sites were to be relocated from their current accommodations to the desert. A string of sprawling new labor camps was to be built along an imaginary perimeter fifty miles beyond the city limits. Each camp would be the size of a small city in its own right, with up to a hundred thousand inhabitants—enough to house the emirate's existing labor force with space left over for the additional thousands expected to join them in the coming years.

The decree came as a surprise to the UPC staff. Placing the camps that far out in the desert represented a direct contradiction of the urban growth boundary in *Plan 2030*, the "sand belt" beyond which no development was to take place.[1] There was more to this principle than just preserving the pristine desert; corralling the city's development would avoid the need to run costly roads and utility lines out to the boondocks. It would also maximize the usefulness of Abu Dhabi's planned transit system and cut down on trips between locations.

The labor camps contravened both of these principles. They were too remote to be serviced by utilities, so everything they consumed and generated—water, fuel, waste, and sewage—would need to be trucked in and out. Compounding the issue further were the thousands of buses that would have to make the long trips to haul laborers between the camps and their construction sites. The labor camp decree was a recipe for inefficiency.

It was difficult to comprehend why the emirate's leadership would contradict their own vision for a sustainable future for Abu Dhabi with such a maneuver, but I soon got a glimpse into their thought processes. The UPC had recently hired a security consultancy to develop a safety and security annex to *Plan 2030*. The TIES Department wound up with the responsibility for the contract, and the Professor had tasked me to manage the consultants in my ever-expanding role of hatchet man. The effort had nothing to do with transport, but the Professor reasoned that my experience cowering behind blast walls in Iraq made me an expert in security.

To work on the annex, the consultancy seconded a pair of their staff to the UPC. Ian, the senior of the duo, was a former British intelligence officer with an intimidating resume: Oxford, Sandhurst, and distinguished military service followed by stints hunting money launderers in the Balkans and interrogating militants in West Bank prisons. He was eloquent, and intelligent to the point of eccentricity, which perhaps explained his habit of wearing thick wool socks with his James Bond-style suits, even at the height of summer. His junior partner, Latif, was an excitable American in his early thirties. He smoked like a chimney and talked an awful lot for someone in the profession of keeping secrets.

Shortly after the labor camp decree was issued, I was discussing it with Ian and Latif and I wondered out loud what the emirate's leaders were thinking. "They're thinking worst case scenario," Ian replied. He explained that the security services viewed the growing numbers of laborers first and foremost as a threat. Just a few years previously there had been riots at a labor camp near Al Ain—the first such civil disturbance in the emirate's history. The army eventually had to be called in to quell the rioters. Then, in 2007, more than forty thousand laborers had gone on strike in neighboring Dubai to protest their poor working conditions. The unrest halted work on high-profile projects and led to Dubai's police chief branding laborers a national security threat.[2] Since then, fear had taken root among Abu Dhabi's upper echelons. "The only thing that scares the establishment more than a nuclear Iran," Latif said, "is the thought of ten thousand subcontinentals rampaging down Airport Road."

Jim Morrison's lyrics to "Five to One" ran through my mind.

Moving the laborers out to the desert was meant to isolate them from the rest of the populace and make them easier to lock down in the event of unrest. The measure may have seemed harsh, but it made cold, perfect sense in terms of security. Though Abu Dhabi's laborers were the ones building the city, they could still be excluded from it.

"So how are we supposed to reconcile the labor camps with the urban growth boundary?" I asked. "I gather that we can consider *Plan 2030* hereby duly amended," Ian replied. The government had elected to color outside the tightly prescribed line of its own plan. It would not be the last such variation.

Over the following months the UPC received a slew of proposals for new labor camps. Their sites arced across the mainland in a sweeping penumbra fifty miles distant from the city. I had the unenviable chore of assisting the Development Review team that was handling the proposals. From the start it was clear that our review was to be perfunctory. Abu Dhabi's developers needed the camps built posthaste in order to comply with the Executive Council's decree, and our approval was a matter of form. My transport-related input was limited to asking the developers how many trucks and buses each camp would require and whether they had a plan to limit trips to off-peak hours. Although the proposals involved plenty of drawbacks in terms of sustainability, their human rights implications were even more unsettling. We faced the prospect of sequestering hundreds of thousands of workers out in the desert, far removed from everything but heat, sand, and each other. Even if those laborers had all come to Abu Dhabi of their own accord, quarantining them like lepers bordered on the inhumane.

The labor camp proposals caused a great deal of hand-wringing among the UPC's expats. They violated our professional standards, not to mention our consciences. Of course, that didn't stop us from approving the proposals as instructed, and no resignations were tendered in protest. What was a little moral compromise when compared with what we were being paid? Besides, the developers' representatives took great pains to assure us that the camps would be built with the comfort of the laborers foremost in mind.

We decided to see for ourselves. Keith, the Development Review manager responsible for coordinating the camp reviews, arranged a site visit to a camp whose construction had anticipated the Executive Council's decree by more than half a year. The camp's first phase had already opened and currently housed several thousand laborers. It bore the bland name of H-1 Labor City and lay southwest of Abu Dhabi, just off the Hameem Road that connects the E11 highway with the eastern end of the Liwa Crescent.

I had ample time to chat with Keith during the hour-long drive. He was Canadian, one of the Vancouver Mafia who had been with the UPC from the start. He had a penchant for pinstripe suits and expensive cufflinks, but he never wore a tie. An old hand at the agency, he possessed remarkable insight into the behind-the-scenes workings of the UPC and Abu Dhabi at large—a particularly impressive feat for a thirty-five-year-old.

As we neared the camp we began to pass laborers walking along the shoulder of the road, alone or in pairs. I couldn't imagine where they were going. Other than the labor camp, the sole feature along the Hameem Road's ninety-mile length was a surreal aluminum pyramid that housed a sheikh's private car museum. Even the nearest ADNOC service station would take hours to reach on foot in the brain-melting heat. Against the backdrop of the apocalyptic desert, the roadside wanderers looked like *Mad Max* extras in their coveralls.

A tall sign at the camp entrance proclaimed "Welcome to Hameem Living City," accompanied by cheerful pictures of smiling families. Evidently "H-1 Labor City" had been deemed passé. We were met at the gate by the superintendent, a bald, beefy South African with a churlish demeanor. He showed us around with a stiff courtesy that implied we were anything but welcome.

The camp was laid out in a square measuring half a mile on each side. The rows of squat concrete buildings were painted the color of the sands from which they rose. The insides of the housing blocks were all the same: utilitarian dormitories with basic furnishings. Laborers were housed eight to a room; they each had a bed and a few square meters of personal space, which was admittedly an improvement on the overcrowded flats that Abu Dhabi's lowest classes typically endured. The common bathrooms at the end of each hall reminded me of the facilities at a sports stadium, complete with trough-like urinals. I was pleasantly surprised to see that each pair of rooms shared a kitchenette. "We learned the hard way that canteens are a bad idea," the superintendent explained. "I used to work at one of the camps on Yas. We had brawls almost every week. The laborers congregate by ethnicity in the chow halls. All it takes is one Pakistani to push an Indian and everything goes to rot."

Between the dormitory blocks were strips of concrete and scrubby grass, "recreational areas" appropriate for pick-up games of cricket and not much else. A mosque sat in the center of every dormitory cluster, even though the majority of the laborers were from India and thus presumably Hindu by confession.[3] In the center of the camp was an empty strip mall with spaces for a smattering of convenience shops, although the superintendent could offer no details as to what would occupy them and when. There was nothing else for the inhabitants to do—no library, no cinema, no gym.

"Kind of like a desert Potemkin village," Keith murmured when the superintendent wasn't listening. To me, a slightly different Russian metaphor seemed more appropriate: the camp was a gulag, only with sand instead of snow. Seventy-five thousand souls would eventually call this place home.

To be certain, none of the camp's inhabitants were likely to starve or be worked to death; indeed, they would even enjoy the luxury of air conditioning. But the camp lacked anything beyond the barest necessities. It had no humanizing features, not even trees. It embodied a utilitarian view of the laborer that made Victorian-era workhouses look positively indulgent. Here the laborer was a machine that needed only to eat, sleep, urinate, and possibly pray— nothing more. There were no guard towers or perimeter walls, but they weren't necessary. The shimmering desert beyond the camp's perimeter promised parched death to any who braved it. There was no escaping the camp, which was precisely the point, but there was no escape inside either—nothing to check the boredom and alienation of living in such a place. I knew that Abu Dhabi's laborers typically came to the emirate to escape grinding poverty in their countries of origin. But when I saw the kind of life that awaited them, I couldn't help thinking that back home, at least they were free.

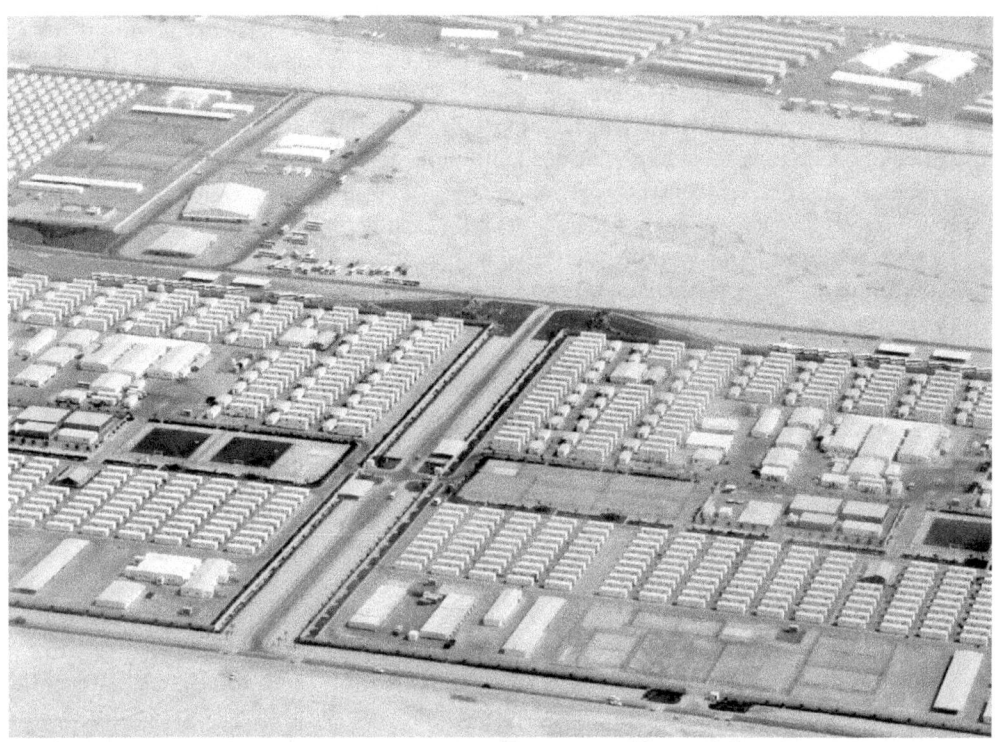

A labor camp. This particular example is on Yas Island.

* * *

The treatment of laborers is a touchy subject in Abu Dhabi and the UAE as a whole. The recruiters who troll the slums and hamlets of South Asia charge between $2,000 and $4,000 to place a laborer in a Gulf job, most of which the laborer himself has to repay from his earnings. On arriving, laborers' passports are confiscated by their employers for "safe-keeping."[4] Unskilled laborers are put to work on grueling twelve-to-fourteen-hour shifts, six or seven days a week, for wages that start at around 500 dirhams (the equivalent of $136) a month. Usually it is years before a laborer is given leave to return home and see his family, and even then he has to buy his own ticket.[5]

Conditions at worksites are frequently appalling. More than eight hundred laborers fall to their deaths across the UAE every year, twice as many as in the entire United States, a country with a construction workforce nearly forty times as large. Expat construction supervisors allege that many of these deaths are suicides on the part of despondent laborers, which are simply classified as "accidents."[6] Work continues year-round, straight through the withering summer months. Construction sites are required by law to cease activity when temperatures hit 50 degrees centigrade—halfway to the boiling point. That is why official weather reports have a curious tendency never to exceed 49.9 degrees, though a casual midday glance at any thermometer between the months of May and September will give a different opinion. The combination of scorching heat, inadequate water supplies, and lack of accessible toilets on construction sites spawns pandemic levels of heat stroke and dehydration. One survey of Gulf laborers returning to India found that more than two-thirds suffered from kidney failure.[7]

For all intents and purposes, laborers have no rights. If a job is finished or cancelled without a replacement, its workers are shipped home at their own expense or simply left to fend for themselves. When Dubai's real estate bubble burst in late 2008, thousands of South Asian laborers were stranded in remote labor camps without food, electricity, transport, and months of back wages they were owed.[8] Laborers are as replaceable as they are expendable; the price of concrete or steel might rise or fall, but labor is always in plentiful supply.

The exploitation of Abu Dhabi's laborers produces plenty of righteous indignation among Western expats, but little concrete action. Nobody is about to lose their seat on the gravy train by agitating for the lower classes. The Emiratis, for their part, make no apologies; laborers come of their own accord and are paid more for their toil than they could expect back home.

Some observers explain the calloused attitudes towards laborers by highlighting the Gulf's thousand-year history of slavery. The dismal practice was widespread even in impoverished Abu Dhabi, and was only banned as late as 1963 under pressure from the British.[9] By then it was a moot point; the oil money had started to flow, and the emirate's citizens discovered that low-paid Asians made inexpensive substitutes for African slaves. As Abu Dhabi developed a more advanced economy, the ever-wealthier Emiratis realized it was more convenient and practical not only to keep the foreigners around, but also to bring in more.

The initial trickle of laborers and other foreigners hired to build the emirate has become a flood today. Foreigners account for three-quarters of Abu Dhabi's 1.6 million residents.[10] That figure describes the emirate as a whole, including the smaller outlying towns where nationals are more prevalent. Tighten the scope to the million or so current residents of the Abu Dhabi metropolitan area and foreigners outnumber Emiratis by a staggering nine to one. It is no wonder that nationals are such a rare sight around town; some expats spend entire multiple-year assignments in Abu Dhabi without so much as speaking to an Emirati. In New York City and Miami, by comparison, foreign residents make up only half of the urban populace—the highest such rates in North America. Even Singapore, Abu Dhabi's role model, counts foreigners as only 40 percent of its population.

Journalists are fond of likening Abu Dhabi's ethnic and economic class hierarchy to a pyramid.[11] At the bottom are the South Asians, who make up more than half of the emirate's residents. Almost 500,000 Indians, 300,000 Pakistanis, and 125,000 Bangladeshis live and work in Abu Dhabi. Most are laborers on construction sites, but they also sweep the streets, collect the garbage, clean the bathrooms in the malls, and serve tea in the city's offices. To be sure, the ranks of South Asians include many accountants, engineers, doctors, and other professionals. Indians (along with their requisite Emirati business partners) own more enterprises than any other ethnic group. But even South Asians who possess these credentials can often be stigmatized like proles.

Southeast Asians make up the pyramid's next level. Filipinos underpin the hospitality and service sectors, manning Abu Dhabi's cash registers, gasoline pumps, hotel desks, call centers, and restaurant tables. Filipinos also account for many of the domestic helpers in Emirati households, along with Indonesians and Malays. Above them on the pyramid are non-Gulf Arabs: Egyptians, Jordanians, Palestinians, Syrians, and Lebanese. They are the rank and file office workers and fill a host of other functions from bank tellers to hospital staff.

The penultimate stratum is comprised of westerners, who can be viewed as either the supervisory lynchpin of the emirate's economy, or as a bunch of overpaid middle-management busybodies. As at the UPC, expats staff a substantial portion of Abu Dhabi's government apparatus. While such widespread foreign infiltration would be unheard of for many governments, its predominance in Abu Dhabi would not have surprised Thesiger, who observed that "Arabs rule but do not administer."[12] And finally, breathing the rarefied air at the top of Abu Dhabi's societal pile are the Emiratis. The pyramid illustration is crude, but it is also broadly accurate.

Although Abu Dhabi can compete with just about any other nation for diversity, there is one critical difference between the emirate and Western countries with a history of immigration. The latter typically offer immigrants some kind of path to citizenship, convoluted though it often may be. In contrast, almost none of Abu Dhabi's foreigners stand a chance of ever becoming citizens, regardless of how many years they may devote to building the emirate's future. The government defends citizenship like the Holy Grail, and for good reason: a UAE passport may not confer immortality, but it does guarantee a pampered life. The only paths to citizenship are to be born to or married to a male Emirati. This policy has as much to do with economics as ethnocentrism; the government simply cannot afford to lavish its welfare on everyone.

Abu Dhabi's foreigners are and always will be merely guests in someone else's house— guests who can be sent home at a moment's notice. If a foreigner is made redundant, his residency visa is cancelled immediately and he is given thirty days to find a new job, leave, or face deportation. Furthermore, a worker can include family members on his visa only with his employer's permission, and then only dependents. A child born in Abu Dhabi to Indian or Pakistani parents, who themselves may have spent decades in the emirate, is thus obliged to find a job upon reaching the age of eighteen or risk being shipped to a mother country he has never seen.

The restrictive immigration policy is a double-edged sword. It keeps the government's welfare outlays in check and preserves the Emiratis' elite status, but it also fosters a transitory and opportunistic mindset among the foreigners who make up by far the majority of the population. Whereas Western nations offer immigrants the opportunity to set down permanent roots, become citizens, and take a stake in the collective future of the country, Abu Dhabi prevents foreigners from any such lasting involvement or commitment. The emirate's foreign residents are destined to be tenants and never owners in every sense.

Ironically, the present situation is no more tenable for the Emiratis than for the foreigners. The Emiratis' privileged lifestyles are completely dependent on the foreign workforce that sustains their economy. The government can deport a few hundred foreigners here and there, but it cannot get rid of them all without facing dire consequences. The pool of Emirati labor is neither large enough nor sufficiently qualified to keep the emirate running. The government pays lip service to correcting the imbalance; the UAE's official demographic strategy calls for Emiratis to make up 40 percent of the country's population by 2021.[13] Yet this goal is slipping further out of reach. The national proportion of Emiratis dwindled from 15 percent in 2006 to 11 percent just five years later.[14] It is all a stark contrast to Thesiger's characterization of the Bedu as "the most self-reliant people on Earth."[15]

As the Emiratis have become an ever smaller and more precarious minority, more than a few have developed a siege mentality. I occasionally heard my Emirati colleagues describe the growing foreign multitude as a danger, steadily eroding the fabric of their society and their very identity. The apparent disconnect between the government's nationalistic rhetoric and the continued rise of the foreign tide even led some to wonder what their leaders actually had in mind. Of course, the taboo on confrontation and the government's unwillingness to brook dissent ensures that such sentiments are never aired publicly. But in private, ordinary Emiratis will sometimes admit that they feel increasingly alienated and adrift. The natives are becoming restless.

Ideally, Abu Dhabi would find a balance, a happy medium that capitalizes on its remarkable diversity while keeping the Emiratis from becoming an endangered species. After all, the population's heterogeneity is one of the emirate's greatest selling points. During the summer of 2009 the Abu Dhabi Commercial Bank ran an advertising campaign in this spirit, plastering billboards across the emirate with the slogan "Ambition: It's the reason 208 different nationalities can live together in harmony."[16] Abu Dhabi's multicultural array helps keep life in the emirate interesting, as was sometimes illustrated for me on occasions when I least expected it.

* * *

My eyes dart around the chamber. Beneath the cheap glare of bare fluorescent bulbs stands a trio of rickety barber chairs, each manned by a diminutive Bangladeshi in a laboratory coat. More of them sit on a bench along the wall. A decrepit fan nudges the stale air. The counter overflows with bizarre grooming instruments. A sink in the far corner appears to double as a kitchen disposal. An antique television on the end of the counter bathes the room in the washed-out hues and tinny soundtrack of Bengali soap opera.

My entrance yields one of those rare moments worthy of cinema. The chatter stops mid-sentence and everyone in the shop turns to stare at me—the barbers, the guys waiting on the bench, even the half-shorn customers reclining in the chairs. All of them bear a decidedly darker skin tone than mine, leading me to conclude that they don't get a lot of Caucasian customers here. Just as I'm about to retreat, one of the barbers smiles broadly, points at my unkempt hair, and nods at an empty spot on the bench. Feeling sheepish, I take a seat.

The same barber finishes with his customer after a few minutes and waves me towards his chair. I try stalling by asking the other guys on the bench if they want to go first, but they motion me ahead. The barber's chair is a museum piece, its two-tone seat flattened by decades of posteriors.

No sooner am I seated than the barber grasps my head in his hands like a vise. I tense up, then relax as he massages my scalp. He looks at me quizzically in the mirror. It's quickly apparent that (a) he wants to know how I'd like my hair cut, (b) he may or may not speak any English, and therefore (c) this is going to be far more interesting than I anticipated. "Short on the sides, and longer on top," I tell him. No reaction. I gesture with my hands. "Short here, longer here." Presumably getting my drift, he tilts his head from side to side like a bobblehead doll, the South Asian gesture of acceptance, and says, "O-K." He launches into the longest, most complicated, and by far most thorough treatment my humble noggin has ever received.

Stage One: The Deforestation. The barber stretches a band of shaving gauze around my neck and wraps me in an apron. Wetting my hair with a spray bottle, he combs it with what looks like a dog brush. The barber reaches below the counter and takes out his electric clippers. The plug has absconded from the end of the cord, leaving a pair of bare, frayed wires. The barber gingerly inserts them into an outlet. A spark, and the clippers whir to life.

The barber shears the sides of my head with industrial rigor. In my experience, most barbers make two or three passes with their clippers before switching to scissors. Not this guy. He attacks my hair with short, quick swipes, switching from one side to another so fast that I lose count. There are no stragglers by the time he's done: The sides of my head are trimmed to the uniform fineness of a championship putting green. The barber attaches a guard to the end of the clippers and prunes the top of my skull. I give him even chances of having learned his technique in the Bangladeshi Army.

Stage Two: The Cut. Finished with the clippers, the barber pulls out his scissors and starts to chop. For twenty minutes the shears are a perpetual motion machine. Even when the barber pulls back to comb or switch to another angle, he continues snipping the air as though possessing a bionic hand that he can't turn off. After the strip-mining of the clippers, I'm amazed that there's still anything long enough for him to actually cut. Nevertheless, when he finishes, my head has been noticeably remolded. It now holds a shape I've never seen before, but it's not entirely unappealing.

Stage Three: The Fine-Tune. The scissors disappear and the barber brings out a smaller set of clippers of the sort typically used for trimming hairlines. He sets them humming and lops off the battered remnants of my sideburns just above the ear. The barber tilts my head forward and draws the clippers across the back of my neck with deliberate slowness, double-checking every few millimeters. Though I can't see it, I'm sure that the resulting hairline is plumb-straight. The barber tilts my head back upright and brings the clippers across the top of my hair like a cropduster making passes over a field, nipping the tops of any stray hairs foolish enough to stick out from the pack. My head now resembles a piece of fine English topiary.

Stage Four: Spelunking. The barber retrieves his scissors, places a hand on my forehead, and points my gaze skyward. Before I realize what's going I perceive a distinct metallic feel and smell as the scissors bore into my nose. This qualifies instantly and unreservedly as one of the most uncomfortable experiences of my life. I writhe in the chair like a worm on a hook as the barber twists the scissors back and forth, every snip bringing an eye-watering jolt of pain. In the brief respite between nostrils I try not to think about the disinfection to which this particular pair of scissors may or may not be subjected between customers. My mind goes blank as the scissors enter the other half of my nose.

Stage Five: The Inspection. The barber hands me a tissue with which to blow the debris from my nostrils. Wiping tears from my eyes, in the mirror I see him standing behind me, grinning and holding up a smaller mirror to the back of my head. I give it a cursory examination before nodding. Even if I were dissatisfied, by now there's not much left on which to make any changes.

I conclude my ordeal to be over and start to rise. The barber puts a hand on my shoulder and gently but firmly keeps me seated. I glance up with trepidation. He raises an eyebrow and asks, "Shaybing?" It takes me a moment to decipher. Shaving. I politely decline, but then notice my five o'clock shadow in the mirror. I'm this far down the path of no return, so why not? I tell him yes. He does the bobblehead thing again and grins even wider, perhaps reassessing the bill.

Stage Six: Scorched Earth. The barber opens a cabinet and produces a sort of lidless blender. He fills it with water, drops in a towel, and pushes a button. While it simmers he arranges his wares on the counter: a box of tissues, a can of shaving foam, several different jars of lard-like creams, and a straight razor, into which I gratefully observe him insert a fresh blade. Steam now billows from the blender. In one seamless motion the barber whips out the towel, twirls it in the air, and swathes my head from eyebrows to throat. The heat incinerates every nerve on my face. Before I can scream, the inferno cools to a gentle roast and I sink back into warm, off-white bliss.

Stage Seven: The Lather. After letting me baste for ten minutes or so, the barber unravels my head and wraps a dry towel around my neck and shoulders. He dips his fingers into a little bowl of water and wets my face with quick slaps of his hand. I get the distinct feeling that he's having fun at my expense, but by now we both know that I'm a pushover and will go along with just about anything. My face sufficiently moistened, the barber smears it with generous swabs of one of the viscous creams. Then he loads up his hand with a mountain of shaving foam and turns me into a yeti, covering not only my cheeks but my forehead and eyelids as well. He says something in Bangla to his colleagues, who look up from their clients and laugh. The barber picks up his razor and lets it dangle menacingly from his hand.

Stage Eight: The Shave. Wads of foam fly from my face as the blade hisses back and forth. My neck is put through its full range of motion as the barber maneuvers my head to allow the razor to come in from every conceivable direction, and several inconceivable ones as well. Every square inch of my face is scoured repeatedly by the disposable steel. The barber even makes good on his tomfoolery by shaving my forehead—although he leaves my eyelids alone, which reassures me that he's not completely insane. Just for good measure, he lathers me up and goes through the whole thing again.

Stage Nine: Mopping Up. By the end of the shave my lopped-off facial hairs are cowering far below the skin—which, apparently, isn't far enough. The barber dabs off the remaining flecks of foam and pulls out a cordless shaver. He stretches varying parts of my face taut against the skull, running the shaver over the flattened skin to mow the exposed stubs down to their follicles. It hurts like nobody's business, but it's effective; the shaver makes chewing noises every time it finds its prey. Gradually the noises become less frequent. The barber switches off the shaver, allowing me to examine my visage's new rubbery smoothness.

Stage Ten: The Dust & Flush. The barber grabs a can of what I presume is talcum powder and dumps a generous quantity onto his palms. He rubs it into my face with sweeping wax-on, wax-off motions, stopping to reload with a fresh dollop. I open my eyes once he's finished and see in the mirror that I'm now a mime. The barber reaches into the collection of vials atop the counter and picks one without looking. From it he daubs a curious yellowish liquid onto a piece of cotton, which he wipes all over my face to mop up the powder he just so vigorously applied.

Next up is a bottle with a label spelled "Eau de Colon," which I hope is intended to mean "water of Cologne" rather than "water of the lower intestine." The barber splashes a liberal amount on his hands and rubs it onto my face. Lo and behold, it's battery acid, or a substance remarkably like it. The barber walks to the sink to wash his hands, leaving me to squirm as the corrosive liquid boils my pores. He returns with a sprayer in hand, and the ensuing torrent of water mercifully brings the pH of my skin back below the threshold of pain. The barber wipes the moisture from my face with yet another tissue; by now we've probably used an entire box. Finally, the barber picks up a colorful little tin with the words "Tibetan Snow" on the front, a fitting moniker for the misty powder inside. When the barber rubs it over my face, the cool tingle does feel like nirvana.

Bonus Stage: The Grand Finale. As if all of this weren't enough, the barber has one more trick up his sleeve. He leans back and cracks his knuckles. We make eye contact in the mirror for the briefest of moments, and I read his intent clearly: This is going to hurt you more than me. The barber claps his hands together, places them against my head, and administers a string of violent karate-like chops to the back of my skull. I'm too startled to react—I'm not sure if it's his knuckles banging together or their reverberation against my skull, but the act makes a hollow knocking sound. The barber segues seamlessly into a head massage, a bewildering flurry of motions that shoves my scalp all around the surface of my cranium. He places his thumb and forefinger on my temples and shakes them like a paint mixer, then attempts to pull the flesh from the back of my neck down into my shirt collar. This continues for ten or twelve minutes, the pattern alternating between bursts of chopping and churning. By the time he's done, I feel like I've been beaten with a meat tenderizer.

Finally it's over, nearly two hours after I first sat down. I rise unsteadily while the barber picks up a broom and calmly disposes of the evidence. Reaching for my wallet, I ask the dreaded question: "How much?"

He pretends not to hear me and continues sweeping. I ask again and he looks up in feigned surprise, as if stunned that I would offer him money. I pose the question a third time. He grins, does the bobblehead thing again, and says "Tbuntie."

Incredible. "Twenty?" I ask, a bit too loudly. Opening my wallet, I pull out a twenty-dirham bill and show it to him just to make sure I heard correctly.

He shrugs. "O-K." Still in disbelief, I pull out another ten dirhams and press the notes into his hands, wanting to pay more, but also not wanting to patronize him. I leave the barbershop feeling like a million bucks, and with my eyes opened to an entirely new realm of grooming, all for the equivalent of eight dollars.

In a city, it is often in the humblest of settings—the hole-in-the-wall shops, greasy-spoon eateries, dive bars, and so forth—where unforgettable people are encountered and the fondest memories are made. Even the richest town on Earth is no exception.

Seven

A Higher Power

Our system of government is based on our religion, and is what our people want. Should they seek alternatives, we are ready to listen to them. We are all in the same boat, and they are both captain and crew. —*Sheikh Zayed bin Sultan al Nahyan*

At the heart of nearly every Middle Eastern city lies the central marketplace, or *souq*. Historically the souq was the primary nexus for both economic and social exchange, with hundreds of small shops lining the sides of winding, often covered alleyways. Shops were clustered by product, so that while strolling through the souq, one would actually encounter a sequence of smaller souqs, each offering a unique sensory experience—the glittering reflections of the gold souq, the vivid aromas of the spice souq, the gentle touch of the hanging fabrics of the cloth souq, and all the while, a succession of proprietors drawing in potential customers with promises of "For you, my friend, I make special price!" Even as modern competition has arisen in the form of shopping malls, many souqs have endured and have adopted a tourist function in addition to their traditional commercial roles.

Abu Dhabi's original souq is unfortunately no more, having been wiped away along with the rest of the Bedu settlement by the first 1960s-era wave of urbanization. It was replaced by the Central Market, an outdoor arcade built in 1972 at the behest of the city's principal planner, the Egyptian Abdel-Rahman Makhlouf. That too was demolished in 2005.

Abu Dhabi still boasts a souq, but of a decidedly different character. Near the center of the island, clustered together on a single block amid a smattering of schools and embassies, lies the collection of Christian houses of worship that residents lightheartedly call the "church souq." The government has a history of tolerance towards the non-Islamic religious practices of its foreign residents; Sheikh Zayed officially opened Abu Dhabi's first church in 1968.[1] However, only other monotheists are permitted their own houses of worship. Since Abu Dhabi does not exactly possess a thriving Jewish population, in practice this tolerance applies only to the city's Christians.

Within the church souq the government has allocated a plot of land to each of the major denominations. The Catholics and the Orthodox each have their own church, as do the Anglicans, in view of the special history between the Emiratis and the British. The rest of the Protestants are lumped together in a single "evangelical" congregation, a curious nomenclature in view of the emirate's ban on proselytizing.

I began attending the evangelical church toward the end of my first summer in the city. The church's catch-all status made for crowded services (held on Friday mornings, the first day of the local weekend), but it also made for a phenomenally international membership, one that matched the city's ethnic panoply. For me, it was one of the more enjoyable of Abu

Dhabi's endless ironies that here, in the heartland of Islam, was one of the most diverse and vibrant congregations I had ever come across. Nowhere else had I seen a church that so fulfilled Jesus of Nazareth's charge to his followers to make disciples of all nations.

Through the church I got to know a group of other young expats living and working in Abu Dhabi who proved to be a breath of fresh air. Although I genuinely enjoyed spending time with my UPC colleagues outside the office, it was nice to have another group of friends with different professions and interests. After morning services most Fridays I would join the church group for brunch. Their varied backgrounds and ethnicities offered insightful glimpses into other dimensions of Abu Dhabi's across-the-board transformation.

The discussion often turned to schools, as the group included a number of teachers, all female and quite young. The Abu Dhabi Education Council (ADEC), the local school board, had seen a 132 percent increase in enrolled pupils just since 2008.[2] In response, ADEC had commenced construction on an additional forty-seven new schools across the emirate, enough to accommodate an additional sixty thousand students. To inculcate these eager young minds, ADEC had hired more than two thousand new teachers, the overwhelming majority of them foreign like the rest of the workforce. Judging by the teachers' annual turnover rate, which approached 60 percent, many of them were less than satisfied with what they encountered in the schools.[3]

"Finland!" said Christine during one such Friday brunch. She was a vivacious young primary school teacher from the Pacific Northwest. "Somebody at ADEC saw that the Finns are consistently number one in the international educational rankings. Now the locals want to copy Finland."

I couldn't resist. "Of course. They're on top of the world." Groans rose from around the table.

Christine continued. "So the ADEC leadership took a trip to Finland and came back with all these great ideas. Now we're halfway into the school year, and we have to change not just our curriculum but also the entire way we teach. The locals think their kids will get smart if they just throw enough money at the school system."

Evelyn, a New Yorker who taught middle school math and science, joined in. "The local culture just doesn't value education. Emiratis are my worst students. Actually, the girls are okay, since most of them really want to learn." She taught boys and girls separately, as was the policy in most schools. "But the boys are just awful. They're rude, they're lazy, and some of them have such short attention spans that I honestly wonder if they're brain damaged. I'll turn around to write something on the board, and right away there's chaos. They think it's cool to fail. They even drag down the foreign students. I had one really sweet kid from Egypt who started off at the top of the class. Now he fails his tests and the local boys give him high-fives."

Creating a knowledge economy is key to Abu Dhabi's transformational vision. A flashy skyline and diversified industries mean nothing if the population isn't smart enough to maintain them. Sheikh Zayed had recognized the importance of education and had made it a cornerstone of the emirate's early modernization, claiming that "the real asset of any advanced nation is its people, especially the educated ones, and the prosperity and success of the people are measured by the standard of their education."

Although Abu Dhabi has made tremendous strides since the late 1950s, when none of its people were schooled, the knowledge economy still faces an uphill battle. An estimated one in six Emiratis is functionally illiterate, a particular disgrace when less wealthy Arab countries like Jordan fare much better.[4] ADEC's own figures show that 95 percent of students graduating from its schools are so ill-prepared for further education that they need two years or more of remedial courses.[5] Although the nascent knowledge economy has dire need of qualified Emirati engineers, scientists, and researchers, four-fifths of local students choose lighter educational tracks such as literature rather than math and science. Fewer than one in five Emiratis complete higher education, and of those who do, fewer still attend the 10 percent of UAE universities that are internationally accredited. Emirati women make up an astounding 72 percent of university students, as the attainment of higher education is one of the few routes for advancement and recognition open to them. Males, on the other hand, have little incentive to learn in view of the jobs guaranteed to them by the government.

Marie, a kindergarten teacher from Namibia, added her say. "We get told all the time that we're not supposed to impose our ways on our students. We're supposed to respect their culture. How do I do that when half of my students don't even have a culture? With most of my local students, their nannies are the ones really raising them. The kids speak more Tagalog than Arabic. It's like their parents have abdicated."

"Don't get me started on Emirati parents," Christine warned. "All the kids at my school are Emiratis, but some have foreign mothers. It's usually a Western woman married to an Emirati man. Those moms actually take an interest in their kids. They pick their kids up after school instead of sending their driver. They come to conferences. I can spot the difference from a mile away. Their kids are engaged and confident, while the full-blooded Emiratis are withdrawn and sullen. Honestly, I pity them. I sometimes wonder if their parents even know they exist."

Evelyn added, "If the parents won't discipline their kids, they should at least allow us to do it. There's one Emirati boy in my class who interrupts me every five minutes. I got so sick of it, but I didn't know what to do, so one day I just wrote his name up on the board. He was mortified. His mom called me the next morning and screamed at me for shaming their family. If we were anywhere else, I would have said that she was the one who should be ashamed."

Kelly, a social worker who had just started her employment with ADEC, asked, "So do you think that the Emiratis who are our age want to change all of this? They must see these things and know something is wrong."

"But if that's how they were brought up themselves, how would they know any better?" Christine responded. "If they've never left the country or seen any other way of life, why wouldn't they think it's just normal?"

Now it was the turn of Martha, a Tanzanian nurse who worked in one of the city's hospitals. "I don't think there's an Emirati in Abu Dhabi who hasn't left the country. The government pays for locals to get medical treatment abroad. You have a sore back? You have the flu? Here you go, a free ticket to Europe. And what do they do when they get there? They spend half their time shopping." Her accusations reminded me of my colleague Sultan, who had disappeared from the office for more than a month while on medical leave in Germany. After returning he had regaled me with tales of the therapeutic benefits of Munich's beer halls.

"You should see the files on some of my Emirati patients," Martha continued. "Two pages of medications, all prescribed by different doctors. All those drugs together do them more harm than good. And the real problems are lifestyle issues; they can't be solved with pills. When we do blood tests, every single Emirati has a Vitamin D deficiency. They never spend any time outside." This seemed bitterly ironic for a people who had spent their entire lives wandering through sun-drenched deserts just a few generations before. As Thesiger noted of the Bedu, "They are a race which produces its best only under conditions of extreme hardship and deteriorates progressively as living conditions become easier."[6]

True to Thesiger's words, the prosperity that the Bedu's modern descendants enjoy has wrought a precipitous decline in their physical condition. Emiratis are, hands-down, some of the unhealthiest people in the world. They are in the top ten fattest nationalities, with more than two-thirds of Emirati men and three-quarters of Emirati women overweight.[7] Abu Dhabi's younger citizens are beset by an epidemic of childhood obesity, largely because their parents do not control what they eat. Researchers have found that Emirati parents consider it normal to give their children money and let them buy whatever they want. The grown-ups' eating habits are no better: one in four adult Emiratis has diabetes, a disease that costs the government half a billion dollars every year.[8] Locals overwhelmingly work in sedentary jobs, and a culture of exercise or even basic activity is nonexistent. Even insomnia has reached endemic proportions; more than two-thirds of locals do not get enough sleep.[9]

The Emiratis' collectively worsening condition is not limited to their physiques. The gilded sledgehammer of wealth and modernity has fractured the social bedrock of the Emirati family—"the foundation of social activity and mutual support,"[10] as *Plan 2030* puts it—into rubble. Divorce is rife, with more than four out of ten local marriages failing, the highest rate in the Arab world and an astounding increase from the almost complete absence of divorce just sixty years ago.[11] One-third of local marriages do not even survive their first year.[12] Money and ennui have bred discontent and rampant infidelity by both husbands and wives. Challenging the local tradition of arranged marriages, ambitious young Emirati men and women increasingly question the wisdom of having their elders pair them up with someone who might not share their perspective and goals in life.

Even more damaging to Emirati society is the collapse in parenting. My teacher friends were not exaggerating when they asserted that the parents of their Emirati students often abdicated their roles. Domestic servants attend to every Emirati household. The typical local villa includes at least one room designed specifically as servants' quarters, often nothing more than a windowless closet adjoining the kitchen. The lowly status of these domestic workers is a far cry from Thesiger's observation that in Bedu homes "servants count as part of the family; there is no social distinction between them and their masters."[13] For Emirati families, the servants' ranks invariably include low-paid nannies to watch the children. One study found that 58 percent of local children spend the majority of their waking hours with their nannies, who typically have no formal qualifications in childcare.[14]

The breakdown in Emirati families has not gone unnoticed. The growing number of servant-raised children has prompted a small but growing public outcry—virtually unprecedented for the Emiratis, who abhor airing their dirty laundry in public—with the angst over this societal shift extending all the way to the top. In 2007 Sheikh Mohammed bin Rashid al Maktoum, the ruler of Dubai, stunned the UAE with a public speech in which he deplored his people's reliance on foreign servants, noting that domestic workers make up a bloated one-tenth of the labor force and outnumber the family in many homes.[15]

Nevertheless, modernity's assault on the individual and familial health of Abu Dhabi's Emiratis continues unabated. If anything, the steadily increasing transformational tempo of the post-Zayed years seems to have exacerbated the strains. Such changes strike at the very heart of Emirati identity, one in which tradition and the family play a central role. Indeed, to outsiders it may look as though the locals are approaching a point of no return. To paraphrase an ancient teacher, what will it profit the Emiratis if they gain the world but lose themselves?

* * *

Despite the pressures of modernization, Emirati traditions and customs are not dead—not yet. Religion in particular still plays a central role in Emirati society and exerts significant influence on life in the emirate. The constitution declares Islam to be the UAE's official religion[16]; the government further defines all citizens to be Muslims and prohibits them—and the rest of the country's Muslims—from changing or renouncing this status. The penalty for apostasy is death, although there are no records of this ever having been applied, and the only Emirati in recent history to declare himself a non-Muslim was let off with a pardon.[17]

Officially, 85 percent of Emiratis across the UAE are Sunni and the rest are Shi'a or other minority sects. Most Shi'ite Emiratis are concentrated in Dubai and Sharjah, due to those emirates' long histories of trade with Iran. Abu Dhabi's Emiratis are almost uniformly Sunni; all of my UPC colleagues certainly identified themselves as such. The distinction has considerable ramifications. Early on, while I was still learning about the basics of Emirati society, I once asked my colleague Sultan whether there were any Emirati Shi'a. He nodded, then looked around before whispering conspiratorially, "But you know, those people aren't real Muslims."

The Abu Dhabi government tacitly agrees, considering all Shi'a mosques to be private and thus ineligible for the state funding their Sunni counterparts receive. As tensions with Iran have risen in recent years, the government has taken a harder stance towards Shi'a foreigners by denying them jobs or refusing to renew their residency permits, perhaps viewing them as potential sleeper agents for the revolutionary regime on the far side of the Gulf. Frankly, this smacks of counterproductive paranoia; most of Abu Dhabi's Shi'a have absolutely no affiliation with Iran, and some have devoted years or even decades of their lives to helping the Emiratis build Abu Dhabi's future.

Abu Dhabi's citizens generally pride themselves on their religiosity, and religious values weigh heavily on the emirate's public and private spheres. The government's Telecommunications Regulatory Authority, for example, blocks Web sites that traffic in pornography, online dating, gambling, or other content that contravenes Islam. Many of Abu Dhabi's malls maintain dress codes banning revealing or inappropriate clothing. Public displays of affection can be grounds for arrest. In 2012 the Abu Dhabi Tourism Police (yes, the emirate has police devoted specifically to tourists) began issuing a pamphlet of advice for foreign visitors, including "Please wear respectful clothing" and "Please avoid any behavior in public places, which could be considered indecent, such as, kissing, cross-dressing etc."[18] Mosques were a standard feature in North Wathba and the other communities that the UPC was responsible for master planning, with one "cluster" mosque for every one hundred or so dwellings and a larger *Juma'a* (Friday) mosque for every one thousand.

Although Abu Dhabi is characterized by its conservatism, it is not nearly as strict as some of its neighbors. The emirate of Sharjah, for instance, bans alcohol and prohibits mixing between unmarried men and women.[19] And religious police, such as the *Mutaween* that dominate public life in Saudi Arabia, do not exist in Abu Dhabi. That being said, the continued importance of religion and other traditions can make Abu Dhabi a cultural minefield for the unaware, full of unwritten rules and taboos. For the many expatriates who seldom interact with Emiratis, this is not so much of a concern, but for those who do, it is a perpetual learning game. Throughout my first year in Abu Dhabi, I feared few things more than committing an inadvertent intercultural transgression around my local colleagues. My gaffes were nonetheless plentiful, and once even threatened to put me out of a job.

As the UPC continued to hire more staff, I was shifted into a small windowless office at the end of the wing, along with Carlo, my Italian colleague on the transport team. To make up for the lack of a view I covered one of our office walls with some maps, including one of the entire Middle East. The office also happened to adjoin our floor's designated prayer room. Thrice daily, during the designated prayer times that fell during working hours, the UPC's Emiratis and other Muslims trooped past our door to pray—the men first, then later the women. From my overlook next to the door I couldn't help noticing who prayed and who didn't; even among the purportedly pious Emiratis, there were quite a few who prayed seldom or not at all.

My vantage point did not escape the notice of Faisal, the UPC's gregarious director of human resources. He took great pains to ingratiate himself with the staff, often dropping by people's offices unannounced and cracking awkward jokes followed by loud, mechanical laughter. Given the power of his position, I found him terrifying. Faisal took it upon himself to check up on Carlo and me at least once a day on his way to prayers, which he never missed. He dubbed me "The Gatekeeper" in honor of my view of the prayer room. I tried to take this as a compliment, reasoning that if a Muslim family could serve for thirteen centuries as impartial keepers of the keys to Jerusalem's Holy Sepulchre,[20] it wasn't too outlandish for me to watch over a prayer room in Abu Dhabi.

At the appointed hour one afternoon I heard a knock on the door and looked up to see Faisal's gleaming grin. "Ah, gentlemen, how are you today? How is my Gatekeeper?" Before I could answer, he noticed the map of the Middle East on the wall, evidently for the first time. "Yes, this is very good. You are broadening your horizons." He stepped forward to examine it more closely.

Suddenly he whirled on me, fury contorting his face. "ISRAEL!" he thundered. "Are you a *fan* of *Israel?*" A knot formed in my stomach as I glanced up at the map, on which the offending country's name was prominently displayed, right in the center. In the UAE, Israel is The Country That Shall Not Be Named. Government censors black out the offending moniker on imported maps and globes, or cover it over with "Palestine." Although the government does not go as far as some of its neighbors in calling for the destruction of the Zionist entity, for the most part, it simply ignores Israel's existence.[21]

"Where did you get that map?" Faisal asked. I told him that I had bought it at a bookstore in one of the malls. It must have slipped past the censors. "I see," Faisal said coldly. "I will have to make a phone call. In the meantime, I suggest that you either take that map down, or remove that word. There are people in this office who would not be happy to see it." Faisal waited until I took a magic marker and blacked out the country's name. Then he stormed out, leaving me wondering if I would have a job the next day.

The entire episode would assuredly have amused Thesiger, who reminds us that the Emiratis' Bedu forerunners were not so concerned with geopolitics just a few generations ago. When the explorer and his Bedu entourage visited Abu Dhabi, he recounted a meeting with Sheikh Shakhbut during which the tottering ruler railed against Jewry. Bin Kabina, one of Thesiger's companions, had no idea what to make of this: "'Who are the Jews?' he whispered. 'Are they Arabs?'"[22]

* * *

I left my apartment one morning and nearly stumbled over a pile of cinderblocks outside my door. Evidently someone had stacked them on the stairwell landing during the night, for reasons unbeknownst to me. By the time I returned from work late that evening, the pile had transformed into a wall that sealed off nearly the entire landing, leaving a walkway barely wide enough to reach my room. At first I thought that the makeshift chamber was meant to be a storage closet of sorts, but over the next several days I observed laborers running plumbing and electrical wires, and I realized that it was intended as a dwelling. The claustrophobic room couldn't have measured more than a hundred square feet.

The same process was repeated throughout the villa during the following weeks. Workers created rough-and-ready cinderblock quarters in any space that was currently empty: in the front hall, in the front and rear courtyards, and even on the roof. Any opening that could fit a bed, a sink, and a toilet was walled off. I thought back to my friend Noor's cryptic comment when we first toured the villa; she must have seen this kind of thing happen before.

In short order the landlord began packing additional tenants into the new rooms, most of them from Abu Dhabi's lower ethno-economic classes. As if illegally subdividing his villa to cash in on every room weren't enough, the landlord evidently saw nothing untoward in wringing even more dirhams out of every last rentable square foot. The chamber on the landing outside my apartment soon housed not one but three people: two parents and an infant. I had no idea how they managed to fit in that space, let alone survive in it. In view of their situation, I wasn't surprised when the domestic unrest started less than a week after they moved in. Every third night or so I would hear them through the walls: the husband and wife yelling in Arabic, the baby wailing, objects being hurled across the room.

The villa soon became the modern incarnation of a nineteenth-century Lower East Side tenement. Trash was frequently left in the common areas, imbuing the villa with a fetid stench. A litter of street cats moved in, whom I learned not to mind as they at least kept out the vermin (not to mention being far more sociable than the other inhabitants). The lights flickered and the taps dribbled under the excessive utility demands. It was hard to tell which was more suffocating: the villa's stagnant air or the wretched, helpless feeling that it imparted. My fellow occupants and I did, admittedly, have a few advantages over our tenement antecedents from a hundred years before: as far as I could tell, all the units in our villa at least had plumbing and air conditioning, although the new cinderblock rooms all lacked windows. Living in the villa would have made for a fascinating anthropological experiment had I not been one of the subjects.

I could have afforded to bite the bullet and move somewhere else, but I stayed—partly out of a sense of solidarity with my fellow boarders. I knew that the situation was being repeated in villas throughout the neighborhood and across the city, making my desire for comfort seem vain.

The misery we tenants came to endure at the hands of our unscrupulous Emirati landlord was made even more galling by the knowledge that he was undoubtedly living like a king and didn't need the extra money he was wringing from the property. Abu Dhabi's Emiratis pride themselves on their piousness, but as I was learning, that didn't prevent some of them from acting with unrighteous rapacity, treating their fellow men as nothing more than revenue streams.

In his 1890 exposé, *How the Other Half Lives*, the muckraking journalist Jacob Riis had chronicled the miserable conditions of New York City's industrial-era tenements. More than a century later and half a world away, the treatise's searing words rang just as true of Abu Dhabi: "How shall the love of God be understood by those who have been nurtured in sight only of the greed of man?"[23]

Eight

Back to Nature

On land and in the sea, our forefathers lived and survived in this environment. They were able to do so because they recognized the need to conserve it, to take from it only what they needed to live, and to preserve it for succeeding generations.—*Sheikh Zayed bin Sultan al Nahyan*

Carlo swiveled in his chair to face me inside the closet-sized office we had shared for a month. "Mike," he said, apropos of nothing, "do you think it's strange that we live on an island ... and there are no good beaches?"

Though I had become accustomed to his spontaneous epiphanies, this one caught me off guard. That particular incongruity of Abu Dhabi's metropolitan landscape had never dawned on me. Carlo had a point. Almost all of Abu Dhabi Island's forty-two-mile coastline is occupied by development, infrastructure, and other manmade flotsam. The city segregates its inhabitants from the waters that surround them—ironic for a settlement that once depended on the sea for its existence. No point on the island is more than a mile from the shoreline, but the water is so obscured by buildings and other obstructions that one rarely realizes its proximity.

The island does retain a scant few interfaces between land and sea. The Emirates Palace Hotel at the island's northwest corner boasts a spotlessly manicured white sand beach, restricted to guests who shell out thousands of dollars a night for a room. Some of the sheikhs' private estates have beaches, but these are similarly off-limits to the hoi polloi. Abu Dhabi's only public strand is the beach that stretches for two miles along the scorpion's head of the Corniche at the island's northern edge. The stretch of sand is backstopped by a path for pedestrians and cyclists along with clusters of refreshment stands. In keeping with Abu Dhabi's conservatism, the beach maintains dress codes and a fenced-off family section for women and children. During the summer of 2009 the UPC began a phased rehabilitation of the beach, boosting its aesthetics by trucking in hundreds of metric tons of fine orange sand carved from of the Empty Quarter's towering dunes. The project came with a price tag of more than one hundred million dirhams.[1]

Unfortunately no amount of terraforming could solve the Corniche beach's water problem. The beach fronts on a shallow lagoon that was created in the 1970s when boatloads of sand were dumped offshore to form a thousand-acre island named *Lulu*, the Arabic word for pearl. Lulu Island acts like a giant cork, trapping water in the lagoon and preventing it from flushing to the Gulf. Wading out from the Corniche beach is thus a nasty experience. The cloudy water stinks like a swamp, and one's feet sink into muck on the bottom. Jet skis and powerboats thrash the lagoon, stirring up silt and leaving an oily film that clings to the skin for days after a swim. I learned early on that the beach was not a place to take visitors, which was just as well during the summer, when the waters of the Gulf are too hot for swimming anyway.

The Corniche beach and Lulu Island epitomize Abu Dhabi's adversarial relationship with its natural surroundings. The modern city requires a staggering amount of resources to exist in its desert setting. Its people consume more water and electricity and produce more emissions and waste per capita than almost anyone else on the planet. On average, an Abu Dhabi resident uses 121 megawatt-hours of energy per year, the third-highest rate in the world—fully four-fifths of which is used to run air conditioners during the summer months. At 10.6 hectares per person, the inhabitants of Abu Dhabi and the UAE as a whole have the unfortunate distinction of generating the largest ecological footprint in the world.[2] Some journalists decry the country's very existence as a form of "ecocide."[3]

Water is Abu Dhabi's direst environmental flashpoint. The average family uses one million liters of water per year—145 gallons every day—more than three times the level recommended by the United Nations and six times that of other Middle Eastern countries like Egypt and Jordan.[4] Much of this water is consumed through indirect uses such as irrigation. Bear in mind that this is in a country with just 19 cubic meters of renewable freshwater resources per person, compared with 110 cubic meters per person in Jordan and 9,044 cubic meters in the U.S.[5] At present Abu Dhabi reclaims just 4 percent of its wastewater for uses such as irrigation.[6] In an emergency, the emirate's on-hand water reserves would not last more than 48 hours.

The scarce groundwater and infrequent rains require the emirate to satisfy its thirst via desalination. The UAE is home to nine of the world's twenty largest desalination facilities, of which its biggest—Abu Dhabi's titanic Shuweihat plant—produces 240 million gallons of desalinated water every day.[7] Desalination is notoriously inefficient, requiring three liters of seawater to generate a single liter of potable water.[8] The residue of this process is hot, salty, sludgy brine that is discharged right back into the Gulf. This despoiling is repeated up and down the coastline not just in Abu Dhabi, but also in the other desalination-dependent city-states that border the Gulf. Brine has caused the Gulf's salinity to soar from its historic levels of 37,000 parts per million to 56,000 today, placing tremendous strain on the Gulf's fragile marine habitats.[9]

Although the Gulf[10] enjoys an outsized notoriety, few outside the region appreciate just how small and fragile it is. The Gulf is just 500 miles long and varies in width from 200 miles to just over 30 at the Straits of Hormuz. It is surprisingly shallow, averaging just 150 feet deep and barely exceeding 300 feet at its deepest; along certain sections of Abu Dhabi's coastline, its waters are no more than 30 feet deep for as far as 30 miles offshore.[11] The Gulf's total water volume varies between 1,700 and 2,000 cubic miles depending on tidal levels.[12] As a Michigander, I cannot help but compare it to the Great Lakes that surround my home state.[13] The Gulf's 97,000 square miles of surface area exceed the 94,390 square miles of Lakes Superior, Michigan, Huron, Erie, and Ontario combined, but Superior alone holds one and a half times as much water—2,900 cubic miles.[14] Indeed, hydrologically the Gulf acts more like a lake than an inlet of the Indian Ocean; the narrows at Hormuz restrict the Gulf to replenishing its waters once every eight or nine years.[15] The Gulf's shallow waters, prevailing northwesterly winds, and extremely high evaporation rates gave it one of the highest natural salinity levels of any major body of water, even before the advent of desalination. Despite these constraints, the Gulf hosts a breathtaking array of marine wildlife, including extensive coral reefs, dolphins, hawksbill turtles, and manatee-like dugongs.

Today, Abu Dhabi and the other cities that ring the Gulf are inadvertently transforming it into the next Dead Sea.[16] The saline discharges from the desalination plants are merely one ingredient in the Gulf's increasingly toxic stew. At the north end of the Gulf, the Tigris and Euphrates rivers spew the filth they have accumulated during their tortured journey across Iraq. Kuwait, Saudi Arabia, Qatar, and the UAE all have sewage treatment plants that are not up to modern standards, while Iran's cities cut to the chase by dumping raw sewage straight into the Gulf. The shallow waters are polluted even further by the thousands of tankers that illegally flush their ballasts when they dock at the Gulf's oil terminals.

The effects of pollution, salinity, and artificial warming pose a dire hazard to the Gulf's flora and fauna. Whereas divers twenty years ago could swim through coral gardens teeming with exotic fish and sea turtles, today "dead reefs stand like gravestones in underwater ghost towns."[17] One of the UAE's most colorful reefs was decimated when Dubai began building the Palm Jumeirah directly atop it in 2001. Gulf fishermen's catches are down more than 20 percent since 1990. In 2008 the waters of the lower Gulf were plagued by "red tides," noxious algal blooms that soaked up oxygen and left huge dead zones in their wake. The algae killed hundreds of thousands of fish in a single day, many jumping onto shore in a vain effort to escape suffocation. The red tides closed beaches and even caused several of the UAE's desalination plants to shut down in order to avoid contamination.[18] Rising levels of pollution are also blamed for "mass suicides" of dolphin pods that have beached themselves near Hormuz.[19]

While many parties share the blame for the Gulf's degradation, including more than a few foreigners in the employ of oil companies, shipping lines, and other resource-hungry enterprises, the lion's share can be placed squarely at the feet of the Emiratis and the citizens of the other Gulf nations. For five decades they have run the show, pursuing development regardless of its environmental cost. The historical origins of this approach can be traced back to the Bedu's view of their harsh environs as an adversary to be feared and endured, not celebrated. As Thesiger noted, "While [the Bedu] are very sensible to the beauty of their language, they are curiously blind to natural beauty."[20] After generations of living at nature's mercy, the Emiratis now have the money and the equipment to literally reshape their surroundings as they wish, carving rivers in the desert and raising fancifully shaped islands offshore. Author Jo Tatchell saw among Abu Dhabi's nationals an obsession with creating permanence where before there was none: "This desire to master nature is a novelty for a race whose culture has been constantly erased by the sand and sea."[21]

Lest any American reader be tempted to look contemptuously upon the Emiratis' brazen abuse of their natural environment, it is worth remembering that the track record of the United States is not exactly untarnished in this regard. Vast areas of the western states in particular were not much more hospitable than eastern Arabia, and were only conquered with similarly high environmental and fiscal costs. Mark Reisner's classic *Cadillac Desert* reminds us that, just like the Gulf's conurbations, Las Vegas and other ephemeral western paradises "were formed out of seas of sand and humps of rock. Sprawling cities sprouted out of nowhere.... The cost of all this, however, was a vandalization both of our natural heritage and our economic future, and the reckoning has not even begun."[22]

Abu Dhabi's new transformative vision was supposed to prevent such a reckoning. The emirate had embarked on a number of initiatives intended to chart a more sustainable course. The most ballyhooed of these was the Masdar development, which would construct the world's first carbon-neutral urban district on a 2.3-square-mile plot near the airport at a cost somewhere between fifty-five and eighty billion dirhams.[23] The district would generate all of its electricity from renewable sources, with solar panels covering roughly 80 percent of its roof areas. Among other innovative features, the entire Masdar development would be built atop an elevated podium housing a unique "personal rapid transit" system of three thousand electric podcars that would ferry the forty thousand residents around the district like driverless personal taxis.[24] Admittedly, the carbon-neutral label was only achieved with some creative accounting, such as ignoring the automotive emissions of the additional fifty thousand office workers who would commute to the district every day and park in garages along its periphery. And it remained to be seen whether Masdar's advances could be adopted cost effectively on a wider scale. Still, it was a step in the right direction.

Abu Dhabi had also lobbied successfully to become the site for the headquarters of the new International Renewable Energy Association (IRENA) in mid–2009, beating out Germany and Austria.[25] Fittingly, the organization would be housed rent-free in office space within the Masdar district. The UPC's troubled Estidama program was another step, however faltering, towards sustainability. Even the creation of the transit system and the national railway would help reduce the emirate's environmental footprint.

But for every stride forward there seemed to be a reactionary lurch back. The UPC's tiny environmental team could barely keep pace with the terraforming ambitions of the emirate's developers and other government agencies. For example, in late 2009 Sheikh Hamdan, the "Ruler's Representative" in Al Gharbia, announced that his office would spend twenty-eight million dirhams to promote the biologically rich Bu Tinah shoal off the Al Gharbia coast in an international competition to choose the world's greatest natural wonders.[26] Shortly thereafter, my colleague Liz found herself scrambling to convince the same sheikh's staff to abandon their plans to dredge the seafloor in the middle of a coastal biosphere reserve just so they could create additional beachfront property for the town of Mirfa. "It's tragic enough to see people destroying the environment in a place like England or America," Liz protested, "but here it just boggles my mind. It's not as though they have a lot of ruinable nature to start with." She wasn't exaggerating; even *Plan 2030* admitted that 93 percent of the Emirate's land mass was "prohibitively difficult to inhabit."[27]

Amid the missteps, one component of Abu Dhabi's strategy to mend its relationship with nature was coming together nicely on Sir Bani Yas, a desert island off the Al Gharbia coast some one hundred fifty miles west of the city. At eleven square miles Sir Bani Yas is the largest of Abu Dhabi's natural islands, which number more than two hundred. The island is shaped like a squashed teardrop and sits three miles north of the coast near Ruwais. Sir Bani Yas is just one of a multitude of salt dome formations dotting the lower Gulf, which were formed by subterranean salt deposits that pushed their way to the surface and accumulated sediment over eons. In addition to its rugged natural beauty, Sir Bani Yas has yielded a treasure trove of some of the Gulf's most archaeologically significant sites, which hint at habitation predating Abu Dhabi's founding by millennia. Along with finds from as far back as the Late Stone Age (ca. 5500 BC), archaeologists have uncovered the remnants of a seventh-century Nestorian church and monastery, a reminder of the eastern Christianity that flourished throughout Arabia until the coming of Islam.[28]

Long after the island's last residents had been lost to the ages, Sheikh Zayed turned Sir Bani Yas into his private nature reserve in 1971. He ordered hundreds of thousands of trees to be planted on the previously sparsely vegetated island as an extension of his vision to green the desert. He also brought to the island his own private wildlife menagerie, thousands of animals including native Arabian species like the sand gazelle, the tahr (a kind of goat), and the endangered Arabian oryx, as well as more exotic animals like ostriches, llamas, zebras, and giraffes. Although the island was Zayed's private property, he often brought visitors to show off his crowning environmental achievement.

After Zayed's death Sir Bani Yas passed into a sort of limbo under his estate. In 2007 the government turned the island over to the Tourism Development and Investment Corporation (TDIC), the state-owned real estate company responsible for developing the emirate's prestigious new tourist destinations. TDIC elected to redevelop Sir Bani Yas as an eco-resort where visitors could ogle the island's wildlife and explore its varied terrain while enjoying a suitably Abu Dhabian level of luxury. The desire for a minimal environmental impact meant that TDIC built little other than an obligatory five-star hotel and an arrival center for visitors coming by boat or plane, preferring to let Sir Bani Yas' rugged beauty serve as the main attraction. It was a brilliant marketing stroke, actually, highlighting the island's remoteness and austerity while adding just enough bling to make it comfortable.

Like many other projects in Abu Dhabi's first wave of post-Zayed development, TDIC's work on Sir Bani Yas predated the UPC's creation and was already substantially complete by the time the company submitted a retroactive proposal to us. The TDIC staff distinguished themselves from their competition by getting just about everything correct on Sir Bani Yas. There was little for the UPC's review team, of which I was a part, to do besides nod and smile. I had the least to say of anyone; TDIC had banned private vehicles from the island, making the transport component of the plans rather perfunctory. Our TDIC counterparts were highly capable and clearly took the project's environmental ethos seriously. We returned their submittals with barely any comments. In return, they took it upon themselves to fly us out to the island. TDIC had officially opened the resort in the fall of 2008, but they were still finishing elements like the activity center and fine-tuning the island's ongoing operations.

The hour-long trip to Sir Bani Yas in TDIC's wobbly floatplane nearly made me foreswear flying. The cabin barely had enough room for anyone besides the pilots; the passengers were me, Keith, a young Emirati woman from his team named Fatima, and Austin, who had used his Al Gharbia connection to finagle a spot on the trip. Once up in the air, the plane tossed back and forth with every crossbreeze and downdraft. "Isn't this great?" Keith shouted over the noise of the propeller. "I used to ride in planes like these when I worked in British Columbia. Made hopscotch visits to remote little towns in the woods. Barfed every time." By the time the plane's pontoons sliced into the bay at Sir Bani Yas, I was tempted to ask whether we could take the boat on the way back.

Celine, the French planner in charge of the project, met us at the visitor's center. She introduced us to Wim, a burly South African game warden replete with knee socks and safari hat TDIC had hired to manage the island's wildlife. We climbed into an ethanol-fueled touring van and headed out along the island's sole asphalt road. Wim drove us through thickets of thorny ghaf trees planted in neat, linear rows radiating outwards from the central hills of the salt dome. On the western side of the island we crossed an imaginary line and the foliage abruptly stopped, revealing rows of dead, stunted saplings stretching to the shore in the distance. Celine explained that when TDIC took over the island, millions of gallons of water were being piped in from desalination plants on the mainland every day just for irrigation. The staff performed triage by identifying the areas most conducive to sustaining greenery, and then simply shut off the irrigation to the rest. "It wasn't a difficult decision," Celine explained, pointing to the rows of tinder in front of us. "These trees had been here fifteen years. Look how much they grew." None of the dead saplings was taller than three feet. I admired TDIC's decision to go against the prevailing local mentality that nature's constraints were merely inconveniences to be vanquished with money. Sometimes sustainability meant working with the desert instead of fighting it.

We drove up into the island's central massif, where the hills were like a time-lapse image of the effects of erosion. The blackish layer of volcanic soil on the surface of the salt dome peeled away in places to reveal pink and ochre mineral deposits underneath. The salt dome offered commanding views of the island's austere beauty in every direction.

Descending from the hills into the artificial forests we finally encountered animals. The variety was striking: bounding herds of gazelles, oryx with their curving scimitar-like horns, loping giraffes, and skittish red deer. While the rest of us oohed and aahed, Wim alternated between driving and scanning the thickets with his binoculars. Finally he exclaimed, "There you are!" and took the van into the bush. We pulled up just short of a watering hole, next to which a pair of cheetahs lounged in the shade of a tree, eyeing us languidly.

"My darlings," Wim said with manifest pride. "Straight off the savannah. We brought them to help with the gazelles. They've been here two months, and they're finally starting to hunt on their own. You should see those cats make a kill. It's a work of art."

The cheetahs had become curious and started ambling towards the van. "Kitties!" Austin squealed from the seat behind me. "Here, take a picture for me." He dumped his camera into my lap and pulled open the sliding glass window next to me. I suddenly found myself five feet away from the business end of a cheetah who didn't look opposed to giving white meat a try.

"Hm ... not supposed to do that, they aren't," Wim said. He hopped out of the van, yelling and clapping his hands. The startling appearance of the six-foot-tall bogeyman convinced the cheetahs to scamper off. "Guess we'll have to work on their fear of people," he said as he climbed back in. "Can't go having them nibbling on the guests, now can we?"

We drove past the excavated ruins of the Nestorian monastery on the island's eastern side. The site was off limits, forcing us to glimpse it from afar. Celine explained that the debate over what to do with the ruins reached all the way to the upper echelons of the government. Opening the site to the public would add a significant attraction to Sir Bani Yas, raising its profile as a destination and giving visitors insight into the history of the lower Gulf. But it would also mean acknowledging that for much of the UAE's history, religions other than Islam prevailed—a sensitive subject for the Emiratis, who define themselves by their Islamic culture. Celine seemed confident that openness would prevail. "The Crown Prince seems to understand. You should embrace history, not hide it."

We ended our tour at the hotel, which stood sentinel-like at the very northern tip of the island, its green grounds looking rather out of place among their stony surroundings. TDIC was only now ramping up its marketing campaign, and guests were still few and far between. We had the restaurant overlooking the placid waters of the Gulf entirely to ourselves.

Over a late lunch Wim spoke in his Afrikaans-tinged accent about the challenges his staff had faced when they first arrived on the island. "The animals had been neglected to the point of abuse. Nobody bloody took care of the place after Zayed died. We went into the giraffe pens and found the shade structures toppled over and the water troughs broken. In this heat, it's amazing they survived." Unfortunately such mistreatment of animals is not uncommon across the UAE. The newspapers often carry stories of exotic animals that are abused or abandoned by wealthy locals who buy them as novelty pets.[29]

"The gazelles, though, now they were breeding out of hand," Wim continued. "Of all the species brought to the island, there wasn't a single predator. I have to hand it to Sheikh Zayed for helping to protect endangered species, but whoever was advising him didn't know what they were doing. In the end, we wound up having to get rid of a lot of the animals. There were too many, and some just couldn't take the climate."

Fatima, the sole Emirati at the table, asked, "What do you mean, you got rid of them?"

"Well, we shipped a few back to Africa."

Fatima hesitated before asking, "And the rest?"

"We culled them. Which is bloody difficult when you can't use a gun."

"Why couldn't you use guns?" I interjected.

"No guns in this country, unless you're Emirati and in the army. The natives don't take

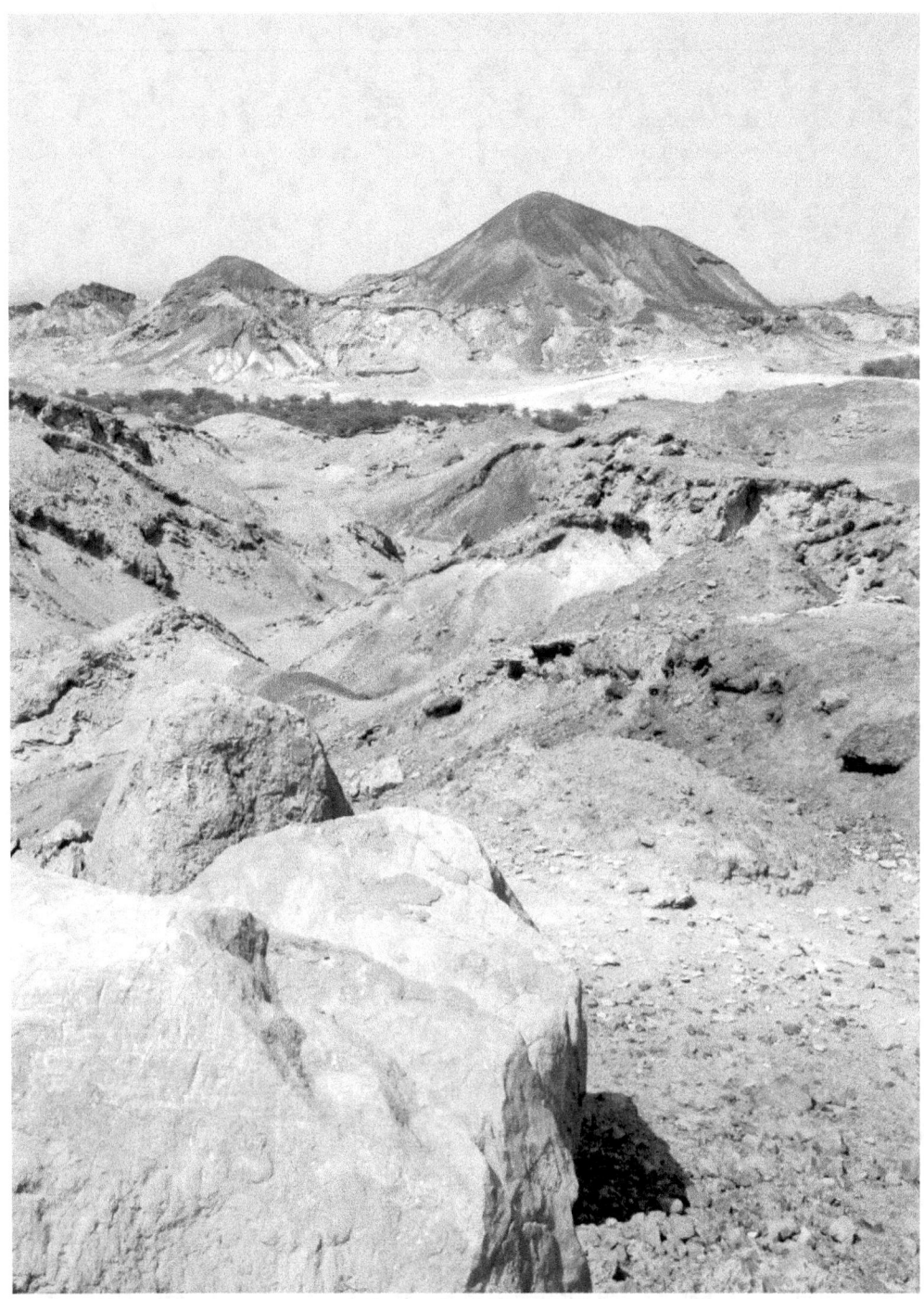

The salt dome on Sir Bani Yas island.

too kindly to that." This was no exaggeration: in 2010 an American military contractor transiting through Abu Dhabi's airport was arrested for having in his luggage nothing more dangerous than a front firearm grip and a cleaning brush. He was eventually released after languishing two and a half months in the emirate's Al Wathba prison, notorious for its overcrowding, rapes, and stonings.[30]

"So, how do you ... kill them, then?" Fatima asked.

Wim smiled. "My dear, there are some trade secrets you really don't want to know."

As we left the restaurant I saw a group of young Emirati men coming in. I overheard one of them speaking to the hostess. "Outside? Are you crazy? Maybe my ancestors liked sitting outside, but I'll take air conditioning."

* * *

The changes that marked the onset of the cooler season (calling it "winter" is just exaggeration) were subtle enough to miss at first. The air, usually laden with moisture, felt a little crisper day by day. Gradually the temperatures subsided to where stepping outdoors didn't induce instant sweat. One early October afternoon I was startled to see a solitary wispy cloud hanging in the sky like a puff of white smoke. It was the first atmospheric phenomenon I'd witnessed since stepping off the plane seven months before.

To mark our emergence from the summer hibernation, Elise invited several other colleagues and me to join her on a kayak tour through one of Abu Dhabi's mangrove forests. Multiple species of saltwater mangroves grow in abundance in tidal lagoons along the UAE coastline. The mangroves are a rich breeding ground for the Gulf's marine species, and they historically served the Bedu as an important source of food as well as wood for fuel and construction. Zayed's desert greening program in the 1970s and 1980s bolstered the mangrove's natural coverage to more than 7,500 acres.[31] Three-quarters of this acreage was in Abu Dhabi territory, much of it in watery glens tucked among the metropolitan archipelago like layers of spinach in a souffle. Although the mangroves surround the city, Abu Dhabi's estrangement from nature makes it easy to forget they are there.

Our kayak tour was slated to go through one of the forests in the Eastern Mangrove Lagoon just east of Abu Dhabi Island. *Plan 2030* had designated the lagoon as a future national park. The tour convened at a tiny inlet next to an electrical substation, the only access point on the island's eastern flank. We had to clamber down slippery riprap to launch our kayaks into the lagoon. With the surrounding islands absorbing the Gulf's waves, the surface of the water was as smooth as glass.

Dale, our guide, was a former commando who had come to Abu Dhabi several years earlier with his diplomat wife. Dale didn't look like the Rambo type; he was soft-spoken and a tad shorter than average, with a wiry physique instead of bulging biceps. To escape being a homebound Mr. Mom, he had taken up kayaking through the mangroves as a hobby. After a while he started bringing along friends, who then passed word to their friends. Before long, Dale had found an Emirati partner, started a business, and hired guides to run daily tours. He had unwittingly struck a chord among Abu Dhabi's Western expats, who were almost frothing at the mouth for any kind of outdoor activity.

We paddled several miles across the open sound to the wall of mangroves on the far side, where Dale led us into a shallow channel that snaked its way through the forest. The mangroves closed in around us like a snug gray-green cocoon. The trees reached up to fifteen feet in height, and their branches were so intertwined that it was impossible to see more than a few paces into the thicket.

A few minutes into the forest I realized something was missing: the noise, the dust, the constant din of traffic and construction that was omnipresent in Abu Dhabi, like a soundtrack playing in the background. I had become so accustomed to it that its absence unnerved me. Here the only sounds were the lapping of our paddles and the chirping of birds. I hadn't realized how badly I needed a nature therapy session like this.

Dale halted and told us to listen to the crackling murmur of the mangroves as they

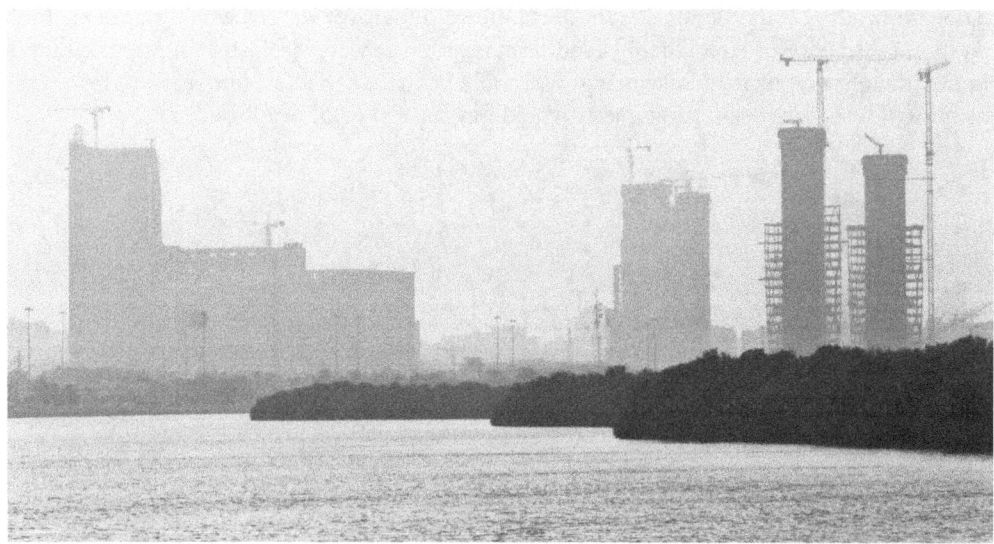

A portion of Abu Dhabi's evolving skyline as viewed from the Eastern Mangroves. At right are the twin beehives of the Al Bahar Towers.

sucked water up through their exposed claw-like roots. He described how the trees filtered the brackish water by secreting its salt in crystalline deposits on their leaves. As we sat stationary in the kayaks, I noticed the barely perceptible movement of hundreds of violescent crabs, each no bigger than my thumb, scuttling among the roots. Dale snatched one up with lightning speed and cupped it in his hands, where it stood flexing its claws in a tiny gesture of defiance. Dale explained that the mangroves provided one of the region's most vital wildlife habitats. Nearly two-thirds of the Gulf's fish population spawned among the trees' roots. They also served as breeding grounds for turtles, sea snakes, and shrimp, and their branches made nests for flamingos, herons, and other birds migrating between Africa and Asia.

We pulled ashore on a spit of sand to rest and eat dinner. As the sun sank behind the trees, we dined on kebabs that Dale roasted on a portable grill. Afterward he ensured that we picked up every last scrap of trash, telling us how he had started bringing school groups out to the mangroves to collect the debris he encountered with increasing frequency. Elise asked if the groups ever included Emirati kids. "Of course," Dale replied, "we get locals all the time. We try to show them that these trees are worth protecting, that this landscape is as much a part of their heritage as anything else. And I think a lot of them actually get it. But by the time they're old enough to do anything about it, most of the mangroves will be gone."

This ominous prediction took me by surprise, and I asked him to explain. Dale said that in his few years of kayaking, he had already seen huge chunks of mangroves slowly choked to death. Dredgers had plowed huge shipping channels through the forests, land reclamation choked off the tides that nourished them, and gigantic new real estate projects were simply paving over mangrove stands on islands like Reem and Saadiyat. Dale looked around at the trees and said sadly, "I figure this forest has maybe four or five years left."

Night fell and we paddled back across the ink-black lagoon beneath a full moon that hung like a spotlight in the cloudless sky. Halfway across we had to fight our way through a school of silvery fish that leapt at us from the waters with uncanny accuracy. One thwacked the back of Elise's head and nearly capsized her kayak. As we neared the shore, I saw the halon glow of the construction site for the Eastern Mangroves Resort, which was being built on the eastern edge of Abu Dhabi Island right next to the watery forest. I found little humor in the thought that its namesake mangroves could be lifeless within a few years of the resort's opening. How many jet-setting guests would pay for a view of deadwood?

Nine

The Short Arm of the Law

I am not imposing change on anyone. That is tyranny. All of us have our opinions, and these opinions can change. Sometimes we put all opinions together, and then extract from them a single point of view. This is our democracy.—
Sheikh Zayed bin Sultan al Nahyan

Khalid looked up from his Blackberry as I walked over to his desk. "We have a problem," I said.

"Umkak, tell me."

"Remember how we gave the preliminary alignment for the railway to the Al Gharbia Municipality? They compared it with their property records and found conflicts with existing plots." I unrolled a set of maps across his desk. "Lots of conflicts."

The planning for the national railway, which Khalid and I were managing, had become increasingly complex. The government had recast Etihad Rail as a formal state-owned corporation and had appointed our general manager to chair the board, thereby drawing the UPC even deeper into the effort to build the railway. Etihad Rail's consultants had developed a preliminary alignment for the Shah Line, and it fell to Khalid and me to help them identify potential conflicts with land uses both existing and proposed. We in turn asked the Al Gharbia Municipality to check the alignment against their property records.

"So what we got?" Khalid asked. He leafed through the maps, which showed satellite images of the desert terrain overlaid with the proposed alignment and outlines of allocated plots.

"There are some scattered conflicts where the alignment passes north of the E11," I pointed out, "and a few more in Madinat Zayed, although it looks like there's nothing built on those plots yet. The bigger issue is in Liwa." I flipped to the map that showed the section of the alignment just north of the Liwa Crescent. "The route passes right along the back of a row of eighty or so farm plots here. We can't move it east away from the farms because there are dunes there, and the earthworks would be hugely expensive." The freight trains that would eventually run along the route would only be able to handle very minor changes in grade, so going through the dunes would have meant flattening the tops of certain sandbanks and filling in the troughs between others. "So it looks like we might have to go through the farms."

Khalid seemed unconcerned. "Mmm ... so?"

"Wouldn't it be difficult to take the properties?" I assumed we would have trouble expropriating the farms, as they had been a special part of the land allocation program that Sheikh Zayed established in the 1960s. The farm plots had been distributed to Emirati families that had relocated to the new Abu Dhabi city. The farms were a way for the families to preserve their connection to Liwa after they had moved. I didn't expect those families to part easily with their land.

"Why this a problem?" Khalid asked. "Government give them the lands in the first place, government can take it away and give them somewhere else." His blasé response caught me off guard.

"So ... what kind of process do we have to follow?"

"What you mean?"

"There's a law that outlines how to compensate someone when we take their land, right?" My prior experience had accustomed me to operating within extensive legal frameworks for government takings of private property. The urban redevelopment agency where I worked in Detroit had managed a number of large land assembly projects in depopulated areas of the city, where large concentrations of parcels had reverted to public ownership. The agency was responsible for acquiring the remaining privately owned properties in order to make the consolidated areas more attractive for redevelopment. Although the use of eminent domain to acquire private property was hardly new, Detroit had given it a novel twist. In 1982 the municipal government had acquired the remnants of Detroit's Poletown neighborhood in order to bulldoze it and allow General Motors to build a new assembly plant in its place—the first time in U.S. history that eminent domain had been used to transfer property from one private owner to another.[1] Michigan's legislature subsequently enacted a bevy of laws delineating excruciatingly detailed requirements for such public takings, including notifying affected property owners, negotiating fair-market-value purchases (or court-ordered seizures in the case of owners who didn't want to sell), and relocating residents to equal or better housing. Taking people's property out from underneath them was not a matter to be taken lightly.

The Abu Dhabi government, however, evidently viewed things differently. Khalid furrowed his brow. "No, there's no law. Why we need law? Law is for what you supposed to *not* do."

"There's no specific process we have to follow?"

"Yes, there's process, but ... well, everybody just know it. We tell Municipality what plots we needs to move, umkak? They send people out to see the property and how much it worth." He flashed his conspiratorial politician's smile. "But they not tell anybody ahead of time that they coming. Otherwise, the property become a lot more expensive."

I knew exactly what he meant. Back in Detroit, an old-timer at the redevelopment agency had once regaled me with the story of how the huge Chrysler manufacturing complex on the city's east side was expanded in the early 1990s. At the time, the project was one of the largest land assemblies ever undertaken in the Rustbelt. The properties targeted for acquisition included several abandoned and dilapidated warehouses, which were surreptitiously acquired by private citizens with alleged ties to organized crime around the time of the project's announcement. When the city made offers on the properties, the new owners negotiated purchase agreements that required the city to pay for the factories and the land they stood on, as well as the taxable value of any leftover equipment that remained inside. This last part was unusual; such "personal property" was typically not included in government takings. As soon as the deals were signed, the cunning owners went out and bought up all of the old industrial junk they could find—presses, lathes, cranes, even scrap metal—and filled the buildings to the rafters. They billed the city full retail value for what were essentially mountains of garbage bought at firesale prices. The city sued to have the obviously fraudulent deals reversed, but the Michigan courts prostrated themselves before the Altar of Property Rights and ordered Detroit to pay up. The owners made a killing.

I was glad to see that Abu Dhabi's government was clever enough to avoid the same ruse. "Once Municipality done the surveys, they make a price and pay the owners," Khalid continued. "Then we give them plots somewheres else."

"That's all?"

"Mm-hmm." It sounded much simpler than I had feared. Working for an autocracy certainly had its advantages.

Khalid flipped to the final map, which showed the rail alignment crossing the Liwa Crescent before turning east toward its terminus at the Shah plant. He squinted and pointed at where the route traversed several irregular patches of foliage scattered among the crescent's dunes. "What's these?"

"Yeah, I don't know what to make of those. They look like agriculture, but they're not square-shaped like the farms to the north. The Municipality doesn't have any records of allocated plots there. Maybe they're just oases."

Khalid looked closer and clucked his tongue in the local expression of disapproval. "No. They's heritage farms. *This* a problem."

"What are heritage farms?"

"Heritage farms is the original farms in Liwa. They been there hundreds of years. They's not have plot records because they was there before Abu Dhabi, umkak?"

"So will they be harder to relocate?"

"Harder? Wow." He leaned back in his chair. "This not something we can do. For heritage farms we have to ask Crown Prince Diwan." The *Diwan* was the crown prince's personal court. When sensitive issues arose, such as the potential expropriation of the heritage farms, the Diwan would engage with the affected parties and attempt to arrive at a solution acceptable to all—a modern incarnation of the traditional tribal forum of the Bedu. If necessary, the crown prince himself would get involved. Ultimately, the Diwan's decisions were binding. Among its other functions, the Diwan was also the sole source of property deeds, known in Abu Dhabi as "affection plans."

Khalid explained, "Diwan have to be the ones to tell these people to go. Some heritage farms, they owned by big people, even sheikhs. You show up without invitation, they come out with guns."

I smiled at this hypothetical scene. I had once read a description of the Liwa Crescent as West Virginia cast in sand, with its pockets of farms nestled among towering orange dunes. Now I completed the picture with a shotgun-toting Emirati farmer yelling at strangers to get off his land—an Appalachian echo in Arabia.

* * *

The rule of law is a nebulous concept in Abu Dhabi. The UAE's 1971 constitution stipulates Islamic Shari'a to be the principal source of law at both the federal and emirate levels.[2] The country's Shari'a-based legal framework is similar to a civil law system, relying on an extensive code of legislation rather than the binding judicial precedents of common law. The constitution gave the responsibility for promulgating the necessary compendium of civil laws to the Federal Supreme Council, the body comprised of the seven rulers of the UAE's emirates. Assisting the Supreme Council in this gargantuan task is the Federal National Council, an advisory legislature of appointed representatives with a mandate to propose laws but no power to enact or enforce them.

Although the Supreme Council has passed hundreds of laws in the four decades since the UAE's founding, and although the rulers of the individual emirates have legislated on many more subjects that the constitution does not enumerate as federal responsibilities, there are still plenty of gaps in the law. The eminent domain issue Khalid and I encountered on the national railway was merely one example of an area for which legislation simply hadn't been codified. The constitution declares that "general confiscation of property shall be prohibited"[3] and can only take place in circumstances specified by law, but as Khalid pointed out, no such law exists.

Just as taking property is a legal lacuna, so is handing property out, at least when it comes to foreigners. In the UAE's early days Sheikh Zayed was adamant that only Emiratis would own the country's land, reportedly instructing the rulers of the other emirates not to sell "even a single grain of sand" to foreigners.[4] After Zayed's death, Abu Dhabi's developers tested this unwritten prohibition by designating new mega-developments such as Reem Island and Raha Beach as "freehold zones" where foreigners could "own" property via ninety-nine-year leases.[5] The developers hoped that this provision would be enough to attract the legions of wealthy international jet-setters they were counting on to fill up their shiny new apartment towers. Despite the government's lip service to an Emirati-heavy future for Abu Dhabi, the developers knew it would be foreigners, *millions* of foreigners, who would continue to make up the vast majority of Abu Dhabi's population well past 2030.

In late 2009 the developers realized that their first freehold zone projects were nearing completion without any laws in place to actually permit the long-term leases to foreigners. They pressed the government to enact a fix, and the Executive Council in turn tasked the UPC and the Municipality to pull together a draft property law from scratch. As with every other project, a team of consultants was brought on board—in this case a group of international legal experts who specialized in "strata law," the European term for regulations that permit condominium-type ownership within a larger building or property, with provisions such as shared responsibilities and rights to common areas.

The process of drafting a new Abu Dhabi strata law went smoothly until it hit the residency issue. The government had given no indication that purchasing real estate in Abu Dhabi would give a foreigner owner any rights of entry, let alone extended residence privileges. As it stood, a foreign owner would either have to get a job in order to obtain an employment visa, or rely on tourist visas, which lasted only thirty days and could not be renewed without leaving the country. The odds were slim that any wealthy foreigner would invest in an Abu Dhabi property without being assured of the right to inhabit it.

Though granting residency to foreign property owners hardly sounded extreme, in truth it was a nonstarter for many Emiratis—both government officials and rank-and-file locals. They believed that granting foreigners any kind of semipermanent status would be the beginning of the end. Foreign residents would eventually clamor for access to the mother lode of Emirati citizenship, and before long locals might face the apocalyptic scenario of foreigners seizing control of Abu Dhabi. Such a prospect wasn't without precedent. Singapore, for example, had let in a steady flow of Chinese immigrants during the first half of the twentieth century who eventually became a majority and declared the city-state independent from its Malay hinterlands in 1965. *That* was certainly an aspect of the Singaporean model that Abu Dhabi's leaders did not want to replicate.

In the end, the Abu Dhabi government punted the residency question up to the national level. The Federal Supreme Council responded with a law permitting foreign property owners to obtain special "investor visas." Such investors would still have to leave the country every six months to renew their paperwork, paying 2,000 dirhams each time—with no guarantee of being let back in.[6]

In essence, the government was sending a message to foreign investors that being able to buy real estate in Abu Dhabi was privilege enough; any further rights, if they came about, would be icing on the cake. It was typical of the "if you build it, they will come" mentality that pervaded the emirate's boom. Such confidence risked losing touch with reality. Notwithstanding all the glorious plans and pictures of the future city, Abu Dhabi was still a tough sell at present. The city offered little to do, its appearance was rather banal, and the climate was too hot even to venture outside for half the year. If Abu Dhabi wanted to attract wealthy investors, it would have to make concessions, of which residency rights were the most elemental. As it stood, Abu Dhabi was still paying people to come and live in the emirate; the recent population growth was entirely due to the influx of workers staffing the boom. For the Emiratis to think that the global elite would flock to Abu Dhabi without basic rights, let alone incentives, was more than self-assurance—it was hubris.

Even if the government were to develop a better solution to the residency issue, Abu Dhabi's legislation leaves many other aspects of life in the emirate in legal limbo. When legal questions arise, either at work or in a personal context, the law is often murky if not silent. Arabic is the only official language for legislation, government decrees, and court proceedings. While this respects the primacy of the Emiratis' culture, it also complicates things for the vast majority of the population that doesn't speak the tongue. Even though most Emiratis and foreigners can handle at least rudimentary English, the government refuses to consider using bilingual verbiage on even basic documents such as traffic tickets.

Where laws do exist, the penalties for breaking them can seem capricious, at least by the standards of punishment to which many of Abu Dhabi's foreigners are accustomed in their home countries. Bouncing a check, even unintentionally, is a criminal offense punishable by jail.[7] Among the waves of expats who fled Dubai during its crash, many were running from postdated checks they had previously written for mortgages, car payments, and credit cards, never imagining they wouldn't have the funds to pay when the checks came due.[8] Profanity is illegal, as is gesturing rudely while driving—an offense I was tempted to commit daily in Abu Dhabi's exasperating traffic.

Punishments for breaking traffic laws are particularly bizarre. According to the Abu Dhabi traffic code there are no fewer than 147 ways to break the rules of the road.[9] Some are straightforward, such as reckless driving and vehicular manslaughter. Upon being convicted of either offense, the traffic police will impound the wrongdoer's car for thirty days and mark twelve "black points" against his driving record, half the limit at which one's license is revoked. Both of those penalties are doubled, however, should someone have the audacity to drive a car without license plates. Driving a "vehicle that causes pollution," in the language of the traffic code, merits a five-hundred-dirham fine, begging the question as to whether there are any vehicles that *don't* cause pollution. Bicycles aren't an option, as they are banned from Abu Dhabi's streets entirely. "Parking a vehicle on pavement" earns the offender three black points, so it is perhaps no surprise that people park on the sidewalk, in the sand, and everywhere else *except* paved parking spaces. The traffic code is almost as chaotic as the roads themselves.

Abu Dhabi's laws do not pretend to treat people equally. The constitution guarantees equality before the law, but only for citizens of the country.[10] In practice, even this promise is a farce. The courts have ruled that a man may beat his wife and children, as long as he does not leave physical marks.[11] Abu Dhabi's sheikhs rule by fiat and are accountable to no one, much less to a piece of paper. And for ordinary Emiratis, one's standing before the law is a function of one's *wasta*, the local version of clout. Wasta is a bewildering blend of social status, familial and tribal affiliations, name-dropping, and favor-calling that traces back to the Bedu. Thesiger observed that among the Bedu every man was a law unto himself: "The country was full of outlaws, who feared no punishment other than the blood-feud and the retaliation of hostile kinsmen."[12] Survival in this merciless milieu depended on one's ability to amass wasta by exploiting relationships and sharing resources when they were plentiful so as to be in a position to receive when they were few. When Abu Dhabi underwent its cat-

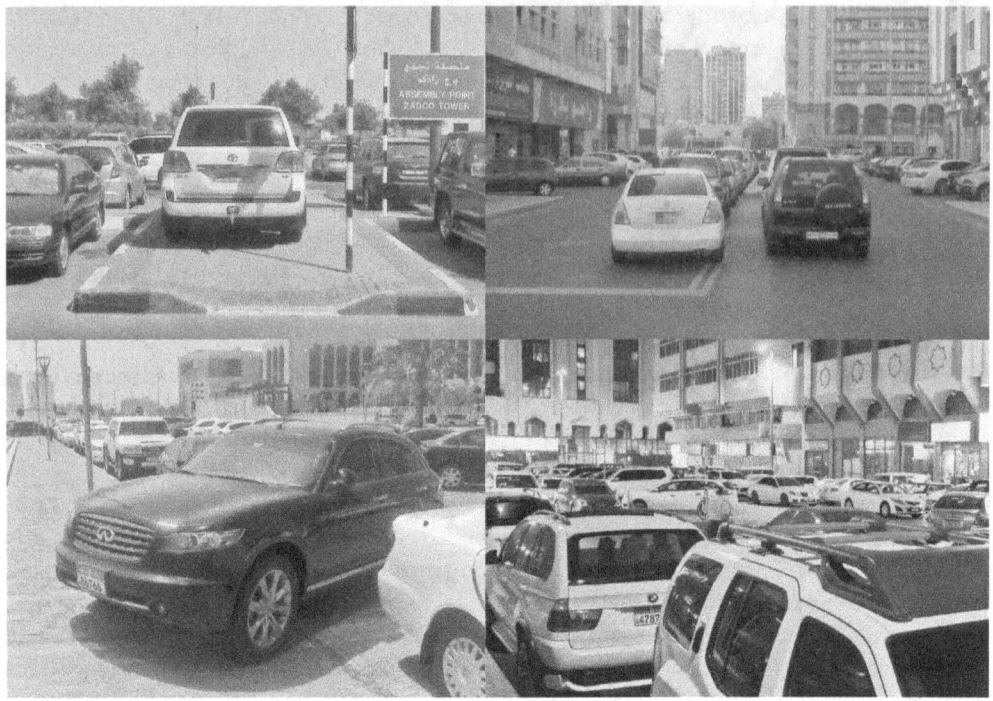

Abu Dhabi's car culture makes for creative parking solutions.

aclysmic modernization in the 1960s and 1970s, its people were unaccustomed to dealing with the bureaucracy inherent to a modern state.[13] Consequently, they often resorted to wasta to circumvent their own laws and institutions, setting a precedent that continues today.

Wasta mentality pervades life in Abu Dhabi. Emiratis constantly employ it to get what they want—the first place in queues, for example—and to extricate themselves from unfavorable situations—say, a traffic ticket. The Emiratis' use of wasta to grease the wheels of everyday life both amazes and enrages foreigners, who of course have none of their own.

Wasta created endless headaches for us at the UPC. My colleagues in the Development Review Department faced a steady stream of Emirati developers and landlords who vehemently protested the changes our agency tried to impose on their schemes. Admittedly, this resistance was not unique to Abu Dhabi; real estate development is a dirty business the world over. Rare indeed is the developer who doesn't fight any regulation or exploit every loophole to boost his bottom line. What distinguished Abu Dhabi's property sharks was their ability to pawn their wasta into special dispensations that overruled the UPC. If a developer's staff didn't like what they heard, they either pressured our general manager into backing down, or if that failed they simply phoned their favorite sheikh and had him deliver the message. Unfortunately it was always the most outlandish development proposals that created the most problems in this regard, and which usually resulted in the UPC being forced to yield. The agency proved unable to uphold one of the key dictums of its own *Plan 2030*: "It is wise to use explicit development principles to evaluate proposed projects and to not succumb to persuasive [developers]."[14]

"Have you heard?" Keith asked as I walked past his desk one afternoon. "This week I've had three separate developers come in and read my guys and me the riot act." He nodded at Sultan and Ismail, the two young locals on his team. "We're talking Emiratis who have been given huge plots of land for literally nothing, and they're upset because we want them to consider the public interest." He reached into his trash can and pulled out a rendering of some bland commercial buildings. "This guy, for example. We asked him to add an arcade to his strip mall to create a decent streetscape. I'm trying to *help* him make a place people will want to shop at, for crying out loud. And what does he say? 'You're taking three meters of my land! It is unjust!' You know what? Go live in Africa for a month and then tell me about injustice." He threw the rendering back in the trash and shook his head. "Sometimes I think I should write a book about this place after I leave. For a people who had nothing fifty years ago, the greed around here can be astounding."

Moving beyond Emiratis, Abu Dhabi's laws treat foreigners as an afterthought. The Constitution guarantees foreigners "the rights and freedoms stipulated in international charters, treaties, and agreements to which the UAE is party."[15] Beyond that, noncitizens are essentially on their own. The concept of human, let alone civil, rights for foreigners is superfluous and based primarily on one's country of origin and income. Western expats typically receive better treatment and lesser penalties than foreigners in the lower classes, presumably because they're more expensive to replace. A Westerner convicted of a lesser criminal offense might be let off with a fine, or at worst a short spell in jail followed by deportation, whereas an Asian found guilty of the same may languish for years in a local prison. The only situation in which a foreigner's social standing isn't an issue is when he runs afoul of an Emirati—in which case, the foreigner is always at fault. Period.

One morning Elise and I encountered Liz coming in to the office almost two hours late. She was wearing the same clothes as the day before, a cardinal sin for someone with her fashion sense. Her hair was unkempt and her eyeliner was smeared, making it look as though she had hardly slept the night before.

"Are you okay?" Elise asked.

"I'm fine," Liz replied, her indignation hinting that she was anything but. "I spent a lovely night at the police station."

Elise gasped. "What happened?"

"I was driving through my neighborhood last evening when a kid ran out in front of my car." I groaned inwardly. Felicia, Liz's sporty little Mercedes roadster, had caused her no end of trouble. Its low-slung seats barely enabled her to see over the wheel, and the engine put out far more torque than she could handle. She hit things so often that the car spent more time in the shop than in her driveway.

Liz continued, "There were so many cars parked on the street that I was driving quite slowly, but I still couldn't stop before I'd bumped him."

"Is he okay?" Elise asked.

"The little bugger's fine. Bruised his arm, that's all. But his parents wanted to take him to the hospital anyway to have him checked out. The police said they had to keep me at the station until the doctors confirmed he was okay."

"But it wasn't even your fault," I protested.

"No, it wasn't. But the kid was Emirati, so of course it was my fault. When the police showed up, the parents started jabbering with them in Arabic and nobody would translate for me. They probably told the police to leave me in jail overnight out of spite. Somehow I don't think it took nine hours in the middle of the night for the kid to see a doctor."

Elise said, "Why in the world did you come to the office? You should have gone straight home."

"I was going to, but the police took my phone and I forgot to get it back. I wanted to tell Ethan that I won't be here the rest of the day. Then I'm going home to get some sleep."

We watched Liz's diminutive frame march imperiously down the hallway toward Ethan's office. Elise sighed knowingly. "At least she was sober."

Despite such examples of overzealous punishments, enforcement of rules and regulations in Abu Dhabi typically ranges from spotty to nonexistent. Police cruisers routinely loiter in the slow lane while drivers rocket past at speeds well over the limit. Throughout my time in Abu Dhabi I tried to find out how many building inspectors the Municipality employed, but I never got a solid answer. The number was small enough that I didn't once encounter an inspector at any of the city's construction sites. The contractors erecting Abu Dhabi's new buildings were essentially left to police themselves.

Food safety is another problem. Although the Abu Dhabi Food Control Authority (FCA) does require restaurateurs and grocers to follow an extensive set of food safety measures, their occasional snap inspections often uncover egregious violations. I had an uncanny knack for picking the worst offenders. During the summer of 2009, for example, the FCA shut down the meat counter at the hypermarket where I shopped when they found unsanitary conditions not suitable to reprint.[16] Another investigation revealed that more than sixty samples of arugula leaves from stores and restaurants across the UAE were contaminated with fecal coliform cells and E. coli bacteria at levels higher than those of a toilet,[17] a situation that prompted me to discontinue my habit of ordering arugula salads at a cafe near the office. Nevertheless, throughout my time in Abu Dhabi, some foodstuff or another would wreak gastrointestinal havoc on me just about every third week.

Enforcement was the UPC's Achilles heel. We had nowhere near enough staff to monitor whether the developers were complying with the requirements we imposed on their projects. Even had we possessed the numbers, we still lacked any legal purview to exact penalties from noncompliant developers or halt work on their projects. The shrewder developers knew this and didn't put up a fight when we reviewed their proposals. They simply accepted our markups and then went out and built whatever they wanted. Despite our official mandate to oversee development across the emirate, the UPC was in many ways a toothless watchdog.

Ultimately it seemed apparent that the law in Abu Dhabi exists first and foremost to facilitate state control over nationals and foreigners alike. The urbanist Yasser Elsheshtawy has pointed out that Abu Dhabi "represents a planned city which, from its very inception, was geared towards controlling and eliminating any kind of informal behavior."[18] The government's rigid social policing is prompted by the dual desires of keeping the burgeoning foreign population under control and presenting to the outside world an immaculate image of a modern, orderly city. Dispensing actual justice comes in a distant second place.

Abu Dhabi's government routinely brushes aside personal rights in the name of public order. Article 31 of the constitution, for example, guarantees "freedom of communication by post, telegraph, or other means ... and the secrecy thereof."[19] In reality, the postal service opens packages originating from abroad and confiscates anything deemed obscene or threatening to the state. Latif, the security consultant, once explained to me how the state security services assign a case officer to every foreigner that enters the emirate. The officer monitors that person's phone calls, text messages, and e-mail transmissions for a month, after which he determines whether the person is worth tracking further or can safely be relegated to passive monitoring. Although Latif's story smacked of conspiracy theory, I was forced to reconsider when he also mentioned that the security services would soon roll out "Falcon Eye," a comprehensive network of closed-circuit TVs to monitor all of Abu Dhabi's major streets. Before long, ugly steel poles sporting mysterious black globes began sprouting from medians all over the city. In Abu Dhabi, Big Brother *is* watching you.

What Abu Dhabi lacks in the way of codified laws, it more than compensates for with unwritten ones: the labyrinthine customs, conventions, and taboos that are forever complicating life in the emirate. The Emirati abhorrence of conflict undergirds a culture of outward civility that constrains public behavior. One gets the sense that everybody in Abu Dhabi is trying hard not to rock the boat. Censorship is rife, both the official and self-policing varieties. The freedom of expression guaranteed in the constitution[20] is not upheld, nor does anyone expect it to be. As the author Jo Tatchell concludes, "Above everything else people in Abu Dhabi want money. Freedom of expression is a luxury that most cannot allow to take precedence."[21]

* * *

Among the group of friends I had met at church was an Alaskan named Marcus, whose towering six-foot-three frame and ruddy lumberjack beard were offset by his gentle demeanor. He was an outdoorsman at heart, proof that one can take an Alaskan out of the frontier but not the other way around. Upon arriving in Abu Dhabi and finding himself surrounded by sand instead of snow, he had adapted by taking up desert camping. As the heat of summer ebbed, Marcus and Arta, his soft-spoken Albanian wife, would often lead our group on weekend excursions to the towering dunes south of Liwa or the rocky mountains of neighboring Oman.

Marcus had also become an expert at dune bashing, the popular Gulf sport that involves death-defying drives up and down sand dunes. Arta allowed Marcus to indulge his passion of custom-modifying SUVs to support his hobby; nearly every part on his Nissan Pathfinder was an aftermarket addition, giving it the appearance of a miniature monster truck. Prior to one weekend camping trip, Marcus offered to take me out into the dunes and teach me the basics of dune bashing in my Jeep. I had embraced Abu Dhabi's car culture by purchasing a four-wheel-drive Grand Cherokee that I had christened Big White, and I was eager to put it through its off-road paces.

I awoke early on a Friday morning with the uncomfortable sensation of having sucked on a hairdryer overnight, a typical feeling thanks to my suffocating air conditioner. I packed my camping gear and headed outside. When I reached the street, I was shocked to find my Jeep listing to one side in its parking space. Two of its tires were slashed and paint was sprayed on the door handles. My friends were equally surprised when they pulled up. None of them had ever heard of such a thing in supposedly crime-free Abu Dhabi. Marcus retrieved his repair kit and helped me patch up the holes.

To replace the tires we drove out to Mussafah, the sprawling industrial district on the mainland just south of the city, comprised of hundreds of acres of dusty warehouses, repair shops, junkyards, wharves, smelters, and other noxious land uses not suitable for the city proper. It had the flavor of a Mexican border town that takes care of its northern neighbor's nasty but necessary business. Marcus was quite familiar with the district, having spent plenty of time in its various chop shops. I followed him down yawning thoroughfares lined with rusted automotive hulks, discarded shipping containers, gigantic sections of concrete utility pipes, and other kinds of heavy-duty debris. Roving bands of laborers added to the postapocalyptic aura, their black welding goggles peering out from shawls pulled tight to ward off the blowing sand.

We turned a corner and nearly plowed into a solid mass of laborers. By now it was early in the afternoon, and the Muslims among the uniformly male residents of Mussafah were gathering at the industrial zone's scattered mosques for Friday prayers. The laborers in front of us, hundreds if not thousands of them, sat and stood in the road in front of a tiny mosque, blocking it from one side to the other. I considered turning around, but on Mussafah's divided roads this was impossible. Instead I inched forward through the crowd, parting their ranks like Moses at the Red Sea. As I crept along, a wall of South Asian faces stared at me through the windows, their blank looks conveying not anger, nor annoyance, nor even curiosity, just a silent, unmistakable message: "You don't belong here. This place is ours."

The following Sunday I went to the police station nearest my villa to file a report on my slashed tires. The rotund Emirati officer behind the desk listened to my story with a look of pained sympathy. He clucked and said, "This is terrible. You must have made someone very angry. These things do not happen without a reason. Perhaps you parked in somebody's space?"

I struggled to contain my ire and told him I parked in the same spot every day.

"Yes, but perhaps you must have been rude to someone in traffic." Okay, with my driving habits, this was not merely possible, it was assured. But how would they have found out where I lived?

"What kind of details do you need for your report?" I asked.

He leaned back and rested his hands on the powder-blue uniform covering his ample belly. "No, a report is not necessary."

"Don't you want to know where it happened?" I stammered. "What if there have been other incidents nearby? You might want to start some neighborhood patrols."

He waved a dismissive hand. "These things are silly. It was children, maybe. A report is not needed."

It dawned on me why Abu Dhabi's crime statistics might be so low: if a crime isn't reported, then it didn't happen. Apparently Abu Dhabi was a police state only up until the point when one actually needed the police. I left the station reminiscing that during my entire time in purportedly crime-ridden Detroit, my car hadn't once been vandalized.

I did eventually get to go dune bashing with Marcus. In the span of fifteen minutes I managed to bury Big White up to its axles twice. We tore off both the front and rear bumpers pulling it out. I decided I might be better off sticking to paved surfaces.

Ten

Faulty Towers

The perfection of architecture is attained not so much by the form of the elements, which is a matter of convention, but by their chivalry of balance and proportion. — *Robert Byron, The Road to Oxiana*

Architectural Tour of Abu Dhabi

A Suggested Itinerary

Today is the big day. You've decided to tour around and see the new buildings that are reshaping Abu Dhabi's skyline. Perhaps you're a visitor to the city, or a resident newly arrived, or maybe you've lived here for years but have never taken the time to seriously reflect on Abu Dhabi's emerging architecture. Here, finally, is your chance to acquaint yourself with the new face of the city in all its splendor. First you must procure a boat. Trying to tour the city by car will only exasperate you, and besides, the full effect of Abu Dhabi's architecture is best appreciated from the water.

Start your tour at Yas Island, where Aldar, Abu Dhabi's largest developer, has created some innovative edifices. That flowing, organic white shell is actually a hotel, the five-star Yas Viceroy. The island's Formula One racetrack cuts right through the hotel at the junction of its two wings, which form a bulging T from above. The critical eye might notice more than a passing resemblance between the hotel's bulbous superstructure and a streamlined lady's shaving razor. The superstructure is actually meant to evoke the nets once employed by local fishermen, and its designers deserve credit for creating one of the few buildings that pay homage to Abu Dhabi's history. At night, the fishnet's iridescent glow slowly slides across the spectrum from red to purple to blue and back again, a mesmerizing effect visible for miles around.

Beyond the hotel rises the red and black hulk of Ferrari World, a leviathan structure that resembles a giant neuron from the air. Ferrari World encloses the world's largest indoor theme park, with the Formula Rossa, the world's fastest roller coaster, located right next door. The park gives Abu Dhabi a tourist attraction unlike any other, but in view of Ferrari's rather narrow market segment, the jury is still out as to how many visitors it can draw.

Across from Yas Island on the mainland sits the Raha Beach development (also by Aldar), a crowded mini-city wedged between the waterfront and the E10 highway. Raha Beach is one of the largest of Abu Dhabi's new projects, a sprawling construction site six miles long and a half-mile wide. When finished it will showcase a little bit of everything: a cluster of circular apartment buildings reminiscent of the Watergate Hotel, a trio of turquoise condominium towers whose glass façades step backwards like one-sided ziggurats, and the centerpiece known as HQ, Aldar's prominent new headquarters and the world's first circular

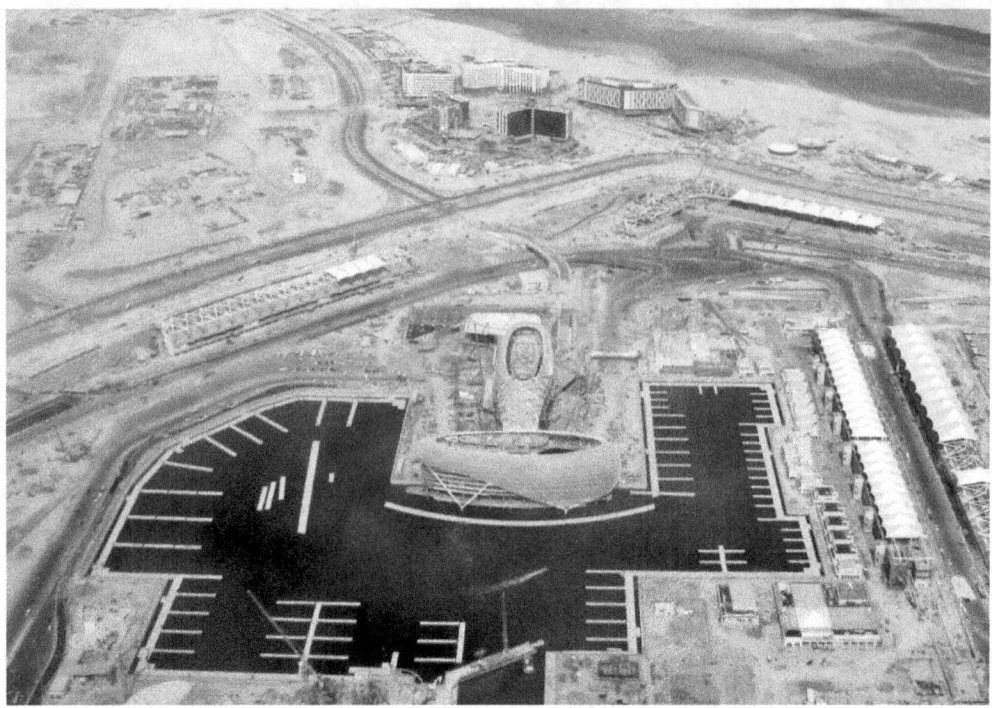

Yas Island under construction, circa September 2009. At the center is the Yas Viceroy Hotel surrounded by the Yas Marina; to its right and left are the grandstands for the Formula One racetrack.

skyscraper, a thick vertical disc whose metallic colors and crisscrossed hatching have already caused it to be dubbed the Silver Waffle.

Motor the length of Raha Beach towards the southern tip of Abu Dhabi Island and pass beneath the undulating arches of the new Sheikh Zayed Bridge, whose short history is already quite storied. The bridge was conceived in 2003 as a much-needed third link between the island and the mainland, relieving the overloaded Maqta and Mussafah bridges and connecting the E10 with the redesigned Salaam Street. The government commissioned the Pritzker Prize-winning architect Zaha Hadid to design the bridge as a suitably iconic gateway to Abu Dhabi. She sketched a half-mile span soaring sixty feet over the channel, supported by three steel arches that swooped above and below the bridge deck like an irregular sine wave.

Building this whimsy became a nightmare. The project's engineers found it nigh impossible to translate Hadid's drawings into a structure that wouldn't collapse on itself. They had to completely rework the design and while simultaneously managing other complications such as the government's eleventh-hour decision to increase the road from two to four lanes in each direction to cope with anticipated traffic growth; each additional lane could accommodate another two thousand vehicles per hour. The arches were manufactured in sections in Thailand and shipped to Abu Dhabi to be welded together on-site. Their free-flowing bulk was so unwieldy that a special crane had to be devised just to maneuver them into place.[1] The bridge ran years past its original 2006 completion date. Work had ground to a halt by early 2009, forcing the Municipality to fire the Greek contractor and bring in a Belgian firm to finish the project by mid–2011. The final price tag rang in at more than a billion dirhams, nearly twice the original budget.

Even as the bridge slowly took shape, its fanciful design turned out to be more than Abu Dhabi's leaders had bargained for. Hadid had intended the undulating arches to evoke the sand dunes of the Empty Quarter. But after the final arch was dropped into place, locals were scandalized to discover that the bridge's profile more resembled a buxom woman lying on her back. Combined with the delays and cost overruns, the unintentionally salacious design reinforced the message that international "starchitects" should be banned from designing key pieces of infrastructure.

As you halt in the Maqta Channel just past the Sheikh Zayed Bridge, you face sprawling hotel complexes on either side. To your immediate left on the mainland is the new Fairmont *Bab Al Bahr*, or Sea Gate. The flat, dark glass of its façade is inlaid with rectilinear lighting strips whose nighttime neon glow resembles the lightcycle tracks from *Tron*. In the daytime, the hotel's boxy profile and slightly raised elevations at either end may remind you of another 1980s icon: the ghettoblaster. Just beyond the Fairmont is the Shangri La, its arched colonnades and latticed balconies paying homage to an Arab golden age that left its mark on Baghdad but actually never touched this part of Arabia. The Shangri La has become an Abu Dhabi institution, both for its collection of excellent restaurants and indoor pseudo-souq of high-end shops and for its status as one of the few venues with the sense of identity, however synthetic, needed to define a coherent place. On the far side of the channel is the new JW Marriott, whose primary purpose seems to be to block the views of the Sheikh Zayed Mosque beyond.

Now come about and head back the way you came. Look to port in the brief gap between the Maqta and Sheikh Zayed bridges, where you will see a nondescript beige building resembling a conical sand castle sitting in the channel. This is the Maqta Watchtower, one of only three structures in Abu Dhabi that predate 1970. It is plain yet noble, with a touch of ornamentation in its serrated cornice and nose-like vents protruding from the smooth façade. The watchtower is arguably the most subtle and well-proportioned building in the city, with just the right ratio of height to circumference. Of the numerous foreign architects who have strewn their litter around Abu Dhabi, it is a shame that none looked to Maqta for inspiration. If anything, the watchtower makes a compelling argument that the Emiratis should go back to designing for themselves.

Pass beneath the Sheikh Zayed Bridge once more, turn to port, and motor up the eastern side of Abu Dhabi Island. Near its midpoint you'll see the towering slab of IPIC Square, the new offices of the emirate's second-richest sovereign wealth fund, the International Petroleum Investment Corporation. The main tower looms over several smaller replicas tapering down in front of it, resembling a cascade of falling dominoes, a curious visual metaphor for a financial institution. You'll also note the twin Al Bahar Towers, which look like skinny beehives. Their façades are covered in an exoskeleton of interlocking triangular panels that dynamically open and close throughout the day to maintain shade on the side of the buildings facing the sun—one of Abu Dhabi's more innovative architectural feats.

You must now steer away from the island to cut a wide berth around the *Qasr Al Bahr*, the Sea Palace residence of Sheikha Fatima, wife of the late Sheikh Zayed and the UAE's First Lady. By all accounts the Sheikha doesn't like mariners coming too close, nor do the sailors on the gunboats stationed nearby. Past the Sea Palace dozens of towers rise from the haze, clustered in groups like megaliths left behind by a race of giants. This is Reem Island, a veritable city within a city. Reem consists of more than a dozen different subdevelopments in various stages of construction; some are still holes in the ground, whereas others are finished skyscrapers. Development in some form or another covers almost all three and a half square miles of the island, with the exception of two puny patches of mangroves barely

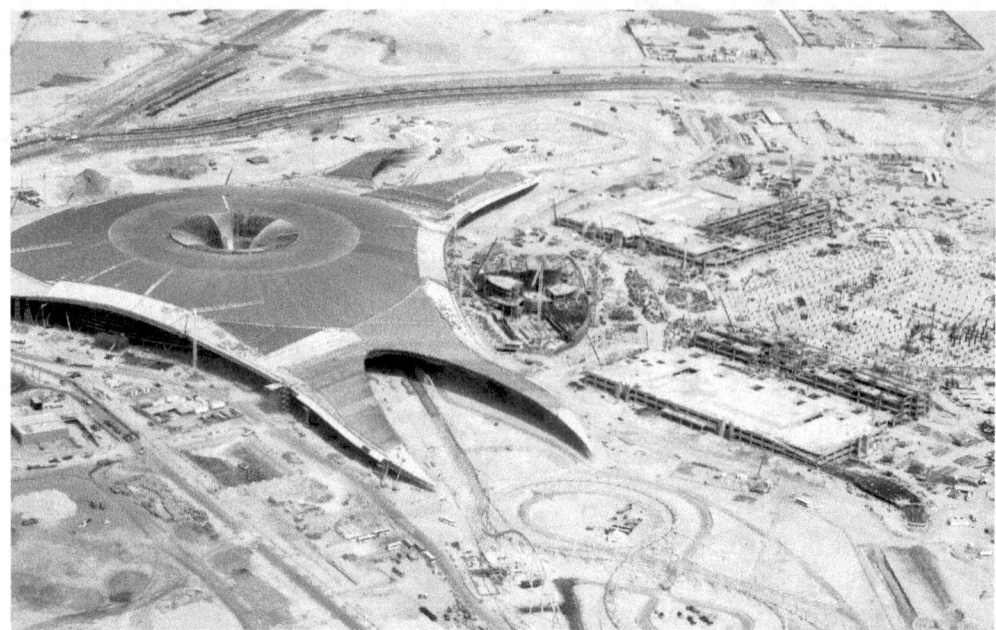

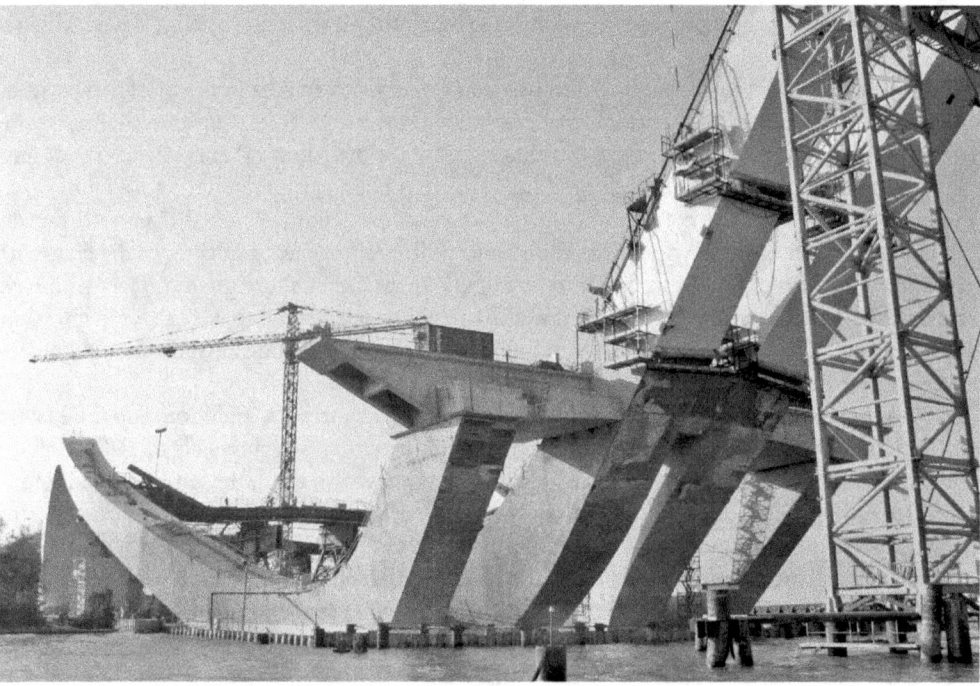

Top: More construction on Yas Island, circa September 2009. At the left is Ferrari World; at bottom right the track for the Formula Rossa, the world's fastest roller coaster. *Bottom:* The undulating arches of the Sheikh Zayed Bridge under construction, circa September 2009.

clinging to life. Reem is the exclamation point in a city of superlatives: one hundred billion dirhams of construction that will yield sixty-five million square feet of real estate and twenty-two thousand residential units when finished.

Seeing it up close for the first time may, unfortunately, be one of the bigger disappointments of the day. First up are the triplet skyscrapers of the Gate Towers, which are linked by an arcing penthouse bridge—an impressive architectural feat, although it is almost a carbon copy of the Marina Bay Sands hotel in Singapore. Imitation, as they say, is the sincerest form of flattery. Behind these are the looming shadows of the Sky and Sun towers, the tallest buildings on the island at seventy-four and sixty-five stories respectively. From a distance they are elegant in their simplicity: dark sentinels keeping a silent vigil over the city. Yet, upon closer inspection, one sees the towers are covered from ground to roof in plates of opaque, reflective glass, a style that afflicts Abu Dhabi's newer buildings like blight. The emirate's architects are obsessed with plastering building façades in colored plateglass and aluminum panels, though it violates all notions of taste. The materials are tawdry and, in the case of the highly flammable aluminum cladding, notoriously unsafe.[2] Moreover, Abu Dhabi's builders can never seem to fit the pieces together quite precise, resulting in façades that appear undulating or deformed. Buildings across the city, from the spectacular to the plain, thus reflect distorted images of their surroundings, giving Abu Dhabi the appearance of a fun house filled with warped mirrors. The newish glass and aluminum buildings require almost constant cleaning to wash away the sand and grime that sticks to their façades. Most do not receive this, giving them a neglected, timeworn appearance almost as soon as they are complete. The façades of the Sky and Sun towers have almost nothing to break their visual monotony, just a few cooling vents and some vertical protrusions that look tacked on. The net effect is underwhelming.

Along the western side of Reem you motor into a circular inlet ringed by the dozen high-rises of Marina Square. Many of them are even worse offenders on the plateglass front; several are nothing more than blank aquamarine walls. Their proportions are all wrong. Some of the towers have skinny, squarish cross sections that look incapable of containing more than four units per floor, while others are squat boxes with garish protrusions topside. The ornamentation varies widely; some of the towers have a glut of balconies, façade accents, and so forth, while others lack them entirely. Marina Square has the cumulative look of a term project from an architecture student in his introductory year. Its three thousand residences were nevertheless slated to be some of the priciest in the city upon their completion. Had the buyers any sense, they would have demanded payment to live there.

Having completed your circuit of Reem, cross over to Saadiyat Island, passing beneath the Sheikh Khalifa Bridge that connects it with Abu Dhabi. At Saadiyat's northern tip you see the earthworks for the quartet of museums that will one day anchor the island's cultural district. If they look anything like the set of scale models on display at the Emirates Palace, the future Saadiyat museums will be a decidedly mixed bag. The design for the Louvre's Abu Dhabi franchise was given to a suitably French architect, Jean Nouvel, who put forth a cubist village over which a huge lattice dome hovers like a giant flying saucer. The Japanese architect Tadao Ando's design for the maritime museum is a minimalist white box sliced to evoke the billowing sail of the dhow boats that once plied Abu Dhabi's waters. The performing arts center, another conception of Zaha Hadid, bears a striking resemblance to a bicycle helmet. The UK firm Foster + Partners received the commission for the Zayed National Museum, designing a cluster of airy steel ellipses meant to evoke falcon wingtips. Last but not least is Saadiyat's crowning glory, the latest installment of the Guggenheim Museum franchise to be designed by Frank Gehry. Apparently the best he could come up with was a confused geometric jumble that looks like a child's discarded tinker toys. Lest you retain any illusions of subtlety, bear in mind that Abu Dhabi's Guggenheim will be nine times the size of its Manhattan counterpart.[3]

Apart from the uneven quality of Saadiyat's future architecture, the more fundamental issue at hand is the notion of the cultural district itself. Sequestering all of these institutions in one corner of the city will make it easy for tourists to bounce among them during the course of a day, but the cultural district risks becoming an institutional ghetto devoid of other character or activity. In planning Saadiyat's cultural district, Abu Dhabi has indulged an obsession that plagues the Gulf; that of single-use districts. Nowhere is this more evident than in neighboring Dubai, with its Media City, Internet City, Health City, Academic City, Silicon Oasis, Motor World, and so on. This segregationist urbanism has long since fallen out of favor in the West, albeit only after catastrophic experiments throughout much of the twentieth century. For the tens of billions of dollars Abu Dhabi is shelling out to import the cultural bounty that the Saadiyat museums will hold, the city would benefit far more by spreading them around.

Leaving Saadiyat you now loop around the Mina Zayed port and head down along the Corniche. The buildings on the waterfront have been the defining image of Abu Dhabi for the last twenty-five years, to the point that they appear on the reverse of the thousand-dirham note, the UAE's highest denomination of currency. The twenty-story façades lining the Corniche are fancy but not flashy, and are punctuated here and there by prominent edifices such as the salmon-hued headquarters of the state oil monopoly.

At this point you might do a double take at what appear to be a pair of giant licorice sticks spoiling the otherwise agreeable downtown skyline. Those two towers deserve special explanation. They stand on the site of the former Central Market, the outdoor shopping bazaar that was built as the new city's ersatz souq in 1972. The market was nothing special to behold: a boxy confusion of shabby concrete buildings and flyspeck shops, some with tarpaulin roofs and sand floors.[4] Most of the shopkeepers were Indian or Pakistani, lending the market an aura more Asian than Arabian. Yet in view of Abu Dhabi's lack of a discernible center or historic quarter, the market was the only place in the city that conveyed a sense of history, place, and tradition.[5] Jonathan Raban noted on his 1979 visit that the shopkeepers, patrons, and loiterers lent the place a unique sense of life; the market's exoticism "was accentuated rather than diminished by the banality of its appearance."[6] The Central Market became a landmark for residents and visitors alike.

As the years wore on, the market's grit and informality increasingly jarred with the sophisticated image that Abu Dhabi's leaders wanted the world to see. As early as 2002 the authorities discussed "upgrading" the market in a manner sensitive to its existing character and atmosphere, even though plenty of residents were quite happy with the "old, burnt, dusty, permanently dying souq."[7] After Zayed's death, these pretenses were dropped. The market was gutted by a fire that many residents believed to have been deliberately started, and the entire area was bulldozed early in 2005.

The government subsequently brought in the doyen of British architecture, Lord Norman Foster, to design a new central market that would redefine the city center. The definition arrived at by Foster's firm was a rather vulgar one: a trio of garish towers—one each for residences, offices, and a hotel—atop a three-story indoor mall replete with wood lattice screens, skylit courtyards, and other pseudo-Arabian elements. The project claimed to epitomize Abu Dhabi's mixture of tradition and modernity, with marketing materials that boasted of how the new complex would "restore Central Market to its former glory, just as it was in the 60s," the speaker evidently forgetting that the market didn't exist back then. The number of towers atop the podium was eventually reduced from three to two—the pair of behemoths you now see jutting upwards from the harmony around them, which are dauntingly christened the Domain and the Trust. The taller of the two, the Domain, was slated to become the city's tallest building at 381 meters (1,250 feet) upon its completion in 2013.[8] Each tower's serrated façade is covered in vertical ripples of (surprise!) plateglass and nothing else, convex

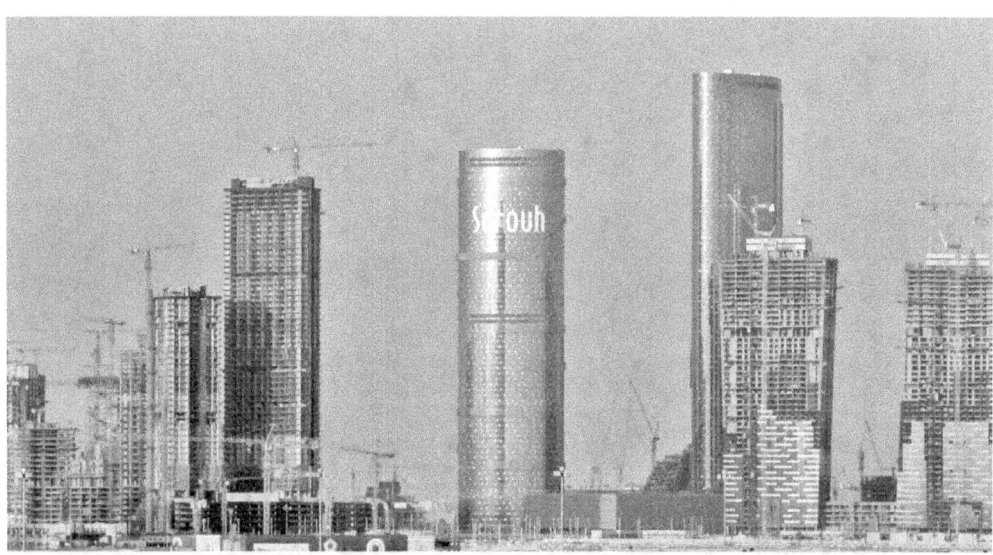

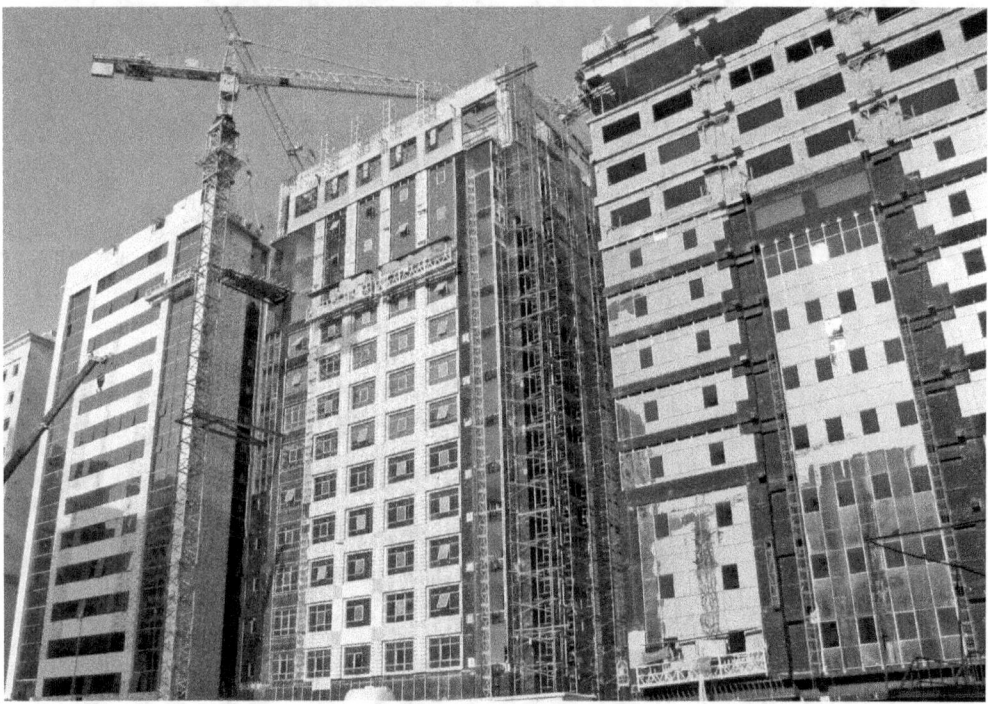

Top: The monolithic Sun and Sky towers standing watch over their brethren on Reem Island, circa December 2010. *Bottom:* A pablum of cellophane and chrome. Tawdry plateglass and aluminum paneling are everywhere.

on the Domain and concave on the Trust. The towers have no other features of interest, other than sharply sloped roofs mimicking sliced bamboo. The new and improved Central Market is not Lord Foster's finest creation.[9]

Mercifully, the tragedy of Central Market is somewhat mitigated by the next stop on your tour. The Abu Dhabi Investment Authority (ADIA) headquarters at the midpoint of

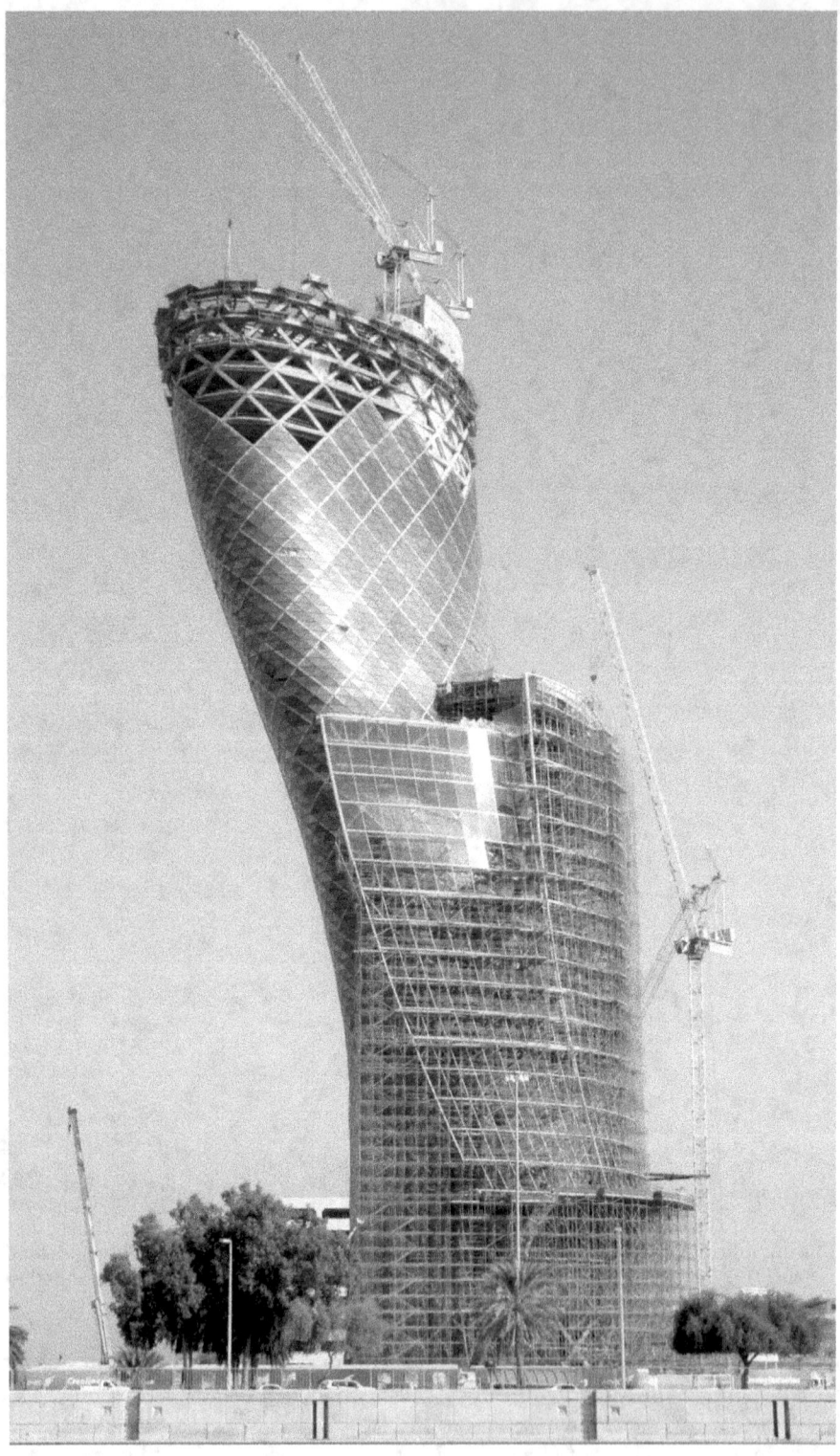

Construction on Capital Gate, the world's farthest-leaning tower, circa September 2009.

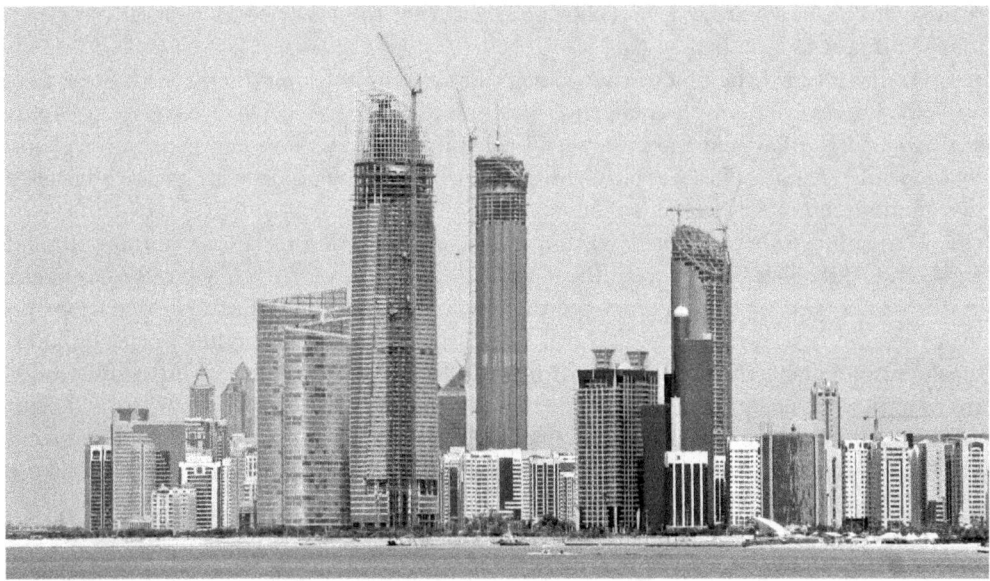

The Corniche skyline, circa March 2011. At the left center, the Landmark soars over the headquarters of the Abu Dhabi Investment Authority. To their right are the bland facades of the Central Market's towers.

the Corniche is the city's most elegant piece of contemporary architecture. It wraps its forty-odd stories in a curtain of glass that curves gracefully back and forth like a rounded W. The design has the subtle touches that are so achingly absent from the city's other façades: transparent glass tinted a faint gray-green, horizontal silver bands lending visual interest and demarcation to every floor, and a gently rising parapet that frames the top. These are simple trimmings, to be certain, but they contribute to a refinement that makes many of Abu Dhabi's buildings look amateurish in comparison. Unfortunately, the subtle elegance that the ADIA building brings to the waterfront skyline is quite literally overshadowed by the new thousand-foot-tall gnomon of the Landmark tower next door.

Reaching the end of the Corniche, you round the scorpion claw that houses Marina Mall and the Emirates Palace. Behind the Palace rise the Etihad Towers, a quintet of office towers resembling an upward-facing claw, clad in (what else?) plateglass of bland blue. After the Etihad Towers there is little to see along most of Abu Dhabi's western edge. Past the pylons of the new bridge to Sheikh Khalifa's private Hudayriat Island is the Al Gurm Resort, a lily pad-like collection of tiny islands with concrete bunker villas on each. Further on, the shorefront is lined with sheikhs' palaces, enormous mansions in all sorts of whimsical Orientalist styles.

Finally you approach a rectangular inlet at the southwest corner of the island. You pull in and come alongside the futuristic bulk of ADNEC, beside which rises the eye-catching Capital Gate tower. Rather than compete with their Dubai cousins for the title of the world's tallest building, Abu Dhabi's leaders have placed their city in the record books with a more horizontal achievement. Capital Gate's tubular form tilts eighteen degrees from the vertical at its midsection, four times the lean of its counterpart in Pisa, before straightening again. Guinness has duly certified it as the furthest leaning tower in the world.[10] The staggered floors are supported by a diagrid exoskeleton similar to the one on London's famous Gherkin. Capital Gate's crook has earned it the nickname of the Broken Arm among residents, who, if there are no locals around, may also point out that the tower bears a closer (and more ironic) likeness to a shofar.

Having reached the end of your tour, you are possibly feeling nonplussed. Sure, there are some impressive examples here and there, but otherwise Abu Dhabi's emerging skyline is a pablum of cellophane and chrome, all colored glass and aluminum paneling in shapes that redefine eccentric. How could the world's richest city wind up with so much tasteless, two-bit, unintentionally comic architecture?

The author Robert Byron might offer an answer. During his 1930s journeys through Persia and Afghanistan in search of the roots of classical Islamic design, which he chronicled in *The Road to Oxiana*, Byron theorized that one could gauge a civilization's character from the caliber of its architecture. If that is the case, then Abu Dhabi's contemporary buildings speak volumes about the city's ethos—little of it flattering. The emirate's expensive edifices are so garish, so amateur, so utterly bizarre that, to echo the British author, "it is difficult to imagine where anyone could have found the architects to design them, even as a joke."[11] For all its vision and forward-thinking rhetoric, Abu Dhabi has discovered the hard way that quality is not something you can rush.

* * *

The dubious integrity of Abu Dhabi's buildings extends beyond the aesthetics of their façades. The use of cheap labor has allowed Abu Dhabi to build at breakneck speed, yet the quality of that construction, done by mostly unskilled workers under minimal supervision, leaves much to be desired. The government has compounded the issue by allowing contractors to largely police their own compliance with the emirate's building code, which dates from the 1960s. Construction quality suffers on infrastructure and buildings alike. The cost-effectiveness of cut-rate labor is sometimes more than offset when roads, sewers, and pipelines have to be rebuilt to correct defects in their construction.

The plateglass that is ubiquitous across the city is an area of particular concern, as many laborers are not trained how to properly set and seal the plates so that they do not pop out in Abu Dhabi's extreme heat. For lunch my colleagues and I would often cross the broiling parking lot of the old Public Works building to the coffee shop in the ground floor of one of the towers along Airport Road, as it was the only eatery within walking distance. On one such occasion Ethan nearly had his arm taken off by a glass panel that burst its seals on the twelfth floor of the tower and came shearing down to the sidewalk. From then on, we always walked to the coffee shop with our gazes turned skyward.

The self-policing nature of construction has given Abu Dhabi more than its fair share of spectacular accidents on building sites. In late summer of 2009, for example, a fire broke out in one of the towers under construction on Reem Island, sparked by a short-circuit that set ablaze materials improperly stored in the building's basement. The smoky plume was visible across the city. Laborers who fled to the tower's top floors to escape the flames and smoke were kept waiting nearly three hours while emergency services sat gridlocked in mid-afternoon traffic.[12] Yet even this was tame compared to Dubai, where entire buildings had been known to collapse partway through their construction.[13]

The problems persist even after a new building is erected, when unskilled, illiterate laborers are employed to finish out the insides. I witnessed this firsthand when the UPC moved offices near the end of 2009. We were scheduled to vacate the old Public Works building and relocate to Mamoura, the sparkling new office complex that the government had built to house its various brain trust agencies. Mamoura A, the complex's first building, contained the Executive Affairs Authority (the staff of the Executive Council) and Mubadala, the emirate's flagship investment company. The UPC was scheduled to move into the recently completed Mamoura B next door, along with the Emirates Nuclear Energy Corporation and the DOT's aviation division, among others.

The UPC staff left our old offices early on a Thursday afternoon so that the movers could pack up our things in preparation for relocating them over the weekend. Less than half an hour after I left the office, I got a call from Keith. "Are you anywhere near Mamoura?" he asked.

"No, I'm at the grocery store. Why?"

"Get over here immediately. You need to see this."

I drove to Mamoura and took the elevator up to the first of the three floors the UPC was to occupy in the new building. Keith was waiting for me. He looked bemused, but said nothing. We walked into the reception area and were greeted by anarchy. The floor had gaping voids where the expensive marble tiles looked to have been set upon with a pickaxe. All variety of cables and wires protruded from open sockets and hung from openings in the drop ceiling. Dozens of laborers in nothing more than street clothes milled around like sheep. For every one of them that was working, four more stood idle or wandered aimlessly. Even the ones doing work seemed directionless. Keith and I watched as a pair of laborers took a glass door off its hinges and rotated it upside-down, then decided the original orientation had been correct and reversed it. Another laborer picked up a fire extinguisher, glanced around, and proceeded to nail it to the wall by its handle. The scene was made even more surreal by the rapid-fire cadence of Malayalam and other exotic tongues.

We picked our way through the reception area and into the main part of the office, where the disarray was repeated on a larger scale. We weaved through the debris and bodies towards the far end of the open-plan floor, where a lone Westerner towered over a group of laborers. We watched as he tried to give them directions from a blueprint using gestures and monosyllables. After the laborers dispersed he sagged into a chair. He was unshaven and looked like he hadn't slept in a week. Keith introduced him to me as the English foreman in charge of our office outfitting.

"It's like 'erding bloody cats," he said wearily. "I doubt one of 'em 'as worked a proper job before. All you can do is try an' find one 'ho speaks some English an' get 'im to tell 'is friends what to do, otherwise.... Well, jus' look a' it!" In view of the trouble that I was having untangling his accent, I could only wonder what the Indians heard.

"I'm guessing we're not going to be moving in on Sunday," I said.

"No, I'll get you in," the foreman replied. "I've got a crew a mates comin' in from Blighty tonight. I'll dump 'is bunch a tossers an' we'll work straight frew the weekend. I tell you, I can do more with six trained blokes than what 'is lot 'as done in a monf." He rubbed his jaw. "After that, I'm never workin' 'ere again."

* * *

My home offered no escape from Abu Dhabi's shoddy workmanship. The tub in my bathroom developed a tilt—possibly prompted by the villa settling on its uneven foundations—so that water ran off the sill and formed a lake on the floor every time I showered. The electrical outlets began having seizures, prompting my air conditioner to finally give up the ghost. The pipes behind the walls started to groan at night, my door became wedged in its frame, and ominous cracks appeared in the walls. The villa was literally crumbling around us.

As 2009 gave way to 2010, I began taking long walks in the evenings, as much to escape the villa as to enjoy the cooler air. I saw the tenement process repeated throughout the neighborhood. Signs of overcrowding were everywhere: villas sprouting cinderblock tumors, dump-sters in the street overflowing with rubbish, single balconies hung with entire clans' worth of laundry, cars double- and triple-parked in the street, on driveways, and in sandy front yards. Idlers began congregating on the street corners at night—first children, then youths, and finally adults, all of them male and either Arab or South Asian. Once more I had the feeling of being a voyeur anthropologist, watching the process of ghettoization unfold before my eyes over weeks instead of years. It was not ghettoization in the stereotypical North American sense, admittedly. Drugs weren't changing hands, houses weren't being torched, illegitimate births weren't on the rise, at least so far as I knew. Slowly but surely, however, the neighborhood was slipping into slumhood.

In early February Abu Dhabi was inundated by torrential rains for three straight days. It took all of an hour for the sewers to be overwhelmed. Flooding brought the city to a standstill by the afternoon of the first day. From our vantage point in the new offices on the sixth floor of Mamoura B, my colleagues and I could see the nearby streets awash and traffic gridlocked in every direction. We stayed at work until the traffic finally cleared at nine in the evening.

That night I arrived home to scenes reminiscent of Hurricane Katrina. The neighbor-hood streets had become shallow rivers, which were forded by drenched vagabonds pushing their earthly possessions in shopping carts. I pulled up onto the sidewalk in front of my villa. People were crowded out front like refugees—angry, wet, miserable people, their household effects piled everywhere, on the ground, atop cars, in their arms. The rain had collapsed the ceilings of the slapdash cinderblock rooms on the roof and in the front and rear courtyards. The first floor was flooded to my ankles.

Amazingly, all the rooms on my floor were spared. I remembered Noor's prescient warn-ing: *You don't want anything on the top or bottom.* I resolved to offer her dinner at the restaurant of her choice.

Eleven

Nadír

No matter how many buildings, foundations, schools, and hospitals we build, or how many bridges we raise, these are all material entities. The real spirit behind progress is the human spirit, the able man with his intellect and capabilities. — *Sheikh Zayed bin Sultan al Nahyan*

If there was one event on the calendar that embodied Abu Dhabi's boom, it was Cityscape, the real estate extravaganza held every spring at ADNEC. Cityscape was the venue for the emirate's developers to showcase their newest mega-projects in a game of unabashed one-upsmanship. For several years running the show had been a scene of rabid speculation. Whenever a developer unveiled a new project, a feeding frenzy would ensue as buyers fought to be parted from their money. Investors from around the Middle East flocked to Cityscape to purchase units in buildings that had yet to break ground. Wealthy buyers scooped up properties by the dozen, sometimes receiving nothing more solid than a highlighted box on a floorplan in exchange for a down payment—no signature, no contract, nothing. A few fancy renderings could result in hundreds of units selling out in mere minutes. It was widely gossiped that the lucky first-comers could then walk out the door and double their money by reselling their promissory titles to the second-tier speculators circling like sharks outside. However, neither I nor any of my colleagues knew of anyone who had actually pulled off this legendary trick. It smacked of a rumor intended to fuel the gambling.

Cityscape 2010 was business as usual, despite the continued economic slump across much of the rest of the world. Judging by the developers' fulsome displays, one wouldn't have guessed that real estate as an asset class had fallen out of favor with global investors. Booth after booth flaunted ever more ambitious, outlandish projects. All of the projects seemed to be targeting the high end of the market, with tower after tower of million-dirham apartments and prime office space. That might have been lucrative for the developers' bottom lines, but it was far from the "range of housing and services targeting all income levels"[1] that *Plan 2030* had called for. Moreover, I had seen the proposals that the developers had submitted to the UPC for many of these projects, and I knew that not one of them included a market study examining the actual level of demand. The developers didn't bother with such twaddle. "If you build it, they will come" had become their overriding mentality.

This year, Cityscape's primary hub of excitement was a giant cube-shaped exhibit rising to the ceiling in the center of the main hall; its geometric superstructure and blue and purple lighting were reminiscent of Disney's EPCOT Center. Inside, one wall was covered with a jumbotron that looped scenes of happy Emirati families among a computer-generated version of the future Abu Dhabi. A scale model of the city made from wood and plastic covered the floor, stretching nearly a hundred feet from the miniature Corniche to the airport. The model depicted how Abu Dhabi would look in 2030 once all of the proposed projects were finished. The level of detail was astounding; even my dumpy villa in Mushrif had its own little box.

The lavish exhibit belonged to none other than the UPC. It had cost our public relations team a cool fourteen million dirhams. The exhibit was designed to send a message to the property illuminati in attendance: Abu Dhabi's experiment in city-building was going fine, thank you very much, just look at all we're doing. But certain elements conveyed more than the management intended. For example, with the entire city shown to scale in three dimensions on the floor model, the scattershot nature of the new developments was all too evident. Clumps of buildings sprang up around the miniaturized city like patches of crabgrass on a putting green. Although the worst offenders belonged to the first wave of developments that had gotten their start before the UPC's creation, there were also plenty of oversized, poorly sited, or simply unnecessary projects that had been approved on our watch. The net effect belied the claim—*our* claim—that there was a powerful and enlightened agency coordinating Abu Dhabi's growth.

Halfway through the weeklong show, I was pulling a shift helping to staff the UPC's exhibit when an excited murmur buzzed through the crowd: the crown prince was on his way! I watched from the mezzanine as Sheikh Mohammed entered at the head of a sizable retinue. As our general manager led him around, a sea of kandoras and abayyas coalesced around the sheikh, squeezing all foreigners aside. It never ceased to amaze me how quickly the Emiratis could put an exclusively local face on affairs when needed. Normally the Emiratis were quite happy to let foreigners take care of things on their behalf. Yet whenever it came to a public event or photo-op, Emiratis were the only ones in the picture, their white robes like the tip of an iceberg with the supporting foreign mass submerged out of sight. Local history would record that Abu Dhabi had been built by Emiratis, for Emiratis. The rest of us didn't count.

Keith came over and leaned on the railing beside me. "I wonder if he gets it," he mused.

"Who?"

"The Crown Prince. You'd think he'd walk around here and see how overblown everything is, and he'd realize that this is getting out of control. They're building too much, too fast, and a lot of it looks like junk. People are going to come to Abu Dhabi and think, the Emiratis happened upon the biggest fortune in history, and *this* is what they bought?"

Keith nodded at the handful of lesser dignitaries clustered around the crown prince; these wore black gossamer *thobe* shawls over their kandoras to signal their elevated status. "See those people—the advisors and the groupies who are supposed to tell the sheikhs the hard truth? I don't think those conversations ever happen. It's like the emperor's new clothes."

"What about people like Larry?" I asked, referring to the UPC's founder.

"What about him?"

"Well, if the Emiratis are too timid, shouldn't an outsider be the one to tell them what they need to hear?"

Keith shook his head. "That's like being a nutritionist to a four-year-old. The first time you tell him 'No candy bar,' you're fired. Larry wants to keep getting paid, just like the rest of us. Besides, he doesn't have much right to tell anyone that they should be curbing speculation."

"Why is that?"

"The Emiratis all fawn over what Legendary Larry did with Vancouver, but they should have looked more closely at his record. He made Vancouver the least affordable city in North America. You never hear anyone mention that, do you? The housing there is more expensive than New York or San Francisco. I'd love to go back to Vancouver, but even with the money I'm making here, I could never afford to live there again."

I actually knew what Keith was talking about. The constant fawning over Vancouver around the office had led me to do some research of my own, in which I discovered that the city's meteoric rise was somewhat overblown. During Larry's decade-long tenure as Vancouver's principal planner, the median price for a single-family home had shot up nearly threefold, to 1.2 million Canadian dollars, by far the highest in Canada. Whereas house prices normally average around three times a city's average household income, Vancouver ran a multiple of nine and a half. Such price inflation might be expected if the city's economy was booming, but in truth Vancouver's economy was only half the size of Detroit's, and its salaries and wages were lower than those of other large Canadian cities.[2]

Even Vancouver's ballyhooed quality of life was more smoke than fire. Jet-setters compared the city's social atmosphere, cultural attractions, and amenities unfavorably to places like London, Hong Kong, or even Toronto. The rapid turnover of property caused by the spiraling prices left many residences empty much of the time; some parts of the city saw up to two-thirds of their properties resell at least once every two years. As a result, there was little sense of community or civic pride. The strongest bonds were to be found among the real estate speculators, who were quick to demonize any doubters foolish enough to question how far property values could climb.[3] And Vancouver's pristine image actually undercut its viability. The city lacked the grit, the rough edges, and the social foment that give a city soul.

I said to Keith, "Yeah, when the sheikhs brought Larry here, I wonder whether they were serious about copying Vancouver. Is that what they really wanted? A sanitized playground for the rich?"

Keith merely grinned.

"Oh ... right. Touché," I sighed.

As the crown prince and his entourage drifted out of the exhibit, Keith and I looked up at the jumbotron. It restarted its cycle of the promotional film the UPC had commissioned for Cityscape. The screen depicted an outdoor amphitheater filled with Emiratis of all ages—men, women, and children, all clad in black and white. I recognized several of my colleagues' faces among the actors. As the sun set behind the theater on the screen, a fanfare sounded and a spectral image of the calligraphic *Plan 2030* logo appeared in front of the crowd. The onscreen Emiratis rose to their feet in measured applause.

"The thing is, at some point this will all hit the fan," Keith continued. "When the bubble pops, people around here are going to wake up one morning and ask who's responsible. And it's going to come straight back to us. The developers are going to say, 'We only built what the UPC allowed us.' Remember the scapegoating in Dubai?"

I nodded. He was referring to the crash that had overtaken the neighboring emirate starting in late 2008. As Dubai's fortunes rapidly unraveled, a number of expat corporate officers had gone to jail on the flimsiest of charges when the companies they managed ran into financial turbulence. "But what do they expect us to do?" I protested. "We can't force them to listen."

"Well, I don't know about you, but I'm planning my exit for when the first big projects start coming online," Keith replied. "When the locals see what they got for their money, it's time to hit the road."

* * *

The slumming of my neighborhood in the early months of 2010 prompted me to broaden the range of my nighttime walks. I started venturing over to the Embassy District several streets away. Although the government had set aside an entire block just south of Mushrif for foreign diplomatic missions, many countries still maintained their embassies in compounds and villas scattered throughout the city, knowing full well that they would just have to move again in a few years to the new Capital District on the mainland. The Embassy District thus had the look of a ghost town, with solitary intact buildings surrounded by empty plots and debris. At night its streets were deserted except for the police standing guard outside the more prominent embassies.

One cool evening I was walking down an empty Embassy District street when I noticed an Emirati female approaching from the other direction, accompanied by what looked to be her housemaid. I crossed to the other side of the street, out of both respect and also my continued irrational fear of local women. As they got closer I hazarded a quick sideward glance—and promptly halted in my tracks. "Mahra?"

The women kept walking, so I called louder and waved. They turned towards me and I saw that the Emirati was indeed my young colleague from the UPC. She removed the earbud headphones tucked under the wrap of her *shayla*. "Well, this is certainly a surprise!" she said as I walked up.

"I could say the same thing. What are you doing here?"

"I live a few blocks over. What are *you* doing here?"

We ascertained that her family's villa and mine were just a few streets apart. "Well, neighbor, is it okay if I walk with you?" I asked.

Mahra's eyes widened and she held a whispered exchange with her housemaid. "Sure," she replied with a hint of mischief. We started down the street with the housemaid following a dozen paces behind. Mahra said, "If my dad knew I went walking with a boy, he'd kill me. And then he'd kill you."

"Oh?" I hoped she was joking.

"My family is very traditional. They don't even want me mixing with Emirati boys besides my brothers. And foreign guys? Out of the question." She was clearly pleased at flouting this constraint.

"Do you come walking here often?" I asked. "I'm surprised I haven't seen you before."

Mahra's smile turned to a frown. "I used to walk around my neighborhood all the time, but not anymore. It was a nice place before, with mostly local families. Now with all these new villas, the whole neighborhood is men. Indian and Pakistani and Arab men. The way they look at me is just horrible. I don't feel safe. The neighborhood doesn't seem familiar anymore." In view of the decline I had witnessed throughout Mushrif in less than a year, I could only imagine how it might have felt to someone who had grown up there.

Mahra suddenly regained her excitement. She grabbed my arm—I panicked momentarily—and began talking about the latest addition to her extensive handbag collection. By now, these staccato changes of topic and emotion no longer surprised me, as they happened all the time in conversations with Emiratis. The younger locals in particular seemed either culturally inclined towards spontaneous conversational redirection or, more likely, possessed of an even more negligible attention span than the youth of the West. I presumed it was a function of growing up among the continual distractions of the latest modern technologies. It was difficult to imagine a people more wed to their Blackberries and mobile phones than the Emiratis. All that perpetual electronic nagging had a discernible effect on their concentration.

We walked past the ugliest embassy in the district, a gray scalene triangle that suggested either a meteorite fallen to Earth or a postmodernist rendition of the Rock of Gibraltar. A phalanx of fences, security cameras, concrete barricades, and frowning guards surrounded the hulking structure. Lest the foreboding design leave any doubts as to whom the embassy belonged, the façade proudly boasted an oversized imprint of the Great Seal of the United

States. It was the local edition of the Fortress America chain that had replaced the diplomatic missions of my home country around the world after 9/11. The building was a monumental embarrassment to every American in Abu Dhabi.

Mahra eyed the fortress. "Every time I come here, I'm scared that the CIA will rush out and grab me," she said with an uneasy giggle.

"Oh, come on. Surely we Americans aren't all that scary?"

"No, you aren't. But your government is. I would never go to America."

"Really?" Her vehemence surprised me.

"No way! I've heard what they do to Muslims at the airports. I wouldn't be able to wear my abayya in public. People would probably spit on me."

I tried to disabuse her of these notions, but she wasn't convinced. It was intriguing to see, for a change, the other side of the mutual misunderstanding between the people of the United States and the Middle East.

"Hey, you should meet Majid, my brother," she blurted, changing topics yet again. "He's studying medicine in London. I think the two of you would have a lot to talk about, since you're both living abroad."

"He's not going to frown on you associating with a Western guy?"

"Oh, Majid will be fine. He's lived in the West for almost a decade now. He won't say anything to Mom and Dad. I'll ask him to give you a call next time he's home."

We reached the far end of the Embassy District and looped around, walking back along the street that separated the embassies from the rear side of ADNEC. Beyond the exhibition centre, the broken arm of the Capital Gate tower came into view. We stopped and watched as the tower's diagrid exoskeleton was backlit by ghostly blue explosions from the welders inside.

"Abu Dhabi's latest world record," I said. "You must be proud."

Mahra frowned again. "I hate all this development. It's ruining the city. Everything is changing. The buildings, the people, everything."

I looked at her with confusion. "Then why are you working for the UPC? We're practically the ringleaders."

She shrugged. "Someone has to bring some sense to this thing, right?"

"So why don't you become a planner? You'd have more of a direct impact than working for public relations."

"I've thought about that, but I'm better off helping people who know what they're doing. People like you."

"Thanks, but I think you're wildly overestimating my abilities," I said. "Besides, it doesn't matter what we expats say if the people who make the decisions don't want to hear it."

"I know," she said quietly. "When I look at what's going on, sometimes it makes me so angry that I don't know what to do. Usually I just write about it in my journal."

"What about writing an editorial in the newspaper?" I suggested. She looked at me like I was mad, but I continued, "Seriously, a young Emirati woman with a perspective like yours? I think people would pay a lot more attention to that than to anything from a foreigner."

She shook her head. "You don't understand. People don't say those kinds of things here. Not in public."

"Well, you could write anonymously."

"They would find me. I still couldn't say what I really think."

"And what's that?"

Mahra gazed up at the unfinished frame of Capital Gate. The lights of the construction site played across her face and twinkled their reflections in her dark eyes. "Sometimes I think we Emiratis are selling Abu Dhabi just so we can get rich. We have bigger villas, but so what? Am I really better off if I have a house but lose my home? Everybody recognizes the problem, but no one says anything. If we could just talk openly, we might have a chance to bring it under control, to slow things down and really think about where we're heading. But we are all afraid of being the first to speak up." Her voice took on an angrier tenor. "Back in my grandfather's time, people said what they thought. Yes, there were arguments. Nobody argues like an Arab! But then they discussed and they compromised, and everyone was better because of it. Now...." Her voice trailed off.

Spoken by a young woman from a conservative family in a traditional society where criticism was unheard of, her words were astonishing. I had heard occasional discontented rumblings among my Emirati colleagues, but never anything so blunt. I wondered how widely these feelings were shared.

We stood in silence for a few moments before resuming our walk. Mahra gazed into the distance in front of us, where the sodium glow of the streetlights seemed to march into infinity down the empty street. "We have already lost so much," she said. "Our traditions, our culture, our identity ... I wonder if we'll have anything left by the time we wake up." Her tone changed from anger to resignation. "Sometimes I feel like I'm a prisoner in my own city."

* * *

The climate at my villa changed quickly from flood to drought. Less than a week after the rains had ceased, I turned on the tap one morning and heard nothing but a distant gurgle. After determining that several other residents faced the same situation, we went outside to the utility box at the back of the villa, where we discovered that the wires to the water meter had been snipped. There was a note from the utility company stating that the villa had been disconnected for nonpayment of bills. Not only was our absentee landlord bilking us on rent, he had simply pocketed the utility fees we had been forced to pay him up front, since the illegally sublet rooms didn't have individual meters. That wasn't the only service that had been shut off. I tried calling the villa's maintenance man, but his phone had been disconnected. It was just as well, since I had never actually seen him at the villa.

Two days later, the water was still out. It was the last straw. With nearly a month still to go on my lease, I packed up my meager belongings, drove out to Yas Island, and checked in to one of the new hotels. Staying any longer in that house of horrors was simply more than I could take.

The situation at work was, unfortunately, little better. The ever more preposterous proposals that Abu Dhabi's developers rained down upon the UPC hit a high-water mark in the early months of 2010. Typical of these was the proposal for Um Lafina, one of the larger islands in the metropolitan archipelago. *Plan 2030* called for Um Lafina to receive only the lightest development, a few "eco-villages" with a parkway winding between them. The sheikh who owned the island had something different in mind. His office submitted a proposal for a self-contained central business district with enough real estate for nearly two hundred thousand people, almost a duplication of the scale of Reem Island right next door. When the UPC staff pushed back against the concept, the sheikh's office made a call to our general manager, who sent word down that the proposal was to be approved with no further questions asked.

Even better was the concept for the Al Ain Wonderland, a luxury resort on the outskirts of the emirate's inland second city. The plans featured an outdoor ski slope down the side of Jebel Hafeet, the only mountain for more than a hundred miles. The absurdity was incredible: an open-air slalom in one of the hottest places on Earth? Even if the developers could figure out a way to keep the snow from melting and becoming the world's largest slip-and-slide, they seemed to have overlooked a more fundamental question: Why would anyone come to Arabia to ski? The more I saw of how Abu Dhabi's future was taking shape, the more it baffled me.

And so it came to pass that, one year to the day after I had first arrived in Abu Dhabi, I drove to the airport to catch a flight. I was heading home for two weeks of much-needed respite. I arrived at the terminal looking forward to falling asleep on the plane and waking up somewhere over Europe, ideally to look out the window and see a landscape of green instead of beige.

The kind lady at the check-in counter looked puzzled when I told her I was flying to Detroit via Amsterdam. "We don't have a flight to Amsterdam today," she said. With a sinking feeling I showed her my ticket. "I'm sorry. That flight isn't scheduled on Tuesdays."

Outside the terminal I phoned the airline's local office. "Hello ma'am-sir," the agent said, using the gender-neutral salutation favored by Filipino service staff across the UAE. "Yes, I have your ticket record here. The Tuesday flights to Amsterdam were discontinued, so we rebooked you on the Wednesday flight."

"When did you do that?"

The tap-tap-tap of a keyboard. "According to your record, in January, ma'am-sir."

"And did you ever send me a notification?"

Tap-tap-tap, then a pause. "No, ma'am-sir."

"You don't say. No e-mail? No phone call?"

Silence.

"Thanks for your consideration." I hung up the phone. Even by the standards of Abu Dhabi's consistently awful service, it was infuriating. I couldn't think of a more fitting end to my first year in the city.

I briefly considered going to the office, but discarded that insanity in favor of heading back to the hotel and lounging by the pool. Abu Dhabi could hold me hostage, but it couldn't force me to work. I spent the remainder of the day sprawled beneath a palm tree amid a pod of lobster-red Europeans. In front of me, past the pool and the narrow channel beyond, the steel innards of Raha Beach's growing buildings rose from the haze. Over the playful splashing of children I could hear the distant clamor of hammers and cranes. At least the dust from the construction was blowing in the other direction.

With my notebook in my lap, I took stock of my time in Abu Dhabi thus far. On the plus side, I had to admit that the emirate was still an amazing place to work. There was simply a phenomenal amount of activity. Where else would I be able to play a part in projects like the national railway? And I did enjoy working alongside such a diverse and talented array of colleagues. Yet the power brokers behind Abu Dhabi's schemes often seemed disinclined to listen to the expats they had hired to advise them. If the leaders weren't going to heed our advice, then why were we here?

Beyond that, life in Abu Dhabi was either feast or famine, mostly a feast of aggravation and a famine of fun. Yes, the diversity was stimulating; every day brought memorable and often amusing intercultural encounters. But the rest of quotidian Abu Dhabi left much to be desired. The traffic, the dessicating climate, the lack of nature, the dearth of things to do, the vulgar architecture, the miserable housing, the traffic, the extortionate cost of living, the biweekly food poisoning, the sensory deprivation, the traffic: it was all a bit much. I hated to think I was staying just for the money, but I had to ask: would I still be here if the

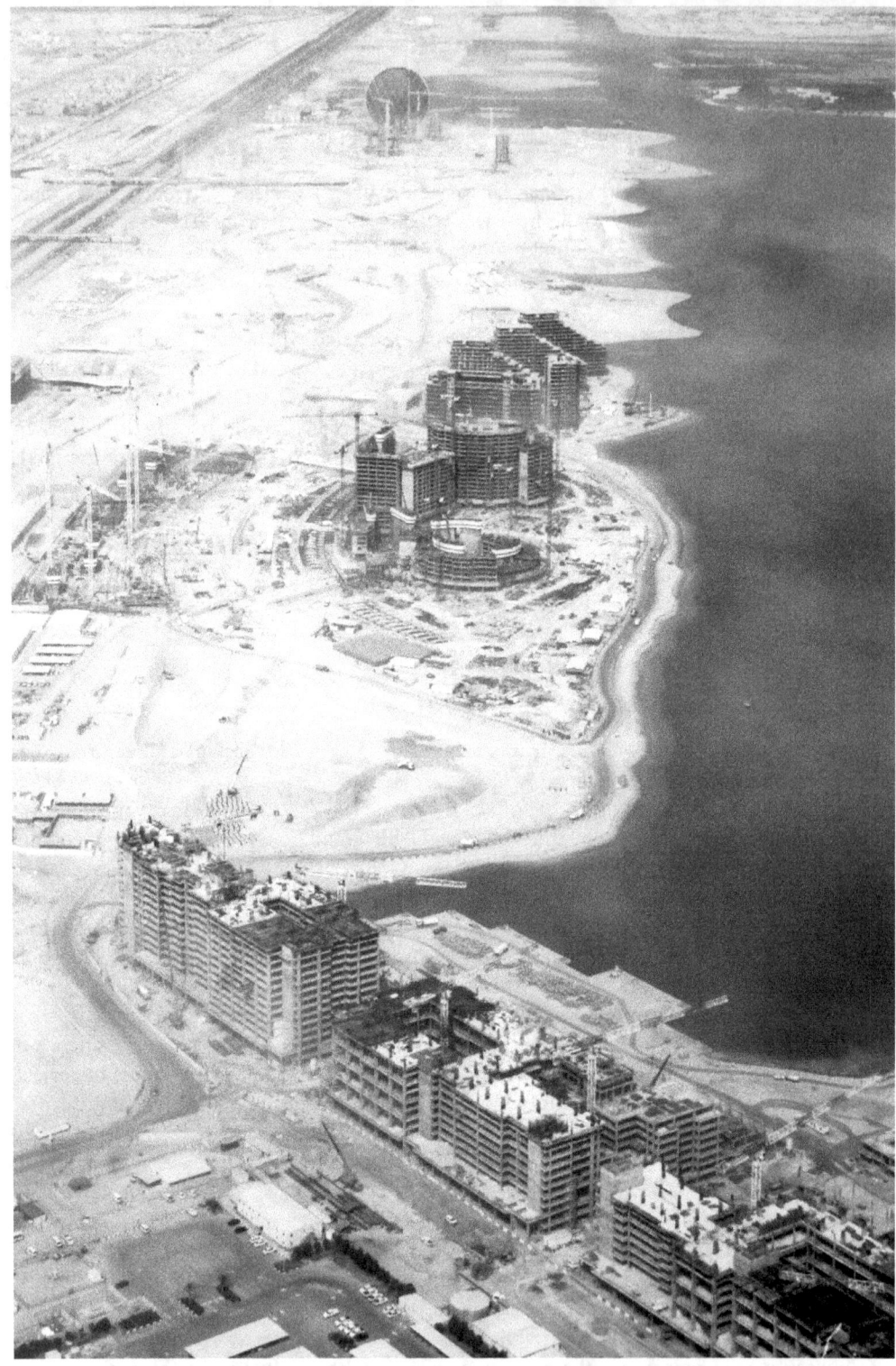

Raha Beach under construction, circa September 2009. In the background is Aldar's HQ.

pay were not so generous? *Abu Dhabi is a golem,* I wrote in my notebook, *with the form of a city but none of the spirit, going through the motions of urban life in a jerking, awkward manner, gazing upon itself with vacant, uncomprehending eyes.*

I closed the notebook, set it aside, and tried to nap. As I drifted off I wondered whether I would make it onto a plane the following day—and if so, whether I would come back.

Twelve

Greener Grass

We have our traditions, customs and ideals that we stick to. We do not imitate the lifestyle of other nations. In the Western community there are lifestyles that do not attract us and hence we will not bring them to our country. —*Sheikh Zayed bin Sultan al Nahyan*

I did come back, of course. There was really no other choice, despite Abu Dhabi's copious frustrations and my mixed feelings about how the emirate's transformation was unfolding. Leaving would have meant returning to the real world, with its responsibilities, humdrumwork, income taxes, chores, and all the other grown-up concerns that were blissfully absent from the life of a Western expatriate in Abu Dhabi. The gilded neverland held me in its thrall.

My first order of business was finding a new place to live. My colleague Austin, the Al Gharbia planner, also happened to be looking to move. Our number became three with the addition of Rhys, an urban designer from Wales who had joined the UPC the previous summer and was looking for something more permanent than his heretofore string of transient accommodations. His primary role at the agency was taking the developers' horrendous designs and reworking them into something palatable. Rhys cut the image of an artistic savant, with his squared glasses, trendy jeans, and inexhaustible supply of crisp black shirts. In previous conversations, he had evinced a sardonic wit that he delivered with perfect deadpan, although I often found his Cardiff accent indecipherable.

Wanting to get as far away from the ghetto as possible, I suggested that the three of us look for an apartment in one of the high-rises on the north end of the island, in what passed for Abu Dhabi's downtown. Austin quashed that idea. "That's where I live now. It's the opposite of what you'd expect. It has all the negatives of city living and none of the positives. The traffic is horrible, there's no parking, and no amenities either, unless you count the smelly Indian grocers. Sure, you can walk, but there's nothing to walk to."

"Except Blitz," Rhys added.

"What's Blitz?" I asked.

Austin guffawed. "Just hope we never take you there."

Rather than dealing with the potential nightmare of another illegal sublet, we decided to look for a modest townhouse that we could rent in its entirety. Owing to the decades-long dominance of the villa, the townhouse concept was new to Abu Dhabi, and the city's architects were still trying to come to terms with designing something halfway between an apartment and a full-blown mansion. Our house hunt reminded me of the plight of Goldilocks as we toured a string of residences that were too small, too big, or—on one awkward occasion—already had someone sleeping inside. At one point our real estate agent showed us a property that had allegedly been a sheikh's private party pad; it came with darkened windows, a disco ball, and zebra-striped wallpaper. Austin was tempted to say yes.

We eventually went to see a townhouse in the Golf Gardens neighborhood. Golf Gardens was one of the most prestigious of Abu Dhabi's new developments, a residential gated community that had just opened in early 2010. The neighborhood sat on the mainland a short way beyond the Sheikh Zayed Bridge, crammed onto an unwieldy triangle of land between the Abu Dhabi Golf Club, the E10 highway, and the private estate of a sheikh. Golf Gardens had been designed as an Emirati community, but many of the locals who bought up the neighborhood's villas and townhouses did so to cash in on the boom by renting them out to expats.

I had driven past Golf Gardens on a number of occasions while it was still under construction and had always surveyed it with disdain. From a distance the development had all the appeal of a pile of shipping containers. Now, as the three of us slowly cruised the neighborhood in Austin's Jeep, things looked even more bizarre on closer inspection. The neighborhood resembled a cubist rendition of Southern California, all right angles, rectilinear planes, and stucco coating the color of stale hummus. The only nonlinear shapes to be found in the neighborhood were the winding streets, whose narrow sidewalks were cluttered with fire hydrants, utility boxes, oversized signs, and towering light poles better suited to a highway. The villas and townhouses were look-alikes, and their worst features were often the most prominently positioned; some streets were lined with solid ranks of garage doors. Seven-foot-tall privacy walls made it impossible to view either the houses' yards or the neighborhood's surroundings. The only gardens to speak of were the leftover wedges of land where the neighborhood's squared plots met at angles, which had been landscaped as pocket parks.

"Whoever designed this place sure didn't care much for the public realm," Austin said as he glanced out the window at a bunker-like villa.

"You know who designed it, right?" Rhys replied.

"No. Who?"

"The same consultants that are working for us on North Wathba."

"They left themselves room for improvement," I said.

We met our agent at the clubhouse at the center of the neighborhood, where he showed us the gym and outdoor pool still under construction. We told him we were looking for something modest. He took us to the far corner of the neighborhood and let us inside the development's smallest townhouse model. The rectangular floorplan was thrice as long as it was wide. The kitchen and downstairs bedroom opened onto a living room that could have accommodated a bowling lane. The upstairs featured a trio of additional bedrooms and a secondary living room, which came equipped with a bar. "Bit odd for an Emirati household, don't you think?" Rhys asked, referring to the bar.

Austin was more concerned with how the house might accommodate the social gatherings for which he was renowned. "We could have the wine and cheese up here ... the karaoke downstairs...." We inspected the rest of the property, which included a two-car garage and front and rear courtyards enclosed by privacy walls. Whereas the front courtyard was xeriscaped with yucca plants and tiles appropriate for the climate, the backyard was covered with freshly laid sod that would undoubtedly need profuse daily watering. Like seemingly everything else in Abu Dhabi, it was one step forward, one step back.

The tour complete, we compared notes. The thought of living here was preposterous. The townhouse had far more space than we would ever require. The resources it would consume—water for the grass, electricity for the lights and air conditioning—were the definition of unsustainable. The neighborhood writ large was an isolated, walled-off enclave of oversized single-family homes that epitomized the worst of suburban sprawl. In short, it was the antithesis of all we stood for as planners. And none of us even knew how to golf. But it was

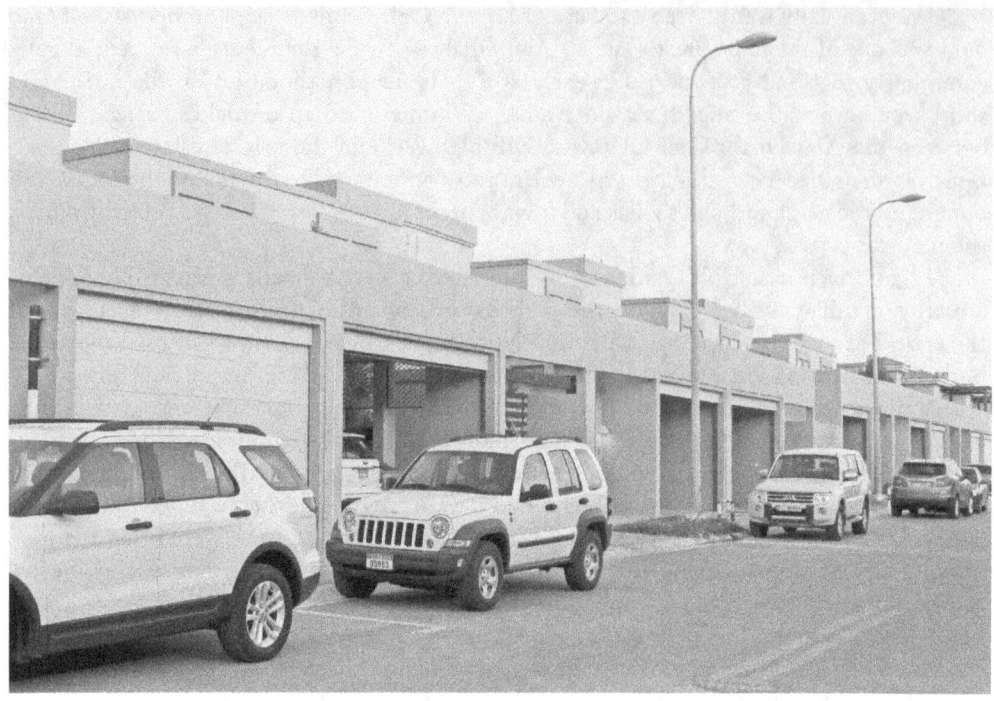

One of the inviting streetscapes in Golf Gardens.

clean, it was quiet, and it was new and therefore hopefully free of the woes that afflicted so much of Abu Dhabi's housing stock.

Rhys asked the agent, "So, hypothetically speaking, if we were possibly somewhat interested, what kind of price range would we be talking about?" Two hundred sixty thousand dirhams to rent it for a year, the agent said, roughly seventy-one thousand dollars.

We conferred among ourselves. It was highway robbery. We could never justify such an expense. Austin turned to the agent and said, "We'll take it."

* * *

In the month or so after the excitement of the Cityscape real estate exposition had passed, Abu Dhabi took a breather as the developers and government agencies regrouped. Abu Dhabi's leaders used the juncture to instill a renewed sense of resolve into the emirate's transformation, which in some cases involved shake-ups to major projects that had been deemed underperforming. The consultants who had been working on the national railway, for example, were summarily fired. There was no advance notice, either to them or to us. One day they were churning out engineering drawings, the next day they were gone. A short while later Etihad Rail brought in another consultancy to take their place. Khalid and I spent weeks bringing the new consultants up to speed.

The UPC's planning for North Wathba had been stalled for several months over what type of transit would serve the community. Our original plans had called for an above-ground extension of the Metro line to run through the center of the community, supported by tram lines reaching down from the Capital District and a network of circulating feeder buses. The low densities resulting from the general manager's ten-thousand-villa requirement had posed a fundamental challenge to the viability of that concept. The DOT was loathe to include fixed transit lines in dispersed locations where ridership might not be high enough to justify the capital costs, but the UPC staff still wanted to offer North Wathba's one hundred twenty thousand future residents an alternative to driving. The drawn-out impasse was finally solved when the Executive Council unilaterally decided that the Metro would not run to North Wathba, and even the tram lines would be downgraded to buses. Until now, the government had shown indifference to the cost of the infrastructure needed to support Abu Dhabi's expansion. It appeared they were starting to have second thoughts.

Regarding the Khaleej Al Arabi highway tunnel, almost a year had passed since the first meeting in which ADNEC's staff had put forth the idea, and not a shovelful of dirt had been turned. The original push to finish the project by early 2011 was now even less realistic. ADNEC's staff had held follow-up meetings every other month or so, during which they complicated matters even more. First they wanted to double the tunnel's length. Then they wanted to include a sprawling outdoor souq in the narrow space between the tunnel and the watery inlet beside it. Next they wanted to expand the souq with a string of luxury villas that would wrap around the northern end of the inlet. The technical challenges and constraints multiplied at every stage. With less than a year to go until the next IDEX in February 2011, the ADNEC staff finally realized the impossibility of the task before them and began talking about having only half of the tunnel and its concrete lid finished by then, so that the defense exposition would have at least a partial venue for its mock battles.

At the UPC, the pace of work redoubled in the wake of the project shakeups, augmented by our new surroundings in the Mamoura office complex. The chaos of the pre-relocation build-out notwithstanding, the new offices had been finished on schedule and we had moved in as planned. The offices were arranged in totem-pole fashion, with the general manager's suite and the other executive offices on the eighth floor, the Development Review Department taking up the seventh, and the Planning Policy and TIES departments splitting the sixth like the peons we were.

The UPC had paid top dirham for a workplace consultancy to design an office that embodied the latest advances and theories. The worker-bee sixth and seventh floors were laid out in open-plan fashion, with informal break-out spaces and dividers between the staff's cubicles that rose only six inches above desk level. I appreciated no longer being confined inside a windowless cubbyhole, but it still took quite some time to get used to looking out on my colleagues' heads and torsos hovering above their workstations. Although such open-plan offices had their origins in postwar Germany as a reaction against authoritarianism, evidently the UPC's management saw no inherent contradictions with Abu Dhabi's own governing ethos.[1]

The office design also exemplified energy efficiency, with zone-specific climate control and motion-activated ceiling lights that turned off when nobody was around—proof that the UPC practiced what it preached with respect to the energy-saving Estidama guidelines. But just like much of the new Abu Dhabi, it was a work in progress. We soon discovered that adjusting the climate controls had no effect on the ambient temperature, which stayed at a constant arctic level, and the lights had the habit of turning on and off at random throughout the day.

The new offices gradually revealed other surprises as well. For the first few months after we moved in, the opposite wing of the sixth floor was periodically infused with a nauseating sewer-like smell, forcing some of my colleagues in Planning Policy to leave the building when it was at its worst. The contractors in charge of Mamoura blamed the plumbing and spent weeks trying to identify the source of the odor, to no avail. When the UPC's general manager gave a tour of the new offices to several members of the Executive Council, they nearly swooned from the stench. That was the final straw. The general manager ordered the contractors to tear the offices apart until they solved the problem. When the contractors opened up the floors, they found scores of discarded water and soda bottles filled with human ordure—parting gifts from the laborers, who had not been given access to toilets while they were working on the building.

On a more favorable note, the UPC undertook one initiative early in 2010 that had an immediate and positive impact on the quality of life of a number of the agency's own staff, as well as on other Abu Dhabi residents. Since the UPC's inception, its staff had fielded a soccer team in the intramural tournament, held every year during the cooler season, which pitted them against squads from the various developers and other agencies. Early in 2010 the UPC's practice field was gobbled up by yet another development, which the Development Review Department had approved under duress.

This did not sit well with the members of the soccer team who worked for Special Projects, which was one of the UPC's support sections. Its half-dozen staffers were all Emiratis or other Arabs, some of whom had been with the Abu Dhabi Municipality for decades prior to joining the UPC and thus retained unparalleled connections among the city's various bureaucracies. The Special Projects staff occupied their own corner of the eighth floor; among other abstruse functions, they were responsible for handling all of the agency's property transactions. Upon losing their soccer field, the property wizards in Special Projects made some calls and got their hands on the affection plan for a sizable parking lot less than a block from our new offices. Within a fortnight the UPC had contractors tear up the asphalt, lay down sod, and construct a full-sized soccer pitch complete with stadium lights and a locker room. Working for the autocrats did have its advantages.

In addition to making the new field available for the soccer tournament, the UPC offered it to several nearby international schools for their various sports teams to use. The schools, which had previously had to make do with makeshift facilities, were immensely grateful. Seeing an opportunity, the Canadians of the UPC's Vancouver Mafia began holding weekly games of Ultimate, the football-like flying disc sport, which were open to all. I was thrilled at the prospect of outdoor activity and immediately joined in, even though, with my skill level, it would have been more appropriate to say I was playing Penultimate. I had a particular problem with accidental full contact; rare was the game I didn't knock someone to the ground. I chalked it up to unrelieved aggression from driving in Abu Dhabi's traffic.

Unexpectedly, the Ultimate games became a cross-cultural exhibition. The Vancouver Mafia was consistently out in force, as were other expats like Elise and Alex. We were all pleasantly surprised, however, when some of our Emirati colleagues began showing up to play. Some of them had never before thrown a disc. One of the most dedicated was Omar, a young Emirati who was a distant relation of the crown prince. Omar drove a gull-winged supercar that cost a half-million dirhams, yet he was one of the UPC's most down-to-earth Emiratis—and also one of the hardest working, often coming to the office on weekends. He displayed the same level of effort during the Ultimate games, diving for catches and hustling tirelessly up and down the field. When his team scored, someone would usually have to stop him and remind him that it was the other team's duty to run to the far side of the field.

My colleague Khalid from the transport team began playing as well. The Ultimate games were the only occasions when I saw him out of costume. The first time he showed up, I didn't recognize him. "Umkak, what we got?" he said, walking onto the field in shorts and a jersey.

"Hey, Khalid, you came!" I said. "Have you played before?"

"No, but my wife told me I need to do something," he replied with a wink. "Too much food, not enough run." I hadn't meant to say anything, but he did look rather doughy without the camouflage of his kandora, as did most of the other Emiratis.

The one exception was Saeed, a young architect from the Planning Policy department, who was thin as a rail. Although he had supposedly never played before, he took to Ultimate like a natural, snagging impossible catches as though his hands were covered in glue. We began to call him Falcon Claw.

After one particularly exhausting game, everyone limped out to their cars. Parked just outside the gate was a hulking H2 Hummer, painted an incongruous baby blue. "Who drives *that?*" Elise said, gawking.

Saeed pressed a button on his keychain and the Hummer's alarm chirped. Everyone looked at him in astonishment. He hopped up into the cab, his sparrow frame dwarfed by the cavernous interior. "Estidama, huh?" he said, pressing the ignition. The engine rumbled and he grinned like a thief. "Sustainability, my arse!"

* * *

My new housemates and I hired a platoon of Bangladeshi movers to manhandle our belongings and the surfeit of furniture that Austin ordered into the Golf Gardens townhouse. My own contribution to the household inventory was rather paltry, as the movers discovered that they couldn't get my furniture out of my old studio thanks to the cinderblock wall outside. I considered thanking the villa's slumlord owner by setting my bed on fire, but thought better of it.

On the morning we were to move in to the townhouse, we retrieved the keys from the agent and walked through the front door. "Oooh, pretty," Austin said, glancing up at the light shimmering on the ceiling.

"Wait ... we don't have a pool," Rhys remarked. We looked out the windows and saw that the fresh sod in the backyard was two feet underwater. We made a frantic call to the Golf Gardens maintenance company. They sent a pair of plumbers who discovered that our connection to the water main had burst. The pipes running into our water tank, which sat in a cement basin beneath a trap door in the backyard, had evidently not been stress-tested properly and had warped in the rising spring heat. The plumbers drained our yard and disappeared down into the water tank to work their voodoo. We would see them often in the coming year.

Austin claimed the upstairs master bedroom, which he labeled the Princess Suite, on the grounds that he needed the extra closet space for all his clothes. Rhys jibed that running out of closets was the last thing Austin needed to worry about. Later, while we were unpacking, I came upon Rhys lining the upstairs bar from end to end with assorted liquors. He looked at me with a bottle in each hand and said, "You do realize that living here is going to turn you into a borderline alcoholic?"

Once we'd finished settling in, we sat in the living room on the overstuffed leather couches and discussed what we should name the place.

AUSTIN: "It has to be catchy. Qasr al-something." *Qasr* is Arabic for castle.
ME: "How about Qasr al-Chrysler?"
(blank looks from the other two)
ME: "You know, because all three of us have Jeeps."
AUSTIN: "Um, no."
RHYS: "What's the Arabic word for alcohol?"

AUSTIN: "Al kuhul."
RHYS: "Yes, alcohol."
AUSTIN: "Exactly."
RHYS: "What?"
ME: "No, he's on second."
AUSTIN: "Never mind. I've got it! Qasr al Deviance."
ME: "That's not Arabic."
RHYS: "Deviance as in behavior, or Deviants as in people?"
AUSTIN: "All of the above."

The name stuck.

Austin hired the Sri Lankan maid who lived with the family next door to clean our place twice a week. At first the thought of domestic help made me feel like a snob, but after coming home one afternoon to find the dishes washed, the trash taken out, the floors mopped, the bathroom sparkling, and my bed neatly made, I was sold. I began to see why many Western expats loved Abu Dhabi's supply of inexpensive servants. Despite my initial reservations, the lifestyle of a modern colonial lord was starting to look good.

Until now, my eremitic living situation had kept me isolated from the more sordid exploits of Abu Dhabi's expatriates. Qasr al Deviance would change that. True to its name, the house would expand my horizons to encompass the full measure of the emirate's expat scene, a let-them-eat-cake variety of decadence not seen since the Roaring Twenties or perhaps the court of the Sun King himself—a lifestyle of lavish dinners at high-end restaurants with bills in the thousands of dirhams, weekend champagne brunches that would put the Romans to shame, spur-of-the-moment vacations to exotic locales all across the Eastern Hemisphere, freewheeling expenditure on everything from take-out dining to plush weekends in Dubai, and underpinning it all, unabashed reliance on Abu Dhabi's army of cheap brown labor to handle the exertion and tie up the loose ends.

Austin threw a housewarming party that was attended by nearly all of the UPC's expats, along with a good number of the rest of the city's Westerners. The evening degenerated into a riotous haze. At one point I walked into the kitchen to see a female colleague lay Rhys flat with a rugby tackle, drawing a cheer from the crowd. I turned around and bumped into the Professor, who was deep into his cups. "Hmm, Michael," he said in his most scholarly voice, "it appears I've spilled my lager on your trousers." I retired to my room around three o'clock while the festivities were still going strong.

In the morning I emerged and was greeted by devastation. Broken glass, cigarette butts, stray shoes, and other debris littered the sticky floor. The kitchen looked like the aftermath of a food fight. For some reason the DJ had fled without taking his turntables. Grace, Austin's senile shorthair cat, sat on her haunches in the middle of the rubble, looking bewildered.

Around noon Austin caromed down the stairs. He picked up a plate of cold quesadillas, mixed himself a rum and coke, and sat on the couch eating this breakfast of champions while surveying the wreckage.

"This is going to take us a while to clean up," I said.

Austin looked at me in mock indignation. "*Clean?* For *ourselves?* Have you forgotten where we are?" He drank another gulp. "I've got a cleaning crew that will go floor to ceiling for three hundred dirhams. I used them at my last apartment every month." It appeared we had a busy social calendar in store.

"How late did you all stay up?" I asked.

He shrugged. "Most people were gone by five, I think. The rest of us snuck over to the clubhouse for a sunrise swim. The Professor went in his drawers." Austin's head tilted back in his trademark Muppet laugh. "I hope I never see *that* again."

Rhys emerged from his bedroom looking like a zombie. "Right, I just thought of a joke. A Texan, a Welshman, and a Detroiter move to the desert..."

Thirteen

Only Sheikh!

The Ruler should not have any barrier which separates him from his people.—
Sheikh Zayed bin Sultan al Nahyan

As the warm spring months once more began their muggy descent into Abu Dhabi's boiling summer, I tried to squeeze in as much time outdoors as I could while the weather was still moderate. Some days I would take long post-lunch walks through the superblock around Mamoura, which was filled with buildings in various stages of completion. In stark contrast to Mamoura's restrained elegance, these buildings were incarnations of Abu Dhabi's worst architectural trends: boxy frames covered in aluminum panels and low-grade reflecting glass designed to be erected as quickly and cheaply as possible in order to start generating rents. The twin cubes of Mamoura looked like blocks of exquisite ivory set among chunks of battered tin.

On other days I would wait for the afternoon traffic to subside before leaving the office and taking long, circuitous drives home, infusing my lungs with fresh air before the inevitable return to climate-controlled sequestration. On one such occasion I took the E10 highway past the exit for Golf Gardens and continued in the direction of Dubai. I wanted to take a spin on the new Saadiyat Highway, which had opened the previous November and had cut nearly a half-hour off the trip between the north end of Abu Dhabi Island and Dubai by bypassing the island's congestion. I had driven out to see the highway once or twice during the later stages of its construction but hadn't been on it since it had opened to the public. Since the highway was the first of many such transport links that would be added to Abu Dhabi's infrastructure over the coming years, I wanted to see how it had turned out.

Driving out of town was like watching a time-lapse video of urban development in reverse. I started among the steel and glass towers at the center of the city, traversed the low-density residential neighborhoods on the southern half of the island, passed the cranes of the Raha Beach construction site, and finally emerged into the desert with Yas Island on the left and the runways of the airport on the right. I reached the whirlpool interchange that marked the start of the Saadiyat Highway, looped up the ramp, and crossed over the narrow channel to Yas. As I traversed the island I could see the superstructure of Ferrari World and the grandstand tents of the Formula One track through the dust. The traffic—mostly dump trucks—gradually thinned until mine was one of the few vehicles on the road.

The highway followed the long stingray tail of Yas and continued onto the sandy spits of the outlying islands. Vivid swatches of green and turquoise in the form of mangrove copses and tidal lagoons opened up on either side. Once again I felt the same sense of relief I had first experienced while kayaking the mangroves, the pressure cooker of the city's noise and dust and heat slowly fading away. Just short of Saadiyat Island the road climbed a low rise, offering a panoramic view of the barrier islands fronting the Gulf. As I slowed to take in the view, I noticed an unmarked ramp splitting off from the highway and leading down the side

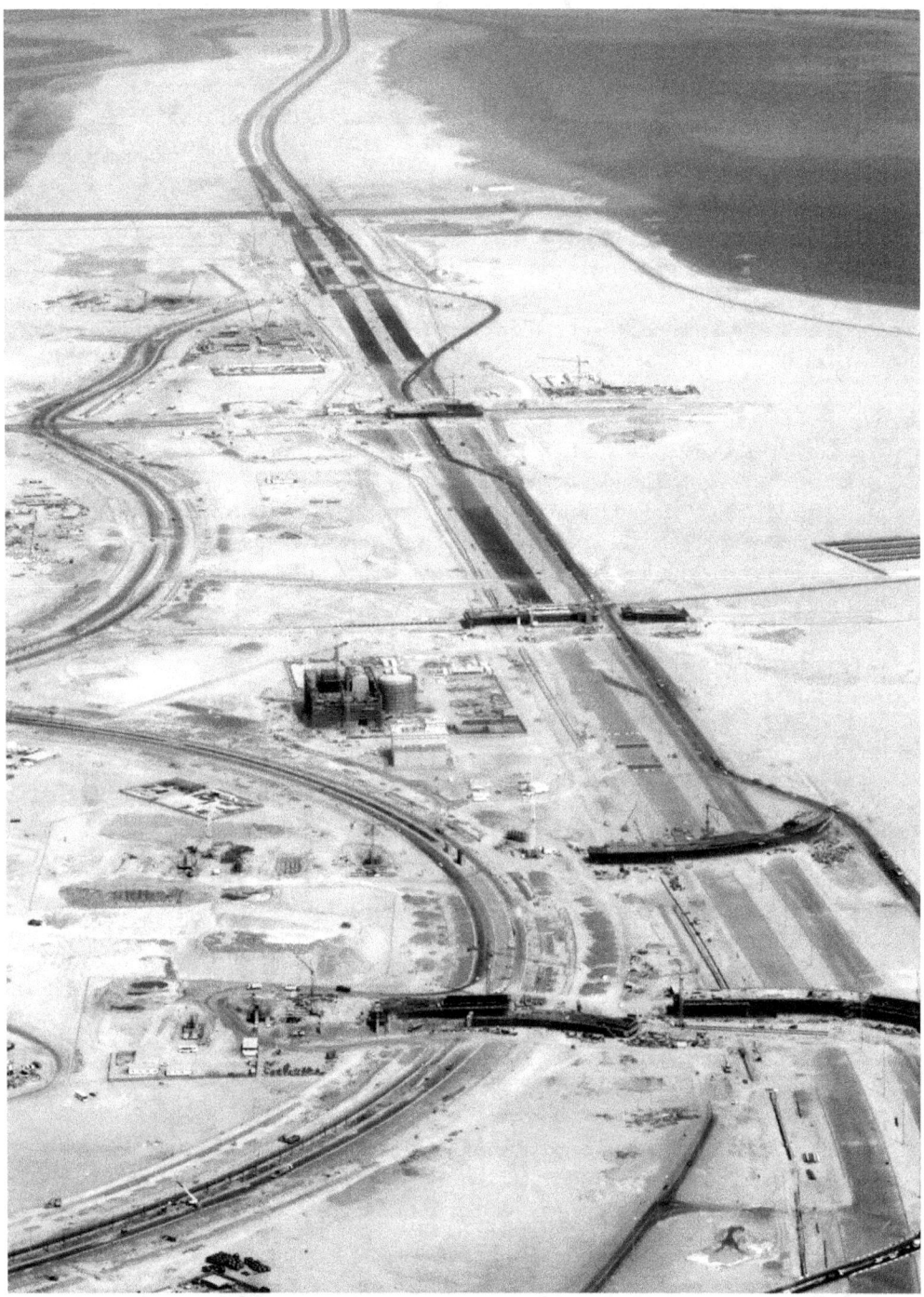

Construction on the Saadiyat Highway, circa September 2009.

of the rise. I turned and followed it to the island's edge, where the pavement ended. A track continued out onto a dirt causeway that disappeared into the mangroves beyond. Curious, I shifted into low gear and continued on.

The causeway cut a twisting course through the mangroves, occasionally making almost ninety-degree turns. Although it looked to have been built to handle vehicles, the dirt was unevenly packed, and in several places I nearly slid down the embankment. After just a few minutes of winding through the mangroves I was thoroughly disoriented. I pressed on until I reached a spot where the causeway widened into a small turnaround, where I pulled over and shut off the engine.

The serenity was profound. The mangroves opened in front of me to reveal an inlet of glistening aquamarine. I could hear nothing but the contented chirping of birds and the burbling of the rising tide as it slowly immersed the mangroves' roots. A gentle breeze wafted through the windows, carrying the pungent aroma of salt and undergrowth. As the air scrubbed my lungs, I realized that I couldn't recall the last time I'd smelled something natural in Abu Dhabi. The city's sensory deprivation was so complete that it escaped notice until something shocked my aesthesis back to life. I could have sat there for hours, letting the birds and the scenery and the smell heal my soul.

A car horn's angry blast startled me from my reverie. I looked up to see a menacing black Chevy Suburban that had materialized out of nowhere. A Goliath of an Emirati emerged, clad in shorts and a Hawaiian shirt instead of the normal kandora. I thought I saw a pistol tucked underneath his arm. His biceps were thicker than my thighs. As he strode up to my window, it occurred to me that perhaps I was out of bounds.

"You. Why you here?" Goliath demanded.

I fumbled for an excuse. "Sorry, I'm just on a site visit. I'm with the Urban Planning Council. *Majlis*..." I racked my brain for the UPC's Arabic name.

"*Majlis*?" He was intrigued.

"*Majlis al-Takhteet al-Amrani*." I handed him my UPC identification card. "Urban Planning Council." I grinned like a fool.

He studied the card, frowned, and leaned in the window, presumably to strangle me. Instead, he wagged a cigar-sized finger in my face. "No *majlis*. Only sheikh!" He pointed in the direction I had come. "You go!"

Not needing to be told twice, I stammered an apology and fumbled with the ignition. As I drove off, Goliath got in his Suburban and followed me back to the road.

Several months later the highway was renamed Sheikh Khalifa bin Zayed Street, in honor of the current president. The next time I drove along the highway, I saw barbed wire framing the ramp to the mangroves and a profusion of signs promising doom for trespassers. The sheikh whose sanctuary I had stumbled upon apparently didn't want to share. The plebeians would have to get their nature fix somewhere else.

* * *

The sheikhs at the helm of modern Abu Dhabi are an inscrutable cabal. They are everywhere and nowhere, controlling the organs of the state and owning huge chunks of real estate and the economy, yet remaining largely hidden from the public eye. Even the extent of their ranks is uncertain. The honorific title of "sheikh" typically refers to one of Zayed's sons, but it also applies to their sons, to other males in the extended royal family, and sometimes to senior members of prominent Emirati clans. The sheikhs are a conspiracy theorist's dream, a real-life secret society that calls the shots and pulls the levers from within Abu Dhabi's shadows. The Emiratis seem to have no problem recognizing their sheikhs, at least the more prominent ones, but to foreigners the identity and role of most of the sheikhs remain obscure. The emirate's self-censoring press offers few insights into their hidden world.

Sheikh Zayed is the great exception to this blanket of secrecy. Zayed cultivated an image as an accessible man of the people throughout his career. When Thesiger first met him in 1948, a full decade and a half before Zayed took over from his brother Shakhbut, the Englishman observed that Zayed already enjoyed a great reputation among the Bedu: "They liked him for his easy informal ways and his friendliness, and they respected his force of character, his shrewdness, and his physical strength."[1] In 1952 Zayed turned down a $42 million bribe from the Saudis to relinquish Abu Dhabi's claim on the Al Ain and Buraimi oases, which he administered, a staggering amount considering that his income at the time amounted to just a few thousand dollars a year.[2] This act earned Zayed enduring respect as a man of integrity as well as a place in the *Guinness Book of World Records* for the largest bribe ever declined.

Even as Zayed ascended from his position as junior sheikh of a marginal backwater to the undisputed ruler of one of the world's richest nations, he never lost his verve. He didn't grow fat or flaunt his personal wealth, unlike other newly wealthy Gulf monarchs. Photographs from his frequent public appearances often show him in his trademark pose, one hand waving to the adoring public, flashing aviator sunglasses and a billion-dollar grin. Details of his personal life were scarce and always flattering, painting a picture of him as a charismatic, humble, and frugal leader.

Now, nearly a decade after his death, Zayed is more popular than ever. His cult of personality has outlived him, attaining almost mythic proportions. Zayed's ubiquitous visage keeps watch over Abu Dhabi from vantage points ranging from three-story billboards to grainy photos on the walls of flyblown diners. Every government office displays his portrait, and no official report begins without a preface invoking his legacy as the father of the nation. The emirate's handful of bookstores dedicate entire shelves to hagiographies of the sheikh.

Abu Dhabi's residents look back on the Zayed years as a simpler, quieter time. Like all nostalgia, this requires remembering the positives and forgetting the negatives to a certain degree. Still, it is telling that even expats have fond memories of Zayed. An Australian friend who had worked in Abu Dhabi for more than a decade once told me, "I miss Sheikh Zayed. When he was here, Abu Dhabi was more than just money."

In contrast to Zayed's fame, his sons are essentially ciphers. Little is widely known about them besides their names. Most of them live in palaces clustered in a restricted area near the island's southwest corner and rarely appear in public. The average Abu Dhabi resident comes closest to seeing a sheikh when one flies overhead in his helicopter. Throughout my time in Abu Dhabi, anything I discovered about the sheikhs came from running afoul of one of their interests, whether it was accidentally traipsing on their land or leveling too many demands on one of their projects.

I complained about this to Latif, the security consultant, echoing Alex's introductory remark about the need for a Who's Who chart for the sheikhs. "It would be nice just to know which sheikh owns what," I said.

Latif got up, closed the door to his office, and locked it. He went over to the safe beside his desk, dialed the combination, and withdrew a tall roll of paper. "You never saw this," he said as he unfurled the scroll. It spilled across his desk and onto the floor.

The paper depicted an annotated family tree of Abu Dhabi's royal Al Nahyan clan that stretched back six generations. Below each family member's name was a biography that included marriages, government positions, commercial holdings, and even personality traits. Latif explained that the chart came from a former foreign intelligence agent who had spent most of his career in the Gulf and now made a hobby of keeping tabs on the region's royal houses. "I have no idea how he gets his stuff," Latif said. "Gulf Arabs are so cliquish, they make the Chinese look like gossips." I certainly shared his perspective; despite my attempts to get to know my Emirati colleagues and their culture, they remained puzzling and often aloof. Thesiger, however, would have not been surprised to hear that some Emiratis were

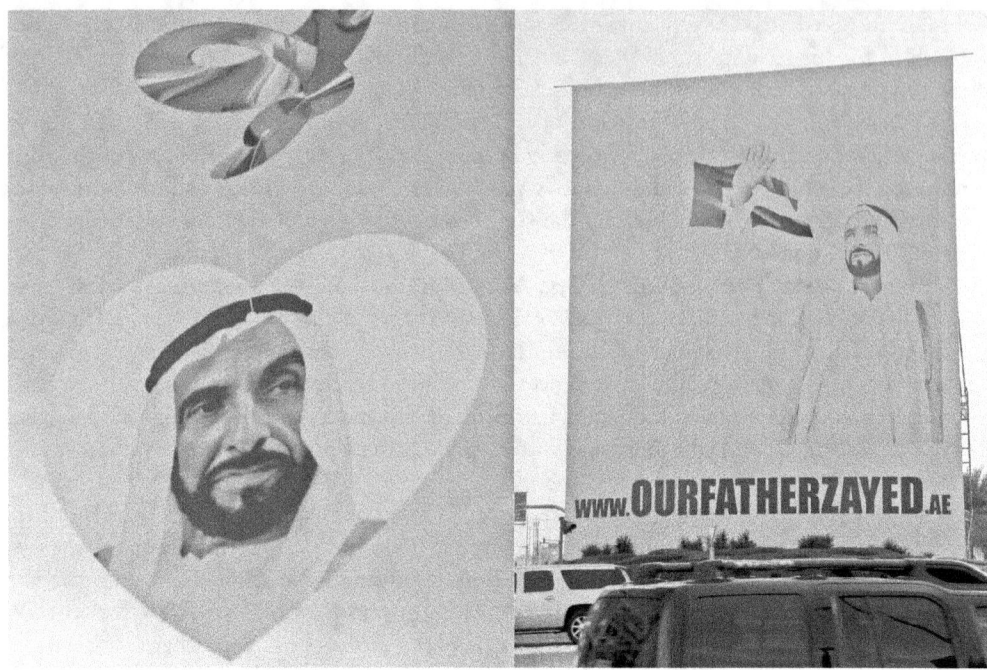

The memory of Sheikh Zayed still watches over his city from vantage points both great and small.

willing to spill the beans on their leaders: "I had learnt that the most effective way to spread a story was to tell it to one or two Arabs under a pledge of secrecy."[3]

I spent a long time poring over the chart. That document alone seemed to contain more information on the behind-the-scenes politics of Abu Dhabi's power brokers than all of the books and articles ever written about the emirate.[4] I concentrated on the dynamics between Zayed's sons, which were far more complex than one might imagine. Although the state presents itself as a monolithic entity without internal dissent or debate, Abu Dhabi has no shortage of political theatre; it simply takes place behind closed doors.

Zayed had a total of nine acknowledged wives over the course of his lifetime, and likely several others that foreign observers missed. He rarely stayed married to more than three women at a time, preferring to keep an open slot within the four wives permitted by Islam. When Zayed divorced one of his wives, he ensured that she continued to enjoy a privileged lifestyle and substantial financial support. Among his wives Zayed fathered a total of nineteen sons and something like a dozen daughters.

Zayed's eldest son, Khalifa, is the most powerful of the brood. Khalifa was born in 1948, the only son of Zayed's first wife, Hassa. Three years after Zayed became ruler of Abu Dhabi in 1966, he appointed Khalifa as his crown prince, the first in line to succeed him. In his role as president of the young federation, Zayed found himself frequently preoccupied with international affairs. Much of the day-to-day administration of Abu Dhabi thus fell to Khalifa, and by all accounts he took his duties seriously. In the early 1980s Khalifa became chairman of Abu Dhabi's Supreme Petroleum Council, which placed Abu Dhabi's (and by extension the UAE's) oil policy under his control.

Khalifa also chaired the Department for Buildings and Social Affairs, the all-important agency that doled out land and loans to locals. Khalifa sweetened his father's already lucrative land policy; under his leadership, not only did the department hand out plots and money, but it also offered to design, construct, and lease residential and commercial buildings on behalf of Emirati owners. The department charged a negligible loan rate of 0.5 percent per annum, with no set time limits or penalties for repayment. In return, the owners received half of the rents for the first ten to fifteen years, after which they were given back their properties. Khalifa's deal made real estate, the classic passive investment class, even more foolproof for Abu Dhabians. It also made Khalifa the main dispenser of handouts, even though Zayed retained credit for originating the system. The department became known colloquially as the Khalifa Committee, and the rents it amassed from properties across the city bolstered Khalifa's already considerable wealth.

Khalifa was quickly proclaimed ruler of Abu Dhabi upon Zayed's death in November 2004. Within a few days the rulers of the other emirates dutifully elected him president of the UAE in his father's place as well. Although Khalifa proved to be an effective ruler, he reportedly possessed little of his father's charm and personality. Foreign diplomats labeled him distant and uncharismatic.[5] He was also dogged by persistent rumors of poor health stemming from an inactive lifestyle. Early in his rule Khalifa retreated to the sphere of federal and international affairs, although he retained nominal control of Abu Dhabi's central institutions. He also sponsored some of the largest real estate projects in the first wave of post-Zayed development, including the colossal Landmark Tower at the midpoint of the Corniche. But aside from his ever-present portraits and the weekly newspaper photos of him entertaining various notables, Khalifa was rarely seen.

Zayed's second wife, Sheikha, also bore him a single son, Sultan, in 1953. In his younger years Sultan was seen as a rising star; Zayed appointed him commander of the UAE's armed forces when he was just twenty-three. Sultan had an affable personality and shunned commercial interests, earning him the respect of many tribal elders and the affection of the people at large. In 1982, however, Zayed abruptly stripped Sultan of his titles and sent him abroad. Some speculated that drug problems precipitated the demotion, while others thought Sultan may have made an ill-advised attempt to depose his father.

Upon returning several years later, Sultan avoided the public eye and focused his attention on cultural affairs and the preservation of Emirati heritage. In contrast to the rest of his brothers, Sultan was renowned for his frugal lifestyle and eschewed property development even after the post-Zayed boom took off. Sultan's humility, personal appeal, and stewardship of local traditions and culture earned him positive marks among his countrymen; my Emirati colleagues always referred to him with emotional reverence. After ascending to the presidency in 2004, Khalifa began quietly restoring some of Sultan's lost political influence, perhaps seeing his half-brother as a bulwark against their ambitious younger siblings.

The rest of Zayed's progeny was split among blocs of full brothers by various other mothers. The largest and most important of these blocs was known as the *Bani Fatima*, the six sons of Zayed's fifth and favorite wife, Fatima, who is still known publicly as the UAE's First Lady. The eldest of the Bani Fatima was Zayed's third son, Mohammed, born in 1961. He became the darling of the family after Sultan's fall from grace, taking over his brother's role as commander of the armed forces. Mohammed graduated from the Royal Military Academy at Sandhurst and was widely seen as the most intelligent and capable of Zayed's sons. He bore the closest physical resemblance of any of the brothers to their father, and he also inherited much of Zayed's charisma. In 2003 the ailing Zayed appointed Mohammed to the entirely new position of Deputy crown prince, breaking with custom to ensure that the talented Mohammed would be next in line to succeed Khalifa instead of one of Khalifa's sons. The reshuffling also meant Mohammed would become Deputy Ruler of Abu Dhabi upon Khalifa's accession to the throne. Whether or not Zayed anticipated that Khalifa would have difficulty following in his footsteps, the venerable sheikh's last significant act was to ensure that Mohammed would effectively run the show in Abu Dhabi. If there was any consternation from Khalifa or other members of the royal family, it was not made public.

Mohammed moved up to the position of crown prince upon Zayed's death and wasted little time consolidating his position. He took up the chairmanships of both the Abu Dhabi Executive Council and Mubadala, the state-owned conglomerate formed in 2002 to make strategic diversifying investments for Abu Dhabi's economy. Mohammed distributed powerful positions among his Bani Fatima brothers. The next eldest, Hamdan, became minister of Foreign Affairs; Hazza took over the internal security and intelligence services; Tahnoun was sent to assist Khalifa as the chairman of the presidential office; Mansour took over the International Petroleum Investments Company (IPIC), the emirate's second-largest sovereign wealth fund; and the youngest, Abdullah, became minister of Information and Culture. Between them the Bani Fatima controlled much of Abu Dhabi's political and economic apparatus. They also maintained substantial commercial interests, such as the Royal Group real estate company. Under Mohammed's leadership as crown prince, this group was the driving force behind the new vision for Abu Dhabi's future.

The crown prince was widely respected not only for his verve, but also for his perceived willingness to put Abu Dhabi's interests above his own. Some even speculated that Zayed had elevated Mohammed to his leadership position because he was the son least likely to use the emirate's holdings as his personal bank account.[6] To be certain, the crown prince was no pauper; he maintained his fair share of commercial interests along with his Bani Fatima brothers. However, he sought to make a name for himself through sound vision and leadership, not his net worth.

The bloc of five sons born to Zayed's sixth wife, Mouza, was less powerful than the Bani Fatima, but it was still a force to be reckoned with. In the month before he died, Zayed appointed the eldest, Saif, to the influential post of minister of Interior, perhaps as a last-minute balancing act vis-à-vis Mohammed and his brothers. Saif's younger brother Ahmed helmed the Abu Dhabi Investment Authority (ADIA), the largest of the sovereign wealth funds that invested Abu Dhabi's oil proceeds, whose assets were pegged at between $800 billion and $1.2 trillion. Although Ahmed's 2010 death in a glider accident in Morocco at the age of 41 was expected to unleash a power struggle among the various fraternal factions over control of ADIA, this never materialized, at least not openly.[7] Hamed, the middle of Mouza's sons, chaired the state-owned airline Etihad.

The remaining sons of Zayed were politically more peripheral, the only public knowledge about them coming from their involvement with various personal businesses and local sports teams. For example, Saeed, the eldest of the four sons of Zayed's wife Ayesha, chaired Abu Dhabi's hometown (Al Wahda) soccer club. In addition to the loss of Ahmed, Zayed's sons had been reduced to seventeen after their brother Nasser's helicopter crashed into the Gulf in 2008.

Once I had finished with the chart and Latif had returned it to its safe, he explained that part of the reason for the sheikhs' nebulous public images was that they spent considerable time abroad, tending to matters of state, business interests, properties, and whatever else billionaires occupy their time with. Sometimes they just needed to get away. Khalifa, for example, was in the process of building a vacation home (more fittingly described as a palace) in the Seychelles.[8]

"And then there's houbara hunting," Latif said, "the sheikhs' favorite pastime." Houbara hunting is a tradition stretching back centuries.[9] Thesiger had noted the Bedu's unique relationship with the ungainly birds: "Hubara [sic] are MacQueen's bustard, a bird the size of a hen turkey; they arrive in Arabia from Persia, Iraq, and Syria at the beginning of the winter and most of them leave in the spring."[10] Zayed himself had once invited Thesiger to join him on a houbara hunt in the dunes near Liwa. The Englishman wrote a stirring description of how Zayed and his retainers deftly employed their pet falcons to flush the bustards from their nests and exhaust them in mid-air combat. Houbara were not easy prey; even when forced to the ground they could outrun the Bedu's *saluki* hunting dogs.

Nowadays, with the help of SUVs and automatic rifles, Gulf Arabs have pushed the houbara to the brink of extinction on the peninsula. Arabs with means, Latif explained, had simply switched to Asian hunting grounds. "They used to go to Afghanistan all the time before 2001," he said, "but now it's mostly the other Stans."

"Why Afghanistan?" I asked.

"The UAE was one of exactly three countries that had diplomatic relations with the Taliban. Not the brightest chapter in Emirati foreign affairs. The sheikhs gave the Taliban tons of money, and the Taliban let them use Afghanistan as their game ranch. They even let the Arabs build an airstrip in the south just for the use of their hunting parties."

Back in the late nineties, according to Latif, a party of Abu Dhabi's sheikhs was hunting in Afghanistan when one of their staff passed word to the CIA that Osama bin Laden was making regular visits to the camp. It was the first time the American intelligence services had obtained a fix on bin Laden's position since Al Qaeda had bombed two U.S. embassies in East Africa more than a year before. The Americans cued up a cruise missile strike that was guaranteed to obliterate the camp and everyone in it, but President Clinton's antiterrorism czar called it off at the last second. They couldn't be sure bin Laden was really in the camp, he argued, and the collateral deaths of Abu Dhabi royals could fracture relations with the UAE, a key Middle Eastern ally. The missiles never flew and bin Laden slipped away.[11]

I interrupted Latif. "How do you know all this?"

Latif smiled and continued. "A few years later, that same antiterrorism czar left the White House and started his own consultancy. The firm opened an Abu Dhabi office and just happened to receive a lucrative monopoly on all of the security work in the emirate." I realized with a start that Latif was talking about his own employer, and the pieces fell into place. "Anyway, normally the Crown Prince tends to ignore his brothers' mischief," Latif said, "but I heard he chewed them out over the bin Laden episode."

Such stories would of course never be made public in hypersensitive Abu Dhabi. Yet there was one area in which the sheikhs' activities could not be veiled: land. The sheikhs owned huge swathes of the metropolitan area, including many of the islands around Abu Dhabi. In the UPC's early days, when Larry and his Vancouver Mafia were developing *Plan 2030*, the greatest challenge had been apportioning Abu Dhabi's growth evenly among the sheikhs. For the most part, each sheikh wanted to fill his lands to the brim with new projects, but there was only so much potential growth to spread around. Even if Abu Dhabi reached its ambitious target of three million residents by 2030, that wouldn't justify a small city's worth of real estate on every sheikh's island.

Larry and the UPC tried to strike a balance by allocating much of *Plan 2030*'s antici-pated growth among the islands controlled by Abu Dhabi's quasi-public development com-panies: Reem Island belonged to Sorouh, Yas belonged to Aldar, Saadiyat to TDIC, and Suwwah to Mubadala. The plan also directed a large amount of growth towards mainland locations like North Wathba, which were owned by the government. Although the distri-bution was bound to make some of the sheikhs unhappy, Larry and the UPC relied on the crown prince, their patron, to convince his brothers to buy in.

The sheikhs' reactions varied widely. Khalifa made it clear that as president he would develop what he wanted, where he wanted. He excluded the north half of his Hudayriat Island from any oversight, obligating the UPC to show the island as a void in *Plan 2030*. Sultan made a similar move with his own island of Umm Sammalia, but for the opposite reason. He designated it a nature preserve that would remain free of development, a rare example of temperance among the sheikhs. Some of the other brothers were rumored to chafe under *Plan 2030*'s constraints, but by and large the crown prince seemed to have given them enough to satisfy their aspirations and avoid any conflicts. Over time, though, the sheikhs and their development companies began to test the waters by proposing projects that deviated from *Plan 2030* or by simply starting to build them without the UPC's knowledge or consent. But as the emirate's leaders would discover, pushing the boundaries of *Plan 2030* was one thing; toying with the laws of supply and demand was another matter entirely.

* * *

Shortly after the UPC moved to Mamoura B, a café-restaurant by the name of Jones the Grocer opened in the ground floor of the building. Jones was an Australian chain that reportedly enjoyed a cult following in its home turf. The Mamoura franchise, the chain's first in Abu Dhabi, became an establishment among the city's upper classes almost overnight. The presence of Jones raised the number of decent coffee houses in Abu Dhabi to exactly one, which accounted for its popularity among expats and Emiratis alike, all desperate to escape the burnt swill served everywhere else in the city. The place was packed to overflowing at lunch and only slightly less busy the rest of the day. Its prices were outrageous, but it was hard to fault the Australians for gouging; they knew a captive market when they saw one.

Prior to a morning meeting next door in Mamoura A, I went down to Jones with Keith and Shamma, the young Emirati woman from his Development Review team. We took seats at one of the few empty tables near the back of the café. Keith was dressed smartly, as usual, in pinstripes and fancy court-jester shoes. Even in one of my better suits, I looked like a pauper in comparison. Yet both of us might as well have been invisible sitting next to Shamma. She was one of the most attractive young women at the UPC, and she knew it. She perpetually allowed her *abayya* to spill open to reveal the form-fitting designer outfits she wore underneath. As we entered the café she drew glances from more than a few male customers, as well as decidedly colder looks from other Emirati women.

We sat unnoticed for several minutes until Keith flagged down one of the waitstaff to take our orders. Jones may have been new on the scene, but it had rapidly achieved Abu Dhabi's characteristically awful level of service. Our coffees took an additional fifteen minutes to arrive.

As she took a sip, Shamma glanced towards the front door. She nearly spat her coffee in my face and grabbed Keith's arm, making me blanch at the violation of the no-touch protocol. "*Look!*" she said, her voice wavering.

Keith and I turned to see a quartet of Emirati men walk into the café. Although one of them was a few inches taller than the others, they looked like ordinary Emiratis, walking with the measured pace of people not troubled by time.

"Do you know one of those guys?" Keith asked.

Shamma didn't hear him. She followed the men as if in a trance, not bothering to conceal her stare. "It's him," she said, almost whispering.

"Who?" I asked.

Shamma whirled to face us, her eyes wild with excitement. "*The Crown Prince!*"

Though I had seen the crown prince at Cityscape, I had been too far away to discern his features. I looked again and finally noticed the resemblance between the tall Emirati and the royal visage I had seen on so many office walls. Sheikh Mohammed looked older and more relaxed than his stern official portrait, in which he is almost sneering. Other patrons recognized him too, and excited whispers rippled through the café. The waitstaff, on the other hand, acknowledged the crown prince's presence but remained surprisingly nonchalant; clearly this wasn't his first time in the café. As his small entourage sat at a table near the entrance, the crown prince greeted several of the waitstaff, shaking hands and chatting with them. I noticed that the staff in question were all Filipinos and Africans, ethnicities that Emiratis typically treat like chattel. Yet here was the crown prince himself, making a point of addressing them like actual human beings.

The sheikh rejoined his companions and the rest of the café made a pitiful attempt to act normal. I looked out the front windows, expecting to see a phalanx of security stationed outside, but there was just a single Emirati with an earpiece standing unobtrusively near the door.

Keith freed his arm from Shamma's grasp and said, "Why don't you go over and introduce yourself?"

She glared at him. "No way."

"Come on, ask for his autograph. Maybe he has a nephew you could marry."

Shamma turned bright crimson. "Keith, stop!" she hissed, but she couldn't hide her flustered smile. She looked like a middle schooler at a boy band concert, wanting to scream at the top of her lungs.

Her reaction was understandable. Sheikh Mohammed was the closest thing Abu Dhabi had to a local celebrity. He led by example, circulating tirelessly among the agencies that did his bidding. Mohammed was not averse to appearing in public, although he was far from a common sight. The crown prince was even rumored to keep tabs on his changing skyline by driving himself around Abu Dhabi in an unmarked car, accompanied only by a submachine gun on the passenger seat and the unshakeable knowledge that this was *his* city. He was Abu Dhabi's living incarnation of power, money, and fame, all rolled into one person. Shamma's star-struck behavior was entirely within reason. I would have been at an equal loss for words had I walked into a Starbucks back in the States and seen President Obama, Warren Buffet, and George Clooney sipping mochas at a table.

Keith looked at his watch. "I hate to interrupt, but we're late for our meeting." We paid our bill and made our way towards the door, passing right by the crown prince's table. Shamma studied the floor in front of her, sneaking sidelong glances in the sheikh's direction. The crown prince looked up and smiled warmly at her as we passed, causing Shamma to nearly trip over her own feet.

As soon as we stepped outside, a sudden compulsion possessed me. "Hang on, I'll be right back," I said, and ducked back through the door. I emerged again after a few minutes to quizzical looks from both my colleagues.

"You didn't seriously get his autograph, did you?" Shamma asked.

"No."

"Did you get a picture with him?"

"Something slightly more memorable."

She was nearly beside herself. "Like what?!"

I fixed her with a level gaze. "If you were to ask the Crown Prince what kind of coffee he prefers, what do you think he would say?"

Keith laughed and Shamma squealed, "Tell me!"

I merely grinned.

* * *

Qasr al Deviance Journal: Week 7

I awaken to the early morning light pouring through the windows and total silence in the house. This is odd; our air conditioning and plumbing systems are normally as noisy as a junkyard. On my way downstairs I flip various light switches and confirm my suspicions: the power is out. The tap in the kitchen issues a thin dribble, indicating that the water pump has also gone.

Rhys hears me fumbling around and emerges from his room. "Towels men gout Vince Magurdy," he mumbles. His Welshness is even more cryptic than normal in the morning.

"What?"

"Power's been out since four-thirty," he enunciates. "I know this because I've been awake since then, lying in a pool of my own sweat."

We open the electrical panel but none of the breakers are tripped. Austin comes downstairs and joins us in puzzling over the outage. We call the maintenance company and they promise to send a technician within the hour. We take turns walking over to the clubhouse to shower before work.

Nearly two hours after our call, the technician finally shows up. He examines the breaker panel, then unscrews an unmarked plate below it, revealing to our dismay and surprise a hidden master circuit breaker underneath. He flips it and the house whirs back to life.

We are not amused. No sooner is the technician out the door than Austin vents his anger. "A *hidden* circuit breaker? Why would you design a house with a hidden circuit breaker? They couldn't tell us that on the phone?"

Rhys is more direct. "Sometimes I feel this city's being built by a bunch of *ab*-solute halfwits."

Fourteen

Grand Designs

And on the pedestal these words appear:
"My name is Ozymandias, King of Kings:
Look on my works, ye mighty, and despair!"
Nothing beside remains. Round the decay
Of that colossal wreck, boundless and bare,
The lone and level sands stretch far away. — *Percy Bysshe Shelley, Ozymandias*

I stood beside Big White in the middle of an empty, windswept lot, one of the few undeveloped plots in the industrial district of Mussafah. In the distance, a silver Mercedes turned off the road and drove across the lot in my direction, sand billowing behind. The car came to a stop a stone's throw away, engine still purring. The driver emerged; his tailored suit, wraparound shades, and shaved head lent him the look of an assassin. All we needed to complete the scene was to unlock our respective trunks and make an exchange of drugs for money or some other sordid deal.

Instead, I handed him a sheet of paper. "Congratulations, you've got your Taxi Village," I said. The assassin, an Australian by the name of Roger, was in reality Abu Dhabi's taxi overlord. The DOT had hired him more than a year before to assist their taxi section. Upon arriving in Abu Dhabi, Roger had discovered that he *was* the taxi section, at least for the time being—a one-man show trying to bring some semblance of order and regulation to the city's motley taxi fleet.

Under Roger's guidance, Abu Dhabi was now in the middle of completely overhauling its taxi services. Roger had created a plan to phase out the city's Taliban Taxis in the years leading up to 2012 and replace them with a fleet of new silver-bullet Nissans. He had also helped the DOT create a new regulatory body, TransAD, which issued a half-dozen concessions to private companies that would be responsible for buying the new taxis, maintaining them, and training and supervising their drivers. The eight thousand Taliban Taxi drivers would be offered a chance to join one of the new franchises, but only after they proved they could read either English or Arabic, which disqualified many.[1] TransAD implemented a host of rules for the new taxis where none had been before, such as regulated working hours, periodic vehicle inspections, and the mandatory use of digitized fare meters to replace the old system of haggling over prices. Even the drivers' uniforms were standardized: out went turbans and baggy pajamas, in came crisp trousers, ties, and epaulettes. Abu Dhabi's leaders hoped the new and improved taxi fleet would make a suitably dignified impression on the international visitors they were courting.

In conjunction with the taxi fleet's reorganization, Roger had previously met with Alex and me to present his idea for "Taxi Village," a combined central depot and housing complex that would alleviate the current problem of having the fleet strewn across the city. He noted that the city's taxi drivers currently paid for their own food and housing; as such, they tended to share accommodations in low-rent buildings downtown. Roger had done surveys and discovered that taxis clogged up to a third of the parking spaces in some downtown superblocks at night, exacerbating the city's already pronounced parking shortage.

"What's even more concerning," Roger had said while making his pitch, "is that there's no way to tell when the drivers start and stop their shifts. Right now they all work on commission. The driver pays a monthly fee to the Emirati who sponsors him, averaging about two thousand dirhams a month. He gets to keep the rest of what he makes, which usually isn't more than another two thousand. So if a guy's had a slow day, he stays out for sixteen, maybe eighteen hours until he's made enough. That's why so many of these poor guys can barely keep their eyes open." He didn't need to belabor the point; like every Abu Dhabi resident, I had endured plenty of terrifying experiences at the hands of narcoleptic cabbies.

Taxi Village was supposed to solve the dual issues of parking and working hours by consolidating the new taxi fleet in one location. The DOT would provide housing and dining facilities for the drivers, and each of the concessionaires would provide maintenance and repair yards for their cars. Taxi Village's space requirements would be lessened by splitting the twenty thousand drivers into two twelve-hour shifts, with one shift on the road while the other rested. That way the DOT could also monitor how long each driver spent behind the wheel.

At Roger's insistence, TransAD had required the concessionaires to offer their drivers contracts with fixed hours and a decent basic salary; the DOT would pick up the cost of housing and meals. Roger hoped it would attract a better caliber of driver from the countries where the DOT was recruiting. "We're talking about Indians and Pakistanis and Bangladeshis who have never left home before," he had said. "They'll have hard enough lives here as it is. Sitting in traffic for hours every day. Hearing abuse from passengers. Being tailgated and cut off by other drivers. The least we can do is give them a bed and good food."

At the time, Roger's comments hit me like a slap in the face. He seemed to genuinely care for the welfare of the thousands of taxi drivers under his authority. He was one of the only expats I had encountered who was taking concrete action to help Abu Dhabi's lower classes. Most Westerners were content to spout righteous indignation at the poor conditions of the great unwashed, but few acknowledged their role in perpetuating the system, much less lifted a finger to do anything about it. Roger's humane attempt to shepherd his cabbie flock cast a stark light on the upper crust's apathy towards Abu Dhabi's nameless laboring classes, apathy to which, I had to admit, I was becoming prone.

Following Roger's pitch I had made it my mission to find a suitable plot for Taxi Village. The search quickly narrowed to Mussafah, as it was the only place in Abu Dhabi with enough space for the project. Moreover, gritty Mussafah was the only politically palatable location for housing thousands of drivers and their taxis, as it was conveniently far away from the more refined parts of town. Even so, I had found it difficult to identify a sufficiently large plot in Mussafah for what Roger had in mind. I eventually came up with an empty plot on the western side of the district, where Roger and I now stood.

Roger wiped off the sand accumulating on his sunglasses and looked at the piece of paper I had handed to him. "What's this?"

"Your affection plan. The DOT now owns this fine piece of real estate." Although the plot had already been given to another agency, I'd gotten it transferred to the DOT with the help of the property gurus in the UPC's Special Projects team. A few calls from them to the crown prince's Diwan, and the DOT had its land. In the supposedly advanced real estate systems of North America, such a transaction would have taken weeks if not months, with attorneys, title agents, and city councils holding things up every step of the way. Working in a young country had its pluses.

"So this is the place," Roger said as he surveyed the lot around us. "Not much to look at, is it?"

"No, but it's the biggest open plot we could find in Mussafah."

"How big?"

"Forty-eight hectares," which was about one hundred twenty acres.

"You think that's enough for the whole fleet?"

"Well, I wanted to talk with you about that," I said. "How many drivers are you planning to house?"

"Twenty thousand," Roger replied, "two shifts at ten thousand drivers apiece. That's what I'm anticipating, anyway, but that number will probably go down. I've done some research on how Abu Dhabi compares to other cities. New York has fourteen thousand taxis for a population of eight million. We have a million people in Abu Dhabi now. Do we really need ten thousand taxis? It'd be overkill even if we get to the three million residents in *Plan 2030.*"

"Yes, but you don't need a lot of taxis when you have a transit system like New York's," I pointed out. "Here, on the other hand, it'll be years before the first tram lines are up and running. Let's say you cut the number in half—ten thousand drivers is still a lot of people to cram into just one plot. Not to mention all the traffic coming in and out at once during the shift changes."

"I assumed we would deal with that by staggering their changeover times."

"Fair enough, but if some major accident or emergency were to happen on the site, you could be looking at a shutdown of the city's entire taxi fleet. So I was wondering if you'd consider splitting the operations across multiple sites. You know, two or three Taxi Villages. It'd be easier to find smaller plots, too."

Roger mulled this over. "Yeah, I think I'd be fine with that. As long as we can still use this one. I'd like to start construction as soon as possible."

"You can start construction tomorrow, if you want. But there's one more thing."

"And that is?"

"A portion of the new fleet will be ladies' taxis, right?"

"Right."

"Which means female drivers, right?"

"Right. Did you know they'll even have pink signs?" The ladies taxis had been conceived in response to complaints from women, residents and visitors alike, about inappropriate behavior by Abu Dhabi's male cabbies. Much of this was expected to diminish with the removal of the Taliban Taxis, due to the higher standards and better vetting of drivers for the new fleet, but the government was taking no chances with its reputation.

I asked, "Where do you plan to house the female drivers? Together with all of the men?"

Roger's eyebrows arched above his shades. "Hadn't thought about that, actually."

"If we give you sites for several Taxi Villages, you might want to think about setting one aside for the ladies. It'd be bad enough to force them to live among the male drivers, but then to put them in Mussafah among a hundred thousand male laborers with no other females in sight..."

Roger caught my insinuation. "Mmm. Might not be the best idea." He turned to look at the dusty warehouses and factories of the industrial zone sprawling all around us. "Can you imagine what it must be like for them here? Poor buggers."

Even after working in Abu Dhabi for more than a year, I was still taken aback by the ease with which the UPC and our sister agencies made landmark decisions that would shape Abu Dhabi for years to come. I was further bemused—and humbled—when I reflected upon my ability to contribute to some of those decisions. I had slept through a good number of my planning classes in graduate school, and my career until now had consisted of weak attempts to appear as though I knew what I was doing. Now my Emirati hosts were looking to people like me for guidance on how to remold their city, spend tens of billions of dirhams, and influence the lives of tens of thousands of residents in the process? It was all a bit much to believe.

The national railway project had been gaining steam throughout the spring of 2010. Khalid and I helped finalize the Shah Line's alignment in Al Gharbia, so that Etihad Rail's new consultants could start the detailed design in earnest. While this was underway, the Etihad Rail board instructed their staff to work with us to identify and safeguard potential corridors for the high-speed passenger line envisioned between Abu Dhabi and Dubai. Although the high-speed line wouldn't start construction for another few years at least, it was important to stake out potential corridors now, so that the railway wouldn't find all of its potential routes blocked by development when it came time to build.

As soon as we began the process of identifying potential corridors for the route, the crown prince himself intervened. Until now, *Plan 2030* had shown the high-speed line running parallel to the E11 from Dubai to the outskirts of Abu Dhabi. There it would dip down into a station at the heart of the new Capital District, then follow a path through the Eastern Mangroves before diving below Reem Island. The line would terminate on the eastern end of downtown at the subterranean Central Station, the future nexus of the Abu Dhabi transportation network, where rail, Metro, tram, and bus lines would all meet. Sheikh Mohammed chose to alter this route in favor of having the high-speed trains pass through Saadiyat Island before arriving at Central Station. Presumably his intent was to enable passengers to hop off at the figurative front door of Saadiyat's new cultural institutions.

On paper the change was simple enough; instead of going beneath Reem, the high-speed line would have to swing east through Saadiyat and then loop back around to Central Station. Putting a new station on Saadiyat could certainly be done, as the island's projects were still early in their construction and could be shifted around. The reconfigured approach to Central Station, however, would be tricky. The station was to be located in the most densely built-up area of the city, on a plot already crisscrossed by utility lines and hemmed in by buildings. It had taken months for my transport team colleagues and me, working with our Etihad Rail partners, to design a hypothetical below-ground box into which the station could fit. Redirecting the high-speed line via Saadiyat would mean that the line would approach the station from a different direction, which obligated us to quite literally go back to the drawing board.

Alex, Khalid, and I met with Henri, the French tunnel expert who had recently joined Etihad Rail. Henri had cut his professional teeth working on the Channel Tunnel between Great Britain and France. His latest achievement was the Gotthard Base Tunnel beneath the Swiss Alps, the world's longest rail tunnel, which had taken fourteen years to build. In comparison with these feats, designing the tunnel for Abu Dhabi's high-speed rail line should have been child's play, but it had Henri stumped. "In Switzerland we were, how you say, drilling through the wilderness," he said. "It was just a matter of finding the path of least resistance. Here, everything is in the way."

We pored over a table-sized diagram that showed the current and future constraints on the Central Station site. The station had to fit within the boundary of a ten-acre plot that was bordered to the west by an existing row of skyscrapers and to the east by another set under construction. Both the tunnel carrying the rail line into the station and the station itself had to avoid the foundations of these buildings. To the north was the trench for the Salaam Street tunnel, another no-go area. On the south it fronted the narrow waterway between Abu Dhabi and Suwwah Islands. A maze of below-grade utility lines wove around and through the area. Complicating things even further was the Metro line that was planned to pass through Central Station on a higher subterranean grade. Into this tangled web we had to weave the station and its approach tunnel, which fanned out into a switching yard as it approached the station's four platforms. The actual station design would be determined later; for now we just needed to carve out a box six hundred feet long by one hundred fifty feet wide by thirty feet tall. It was like playing chess in three dimensions.

Henri said, "With the line now coming from Saadiyat, the north-south placement for the station no longer works. The line would have to make a giant U-turn to enter. To build that kind of tunnel would be prohibitively expensive. And it would take us beneath the building foundations on Suwwah. Impossible."

"What about just turning the box east-west?" I said, tracing the diagram with my finger. "The station box would protrude into the water, but it's going to lie below the depth of the channel anyways, right?"

Henri shook his head. "Yes, but the station and tunnel will still be too shallow to bore. We're going to have to use cut-and-cover." Whereas tunnel boring mimics the burrowing of a mole, the cut-and-cover method involves digging a giant trench, filling it with concrete tunnel sections, and then reburying it—the same technique that was being used on the Salaam Street tunnel. Henri said, "To do that underwater we would have to block off and drain the waterway. Too expensive again."

Khalid said, "Can we just shift it in from the water?"

"That would mean that the rail and Metro stations won't overlap," I pointed out.

Now it was Alex's turn to demur. "No, the Metro station should stay at least partly on top of the rail station, so that people can transfer between them. Otherwise it defeats the purpose of having both on one site."

Henri leaned back in his chair. "Then we're stuck." Proverbially speaking, if the three most important rules about real estate are location, location, location, then their corollary is that the important sites are always the most impossible to work with. No matter what one wants to put there, everyone else wants a piece as well.

We stared in frustration at the jumbled diagram. Finally I said, "We could just try to force it." I went to my desk and returned with my most technologically advanced tools: a ruler, an eraser, and some colored pencils. For the next hour the four of us sketched out various shapes and directions for the station and its approach tunnel. At one point we thought we had a solution, until we saw that the tunnel would clip the supporting foundations for the Sheikh Khalifa Bridge between Saadiyat and Abu Dhabi. With a little more fine-tuning, we got around the foundations and settled on an alignment that just might work.

"It's not pretty, but it fits," Alex said.

Henri took the sketches back to his office to have his engineers digitize them. He later called us to confirm that our guesswork had run the gauntlet. Admittedly, it was only a start, and a rudimentary one at that. It would take years more to flesh out the Central Station's design and build the real thing. Yet I took pleasure in thinking that everything to follow— the countless man-hours and billions of dirhams that would go into building the lynchpin of Abu Dhabi's transportation network—would be steered by our preschoolish scribbling.

For every such delusion of grandeur, my colleagues and I also had plenty of powerless moments. For example, the developers on Reem Island came back to the UPC to modify

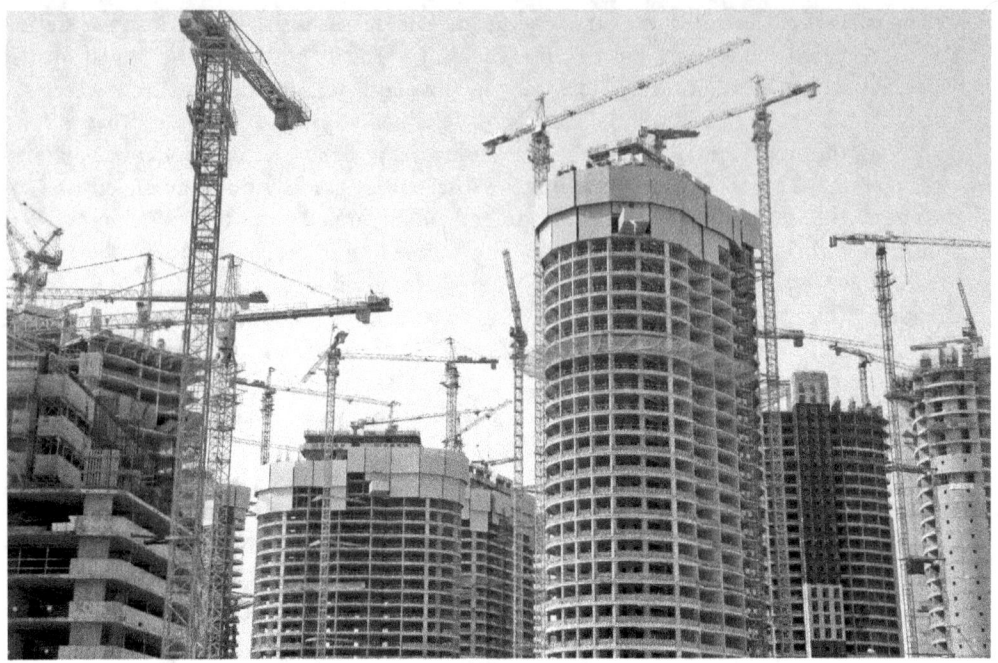

Reem Island's budding skyscraper forest, circa March 2011.

their approved master plan, having decided that their hundred or so anticipated towers weren't going to be enough. They wanted to remove the two small mangrove stands that were the island's only remaining patches of nature and replace them with more real estate. Rhys was given the unenviable task of determining which of the two groves should be retained and producing a design for how it could be preserved among the encroaching buildings. It was a fool's errand; in the end the developers simply ignored the UPC's advice and elected to replace both mangrove stands with pavement. Rhys lamented afterwards, "You know, I just don't understand. Does anyone in this city bother to consider that if all these newcomers actually materialize, they might want to look at something besides wonky buildings?"

* * *

In addition to the Sheikh Zayed Mosque, the other defining symbol of modern Abu Dhabi is the Emirates Palace, the squat salmon-colored edifice near the northwest corner of the island. Built in a neoclassical Arabian style at a cost of eleven billion dirhams, it was the most expensive hotel ever built until surpassed in 2011 by Singapore's Marina Bay Sands.[2] Standard rooms at the Emirates Palace rent for $1,000 a night; suites go for thirteen times that amount. In the unlikely scenario that the hotel's rooms were to be fully booked, staff would still outnumber guests six to one. The hotel's sixty acres of sprawling interior space drip with gold leaf and boast more than a thousand Swarovski chandeliers, a tea room that serves gold-flecked chocolate, a vending machine that dispenses tiny gold bars, and a seven-star rating (admittedly self-awarded). In a city of superlatives, the Emirates Palace is the exclamation point.

On a balmy summer evening my housemates and I met up with Liz and Elise beneath the palace's golden dome, which yawns larger than that of St. Paul's Cathedral in London.[3] We made our way down the ranks of escalators and through the colonnaded hallways to the theatre, where the gold-leaf theme continued throughout the upstairs balcony and onto the ornate frame around the stage. The rows of cushioned seats were spotless, a pleasant contrast to the sweat- and soda-stained recliners of the cinemas in the malls. A stylized gilt falcon resembling the national crest cast its pupil-less gaze down on us from the ceiling above the stage, prompting me to wonder about the fascination with avian motifs that seems to be a common theme among autocratic regimes throughout history.

We were here for the Abu Dhabi Film Festival, one of a handful of cultural oases on the calendar. In its three short years the festival had already gained a broad following among Abu Dhabi's culture-starved expats. The government had coaxed the former director of New York City's famed Tribeca Film Festival into taking the helm of the nascent Abu Dhabi event. Shortly after his arrival, the director gave an interview in which he admitted that film festivals had become a commodity; every city looking to make a name for itself felt obligated to have one. Yet he was adamant that Abu Dhabi's festival would be more than just a me-too impulse. He wanted it to nurture a legitimate culture of both film-going and film-making in the emirate.[4] Observers remained divided on whether the necessary foment could take root in a society so straightjacketed by taboo and self-censorship.

We found our seats and the murmur of the theatregoers quieted down as the festival director strode onstage in a blazer and a pair of neon-yellow tennis shoes. He lectured the sold-out crowd on the importance of what we were about to see: a restored, full-length version of *Metropolis*, the German director Fritz Lang's epic masterpiece, which was one of the most expensive films ever made when it was released in 1927. With a running time of 153 minutes, the director's version was also deemed far too long to be shown in theaters. The studio wound up cutting more than a third of Lang's footage, rendering the plot nonsensical. The material left on the cutting room floor was thought to be lost forever until a deteriorated print of the original film was found in a Buenos Aires vault in 2006. It took an international team of restorationists four years to put the missing scenes in viewable condition. The restored film had premiered in Germany in February 2010 and was subsequently shown in select international venues, of which the Abu Dhabi festival was one of the very few.[5] I could only imagine how much the emirate's leaders had paid for the privilege.

The director's enthusiasm threatened to overwhelm him. He spoke of how *Metropolis* had given the world an enduring vision of the city of the future. "And now, we're watching it here in Abu Dhabi, the true city of the future." His hyperbole drew polite applause as he left the stage and the lights dimmed.

It wasn't until halfway through the movie that the irony finally hit me. Lang's city of the future was shown to be a stark dichotomy. A ruling class of wealthy, leisured elites whiled away their time in skyscraper fantasylands above the clouds while far below them the nameless working masses toiled away their lives in an infernal machine dystopia. I traded glances with my colleagues in the seats beside me, who evidently shared my thoughts: *Metropolis* suited Abu Dhabi all too well.

* * *

Qasr al Deviance Journal, Week 15

The power is out again. It happens every four or five days now. Simply flipping the master breaker no longer does the trick. The problem is in the concrete chamber beneath our backyard, which keeps flooding. This shorts out the water pumps inside and brings down the electricity throughout the entire house. Every time this happens, the maintenance company is obligated to send a team of plumbers to pump out the chamber. During the first few visits they simply emptied the water into the yard—not exactly a surefire means of avoiding more flooding. We finally convinced them to bring a longer hose in order to pump the water through the house and into the street. Our sod appears not to have withstood the repeated inundations; the grass is slowing turning amber.

I am not sure if the plumbers will return after the last such visit. When they arrived, Austin was in the kitchen chopping onions in preparation for one of his dinner parties. I believe he may have been drinking, which would explain why he did not think it odd to answer the door wearing a bathing suit and ski goggles and wielding a kitchen knife. It would also explain why he ran down the street after the terrified plumbers, waving his knife and hollering for them to come back.

Speaking of streets, the development company responsible for building Golf Gardens has apparently decided that the neighborhood's anemic sidewalks are not already cluttered enough and has chosen to add more obstructions. Over the last few weeks they have had contractors install crash barriers made of metal pipes next to every single sidewalk fixture—including the oversized streetlights, the utility boxes, the stop signs, and even the little geranium patches. It seems a bit excessive; the locals' driving and parking skills are bad, but they're not *that* bad. The barriers are rendered all the more garish by their red-and-white-striped paint scheme, giving the neighborhood's streets the appearance of being lined with candy canes.

In other news, the main wet wall in our living room has owned up to its name. A leak has developed somewhere in the pipes inside, leaving a sticky film on the wall and a small puddle on the floor next to it. Despite our attempts to convince her otherwise, Grace the cat prefers this elixir to the water in her bowl. I come downstairs every morning to find her licking the wall. The mystery liquid appears to be psychedelic, as Grace then stumbles around the living room howling like a banshee. The first time I saw her in this state, I put her on my lap to calm her down. Evidently the druggy liquid also impacted her motor skills, as she could not retract her claws and thereby ruined a perfectly good pair of my pants. I am thinking of sending the maintenance company the bill.

Fifteen

Lonely Hearts Need Not Apply

Sans hope of gain, love's not worth a grain.—One Thousand and One Nights

The darkened restaurant had a sultry feel. Strains of bossa nova mingled with the smell of fattened calves from the kitchen. I surveyed the other patrons. To one side, a table full of Chinese businessmen chatting loudly and all wearing the same suit. Opposite them, a gaggle of European tourists—Germans, judging by their accents and overflowing mugs of beer. At a back table were a pair of stylish young couples, both genders wearing skin-tight pants and half-unbuttoned shirts, the unmistakable hallmarks of the Lebanese. All four of them glanced up as the hostess walked past with an elderly Emirati couple in tow, the husband carrying a cane and the wife clad in a full *niqab* veil that obscured her face.

I glanced at my companions around the table. All three of them were locals. On my left was Hamdan, who was large for an Emirati, well over six feet tall, with a bulging waistline that his kandora struggled to conceal. Abdullah, on my right, was the exact opposite: short and skinny, with nervous eyes barely visible beneath the low-pulled brim of his baseball cap. And directly across from me was Mahra's brother Majid, averaging the other two in height and build. He was in town from London and had invited me to join him and his friends at Chamas, the Brazilian steakhouse in the swank Intercontinental Hotel. The Intercon, as it was called, was one of the city's iconic establishments, boasting a half-dozen restaurants and occupying its own little grassy knoll on the west coast of Abu Dhabi Island, just north of the crown prince's Diwan. Along with the mound housing the Emirates Palace, the Intercon's hill was one of exactly two promontories in the otherwise pancake-flat city.

"Have you been here before?" Majid asked. He spoke flawless English, just like his sister.

"Nope. First time," I replied.

"You're going to love it. I come here whenever I'm home."

I asked how London was treating him and he copped a flawless Cockney accent: "Enh, it's fuw 'a punters an' fiefs."

A waiter came by to explain the service, an all-you-can-eat affair with roving servers who would bring various varieties of grilled *churrasco* meats to the table. After he left, Hamdan added, "Remember to eat your money's worth." We had each paid upwards of four hundred dirhams for the meal. Hamdan clearly relished the challenge.

"Actually, I've been liking London less and less," Majid continued. "Mostly because of work. As a resident, I'm the lowest guy in the hospital. Even the nurses boss me around. I'm always on night shift, and we see some crazy stuff at three in the morning. Last week the paramedics brought in a guy who'd been shot point-blank. Half his face was missing. He was gone before we got him to the operating table."

I asked whether he saw a lot of these gunshot victims.

"All the time. It's the drug trade. London's the new Amsterdam. I've been there five years and it's a lot worse than when I arrived."

"How long do you plan to stay?"

"I finish my residency this year and then I'm out. The worst part is the money. They pay me next to nothing to start with, and after taxes it comes out to maybe ten pounds an hour. If I had known all the crap I'd have to put up with, I'd never have done this. I would have skipped med school and taken a cushy oil job like Hamdan here."

"Hey, I tried to warn you," Hamdan retorted.

The conversation was interrupted when the first server arrived with a seared chunk of beef impaled on a sword. No sooner had he sliced pieces onto our plates than another server materialized with chicken wings on skewers. He in turn was followed by another server bearing lamb chops, then another with roast duck, and so on. The deliveries continued in rapid succession, meat piling up on our plates much faster than we could put it away.

Between mouthfuls Majid told me that he was in town primarily to prepare for his upcoming wedding. "It's freaking expensive, man. I keep telling my dad we should let the government pay, but he wants to do it the old-fashioned way."

"How long have you known your fiancée?" I asked.

"Well, she's a distant cousin on my mom's side. I saw her at some family events while we were growing up, but that was a long time ago. I never really talked with her until the last time I was home, when my parents introduced us."

"So it was love at first sight?"

He paused. "She's okay. She doesn't want to continue her education, which was a surprise to me. I didn't find that out until after I'd agreed to the marriage. I don't want her just sitting around the house."

I waited for him to continue. When he didn't, I prodded, "So ... do you like her?"

He thought for a moment. "Yeah, she seems like a nice girl." Another pause. "My mom really wants me to get married, so I guess it's just the right thing to do."

His ambivalence silenced the rest of my questions. Abdullah piped up to tell me, "You know, you can order a drink if you want. We're not going to be offended."

I demurred, saying I had to drive myself home.

"Well I'm sure going to have one," Hamdan announced. He flagged down our waiter with one hand while flipping through the drink menu with the other. "Bring me one of these ... whatever this is, the one with the pineapple."

"A caipirinha, sir?"

"Yes, that." As the waiter walked away, Hamdan yelled after him, "With an umbrella!"

Majid and Abdullah pulled out packs of cigarettes and lit up. The waiter returned with Hamdan's drink, complete with miniature parasol. Hamdan drained half of it in one gulp. For a brief moment I had an epiphany: here I was, sitting with a cadre of smoking, drinking Emiratis in the midst of such a cosmopolitan retinue, all of it taking place in Abu Dhabi, the last place on Earth where one might expect such a thing. Surely it couldn't get much more surreal.

At that moment the band exploded into samba and the doors to the restaurant swung open. In sauntered a quartet of achingly beautiful young women clad in Carnival regalia, feather plumes on their heads and their posteriors sporting jeweled thongs that made bikinis look conservative. The women halted among our section of tables and the band fell silent. Every eye in the restaurant was on the statuesque beauties as they slowly raised their hands. The band struck back up with a vengeance, the drums pounding out a throbbing tribal beat. The dancers began twirling in rapid fluid motion: hips gyrating in impossible circles, high-heeled shoes clacking on the marble floor, sequins glittering, smiles flashing, sweat glistening on flawless skin.

I watched in awe, spellbound by the lurid display. I managed to tear my eyes away for a moment to glance at my companions. Beneath the brow of Abdullah's hat, his skittish eyes darted back and forth between the floor and the feminine hindquarters orbiting a few feet from his face. No such dilemma appeared to afflict either Majid or Hamdan, who both stared openly. The other diners displayed a similar range of reactions. The Chinese salarymen eyed the dancers with barely concealed desire. The Germans clapped and shouted and looked ready to join in. The Lebanese women cast arctic looks at the competition while their men wisely averted their eyes. I peered around the nearest dancer to see the older Emirati couple frozen in place, staring down at their plates with obvious discomfort.

The drums echoed a final beat and the dancers halted, arms aloft, beaming practiced smiles at nobody in particular. The restaurant broke out in applause, the Germans throwing in a few whistles for good measure. The dancers bowed and sashayed back out through the doors. My companions and I craned our necks to watch them leave. Once they were gone, I turned back to Majid. "Did you know that was coming?" I asked.

He smiled. "Of course. Why do you think we come here?" Hamdan nursed his caipirinha while Abdullah lit another cigarette with shaking hands. Out of the corner of my eye I saw the older Emirati couple get up from their table and leave.

"How does the restaurant get away with that kind of thing?" I asked. "Isn't it a bit risqué for Abu Dhabi?"

Hamdan was quick to answer. "People do things in hotels that they can't do elsewhere here." As if to emphasize the point, he drained the rest of his drink. "Every business has an Emirati sponsor, right? So whoever owns this place probably just has a lot of *wasta*. And besides, we're in Abu Dhabi, not Saudi."

We returned to our food, though by now our stomachs had begun to register our gluttony and we couldn't eat much more. Majid tried to flag down our waiter, but to no avail. His friends did the same, but the waitstaff all appeared to pay them no heed. While the Emiratis' frustration grew, I noticed a waiter standing idly at the till; I waved at him and he came over immediately.

After the waiter left to retrieve our bill, Majid said angrily, "See, that's what gets me. In London, I look like a foreigner, and people sometimes treat me differently because of it. Although it's wrong, I can understand it there. But this is *our* city, and it's like we're invisible." His friends nodded in agreement.

I tried to assuage their concerns. "Look, it's just some waiters in a restaurant."

From beneath his hat Abdullah said, "This happens everywhere we go."

Majid looked around at the multiethnic crowd. "Yeah, I know, it shouldn't be a big deal. It's just that every time I come back, Abu Dhabi seems less like the home I remember."

* * *

Though Majid didn't seem particularly thrilled about his impending arranged marriage, simply by having the prospect he was far more fortunate than most of Abu Dhabi's male residents. Abu Dhabi is a city awash in single men. Its gender imbalance is one of the widest in the world, with nearly three male residents for every female.[1] The gap varies widely among the different strata of the socioeconomic population pyramid. Emiratis are more or less on par in gender numbers, with 1.05 men for every woman. The Western expat stratum is more man-heavy, skewed by the male-dominated oil industry. Among some of the lower ethnicities, the trend actually seems reversed; there are far more female Filipina service workers and Indonesian nannies than there are men from their respective countries.

It is at the bottom of the social scale that the disparity is most severe. Male laborers invariably come to Abu Dhabi unaccompanied; the ratio of South Asian men to women is in the hundreds. Those who have families back home are allowed to visit them just once every couple of years, if they can afford the airfare. The result is that Abu Dhabi is inundated with lonely, young, and decidedly unhappy men, a deluge that even the Weather Girls would find excessive.

This is more than just an idle concern; it has serious implications for public safety. The specter of male predation in Abu Dhabi casts ominous tones over a city that otherwise takes pride in its supposed lack of crime. As many as 70 percent of rapes go unreported, largely because female victims in such a conservative society fear the very real potential for social stigmatization, recriminations by employers, or even prosecution for having sex outside of marriage.[2] Shortly after I arrived in Abu Dhabi, a female friend visiting from abroad was accosted by a landscaper as she walked along the Corniche in broad daylight. Some of the malls have gone so far as to ban laborers from visiting on their rare days off, in response to mounting complaints from women shoppers of being leered at by roving bands of males.

Abu Dhabi's gender imbalance is repeated across the boomtowns of the Gulf. No other region of the contemporary world has such a lopsided distribution of the sexes. Even in China, where a parenting culture that overwhelmingly favors male children has combined with the communist government's one-child-per-family policy to skew the country's birthrates, the ratio of men to women is only 1.15.[3] Yet for all its contemporary uniqueness, the Gulf's gender imbalance is not entirely without historical precedent. For example, from the 1850s to the 1900s, throughout the great industrial expansion in the United States that followed the Civil War, a significant portion of the population of American cities consisted of bachelors. They worked in factories, lived in lodging rooms and flophouses, and whiled away their free time in the saloons, billiard halls, and brothels that cropped up to service their needs. This "bachelor transient subculture" grew to the point that it began to scare members of respectable society, leading to the creation of America's first public police forces in burgeoning cities such as my hometown of Detroit.[4] Although the modern Gulf is certainly much different than nineteenth-century North America, it is worth noting that boomtowns share more than a few similarities across time and space. Abu Dhabi's gender imbalance is perceptible in more than just the faces on the street; it has left its mark on the very fabric of the city. Even the city's name is a badge of masculinity. When the settlement was founded in the 1700s, it was simply called *Mleih*, "salty," because of its brackish water. Only later did it become Abu Dhabi, *Father* of the Gazelle.[5]

After living in the city for more than a year, I began to posit a link between Abu Dhabi's surplus testosterone and the banality of its built environment. A city's spaces are like children in that one can easily tell whether they are loved. The presence of beloved urban spaces is fundamental to making a city a cohesive community rather than merely a mass of people living on top of each other. In his *City of God*, for example, Augustine of Hippo argues that a community is defined and bound together "by a common agreement as to the objects of their love" more than by any other trait.[6] The characteristics of a beloved urban space are readily discernible: they are well known, cared for, and above all, frequented—people enjoy spending time with what they love. Some places are easier to love than others: a cozy park, for example, versus what author Lawrence Osborne calls "the great doomed urban spaces that seem to surround elevated roads and their pillars."[7] Sadly, there are very few places in Abu Dhabi that feel loved. The city exudes a coarse, functional impression; little of it seems to have benefited from a tender feminine touch, and even less of it seems to be the recipient of any unprompted affection.

Like Majid, Abu Dhabi's Emiratis are exempt from the emirate's widespread curse of singleness, at least in theory. The tradition of arranged marriages all but guarantees every Emirati a spouse. When the Bedu of long ago established this practice, they had in mind more than just the propagation of their race; it was also a means of cementing ties among families, clans, and tribes. Abu Dhabi's modern restrictions on citizenship and inheritance have reinforced this kin-based pattern. One-third of contemporary Emirati marriages are between close relatives such as first cousins, and the number is rising. Thesiger's observation of the Bedu rings even more true of their descendants: "No race in the world prizes lineage so highly ... and none has kept its blood so pure."[8] Yet this inbreeding has also constrained the Emiratis' gene pool and led to a increase in genetic disease. No fewer than 241 genetic disorders have been identified among the UAE's citizens, the second-highest rate in the Arab world.[9] Common diseases such as diabetes, breast cancer, and Down syndrome have reached epidemic proportions. The filial solidarity of Abu Dhabi's Emiratis is a mixed blessing.

With such emphasis on the family, it is no surprise that Emiratis keep their home spheres closely guarded. In more than a year of working with my local colleagues, the only time I had met one of their family members was when Mahra introduced me to Majid. Hence it was a surprise when Khalid invited Alex, Carlo, and me to his brother's wedding. He mentioned it offhand at the office one afternoon, clarifying that he actually meant brothers in the plural sense. Two of his younger siblings were going to marry their respective fiancées in a traditional ceremony. It was sensible of Khalid's family to hold two weddings for the price of one. As my conversation with Majid had alluded to, even with the government offering to pick up part of the tab, Emirati weddings often cost a fortune, between catering for several hundred relatives and friends and renting a hall big enough to fit them.

Most of the other guests had already arrived by the time we showed up at the wedding hall in the inland city of Al Ain, Khalid's hometown. The three of us Westerners looked like fish out of water in our suits and ties, the only non-Emiratis among the scores of attendees loitering in the outdoor courtyard. The crowd was solely men, in keeping with the Emirati tradition of holding separate ceremonies for men and women.

Khalid was ecstatic when we found him among the crowd. "Wow ... wow! Thanks so much for coming!" He seemed genuinely surprised that we had taken him up on his invitation. He quickly composed himself and switched into the mode of the host, presenting us in rapid succession to his brothers, his father, and a slew of other Emirati friends and family.

The doors of the wedding hall opened and the guests thronged inside. I lost sight of my colleagues in the crush, but I was more concerned that we were all funneling through what appeared to be the building's only entrance. I wondered how everyone would get out again if there were a fire. I made a mental note to check later on whether Al Ain—or Abu Dhabi, for that matter—had a fire marshal.

I rejoined Alex and Carlo inside and we surveyed the cavernous hall for seats. We looked to be out of luck: all of the tables were claimed. Then I noticed a swarthy Emirati waving to us from a table at the far side of the hall. It was Rashid, a young local from the UPC who had recently been assigned to work with Austin on the Al Gharbia plans. Not only was I relieved to see someone I knew, I was particularly pleased that it was Rashid. He came from a family of modest means (in Emirati terms, anyway) in the northern emirate of Ras al Khaimah and was one of the kindest Emiratis in the office. Although Rashid's English was limited, it put my paltry Arabic to shame.

"Rashid, what a surprise!" I said as we joined him at the table. "Do you know Khalid's brothers?"

He thought for a moment. "Yes, I knows him brothers," he said, baring an ivory grin that gleamed against his dark complexion. "I knows everyone."

We took our seats around the table, which was piled high with all sorts of exotic dishes. It was my first opportunity to sample authentic Emirati food. In all of Abu Dhabi there is only a single restaurant that features authentic Emirati cuisine: Mezlai, at the Emirates Palace. There are plenty of other eateries that serve dishes most people view as "Middle Eastern"—hummus, falafel, tabbouleh, and the like—but these are actually Levantine in origin and have more in common with the food of Greece than with that of the Gulf. The sparse vegetation and the historic poverty of the peoples of eastern Arabia produced a traditional cuisine that was quite different.

Rashid began to unwrap the various bowls and platters, intending to serve us. I started to protest, but he would have none of it. "No, please, you sit. This our hospitality." Rashid wielded his plate like a trowel, carving into the mountain of rice and meat in the middle of the table and dumping piles onto our plates. We passed around the half-dozen side dishes, the likes of which I had never before seen.

Our Emirati colleague took his seat and demonstrated how to eat in the traditional way. He scooped up a handful of rice in his hand, rolled it between his fingers, and popped it in his mouth. We did our best to imitate him, succeeding in strewing rice everywhere except our gullets. Rashid graciously refrained from laughing as I lurched forward over my plate to avoid piling more rice on my lap. "You doing well," he said. "It taste better with your hands, yes?"

The only sound to be heard throughout the hall was the juicy murmur of food being chewed. So intense was the attendees' collective concentration on eating that I had a momentary vision of being surrounded by kandora-clad locusts at the other tables. Behind the giant curtain that separated us from the other half of the wedding hall, however, a rather wild party seemed to be taking place. Through the thick fabric I could make out the reflection of disco lights flashing in time with the beat of amplified Arabic music. "What's going on over there?" I asked. "Another wedding?"

Rashid shook his head. "Same wedding. Ladies' ceremony." Female expat colleagues at the office had told me stories about the ladies' ceremonies—frequently raucous affairs with dancing and singing. Such a ceremony was one of the only occasions when Emirati women could discard their *abayyas* and indulge their tastes for fashion, even though they were only showing off for one another.

I asked Rashid, "Are they dancing over there?"

"Yes. Dancing. Men eat, ladies dance. This how things go."

"Have you ever seen one of the ladies' ceremonies?" Carlo asked.

"No! *Haram*." Forbidden. Rashid shook his head for emphasis. Perhaps to change the subject, he pointed at one of the myriad dishes of food. "You not tried *harees*!" I looked down at a bowl containing an ashen pudding, which I had assumed was a dessert. Without waiting for a response Rashid took a spoon and began to stir the pudding. It fought back with the viscosity of sludge. He lifted the spoon from the bowl, stretching a cord of the rubbery concoction across the table until it broke off. He dolloped the heaping spoonful onto my plate and repeated the process around the table. I picked up a fork, raised the lump to my mouth, and bit into it. In both taste and texture, harees bore a surprising resemblance to the paste I recalled eating in kindergarten, only with chunks of meat mixed in.

"You like harees?" Rashid asked eagerly. I tried to smile without wincing. I took several more bites of the goo so as not to offend him before discreetly returning to safer fare.

Carlo poked at the brown gristle atop his rice and leaned over to me. "What do you think this meat is?" he whispered.

I had wondered the same thing myself since first tasting it at the start of the meal. I took another bite but still couldn't place it. "Roast beef, maybe?" I said. "But I've never tasted it cooked this way."

Alex chimed in, "I thought it was lamb."

Rashid listened to our exchange in silence, grinning the entire time. Now he saw his moment. "This?" He pointed to the meat in the center of the table. "This camel."

"Okaaaay," Alex said, halting his meat-laden fork halfway to his mouth. I felt sheepish for not anticipating that this Gulf delicacy would be served at the wedding. Emiratis no longer rely on camels for the transportation and nourishment they once provided their Bedu ancestors, but they still prize camels for their status—and their meat. For my part, I found the camel not all that bad, just a tad gamier than roast beef, with a salty aftertaste. Alex left his untouched for the rest of the meal.

I noticed that the murmur of dining had abated, and I glanced around to discover that we were among the few people still eating. Barely fifteen minutes had passed since we first sat down, yet most of the guests had already wolfed down their meals and were making their way back outside. Not wanting to be left behind, we crammed a few more bites into our mouths before heading to the bathrooms to wash our five-fingered utensils.

While we were standing at the sinks, Carlo suddenly cursed in Italian. He held up his left hand. "I just realized I was eating with this the entire time." Though this was understandable, as he was left-handed, Carlo was clearly worried that he had committed a gaffe. Historically, the left hand in Arab culture was reserved for unclean functions. Even now, in the era of bidets and antibacterial soap, Emiratis never eat southpaw.

"I wouldn't worry about it," I reassured him. "I don't think anyone noticed. Besides, you ate the harees, so Rashid can't be mad at you."

We walked out of the restroom and into a very different scene. The hall, nearly empty just a few minutes ago, was swarming with Pakistani and Afghan laborers ravenously picking over the leftovers on the tables. Before the wedding I had seen them loitering in the parking lot outside the hall. Now I made the connection. The Emiratis' extravagant weddings probably always had far more food than the guests could hope to finish, so once they were done, the hosts let the laborers have the leftovers in a rare display of charity. Every table in front of us was now a blur of activity, the laborers devouring as much as they could while sweeping the rest into plastic bags—rice, meat, cans of pop, whatever was left on the table. From the frantic way they went about it, I wondered if they hadn't eaten all day. Within minutes the entire hall was picked clean. The laborers dispersed as quickly as they had appeared.

Carlo broke our silence with his sage insight. "This place has so many contradictions," he said. "The Emiratis would never even consider disgracing themselves by eating with these people. But then they do things like this. Think about it. How many weddings do you attend back home where the leftovers are given to the poor?"

We walked back outside to the courtyard, where the guests were once more milling around. I was surprised to see that fewer than half had stayed; the rest had evidently left after eating. A group of local musicians was performing a *yolla*, a traditional dance, in the middle of the courtyard. A trio of drummers thumped out a plodding rhythm while a dozen singers arrayed themselves in two parallel lines facing one another. One of the lines sang a hypnotic chant, swaying back and forth. They leaned forward on their cane-like camel sticks as they crescendoed up to a yell and back down again. The other line then mimicked the display, trying to outdo their counterparts in volume. Between the two lines a young Emirati boy paced in a circle, twirling a silver facsimile of an AK-47 above his head.

Khalid found us in the thinning crowd. "Thank you for coming. Really, it mean so much to me. Tell me, what you guys think?"

We offered our enthusiastic praise for the food, then I asked, "So ... what happens now? Everyone just goes home?" Although I tried not to sound disrespectful, the evening seemed strangely anticlimactic.

Khalid smiled. "Some people stay longer. Close friends and family. But yes, most people go home. Our weddings start late, and people must work tomorrow, umkak?"

Alex approached it from a different angle. "When do the bride and groom actually, you know, get married? Is there another ceremony after this?"

"Ah, yes." Khalid clasped his hands, clearly relishing the chance to expound on one of the finer points of his culture. "In our traditions the husband and wife first meet when the families arrange. Her father talks with his father, and they say how the marriage will go. Then the husband and wife go to the court and sign the papers, and that when they actually married, umkak? But this just a legal thing. He does not take her home. That is only after the ceremony. Sometimes it's a long time between! One of my brothers, he married his wife one year ago. But only tonight, when she leave the ladies' ceremony, then he takes her home."

Khalid grinned slyly. "I think he is very much ready. He been waiting a long time for what happen then."

* * *

For most of the Western expats I came across in Abu Dhabi, dalliances were plentiful, but legitimate love was scarce. "Abu Dhabi's dating scene is a minefield," Elise proclaimed at one champagne brunch. "What kind of people do you think come here? Broken people who love money." She distinguished between "relationships," as she called them, and the many flings she bounced between.

Austin voiced a similar complaint. "My dates here are like London buses. You wait for ages, then five show up at once."

Abu Dhabi's Emiratis are not the only ones whose marriages were strained; plenty of expat unions do not survive the emirate. There is even a term for idle expat housewives with little to occupy them besides shopping and affairs: "Khalidiya Kates," named after the tony part of town. For many among the foreign upper crust, Abu Dhabi is a transient, superficial, lonely place.

I was thus a bit skeptical when, some time after we moved to the Qasr, Rhys came home from a weekend in Dubai with his head in the clouds. "I think I've found the woman of my dreams. She's cute, she's Welsh, and she's a fan of wine and rugby," he said.

"Where'd you meet?" I asked.

"At a club." Sure, I thought, that's bound to last.

Much to everyone's surprise, it did. He and the young woman, Seren, went from interested to dating to inseparable in a matter of weeks. Theirs was the only expat relationship I saw that seemed remotely likely to endure.

I first met Seren several weeks later at a going-away party for one of our colleagues, a grandfatherly American the UPC had hired to salvage the Estidama program. He had lasted less than a year before the management made him a scapegoat for the continuing debacle and let him go. Though I felt bad for him, my concern was mitigated when I saw a copy of his six-figure severance package left sitting on a copier.

On a weekend evening the UPC's expats gathered at the new Crowne Plaza hotel on Yas Island for the party. The occasion was more congratulatory than regretful; our colleague was escaping Abu Dhabi, for which the rest of us all envied him to a degree. I took a seat at the large table on the outdoor terrace next to Liz, Austin, Rhys, and a lovely young woman

I presumed to be Seren. She was even more charming than Rhys had described, a full head shorter than him, with a singsong Welsh lilt and the smile of a cherub.

"I hear you're a rugby fan," I said.

"Well, I know a good bit more about it than him," she said, elbowing Rhys in the ribs. I was pleased to see that she could clearly hold her own.

Austin interrupted, pointing and uttering scornfully, "Oh, now *that's* classy."

We turned to see what had drawn his ire. One of our newest colleagues, a portly Australian who had been with the UPC less than a month, sauntered onto the terrace with a miniskirted Asian woman clinging to each of his arms. The ladies were obviously working. I wondered whether they were in the profession by choice.

The UAE bears an unfortunate reputation of laxity regarding human trafficking, with more than ten thousand victims split mostly between Dubai and Abu Dhabi.[10] Although Abu Dhabi enjoys a marginally cleaner status than Dubai, its sex trade is rapidly expanding. Officially acknowledged cases of sex trafficking in the capital rose more than fourfold from 2007 to 2009, although unofficial estimates are much higher.[11] To be sure, some women come to Abu Dhabi of their own accord, drawn by the promise of earning more in a few evenings than they could in an entire month back home, particularly light-skinned women from the former Soviet Union, who command high prices from the locals. Yet, for every woman who freelances many more are forced into prostitution, lured to the emirate by international traffickers promising jobs as waitresses or secretaries. When the girls arrive, the traffickers take their passports and require them to pay off their airfare by servicing up to ten clients a night. Victims of sex trafficking are usually kept in squalid confinement, often in nondescript villas in the middle of otherwise ordinary neighborhoods.[12] Although the government points to strict federal anti-trafficking laws[13] and occasional high-profile busts as evidence of its commitment to curb the problem, officials have also gone on the record stating that the problem is "natural" for a rapidly developing city like Abu Dhabi.[14]

My expat colleagues certainly indulged in their share of vices, but they didn't buy sex, at least not openly. For the Australian newcomer to crash the party with a pair of hookers, each of whom cost him perhaps an hour's wages, was as incongruous as it was odious. We watched as the Australian walked over to another group to show off his conquests. "*Absolutely unbelievable,*" Rhys said, employing his characteristic form of emphasis. "He was talking just this morning about how he has another month before his wife and daughter join him here."

"Looks like he's enjoying his freedom," I said.

"That's atrocious," Liz added.

We saw one of the ladies make a show of grabbing the Australian's ample belly and give it a playful shake. He made a face like an excited schoolboy.

Rhys stood up and said, "Right, I've seen enough for one evening." As he and Seren made for the door, he paused next to the Australian, and I barely caught his words: "You know, we put you people on the boats for a very good reason."

* * *

Qasr Al Deviance Journal, Week 22

During the latest visit from our plumber friends, the portable pump they use to drain our pump room suffers a breakdown. Oh, the irony. I start to wonder whether my housemates and I are the unwitting dupes in some kind of reality-TV prank show, and am half-tempted to look around for the hidden cameras. Instead, Rhys and I watch from the living room as one of the plumbers opens the trap door to the second underground chamber, the one containing our water reservoir, the same water that flows through our taps. The plumber climbs partway down the ladder and proceeds to test the water level by dipping his bum in the drink. Rhys and I can only trade glances.

I have lost count of how many times the plumbers have bailed us out. Though I am grateful for their assistance, I would prefer that they identify the root cause of our pump room flooding so as to render their periodic visits unnecessary, and so that we do not endure any more waterless, powerless mornings. Unfortunately, the cause is elusive. First the maintenance company told us that the sprinklers were to blame—but we have none. Then they thought it was overflow from our water tank. The latest culprit is our neighbor's pool, which is allegedly seeping through its liner. If this is correct, I can only wonder what it's doing to the Qasr's foundations.

The leak in the wet wall has been fixed, although not before the wall turned into moldy cheese. A repair crew had to burrow down into the vertical pipe run from the roof to find the cause: a hairpin leak in the pipe leading to Austin's shower. Although Grace the cat has been deprived of her hallucinogens, she appears to be suffering from flashbacks, wandering around the house howling like a banshee. When Austin recently went out of town, she was inconsolable until I let her sleep in my bed. I woke up to find that she had pushed me halfway onto the floor.

The plumbing fiasco has taken a toll on the Qasr's pipes. They now rattle and whine day and night, giving the house a factory-like ambience. The noises are particularly pronounced in the ceiling above Rhys' room, making it a challenge for him to sleep. On the days we do have water, the flow from the taps and showers rises and falls from the inconsistent pressure, causing us no shortage of hilarity when washing dishes or showering. Only none of us is laughing.

The despoiling of the neighborhood's sidewalks continues. First the developer installed bright orange signs on every corner, each displaying some kind of indecipherable code. Perhaps they are way-finding references for the battered ice cream truck that now slowly cruises the neighborhood twice a week, its pied-piper music sounding like a 72 rpm record being played at 33. Then the utility companies came in and marked their underground lines with dozens of what look like knee-high tombstones, all painted canary yellow and bearing silent witness to what lies beneath. During one of my recent evening walks I stopped for a moment of silence at the resting place of the Abu Dhabi Water and Electricity Authority's 11-kilovolt distribution line, cherished son of his 33-kilovolt parents and proud sire of an entire brood of 440-volt domestic connections. May he forever rest in peace.

In other news, the garage door has developed an attitude. It now opens only halfway before halting; I have to press the opener multiple times to make it go all the way up. Rhys and I spend a Saturday morning trying to fix it. He climbs atop a ladder and gives the guide wheels a good spraying with a can of lubricant. "Right, try it," he says. I press the button on the opener. The motor box whirs and the chain stretches taut, splits, and falls to the floor with a metallic clatter. Rhys looks down at me and says, "It's like Tom Hanks in *The Money Pit*, innit?"

Sixteen

Cracks in the Façade

Our material progress will do more harm than good unless accompanied by social progress serving as the foundation for a civilization in which we can create a society which can enshrine and preserve these traditions.—Sheikh Zayed bin Sultan al Nahyan

Ever since I had arrived in Abu Dhabi, one crucial detail about the emirate's ongoing boom had eluded me: at no point did I know exactly how much development was underway. I couldn't pull up the numbers and say there were so-and-so many buildings under construction or so-and-so many miles of roads, and so forth. I was not the only one whom this information eluded. No one else at the UPC knew it either. For that matter, neither did anyone in the various other government agencies, nor the developers, nor in all likelihood the sheikhs themselves. For all of the emirate's fixation with control, nobody could answer the question with any precision. Things simply changed too rapidly. Every week brought announcements of new projects. Even in the transport sector, the numbers were fluid. If one week there was a hundred billion dirhams of new transport infrastructure in the works, the next week it might be a hundred and twenty billion, and so on.

More than any other entity, the UPC should have known best how much real estate and infrastructure were on the books, but in reality, the agency was flying blind. Its lack of enforceable powers meant that the agency depended on the emirate's developers to report on the number and scale of their myriad developments, and those statistics were highly suspect. Only the developers knew what they were actually building. Even they seemed not to fully grasp the magnitude of their respective portfolios, let alone what the competition was doing, seeing as how none of them ever bothered to conduct market studies. Various real estate consultancies had issued their own surveys, but they were just as reliant on the developers' self-reporting. The bottom line was that even the people in the center of the development maelstrom were in the dark as to its full scope and intensity.

Oddly enough, it turned out to be the UPC's scrappy little transport team that came up with the best means of deriving an answer to this vital question. Lakshmi, our technology guru, maintained a database that tracked Abu Dhabi's developments—existing, under construction, and proposed—with a breakdown of how much square footage each development devoted to residential, commercial, retail, and so forth. The transport team drew on these numbers to anticipate the city's population distribution, which we then used to ensure that the various infrastructure investments were directed to appropriate locations. Despite Lakshmi's best efforts, the database was perpetually out of date; new projects sprang up too quickly to keep pace. Nevertheless, it was the closest thing to a comprehensive inventory that the agency possessed.

In August 2010 the Professor made it our goal to get a definitive grasp of the city's development quantum. The second week of August marked the start of the Islamic month of Ramadan, the one time of year when things slowed down. The reduced working hours and the effects of day-long fasting on Abu Dhabi's Muslims brought a month-long reprieve in the city's blistering pace of transformation. The Professor wanted to take advantage of the hiatus in new project announcements to catch up with what was already on the books. He directed us to collect updated statistics from the developers on all of their projects, which we then fed into Lakshmi's database. Crunching these numbers was all Lakshmi did for the entire month.

At the same time, the UPC was preparing to update *Plan 2030*. When Larry and the Vancouver Mafia had produced the original plan, they had proposed that it should be updated once every five years. Yet by the middle of 2010, less than three years later, a revision was already sorely needed. The slew of unanticipated developments not contemplated in *Plan 2030* had cut back even further on the plan's already limited ability to oraculate the future. The document's original strategic assumptions were also starting to look overly optimistic. For example, to reach the desired three-million-strong population by 2030, the plan relied on Abu Dhabi's economy sustaining an annual growth rate upwards of 7 percent throughout the period. That figure may have been realistic in the years between 2004 and 2008, when the pent-up demand of the late Zayed era was unleashed and the protracted global recession had not started to bite. In 2010, however, the emirate's economists began to predict more modest 4 to 5 percent growth over the next decade. The UPC staff used this lower growth rate to calculate the revised *Plan 2030*'s population goal. Although Abu Dhabi could always pump more money out of the ground, it was not entirely immune to economic forces beyond its borders.

It was towards the end of Ramadan when Lakshmi wrapped up her work. The Professor called an internal meeting of the transport team to discuss the results before disseminating them throughout the agency. He began by giving us the revised population projections. "The original population forecast in *Plan 2030* was 3.1 million residents," he said. "Now we're looking at no more than 2.6 million, and that's in the best scenario, if the five percent growth rate holds. It'll be less if the economy takes a dive." He paused to let this sink in, then said, "Lakshmi, why don't you tell us what you found?"

All eyes turned to Lakshmi. On the table in front of her was a stack of printed spreadsheets, thick as a dictionary, which she flipped through with visible unease. She cleared her throat and said, "I've added up everything—existing population, developments currently under construction, and proposals that have already been approved. If all these projects are completed, and if nothing new is proposed from today forward, then in 2030 Abu Dhabi will have enough real estate for...." She double-checked her figures. "Five million people."

Alex chortled and Carlo let out a low whistle. The data confirmed what we all knew instinctively but had been unable to prove—until now. Abu Dhabi's exuberance had frothed into a spectacular rash of overbuilding. Its magnitude, however, was truly surprising. Even in the best case, the city would have twice as much real estate as it needed. Lakshmi's numbers showed that Abu Dhabi would add fifty thousand new villas and apartments just by 2013. The boom had become a binge.

"Umkak, that not good," Khalid said. "What we gonna do?"

"I don't mean to tell you how to spend your money," I said, "but you might want to hold off on buying that investment property you were talking about."

* * *

The Ramadan month that year proved to be revealing in other ways as well. Whether from the effects of the daily fasting or as a result of the increased personal reflection that this self-restraint is supposed to encourage, my local colleagues and the rest of the city's Emiratis seemed to let their normally impenetrable guard down ever so slightly.

As the high point of the Islamic calendar, Ramadan is a unique time in Abu Dhabi. The government requires all Muslims, Emirati and foreign alike, to observe the Ramadan fast, abstaining from food or liquid from dawn until nightfall. While non-Muslims are not expected to adhere to this rule, they must respect it. Eating or drinking in public during daylight hours is punished by a fine—one of the few such penalties that are strictly enforced. Restaurants are not allowed to open until dusk, although some have enough wasta to get around this restriction. Jones the Grocer, for example, simply hung opaque white sheets in its windows and kept serving its overpriced coffee to the city's caffeine-addled expats right through the holy month.

The word *Ramadan* stems from an Arabic root that denotes intense, scorching heat. Because of the lunar nature of the Islamic calendar, Ramadan falls ten to twelve days earlier every year on the Gregorian calendar. During my two years in Abu Dhabi the month coincided with the withering peak of summer, effectively putting the city into slow motion for four weeks. People moved with torpor in the heat, whether they observed the fast or not. Even the traffic flowed markedly slower during the daylight hours, as though bogged down in the superheated asphalt like dinosaurs in the La Brea tar pits.

This languor was reversed in the hour before sundown, when the city's Muslims rushed to the homes of friends and family to break the fast with traditional *iftar* dinners. As a result, one of the most visible effects of Ramadan was a marked deterioration in the already execrable safety of the roads during the madcap pre-iftar surges, causing countless accidents from fender benders to fiery conflagrations. Even post-iftar, the roads remained crazy well into the night as local drivers unleashed the built-up tension from the daylight hours. After the first few days of Ramadan I became accustomed to driving even more defensively than usual, doing my best to steer clear of the tint-windowed kamikazes as they tore around corners and raced along straightaways. But nothing could prepare me for the terrifying experience of witnessing such driving from the other side of the windscreen.

At Khalid's invitation, I met him for an iftar dinner one Ramadan evening at the Yas Viceroy. The hotel's interior looked even more space-age than that of ADNEC. Every visible surface was covered in white, from the flowing walls to the podlike chairs in the lobby to the streamlined frame around the obligatory photo of Sheikh Zayed behind the reception desk. We dined in the waterfront restaurant overlooking the Yas Marina and its resident collection of super-yachts.

Though the sumptuous dinner buffet was already set out when we arrived shortly before dusk, the restaurant's patrons had to wait for the official announcement of sundown before eating. When the maitre d' came around to the tables to let the guests know they could commence, it set off a race for the buffet that rivaled the Formula One competition held every November on the track surrounding the hotel. I was taken aback by the haste; in my limited prior experience with iftars in Iraq, my Muslim colleagues had preferred to break their fasts gently with dates and water before adjourning for prayers and then moving on to more solid fare. The diners at the Viceroy, in contrast, swarmed the buffet and appeared to all return with two or three plates apiece, which they attacked with zeal. I began to understand why many of Abu Dhabi's Muslims actually gained weight during Ramadan from gorging on fatty iftar dinners.[1]

Over the meal I asked Khalid whether he was still concerned about Lakshmi's findings regarding Abu Dhabi's impending real estate glut.

"Enh, not really," he said between bites of food. "The developers know what they doing."

"How can you be so sure?" I asked.

"That why we have you people, umkak? We bringed the best in the world here to help us build Abu Dhabi. We figure something out." I couldn't tell whether Khalid had legitimate confidence in the abilities of the emirate's "Foreign Legion," or whether this was just bluster. Despite having worked with him for more than a year, I still frequently found him impossible to read. Although gestures such as inviting me to his brothers' wedding and to this iftar demonstrated an obvious effort on his part to bridge the gap, there was still something sphinx-like about him, a sense of reserve or caution or enigma that never seemed to fully go away.

"What you think about the railway?" he said, changing the subject. The planning for the national railway was still chugging along. We had managed to resolve most of the plot conflicts along the Shah Line's route in Al Gharbia. Some of the heritage farms in Liwa had proven impossible to relocate, despite intervention from the crown prince's Diwan. Furthermore, Etihad Rail's consultants had set a maximum design gradient of 1 percent, meaning that the track could not rise or fall more than a foot for every one hundred feet of its length in order to avoid overtaxing the locomotives that would pull the lengthy trains of sulfur wagons. Despite these constraints, we had worked with the consultants to devise an alignment that would keep the costs of earthworks to a minimum. The consultants were now putting the finishing touches on the detailed design. Soon, they would be ready to present the whole thing to Etihad Rail's directors and the Executive Council in order to obtain their approval to start construction.

"Do you really think it will get built?" I asked. I still found the prospect of the railway's creation hard to believe. My experience had accustomed me to expect the worst: the more grandiose the project, the higher its likelihood of cancellation.

Khalid nodded. "Of course. *Inshallah*." If God willed it. I couldn't argue with that.

Though I felt quite sated after my second trip to the buffet, Khalid kept going. I worried it would look rude to finish first, so I felt obliged to continue to make an effort, much to my stomach's chagrin. After stuffing ourselves for two hours we finally called it quits.

We waddled like overstuffed penguins out to the lobby. I had taken a taxi to the hotel, and I told Khalid I would do the same to get back to the office, where Big White was parked. He wouldn't hear of it. "No way, boss. You ride with me." Khalid gave his ticket to the valet, and a minute later I found myself ogling his car, an ivory Porsche 911 Carrera S that gleamed as though it had just rolled off the assembly line in Stuttgart. Khalid had bought the car just a few weeks before. I settled into the cozy embrace of the passenger seat, the scarlet leather interior still smelling new. As we left the hotel and turned onto Yas Island's main road, Khalid goosed the accelerator and slingshotted us around the corner.

Now here, perhaps, was something on which we could relate: cars. "Feels like we're driving on silk," I said. "Are you happy you bought it?"

He smiled. "I tell you what it is, umkak? This car is the net—the best net for catching fishes."

I cocked my head. "What's that mean?"

He shot me a skeptical look. "Come on, you kidding me." When I persisted with my ignorance, he clarified, "Fishes. Girls. I pull up to the stoplight, and the girls, they roll down windows and ask me for directions. All kind of girls—Lebanon girls, Jordan girls, even Emirati girls! And you know, they not need directions, they know where they going. Sometimes they just looking to race."

By this point we were on the highway, traveling just above the speed limit of one hundred twenty kilometers an hour. At such a leisurely pace, the Porsche felt like it wasn't even trying. "The girls think they can outrun you in this thing?" I asked.

"No way! But that not the point." He looked at me sternly and said, in all seriousness, "You making a lot of money while you here, umkak? When you go home, you buy one of these. Maybe then you finally get you a wife." He settled back into his seat with a sigh. "If I was not as good of man ... wow. This car would keep me busy."

Although it was taboo to ask an Emirati about his spouse, I couldn't resist. "And your wife? She doesn't mind the attention you get?"

Khalid shrugged. "She already know I am looking for another."

"*Another* Porsche?"

"No. Another wife."

I lapsed into silence. The Emirati custom of taking multiple wives was far from uncommon, but I wouldn't have picked Khalid to be in the running for another marriage. He seemed too young, for starters; though I didn't know his exact age, it couldn't have been much more than thirty. The revelation was yet another reminder of how little I understood my hosts. Every time I felt I was finally lifting the curtain ever so slightly on their perplexing psyche, they proved me wrong.

"Anyway, my wife can't complain," Khalid continued. "I buyed her a Cayenne. You know, big enough for the fam–"

He was cut off by a high-pitched whine as a pair of heavily modified Audis with neon underglow lights tore past on either side of us, racing each other recklessly down the highway. The effect on Khalid was like waving a red flag in front of a bull. He downshifted, dropped the clutch, and stepped on the gas. The engine roared a Teutonic war cry as we gave chase.

Palm trees flashed past outside the window, blurring together in the Martian glow of the overhead lights. I sank deeper into the passenger seat and glanced at the speedometer just in time to see it climb above two hundred kilometers an hour. Khalid's face was utterly emotionless as we weaved through six lanes of heavy evening traffic. He muttered something in Arabic and flashed his brights spasmodically. I looked forward to see us barreling down on an unbroken phalanx of cars spanning the width of the highway. At the last possible second, Khalid swerved onto the left-hand shoulder and looped around the congestion, missing the nearest car by inches. A knot formed in my stomach as I realized that he could very well kill us.

As we shot across the city, I tried to focus on the scenery instead of on our impending destruction. We passed the steel skeletons of dozens of new skyscrapers, the ethereal blue and green lights of construction cranes dotting the inky darkness above them. Harsh white fluorescence lit the half-finished buildings from inside, silhouetting the hordes of laborers still toiling away on the midnight shift. I focused on one building and, for a brief moment, saw a trio of South Asian faces peering out into the night, lit hauntingly by the spectral bluish flare of an arc weld. Then they were gone.

The Audis exited the freeway ahead of us and I breathed a sigh of relief. But Khalid was not about to let his quarry off that easy. He pulled onto the ramp in pursuit. What was already a disquieting experience now became harrowing as we rocketed through a maze of quiet residential streets. Khalid gunned the throttle on the straightaways, then slammed on the brakes at the roundabouts just long enough to find a hole in the cross-traffic. There was no margin of error. One misjudgment, and we were finished.

I had witnessed this kind of suicidal driving by Emiratis on an almost daily basis, but always from inside my own car, never from one of theirs. Seeing the nihilistic mentality firsthand was disturbing. Khalid was utterly indifferent to the danger—both to us and to the other drivers on the road, not to mention any unfortunate pedestrians—as we played cat and mouse with the Audis through the neighborhood.

Thankfully, Khalid soon succumbed to that other defining Emirati trait: the short attention span. He turned right at a roundabout and the Audis sped away. "Hmm ... that was fun," he said.

When we reached the office, I climbed out of the car onto disco legs that wouldn't stop shaking. "Next time, you drives," Khalid called after me. As I watched him leave, I couldn't help thinking that our drive was an apt representation of life in the fast-changing city—indeed, of Abu Dhabi's entire transformation. The Emiratis were behind the wheel and the rest of us were merely along for what had promised to be a wild ride. But what began as a thrill now seemed increasingly in danger of spiraling out of control.

* * *

The smoke from the shisha pipe made my head spin. My housemates and I were enjoying a rare cool evening in the Qasr's backyard. Our grass had long ago died from the repeated flooding, and the yard had reverted to sand. It wasn't altogether unpleasant, as we didn't have to water it—or rather, our Sri Lankan maid didn't have to water it—and Grace seemed to enjoy having an extra-large litter box.

Omar, one of the Emiratis on Rhys's team, had joined us. He was one of the more westernized of the UPC's locals and made regular if fleeting appearances at expat socials. He almost never wore a kandora outside the office, preferring shorts and T-shirts instead. On this particular evening he had been partaking freely of the shisha, but his liberalness evidently didn't extend to alcohol. When Austin offered him a rum and coke, Omar politely declined. Austin shrugged and fetched himself a larger glass.

The conversation had turned to travel, and Omar was heaping scorn on his countrymen's travel habits. "When my friends go abroad, all they want to do is shop. They go to London or Kuala Lumpur, stay in five-star hotels, and spend two weeks replacing their wardrobes. The Saudis are even worse."

Rhys said, "I love it when the rich ones bring their cars with them. Did you know that cars with Gulf plates account for the most unpaid parking tickets in London?" He cited a recent story that had made its way around British expat circles, about how the London police had booted a pair of Qatari-owned supercars—a Koenigsegg and a Lamborghini—for parking illegally in front of Harrod's department store.[2] "They should do everyone a favor and just stay home."

Omar said, "Well, not me. I go to interesting places. I've been to twenty-six countries, you know."

"What's your favorite?" Austin asked.

"Poland. The girls, man."

"Have you ever been to Yemen?" I asked.

Omar nearly choked on the shisha pipe. "*No*. Why in the world would I go *there*?"

Yemen is the black sheep of the Gulf family. It has little oil and is thus the only nation on the Arabian Peninsula excluded from the rich boys' club of the Gulf Cooperation Council. Yemen's neighbors view the country as both a charity case and a ticking time bomb. With 24 million people each earning an average of one thousand dollars per year as of 2009, Yemen is the poorest country in the region and one of the poorest on Earth.[3] Its woefully corrupt government is too preoccupied with battling separatist rebels and the local chapter of al Qaeda to make any progress on the sclerotic economy. For Yemen's neighbors, the nightmare scenario of millions of impoverished Yemenis spilling over the borders in the wake of a civil war or a humanitarian crisis is a very real possibility.

As it stands, much of Yemen's working-age population is already spread around the

Gulf as long-term migrant labor. The earnings they remit to Yemen keep the country afloat financially. Of particular note, Yemenis comprise a large portion of both the UAE's armed forces and the police. The logic is both racial and economic. There are far too few Emiratis to fill the ranks, but security is one arena that can't be trusted to non-Arabs. Yemenis are the cheapest Arabs, so soldiers and policemen they become.

Unfortunately this role doesn't earn Yemenis any more respect from their Emirati cousins, who view them as hillbillies. The contempt for Yemen is all the more curious given the country's role as the font of Arabian history. The tribes of the peninsula, the forerunners of the modern Emiratis and Saudis and Qataris, all originated in Yemen.[4] Sheikh Zayed himself was able to trace his roots back to Yemen, and he certainly appreciated the value of this history, as one of his most famous quotes reflects: "He who does not know his past cannot make the best of his present and future, for it is from the past that we learn." The Yemen connection prompted Zayed to make the country one of the first and largest recipients of UAE foreign aid. Even after Zayed's death, the UAE continued to devote substantial sums to Yemen—2.4 billion dirhams in 2009 alone—primarily through its international development agency, the Abu Dhabi Fund for Development.[5]

Though I had never been to Yemen, it had held my fascination since my first trip to the Middle East nearly five years before. The country boasted some of Arabia's oldest cities, its predecessor states having given birth to formidable empires while the rest of Arabia was empty wastes. Yemen's stature was such that the Romans dubbed it *Arabia Felix*—Arabia the Fine. The present-day country, in contrast, is well off the beaten path, sufficiently poor and unstable to deter most travelers. Which made it all the more irresistible.

Omar did not share this view. When I pressed him about his disdain for Yemen, he listed the Yemenis' faults. "They're animals. They're thieves. They're lazy and rude." I traded a knowing glance with Rhys. These criticisms came from a guy who was absent from the office without excuse at least one or two working days a week and who never made eye contact with the Indian kitchen staff who brought him his tea.

"You don't have any interest in the history there?" I asked.

Omar took another long pull on the shisha. "What history? Those people had their chance, and they're still in the dark ages." He gestured to the dull suburban façades that surrounded our backyard. "It took us fifty years to do what they couldn't accomplish in five thousand. This is Arabia now."

In spite of Omar's self-assurance, those same façades concealed remarkable dysfunction. Our Emirati neighbors—about half the population of the Golf Gardens community—were profoundly reclusive. They all erected five-foot-tall concealment fences atop their already towering backyard walls and balconies, despite having abandoned the built-in privacy of traditional Arab house designs for semi-detached townhouses and villas. Nevertheless, I managed to catch scattered glimpses of their lives during my evening walks through the neighborhood.

Walking around Golf Gardens was like a free ticket to a luxury car show. The neighborhood servants would wash down their masters' chariots every evening, squandering quantities of water that Abu Dhabi really couldn't spare. Some households seemed to go through cars like groceries, sporting a new model in the driveway every week. During one circuit of the neighborhood I counted two Lamborghinis, one Ferrari, half a dozen Maseratis, four Bentleys, a score of Porsches, an Aston Martin, a Rolls-Royce, and one Ford F-250 kitted out with giant wheels and vertical exhausts like a monster truck. I didn't even bother tallying up the Mercedes, BMWs, and Jaguars. Every last one of these vehicles was in pristine condition, inside and out, all thanks to South Asian hands. The servants kept the four-wheeled trophies polished, watered, oiled, tuned, and gassed. All the Emiratis had to worry about was driving—all the more ironic, given their ineptitude at this very skill.

During my walks I usually caught sight of Emirati children playing outside. They were always under the nominal supervision of their Indonesian and Filipina nannies, whose authority was nonexistent and whose scoldings were mere suggestions. Predictably, the urchins often ran amok, tearing around the neighborhood with impunity. The minders would trail behind, pleading with their charges to stop running out into the street or knocking over the garbage cans or pulling up the geraniums in the irrigated flowerbeds. On my way back from exercising at the clubhouse one evening I came across an Emirati preschooler throwing a temper tantrum. He was rolling on the ground screaming at the top of his lungs, and when his nanny came close he spat at her. She took it like a Stoic; to actually restrain the gremlin would have probably cost her her job.

Despite the fences atop their walls, our Emirati neighbors across the street from the Qasr didn't bother to hang curtains in their second-story windows. I could thus see straight into their upstairs living room from ours. Their gigantic flat-screen television was always on. Even when I woke up in the middle of the night and peered outside, their upstairs windows were invariably lit with a flickering blue glow. The family appeared to take shifts absorbing the TV's enervating rays; there was always someone watching from the sofa, but rarely more than one. Of course, the transparency went both ways. I often wondered what they thought when they looked across the street and witnessed Austin's monthly house parties.

It was these minute, almost trifling, clues that finally helped me understand the full measure of the locals' predicament. Initially I found it all too easy to disdain the Emiratis, to chuckle condescendingly at the ease with which they took credit for the achievements of their foreign workforce or to rage at their incompetent driving. Or I could simply write them off as incomprehensible. But disdain gradually gave way to sorrow as I came to realize the tragic truth: the Emiratis are a people traumatized by their success. No other group in history has experienced such a meteoric, shattering rise. In just fifty years they have gone from being desert nomads on the perpetual brink of starvation to being the wardens of a modern country with one of the highest standards of living in the world. And it has nearly ruined them. Their traditions have been all but erased, their society has been warped, and their very identity has been trampled beneath the clanking tank treads of progress.

When Jonathan Raban visited Abu Dhabi in the late 1970s, he expressed confidence that the Bedu would survive the modernization with which they were then grappling: "The Bedu had met the century head on, but they had been able to deal with it in the family. Everything had been focused inward: inside these boxes of cinder block and cement, the unmanageable century had been reduced in scale so that it could be dealt with at a domestic pace in a domestic space. It could be coped with, if it was taken inch by inch."[6] Now, thirty years later, the unmanageable century has perhaps proven to be really unmanageable after all. Those boxes of cinder block and cement have been replaced with lavish villas, yet the Emiratis' state of affairs is markedly less secure. They have custom-ordered a modern life, a modern city—a veritable monument unto themselves—and now it threatens to consume them.

* * *

Qasr al Deviance Journal, Week 28

After a long, drawn-out battle, our garage door has finally won. It is stuck in the down position and refuses to budge. My housemates and I have become experts at wedging our three bulky Jeeps into our two-car driveway. If this whole urban planning thing doesn't work out, perhaps we can get jobs as valets.

The house's air conditioning system has become self-aware. It taunts us by shutting off at odd hours of the night, only to restart when one of us gets out of bed and goes to turn it back on. It also seems to be growing increasingly ineffective, the airflow from its vents somewhat resembling the breath of a wheezy old man with ice cubes in his mouth.

Our clanging pipes have forced poor Rhys to seek refuge elsewhere. He now spends three or four nights a week at Seren's apartment just so he can sleep. He still clings to the hope that pestering the maintenance company will fix our problems and enable him to return, but he is being disabused of this notion. After his most recent phone call with the maintenance company's helpless help desk, Rhys e-mailed Austin and me a transcript of the conversation:

RHYS: "Hello?"
MAINTENANCE COMPANY: "Hello, ma'am-sir, we are phoning to confirm your appointment for window cleaning."
R: "Actually, I wanted my pipes fixed. And also water and electricity."
MC: "Oh. Can I confirm the appointment for the window cleaning?"
R: "If you want, but I would really like water and electricity."
MC: "Can they come at 2pm tomorrow?"
R: "We will all be at work."
MC: "It's okay, they can do it when you are in work."
R: "Really? How will they access the backyard?"
MC: "Oh. Is it okay if they just do the front?"
R: "No. We would like both sides of the house cleaned. Also, can we have our water and electricity sorted?"
MC: "Yes, let me confirm the appointment. I see it's booked for Wednesday at 8:00 a.m."
R: "No, it's not. It's meant to be tonight. Can they look at it as a matter of urgency? I can't sleep there at the moment."
MC: "Okay, sir. Is Wednesday acceptable?"
R: "NO. It needs to be sorted immediately."
MC: "Okay, sir, I will ring later."
R: "What? Fine. Please call me back within the hour, so I can figure out where I'm sleeping tonight."
MC: "Okay, sir. I will this call you this afternoon. The window cleaners will come at 2:00 p.m. tomorrow, okay?"

The developer has done all it can to render Golf Gardens' sidewalks impassible with fixtures and is now working on the streets themselves. When we first moved in, the neighborhood streets already featured speed bumps every hundred feet that were so outsized even Big White couldn't tackle them at more than three miles an hour without tossing its passengers around. Evidently those weren't enough. The developer has now installed smaller secondary bumps at every street corner, making each trip through the neighborhood feel like a ride on a midget rollercoaster. The way things are going, Golf Gardens is becoming a real concrete jungle, thick with all sorts of manmade undergrowth. Apparently nobody has told these people that sometimes less is more.

In other news, last night I had a peculiar dream in which I found myself standing out in front of the Qasr. I wandered up and down the empty streets before coming to the house of a neighbor. When I knocked on the door, it opened of its own accord. The interior, vast as a warehouse, was bare but for one wall, from which a giant television cast its lunatic images. In front of it sat all the neighborhood children, transfixed by the synthetic scenes unfolding in rapid sequence before them.

"Children, where are your parents?" I heard myself say.

As one, they turned and gazed at me, but with glowing blue screens instead of eyes. I awoke, cold with sweat, their hollow choral reply still echoing in my ears:

"We have no parents."

Seventeen

Guests Behaving Badly

The British have been in the Gulf for two hundred years, and in all that time what have they done for the Arabs? What did the British bring? Fornication and the whiskey bottle.—Arabia: A Journey Through the Labyrinth

R andom left the police station and walked across the parking lot to where Austin and I were waiting in my housemate's Jeep.

"Sorry it took so long," Random said once he was inside. He was clearly perturbed. "There are six Emiratis in there whose job is to drink coffee, and it took the other guy forever just to look up from his Blackberry." Random was from Canada and had been in Abu Dhabi only a few weeks; Austin had befriended him shortly after his arrival. Random wasn't his real name, of course, but Austin had a curious habit of addressing his friends by nicknames he devised. Random actually had it relatively easy; Austin's other acquaintances included Blackpool, a surly chap from the English city of the same name, and Trolley Dolley, a South African flight attendant.

Random was still wading through the bureaucracy of getting set up in Abu Dhabi. On that particular morning Austin and I had picked him up on our way to the office and had taken him to the police station to retrieve his new driver's license. We waited for nearly forty-five minutes. Austin was just about to text him to take a cab when Random emerged.

"Please tell me that you at least got your license," Austin said.

"Barely. The guy at the desk wanted me to go away. He said my name wasn't in the system. I told him I had just submitted my application on Monday and I wasn't leaving until he looked again. 'Ah, yes mister, here you are! Computer is slow today.'"

I asked, "How's your photo? Did they take it with your eyes closed?"

"No, there's no photo on it."

Austin and I exchanged questioning looks. "How can you have a driver's license with no photograph?" I asked.

"It's not my driver's license." Random held up a little blue booklet. "I was getting my liquor license."

Austin erupted. "Your LIQUOR license! You didn't tell me you were getting your *liquor* license!"

"Why do you want one of those?" I asked.

Random looked bewildered. "Isn't that how you buy alcohol here?"

Austin banged his head on the steering wheel. "I can't believe you made us late for *that*."

"I know you Canadians missed out on Prohibition," I said to Random, "but I assume you're familiar with the concept of a speakeasy?"

One of Abu Dhabi's greatest incongruities is that alcohol is a defining element—some would say *the* defining element—of expatriate life in the conservative Islamic emirate. The only places permitted to sell alcohol are restaurants in the city's hotels, and they are ostensibly supposed to serve it only to non-Muslim foreigners who possess a liquor license. Tourists cannot obtain liquor licenses, meaning that every tourist who takes a drink is technically breaking the law. Residents, on the other hand, are allowed to obtain liquor licenses, but they are prohibited from drinking in "tourist establishments," i.e., the hotels. Even Emirati judges who handle alcohol-related cases have gone on record admitting that these regulations are inconsistent and confusing.[1] The general consensus is that the government maintains this catch-22 arrangement so as to have a ready-made excuse to jail or deport any foreigner, whether resident or tourist, who crosses behavioral lines while under the influence. Of course, enforcing such restrictions would prompt many foreigners to stay away. So the authorities generally look aside as the booze continues to flow, a necessary evil for Abu Dhabi to gain its desired international stature.

In practice, Abu Dhabi's residents and tourists rarely have problems obtaining a drink. UAE federal law makes it a crime only to *buy* alcohol without a liquor license; hotel restaurants can *sell* to whomever they want, even minors. None of the hotel restaurants ever ask to see liquor licenses, nor does Spinneys, the one supermarket in town that is allowed to sell alcohol. It is not uncommon to see locals drinking in hotels, all the more incongruous as they are doubly banned from consumption on the dual basis of being Muslim *and* Emirati. For example, at Brauhaus, the German restaurant at the Beach Rotana hotel, one can usually spot at least two or three kandora-clad locals with towering steins of lager in hand.

For homebound consumption, it is easier and cheaper, not to mention far more interesting, to skip the official establishments and visit one of the city's unaccredited liquor stores. Knowledge of these hush-hush outlets is passed around the expat community by word of mouth, although they aren't terribly hard to find. The powers that be assuredly know of their existence; nothing in Abu Dhabi stays hidden from the state security apparatus for long. Presumably whoever runs these speakeasies simply has enough *wasta* to convince the authorities to look the other way.

Shortly after we moved to the Qasr, my housemates introduced me to their favorite such off-license store, the aptly named High Spirits. It was hidden behind an unmarked side entrance to the ancient (by Abu Dhabi standards at least) National Hotel, a decrepit 1970s-era glass box that sat right around the corner from the Supreme Court, of all places. High Spirits' shelves were stocked year-round with everything from absinthe to whisky. Customers exited with their illicit purchases cloaked in black trash bags, as though that would fool anyone. Foreigners weren't the only patrons; quite a few Emiratis also frequented the store. They would park in the sandy lot outside, honk to summon a runner, and crack their black-tinted windows to dictate their orders.

Abu Dhabi's two-faced policy on teetotaling and the dearth of other activities have the unfortunate effect of magnifying the abuse of alcohol, particularly on the part of Westerners. The emirate is blissfully free from public drunkenness, but dipsomania abounds behind closed doors of both structural and automotive varieties. The sumptuous buffets of the city's ubiquitous Friday brunches are merely excuses for expats to drink copious quantities of champagne. Many expats seem even more inclined to get behind the wheel after drinking than they would normally be back home. A third of respondents to one survey reported knowing someone who drove drunk within the previous twelve months[2]—despite traffic laws that forbid *any* blood alcohol content and penalties for drunk driving that include automatic revocation of one's driving license, a hefty fine, and possibly a lengthy jail sentence, deportation, or even lashings.[3] During the prolonged summer, when even the Gulf is too hot to swim in, drinking is essentially the only pastime for the expats who remain in Abu Dhabi, a diversion they pursue with almost pathological abandon. After all, in a city defined by excess, why should the consumption of alcohol be any different?

* * *

The Sheikh Zayed Bridge opened with great fanfare in November 2010, a mere four years late and profoundly over budget.[4] The southern half of the reconfigured Salaam Street was finished around the same time. The entire city breathed a sigh of relief as crosstown road capacity increased by 50 percent almost overnight. My housemates and I, instead of commuting to work via Airport Road, could now hop on the E10 highway just before the bridge and cruise all the way to Saada Street, a block south of Mamoura, without hitting a stoplight, cutting our typical drive from fifty minutes to fifteen.

Its risqué design aside, the Sheikh Zayed Bridge made for a spectacular entrance to Abu Dhabi. It catapulted drivers over the Maqta Channel and offered sweeping views all the way to Mussafah. Despite absorbing a substantial amount of traffic from Airport Road in the weeks after the bridge opened, its eight lanes were never close to full. For a while it was thus common to see cars parked on the bridge in the rightmost lane while their drivers stood at the railing taking in the view. That came to an abrupt end when a pair of tourists were arrested and jailed for snapping photos from the bridge, which the security services claimed to include a picture of the sensitive oil refinery on Umm al Nar Island.

This was merely the latest in a string of incidents in which the authorities had become ever more paranoid about photography. The security services made it clear that they would hold photographers responsible for taking pictures of sensitive installations, even if there were no signs posted. But exactly what constituted a "sensitive installation" was anybody's guess. Clueless shutterbugs thus found themselves stripped of their cameras, thrown in jail, and fined for photographing subjects as innocuous as the Yas Marina racetrack and the broken arm of the Capital Gate tower.[5] For a city that wanted to attract international visitors, it was a self-defeating policy.

One warm December afternoon my housemates and I were driving home on the newly opened Salaam Street on one of the rare days when the three of us managed to carpool. We had no excuse not to do so every day, other than the mornings we woke up without utilities and had to stagger our showers at the Golf Gardens clubhouse. Yet most mornings we just couldn't be bothered to coordinate, and thus would wind up taking two or even all three of our Jeeps to the office. And why not? Gas was cheap, and we were living in a city that, for all its rhetoric about sustainability, still epitomized waste. Even the UPC, which was supposed to be setting the standard with its Estidama program, had selected for its company cars a trio of gas-guzzling Cadillac Escalades.

I was dozing off halfway through the drive when Austin suddenly slammed on the brakes. Traffic in front of us had come to a halt. We inched along as a line of orange barrels reduced the four lanes to one. A bit further along we saw why: work crews with grinders and jackhammers were chewing away the top layer of pavement to reveal the base course underneath.

I raised Khalid on the phone, having to shout to be heard over the din. "Do you know they're tearing up Salaam?" I said.

"Yes. So?"

"Why?! It was just finished. The asphalt was barely dry!"

Khalid was unfazed. "The Municipality getted complaints that the road was bad. They sended out inspectors and finded the contractor builded it wrong. So they make him do it again." That at least accounted for why the road had already felt rutted within days of its opening. Once again, Abu Dhabi had gotten exactly what it paid for.

We made it through the bottleneck, but traffic continued to crawl even as the lanes reopened. Finally we reached the head of the pack. A Toyota Corolla puttered along in the fast lane with a line of irate drivers bunched up behind it. As we approached in the next lane over, the car slowly drifted until it straddled the white line, half in our lane.

Austin bashed the horn and the car jerked back into its lane. As we sped past, Rhys craned his head to look. He turned back and stated, sotto voce, "Would it surprise you gentlemen to learn that the driver of that car was from the Indian subcontinent?"

Westerners react to Abu Dhabi's endemic classism in different ways. It is easy to blame the Emiratis for creating such a stratified system. Waxing indignant about the emirate's unjust hierarchy is standard fare at expat socials. In reality, there is plenty of guilt to share. The locals may be the puppet masters running the show, but from the penultimate level of the emirate's population pyramid, Westerners enjoy a plethora of benefits from the laboring masses as well. Unlike our Emirati neighbors, my housemates and I didn't have a cohort of domestic servants to wait on us hand and foot. But we did have our biweekly cleanings from the Sri Lankan maid, our routine visits from the plumbers, and our floor-to-ceiling power washings from Austin's cleanup crew after each of his bacchanal parties, all for a fraction of what they would have cost back home.

I found the life of a neocolonial to be bizarre. My expat colleagues and I all came from modest middle-class backgrounds in our respective countries of origin. We now found ourselves whisked halfway around the world, dropped into positions of privileged mandarins, paid stupendous amounts of money, and given access to a labor force that could handle any chore for a nominal fee. Sometimes the conveniences of such a lifestyle bordered on the absurd. As though fast food couldn't get any lazier, in Abu Dhabi even Burger King and Hardee's offered delivery. Their motorbike couriers were a common sight, ferrying soggy buns and lukewarm discs of processed beef to homes and offices all over the city. In such a coddled milieu, sloth was inevitable.

It was hard not to let the sense of aristocratic privileges go to one's head. The longer I stayed in Abu Dhabi, the more I felt infected by a pernicious, creeping snobbery. It often manifested itself in impulsive outbursts of scorn for the emirate's endless irritations. Trifles like the uniformly bad service in restaurants, the atrocious skills of other drivers, and even unintelligible phone conversations with the maintenance company all sent me into a barely contained rage. Those beneath me on the social scale were not deserving of my patience.

Elise and I went downstairs to Jones the Grocer one morning for a coffee. I ordered my usual, a double macchiato with a blueberry muffin. "Sorry, ma'am-sir," said the Filipina waitress, "no more blueberry muffins today."

"Okay, I'll take a carrot muffin instead."

"No, ma'am-sir, no carrot either." The waitress winced, as if anticipating my blowup.

"Then what's the point of this?" I hissed as I flung the menu back at her. "Fine. Surprise me. Whatever you've got."

Elise waited for me to cool off and then gave me a withering look. "Was that absolutely necessary?"

"What? Oh," I said, chagrined. "Did I really just do that?"

Some expats tried to defuse the feeling of lordliness by resorting to over-the-top humor, taking Abu Dhabi's socio-ethnic disparities to their rational, absurd conclusion. In any other context the jokes would have been tasteless; but in the emirate's pressure-cooker setting, sometimes they were the only way to cope. For example, when the topic of domestic help or some other service rendered by the labor force cropped up at expat socials, the catchphrase was "what can brown do for you?"—a snide riff on United Parcel Service's marketing slogan and the prevailing skin tone of Abu Dhabi's underclass.

When the security services rolled out their latest Big Brother initiative by requiring all residents to obtain a national identity card, Rhys called me from the registration office. "What's long and brown and smelly?" he asked.

"Do I really want to know?"

"It's the line here at the national ID office, and I'm standing in it with half of Mumbai."

Liz was the first to coin a term for this hyperbolic humor. She called it racialism, as opposed to overt racism. "Stop being such a racialist," she would admonish when anyone made a particularly crass remark.

As time passed it became harder to tell where the jesting stopped and actual contempt began. For one of his monthly parties at the Qasr, which consistently reduced our house to ruin, Austin seized on the idea of hosting a Chav Night, "Chav" being the derogatory term for the English underclass, supposedly derived from "Council Housed And Violent." Rhys made up elaborate posters advertising the event. Anticipation around the office built up for weeks beforehand. When it came, most of the UPC's expats showed up wearing tracksuits, raunchy skirts, frizzy hair, and other ironic apparel. None of them showed any concern at the inherent elitism. Though I was normally no stranger to the joking, Chav Night was a bit too much for me. I bowed out and went to Dubai for the evening.

* * *

Qasr al Deviance Journal, Week 33

Midway upon the journey of our stay in the Qasr, I found myself within a living room dark, for the straightforward pathway had been lost. I cannot well repeat how there I entered, so full was I of the dissipate life to which I had succumbed. I looked aside, and beheld my housemate from the land of Wales ensconced there upon the leather couch, devouring the last of the Vietnamese takeout we had summoned. Across from us did unfurl on the moving screen that most bizarre of rituals, the strife I had heard christened rugby.

Before mine eyes did one present himself who seemed dressed for the rodeo. When I beheld him in the living room vast, "Have pity on me," unto him I cried, "for I am lazy and want not to go out."

He answered me: "No choice in the matter hast thou, for it is Friday, and we shall go out. Therefore I think and judge it for thy best thou follow me, and I will be thy guide, and lead thee hence through the infernal place, where thou shalt hear the desperate lamentations, shalt see the foreigners disconsolate, who cry out each one for the way up from this oblivion; and thou shalt see those who contented are within the decadent mire, because they hope to ne'er return to the real world."

The Welsh and I traded glances and knew it futile to debate. Then the Texan moved on, and we behind him followed and entered on the deep and savage way, descending through the rings of that most dire of underworlds: Abu Dhabi's nightlife.[6]

First Circle: Sloth. The rooftop bar at ADNEC's recently opened aLoft hotel offered a commanding view of the city at night. The downtown skyline shimmered in the distance to the north, while across the inky black waters in the other direction the stygian flares of Mussafah's mills lapped at the sky.

Ethan and Liz joined our trio, arriving within minutes of each other. The conversation turned to the two questions that cropped up at every gathering, the questions that were perpetually on the mind of every expat in the emirate: how long to stay and what to do next?

"I'm looking at PhD programs," Ethan said. "Maybe MIT or Penn. Any job is going to be a letdown after Abu Dhabi, so I figure I might as well do something that engages my brain."

"Well, I've finally settled on what's next for me—Australia," Liz proudly announced. She was forever vacillating; the week before she had been set on doing a master's degree program in North Carolina, and the week before that it was something in South Africa.

"And what's your Magic Number?" I asked. The Magic Number was the term Abu Dhabi's expats used for the elusive savings thresholds that, when attained, would enable them to consider moving on. Liz quoted a figure that was entirely realistic based on her salary but, in view of her profligate spending, would take her the better part of a decade to amass. That was the trick about Abu Dhabi. Expats loved complaining about the place, but when it came down to it, the prospect of returning to reality was even more horrifying than staying. And so, whether intentionally or subconsciously, many of my colleagues and friends lived it up and spent freely, pushing their Magic Numbers ever farther out of reach and thus delaying the departures that attaining their financial goals would have made possible.

"What about you, Rhys?" Ethan inquired.

"Oh, I figure I've got another two years 'til I pay off my house in Cardiff," Rhys said. "By then my skills will have atrophied to the point that I won't be able to work anywhere else, so I'll rattle around here for another decade or two and spend the rest of my days in a wine-soaked stupor at the British Club."

The talk had turned too introspective for Austin's liking. He made some phone calls and we were off.

Second Circle: Avarice. Liz came with us to the Yacht Club at the Intercontinental, where Seren joined us as well. We sat outside on the terrace overlooking the half-moon marina and ogled the sixty-foot boats, all of them gleaming white. Most belonged to Emiratis and were purely for show; their owners took them out no more than once or twice a year. "What a waste," Austin scoffed. "If the locals actually had to earn their pay, they might actually appreciate what they buy."

After the third round of over-priced cocktails, we were all utterly enamored with the prospect of pooling our funds and jointly buying a boat of our own. "But I *want* one," Rhys whimpered.

"It'd mean we couldn't afford any more weekends in Dubai," Seren told him.

This caused him to momentarily sober up. "After the last one, I realized we dropped six thousand dirhams in two days. A thousand quid. I've *ab*-solutely lost the concept of the value of money here."

My gaze turned towards the water and I saw a couple strolling alongside the boats, the male wearing dock shorts and sporting the amber hair of a foreigner, and the female clad in an abayya, most likely an Emirati. What's going on *there?* I wondered, for such pairings were never seen.

Third Circle: Despair. We made a stop at Hemingway's, the bar at the city's aged Hilton hotel, where one of Liz's friends was having a birthday party. Though Hemingway's was a popular expat hangout, I tried my level best to avoid the place. The bar was decked out in kitsch meant to pay homage to the author and was a confusion of fishing gear, bullfighting photos, and pseudo-Cuban furniture. There was a carved stone likeness of the old man's face above the entrance. Had the carving been real, it undoubtedly would have wept at the caricature of the place.

If there was one authentic aspect to Hemingway's, it was the crowd—Abu Dhabi's answer to the Lost Generation of which the author had written, a baleful collection of expats drowning their ennui in alcohol while the cover band attempted in vain to resurrect the 1970s. The birthday party gave the bar an even sharper poignancy than usual, the revelers all seemingly intent on employing prodigious amounts of drink and dessert to chase away the looming question of what exactly they were doing with their lives. Liz paid her courtesies and we lingered half an hour before moving on.

Fourth Circle: Lust. Blitz, the shady nightclub that Austin and Rhys had warned me about, took up the entire mezzanine floor of the tawdry downtown Novotel. It was reached from a side-alley entrance that led to a narrow stairwell littered with cigarettes and empty plastic cups. Inside, the low ceilings and crush of sweaty bodies contributed to an atmosphere of pure claustrophobia. A pall of smoke hung in the air, deafening music throbbed from the speakers, and every footstep stuck to the layer of gunk on the floor.

The patrons were mostly from Abu Dhabi's middle economic strata: men in their thirties and forties from Egypt, the Levant, and Pakistan mingling with Filipina, Chinese, and Burmese working girls, like the Asian continent's version of East meets West. The arrival of us Westerners attracted the attention of a number of the girls, who presumably imagined that they might be able to extract more from us than from their normal clients. I received dozens of come-hither glances—and my derriere received just as many pinches—as we pushed through the crowd. One girl grabbed Austin's arm, looked deep into his eyes, and said, "Tonight, I go home with *you*." Austin did his Muppet laugh and told her that was doubtful.

We reached the edge of the dance floor, where Alex and his wife sat at their usual table, watching the tattooed musicians and miniskirted singers of the Filipino cover band. For some bizarre reason, Blitz was Alex's favorite haunt.

"Hey, good to see you guys," he yelled over the clamor. "Guess what?"

"What?" I yelled back.

"It's my birthday today. I'm turning forty."

"Seriously?"

"Yep." He grinned, and said in all seriousness, "No place I'd rather spend it."

Fifth Circle: The Sum of All Vice. At half past one in the morning we reached a seedy dive tucked among a cluster of similarly squalid establishments in a forgotten corner of the city between downtown and the Mina Zayed port. The darkened interior had an almost palpably sinister feel. A single spotlight penetrated the gloom to illuminate an empty stage, in front of which were arranged tables with bottles of Jaegermeister and cheap scotch. The patrons were almost all Emirati men who sat hunched over their glasses at the tables or coiled on couches at the dim edges of the room. Half of them were accompanied by what appeared to be paid companions—of both genders, no less. By the looks of things, chubby Filipina girls and thin young Arab men were the commodities of choice. The presence of the latter might have been a surprise to Thesiger, who had observed that homosexuality was almost nonexistent among the Bedu: "They sometimes joked about goats but never about boys, and evidently thought the practice ridiculous and obscene."[7]

We took seats at the bar in the back. "*This* is the place you're always talking about?" I asked Austin.

"Watch. You'll see."

In a few minutes, the speakers on either side of the room crackled to life and began playing an Arabic tune with all the acoustic fidelity of an old transistor radio. A trio of dancers sauntered out onto the stage. Their faux-Arabian belly-dancer outfits notwithstanding, they looked decidedly Eastern European. The girls began to move about the stage, their faces empty of emotion. I wondered whether they were working here of their own accord.

Another spotlight came on. Out from the shadows walked a whale of a woman with a microphone in her hand. Her face was caked in makeup and her belly-dancer outfit struggled mightily to contain her girth. To the Emiratis at the tables in front, she might as well have been Cleopatra. They leaned forward as she lifted the microphone to her rouged lips and began to sing. It was dreadful, a spine-grating, off-key warble that sounded like an opera singer being drowned. The locals were spellbound.

A heavily marinated Emirati sidled up to the bar and seated himself unsteadily on the stool next to me. "You like?" he said, nodding towards the stage.

"It's ... unlike anything I've seen," I replied.

He mumbled something to the bartender, who poured him a glass of hooch. He downed it in one gulp and nearly fell off his perch. Placing his hand on my shoulder to steady himself (thereby revealing the huge Rolex on his wrist), he leaned in as if to tell me a secret. "Best time ... Abu Dhabi...," he slurred with breath that smelled like a distillery. I couldn't tell what he meant: that the best time was to be had in Abu Dhabi or that this *was* the best time to be had in Abu Dhabi? He leered for a few more seconds, then slid off his perch to grab the arm of a working girl as she walked past. I watched them make their way towards the door, zigzagging as she tried to keep him on his feet.

I turned to Austin. "Let's go. This is the creepiest place I've ever been in my life."

"Come *onnnn*," he whined. "If we leave now we'll miss the best part."

"Which is?"

"What do you think?" he replied, indicating the dancing girls.

I dug some bills out of my pocket and slapped them on the bar. "I'm going. When you leave, don't forget her," I said, nodding at Liz, who was fading in and out of consciousness on the stool next to him.

Austin dismissed me with a wave of his hand. "Fine. Whatever."

The music, the smoke, and the otherworldly glass-eyed visages of the Emiratis all swirled around me as I walked to the door. A fine ending to another night of what passed for entertainment in this town.

But the night was not over. Some time after I had returned home and fallen asleep, a commotion roused me from my slumber. I rubbed my eyes and looked at the clock: it was almost four in the morning. I grabbed some clothes and fumbled my way downstairs.

Austin sat on the living room couch. He looked to be in shock. In front of him, Liz was splayed out on the floor. "The brakes," she moaned, "the stupid brakes locked up. It wasn't my fault."

Rhys came in through the front door. "You are not going to believe this."

I followed him outside. Parked in front of the Qasr was Felicia, Liz's sleek white road-ster—or what was left of it. Both tires on the driver's side were shredded, the rims were bent beyond repair, and the front fender was pulverized. Rhys and I went back inside, coaxed Austin from his daze, and tried to work out what had happened.

At the end of the evening Austin and Liz had gone back to her place for a nightcap, after which she had insisted on driving him home. By Austin's own admission, she had been too drunk to walk, much less to drive, but he didn't want to bother with a taxi and thus agreed. In her loaded state Liz had failed to slow down before trying to take the turn off of the highway and into Golf Gardens. She had launched her car over a six-inch concrete curb at nearly a hundred kilometers an hour, and then rolled on its rims the rest of the way to the Qasr. Felicia now sat in front of our house in a sad, smoldering heap.

I threw Liz's tiny frame over my shoulder and carried her up to the spare bedroom. After we tucked her in, she continued mumbling that the brakes were to blame until she finally drifted off to sleep.

Back downstairs, Rhys said, "I expect this will change her behavior not at all."

Sadly, I had to agree. At various points, we had all joked about needing to escape Abu Dhabi before it ruined us. But in our friend Liz's case, we worried that staying much longer could very well mean her demise.

Eighteen

The Calm Before the Storm

It is characteristic of Bedu to do things by extremes, to be either wildly generous or unbelievably mean, very patient or almost hysterically excitable, to be incredibly brave or to panic for no apparent reason.... Probably no other people, either as a race or as individuals, combine so many conflicting qualities in such an extreme degree. — *Wilfred Thesiger, Arabian Sands*

A funk settled over Abu Dhabi in early 2011, as though the emirate itself were taking a deep breath. The entire city seemed to be waiting for something big to happen without knowing what that something was. At the UPC, the unrelenting flood of project proposals from the emirate's developers tapered off to a trickle. Monumental projects that had until recently commanded everyone's attention suddenly dropped off the radar. There was a sense of foreboding around the office, fueled by rumors that the emirate's leaders were having second thoughts about all of their pharaonic plans after seeing more realistic estimates of the eventual costs.

The interlude reduced my workload to almost nil. Most of my major assignments, including the Khaleej al Arabi highway tunnel and the North Wathba master plan, all went into holding patterns while the government tried to figure out what it was going to do. Not that I minded the slowdown. When I had joined the UPC in early 2009, the work tempo had been nonstop, and I had felt like I was earning every dirham in my paycheck. The present change of pace was a welcome respite. Half the time I found myself looking for things to do. I attended other agencies' seminars and workshops just for the lunch buffets. When the transport team needed to send a transmittal to another office, sometimes I would hand deliver it myself rather than sending it by courier simply to pass the time. I had become a six-figure errand boy.

The national railway was one of the few projects that continued moving forward. Etihad Rail's consultants had put the finishing touches on the designs for the Shah Line. The company had also commissioned a market study to estimate the share of freight and passenger traffic the railway would absorb once its various phases were complete. The study would thereby demonstrate whether the government could expect to turn a profit on the tens of billions of dirhams that the railway's full build-out would cost. All that remained before construction could begin was to present this business case to the Etihad Rail Board of Directors and the Executive Council.

It was characteristic of Abu Dhabi's automotive obsession that the railway was the only one of the emirate's myriad public works initiatives that had to prove its worth. Indeed, it was the only project of any kind that involved a market study. The government had approved hundreds of kilometers of new highways and roads without so much as blinking. But when it came to laying tracks in the sand instead of asphalt, the higher echelons seemed to suddenly rediscover their sense of scrutiny.

Prior to delivering the final market study to their board, the Etihad Rail staff convened a stakeholder meeting to present the results. They invited participants from across the Abu Dhabi government and from the other emirates as well. The Abu Dhabi DOT sent an entire vanload of staff, beefing up their numbers somewhat needlessly, in my opinion. I wondered where their sudden interest in the project had come from. The Professor, Alex, Khalid, and I attended on behalf of the UPC. We joined the other stakeholders crowding into the boardroom of Etihad Rail's gleaming new offices on the top floor of a new office tower on the edge of downtown, which afforded us a commanding view of the construction on Reem Island trailing off into the haze to the east.

The first forty-five minutes of the meeting were the standard free-for-all: the presenters fielding repeated interruptions from the peanut gallery; the tea staff circulating to take and deliver orders; attendees holding cell phone conversations in their imaginary cones of silence. Finally we got to the meat of the presentation, the projected traffic numbers for the railway. They were resoundingly positive. Even in the most conservative scenarios, which assumed that the UAE's economy would grow at an anemic rate and that the railway would capture only a modest portion of the corresponding growth in traffic, the railway made solid financial sense. The Etihad Rail staff admitted that they had thought it would be necessary for the railway's freight business to subsidize its eventual passenger operations, but the passenger traffic estimates exceeded all expectations. The proposed high-speed rail service between Abu Dhabi and Dubai, for example, was projected to capture anywhere from one-third to one-half of the commuter traffic between the two emirates, a market share that few rail corridors could boast, even in train-loving countries such as France and Japan. The national railway would more than pay for itself.

When it came time to take questions, hands shot up around the room. Before the presenters could call on anyone, however, one of the DOT's hoary traffic engineers stood up and began to pontificate. "Yes, these numbers are very interesting. And it is important to consider all the options, so as to obtain the best value for the money. I am wondering, did you consider any alternatives to building a railway? For example, building more highways or widening the ones we already have?"

I had to make a conscious effort to avoid slapping my forehead. The fatuity of the question was simply astounding. Even setting aside the financial analysis that had just been presented, there were plenty of compelling reasons to build the railway, such as the safety improvements that would come from taking trucks off the road. There was also the international prestige of having a modern rail system. More to the point, the entity in whose offices we were sitting was called Etihad Rail for a reason: the government had created it to build *railways*, not to feed the DOT's highway appetite.

Fortunately one of the Etihad Rail staff handled the question with aplomb. "Yes, you might say we considered highways," he said, "but it's difficult to make any money with those. You chaps know plenty about that, don't you?" His was presumably referring to the DOT's efforts to establish a public-private partnership on the E11 highway in Al Gharbia. The department's negotiations with financial institutions had gotten bogged down and didn't look like they would be going anywhere soon, as the banks simply couldn't see a way to make enough money off the deal to justify their involvement. The barb hit the mark, and the DOT representative sat down in humbled silence. The meeting concluded with the participants agreeing to endorse the market study's findings for the board and the Executive Council.[1]

Even if the railway and Abu Dhabi's proposed transit network were built, it was clear that meaningful changes in the emirate's transportation mindset would be a long time coming.

The emirate depended on its cars as much as its economy depended on oil, and any significant alterations would probably take the full twenty years until *Plan 2030*'s horizon, if not beyond. Having lived in the emirate and dealt with its transport issues on a daily basis for nearly two years, I had come to a certain detente with this reality. Abu Dhabi's traffic still drove me insane, but at least now I understood that it was unrealistic to expect things to get better overnight.

For every step the government took to improve the city's transportation, there was often another step back. For example, in late 2010 the Professor had finally managed to get the UPC's street design manual finished and ratified as official policy by the Executive Council.[2] The manual included a whole host of traffic-calming measures that could be applied to reduce speeds and increase safety on the emirate's roads without reducing their efficiency.[3] My colleagues and I were thus stupefied when the Abu Dhabi police announced shortly thereafter their intent to raise the speed limits on some of the most heavily trafficked roads in the city, ostensibly to make them safer.[4] The police's in-house traffic experts reasoned that if speed limits were too low, some drivers would obey them while others wouldn't, leading to more accidents. That kind of backwards logic flew in the face of the research that underpinned the UPC's street design manual. It was not the first time that various government organs had been at cross-purposes, and it would probably not be the last.

In light of Abu Dhabi's seemingly bottomless pool of contradictions, it was no longer surprising when the *Gulf News* opened its weekend edition with a gushing front-page editorial about "an ascendant Abu Dhabi seeing its moment in history.... [I]t wants to be first in all fields, rebrand itself as a global city, and become a trendsetter in the region."[5] Buried deeper in the same paper was an article describing how, on the day before, a single overturned lorry in downtown Abu Dhabi had set off a chain reaction of cascading gridlock that brought traffic to a standstill for hours across the island.[6] The emirate still had a long way to go.

Had the government truly been serious about improving the safety of Abu Dhabi's roads, there was one particular measure that would have been easy to implement. The emirate's technology-addicted residents were just as glued to their mobile phones and Blackberries while driving as they were at any other time, which contributed significantly to the number of smashups. When the city's Blackberry services suffered a three-day outage later that same year, accidents fell by 40 percent.[7] All the authorities had to do to make the roads nearly twice as safe was turn off the phones.

* * *

After we got off of work I drove Liz out to Mussafah to pick up her car. After letting the damaged Felicia sit for more than a week where she had left it in front of our house, Liz had gotten a wrecker to retrieve the car and take it to the mechanic. However, she had already been through so many collisions that her insurance agency refused to pay for repairs at the Mercedes dealership and instead forced Liz to take the car to a dodgy Mussafah chop shop. It took them nearly a month to put Felicia back together.

As we drove out of the city Liz talked about how she was looking forward to having Felicia back after dealing with the hassle of taxis. I wanted to say something, but I struggled for the right words. I was genuinely concerned for Liz's well-being—physical and financial— if she persisted in driving that car. Slick though the roadster may have been, its performance was clearly beyond her control. Hoping not to offend her, I said, "Have you thought about whether that car is perhaps a bit too ... jumpy for you?"

"Look, I know what you're getting at," she replied, causing me to wince. "And I completely agree. The car is just too much for me to be driving all the time."

I was taken aback. It was the first sensible thing she had said regarding her car in ... well, ever. "So you're going to do something about it?" I prodded.

"Of course," she said. "I've got it all figured out. I'm going to get another car to drive during the week. Something big so that other drivers won't hit me. Then I'll just take Felicia out on the weekends."

She was so perfectly serious that I didn't know whether to laugh or cry. Back home she would never have been able to afford such nonsense, had it ever even crossed her mind. But that was the effect of Abu Dhabi's expat lifestyle, with its insidious tempting whispers: *Go on, buy it. You can afford it, after all. So what if you have to stay another year? You'll have plenty of time for frugality when you go home.*

I dropped Liz off in Mussafah and headed back in the direction of the Qasr. By now it was early evening. I pulled into a service station only to see a long line of cars in front of the automated car wash. For nearly a week I had been trying to get Big White cleaned. I was scheduled to go on vacation the following weekend, and I didn't want to leave a dirty vehicle behind. Every day on my way to and from the office I had driven out of my way to various service stations only to encounter long lines at each one. The automated car washes were agonizingly slow, and I didn't have the patience to wait.

Since I was already at the station, I figured I might as well fill up. I pulled alongside one of the full-service pumps. "Fill it with special, please," I told the Filipino attendant. As he disappeared around the back, I turned on the radio and reclined in my seat, enjoying the mild evening air wafting through the open windows.

I saw movement out of the corner of my eye. I turned to see the attendant standing at the passenger-side window, listening to the music. He matched my gaze and raised an eyebrow. "'Careless Whispers,' sir?" he asked.

"Excuse me?" Then I paid attention to the radio and heard George Michael's crooning voice. "Oh, right."

Much to my surprise, the attendant started to sing along. He had a remarkable voice. I turned up the volume, which encouraged him all the more.

The attendant then stepped back and belted out the chorus at the top of his lungs. As if that weren't sufficiently surreal, the other attendants joined in, serenading the station's customers. They were amazing, hitting the notes in perfect harmony, as though they had been rehearsing this for weeks. Although any resident of Abu Dhabi can attest that Filipinos enjoy a reputation as the city's most musical nationality, this was something else entirely. I looked around and saw a mixture of bewildered looks and smiles on the faces of the other drivers.

The attendant came to my window after capping my tank. I tipped him with all the spare change I had on hand. If a talent scout were to refuel at that station, I thought, he would make the find of a lifetime.[8]

I pulled up to the Qasr and wedged my Jeep into the driveway behind those of my housemates. On my way to the front door I chanced to look in the garage—and abruptly stopped in my tracks. There was a faucet. And a hose. The gears in my head started to grind. Didn't we have a bucket somewhere in the house? And soap? Vague memories of an activity I once enjoyed long ago began stirring in my subconscious. What about a washrag? Yes, I'm sure we had one somewhere. And maybe even a towel.

I had a sudden revelation: lo and behold, *I* could wash my car! I felt like a complete imbecile, standing there next to the garage having just mastered the obvious. I had spent a week ransacking the city for an open car wash, and not once had it occurred to me that I could wash the stupid thing myself. Was this the level of indolence to which Abu Dhabi had reduced me? Had I become so utterly useless as to forget how to accomplish even the most menial tasks? Never mind. I was so elated at rediscovering this token of self-reliance that I threw on my bathing suit and washed not only my Jeep but my housemates' as well.

* * *

The difference was palpable as soon as we stepped off the plane. Gone was Abu Dhabi's pressure-cooker atmosphere. I took deep breaths of thin, crisp mountain air. We had arrived at the airport outside Sana'a, Yemen's capital. My long-standing fascination with Yemen had finally motivated me to book a trip, and I had convinced Elise and Lindsay, a friend of ours who worked at a consultancy, to join me for a long weekend in Sana'a. It had taken two months and a series of trips to the Yemen embassy to play the visa game: one trip to pick up the visa forms, a second to drop them off with our passports, a third to drop them off again along with letters of no objection from our employers (a requirement not stipulated on the forms), and a fourth to retrieve the passports with the visas freshly glued to the pages. And now we had arrived. Sana'a sat on the southwest Arabian plateau at more than seven thousand feet above sea level. The air made me feel slightly delirious, as though some great burden had been lifted from me.

An Emirati from our flight chatted with us as we walked across the tarmac to the terminal. "It is beautiful, no?" he said, pointing to the mountains in the distance. "I come here three, maybe four times a year. Abu Dhabi is ugly too much. Sometimes you must escape." I couldn't have agreed more.

On the drive from the airport to the city, it was evident that we were in for a far different version of Arabia. Our rickety taxi bounced along the potholed road. The scattered traffic drove with a free-for-all manner but in a strange slow motion, as though all the drivers were drugged. Men of all ages lounged in the doorways of the dilapidated shops that lined the road. Their cheeks bulged with golf ball–sized wads of *qat*, the mildly narcotic leaf that most Yemenis spent hours chewing every day, according to my guidebook. Qat was both a national pastime and a scourge that consumed more than half of the country's arable land and meager water resources, all for a product that had no export value and left its consumers stoned for a good portion of every working day.[9]

Whether from the effects of qat or not, Sana'a had the feel of a sleepy provincial town—strange for the capital city of the second most populous nation on the Arabian Peninsula. The driver took us to the historic old city, where he slowed to a crawl inside the warren of tightly packed buildings and narrow streets. We checked in to our hotel, the Burj al Salam, a modern establishment that had been built using the same design and techniques as the innumerable tower houses that packed the old city, some of which were hundreds of years old. An impossibly steep stairwell traversed the hotel's ten stories, each of which had a handful of rooms opening onto a cozy internal landing. The quaint rooms featured half-moon windows with traditional stained glass that bathed the walls in rainbow light. With their low ceilings and simple, homey furniture, the rooms' ambiance was exquisite. The hotel offered modern conveniences but carried the weight of centuries in its walls.

We quickly settled into a daily routine. We would rise late, take a leisurely brunch, and then wander the labyrinth of the old city until dark. The heart of Sana'a looked like something out of a fairy tale. Its hundreds of mud-brick towers were decorated with elaborate white plaster friezes and cornices that made them resemble life-size gingerbread houses. This remarkable architecture dated back almost two thousand years. By the third century of the Common Era, Sana'a had already become famous for the first skyscraper in recorded history, the Ghumdan Palace of the resident Sabaean king.[10] Though some legends claimed that the palace soared as high as twenty stories, its actual height was probably more consistent with the six-to-ten-story buildings still prevalent throughout the old city. What is certain is that the people of ancient Yemen were erecting towers when Hong Kong was merely a salt mine and Chicago nothing more than a swamp.

Thesiger had been deeply moved when he had first encountered Yemen's traditional architecture in Sana'a and in the country's eastern Hadhramaut Valley. He had also foreseen its inevitable decline in the face of newer styles: "[The Yemenis] have evolved an architecture which is simple, harmonious, and beautiful. But this architecture is doomed, for the Arabs' taste is easily corrupted. New and hideous buildings, planned by modern Arab architects, are already rising in these ancient cities. My companions when they saw them were deeply impressed. 'By God, that is a wonderful building!' It was useless to argue."[11]

The tower house architecture was a fitting visual metaphor for the old city's layers of urban life. The twisting, turning streets and countless alleys and side passages were lined with brilliantly decorated façades that gave little hint of the secret worlds within. Through low doorways we discovered art galleries, cafés, and even the shop of a metalworker who specialized in elaborate door hinges. One nondescript hovel housed a coffee grindery with a tethered camel plodding in circles around a giant pestle. In the bustling souq we entered a shop merely to browse and left more than an hour later, sporting traditional goatskin coats and curved *jambiya* daggers. We dined on flat bread and *salteh*, the hearty Yemeni stew of meat, vegetables, and fenugreek froth. Everywhere we wandered brought a profusion of strange sights, smells, and sounds.

Sana'a was atmospheric, historic, poor, and interesting, everything Abu Dhabi and the other instant cities of the Gulf were not. Its buildings didn't scream for individualized attention, but rather contributed their subdued refinement to a whole that was so much more than the sum of its parts. None of the urban schemes of Yemen's wealthier neighbors could hope to match Sana'a's grandeur. If the Romans had known Yemen as Arabia Felix, then the Gulf was Arabia Faux.

In the evenings we retired to the hotel's rooftop terrace to eat dinner and take in the view. The towers of the old city spread before us in every direction like an intricate urban puzzle. As dusk settled over the city, the beige and brown façades faded through the spectrum of orange, red, and purple. Soft green and pink lights came alive and illuminated the cigar-shaped minarets that punctuated the skyline. The vista redefined exotic. One could look on Sana'a for hours and not grow bored.

On our final evening in the city, we sat gazing over the skyline with melancholy, knowing that we would soon have to depart. Elise voiced what we all were thinking. "This place makes Abu Dhabi look pretty bad."

Lindsay agreed. "It amazes me how well this city has stood the test of time. Some of these towers are hundreds of years old. How many of Abu Dhabi's buildings are going to last even a decade?"

For my part, I couldn't help thinking that Sana'a revealed the true extent of what Arabia has lost. The Arabs had once boasted their own rich urban tradition, with which they built some of the most distinctive cities in the world. Now the Arabs of the Gulf are raising a new line of monumental cities, but these are mere shells, echoes of the peninsula's former achievements. With all of Abu Dhabi's talk about preserving the essence of the traditional Arab city, Sana'a made it all too clear how far that was from the truth. I wondered aloud whether any of Abu Dhabi's leaders had visited Sana'a along with their trips to Vancouver and Singapore.

"It wouldn't matter if they had," Elise replied. "The sheikhs aren't to blame. It's the people around them that are the problem." She explained how she had often presented project proposals to the crown prince himself when she had worked for one of the development companies he and his Bani Fatima brothers owned. "He would nod and listen to everything without making any commitments. With all the proposals that people show him, I guess that's the approach that he has to take—don't agree to anything on the spot. And then a couple of days later, our bosses would tell us that the Crown Prince had approved whatever we were proposing. But I never saw anything in writing."

Lindsay shared this view. "The people in the sheikhs' inner circles, the ones who are actually running the development companies and the government agencies and the sheikhs' personal offices—they're absolutely drunk with power. I know it sounds silly, but it's like something out of *Aladdin*. The sheikhs are the equivalent of the well-intentioned sultan, and the people around them are the evil vizier. They're the ones who cook up all this garbage, these awful projects, and they sign off on them as though the sheikhs themselves have approved."

Elise concluded, "Somebody needs to tell the sheikhs that they should take a close look at what their staff are up to before it's too late."

As we took to the skies the following morning, I looked out the window at the mythical skyline below. I thought of Ibn Khaldun, the great Arab historian, who had praised ancient Yemen's virtues and had also offered an explanation for its decline, which was already well underway when he wrote in the fourteenth century. In his eyes, the Bedu were to blame. The nomads had come in from the desert, had taken over the great ancient Arabian civilizations, and had run them into the ground:

"It is noteworthy how civilization always collapsed in places the Bedouins took over and conquered.... The Yemen where Bedouins live is in ruins."[12] This was no bigoted Western iconoclast speaking, but a fellow Arab, castigating his desert-dwelling cousins: "Bedouins are a savage nation, fully accustomed to savagery and the things that cause it. Savagery has become their character and nature. Such a natural disposition is the negation and antithesis of civilization." For Ibn Khaldun, the Bedu could not escape their wilderness nature, even when they tried to put down roots. The desolation of the desert followed them wherever they went. As I watched Sana'a fade into the distance, I wondered if the great historian would expect the same of Abu Dhabi, the latest endeavor of the Bedu to create an enduring civilization of their own.

Rhys had offered to pick me up from the airport on my return. I was thus surprised to see Austin's Jeep parked outside the arrivals area, with Austin behind the wheel and Rhys in the passenger seat. As I got inside, I said to Austin, "Weren't you supposed to be at the concert?" He and a few friends had bought tickets to see Tiesto, the overrated Dutch DJ, who was in town to play a show at ADNEC's exhibition hall.

"Yeah, well, we showed up early and snuck inside while they were still doing sound checks. The sound system almost brought down the house. I mean, literally almost brought down the house. The rafters and the ceiling started shaking. I thought the roof was going to collapse."

"That's what you get when build on the cheap," Rhys remarked.

"So they cancelled the show and gave some bogus excuse about a 'technical problem,'" Austin said. "I swear, sometimes I think I should write a book about this place."

On the way back to the house Rhys mentioned, "By the way, you missed it—the opera was in town."

"I didn't know that. Did you go?"

"'Course we did. It was brilliant. Best thing I've seen in years." He paused. "Oh, wait, that's right. There was no opera, because there's *ab*-solutely no culture here. We stayed in, got pissed, and sang karaoke until two in the morning."

* * *

Qasr al Deviance Journal, Week 45

Despite all our efforts, the Qasr continues to crumble around us. Having exhausted our patience with the maintenance company, we turn to the UPC management for help. My housemates and I trudge upstairs one afternoon to see the agency's procurement manager, who is nominally responsible for arbitrating lease issues on behalf of the staff.

"Come in, please, come in," he beckons when we knock on his door. The procurement manager looks like an Emirati Santa Claus, jovial and pleasantly plump, with dark stubble instead of the fluffy white beard and a checkered headdress in place of a stocking cap. He wears an expression of perpetual befuddlement, as if he is always trying without success to pull something from the recesses of his memory.

"Please, gentlemen, what can I do for you?" he inquires once we are seated.

"Well, we were hoping you could help with our house," I tell him. "We've been having some problems and, er, the maintenance company hasn't ... well, they haven't been very respon—"

"They've been *ab*-solutely useless," Rhys finishes. He enumerates the woes we've endured over the past eight months, ticking them off on his fingers. From time to time, Austin and I chime in to underscore a particularly deplorable point.

Amazingly, our tirade seems to be working. As the list grows longer and longer, the procurement manager turns his gaze out the window. The troubled look on his face shows that he is weighing our ordeal; he even acknowledges our complaints with occasional clucks of disgust. Finally, someone is listening!

When we reach the end of our inventory of indignation, there is silence. The procurement manager rocks back in his chair and glances up at the ceiling, undoubtedly contemplating the various ways he could use the UPC's clout to resolve our situation. Will he call the maintenance company and badger them into finally doing something meaningful? Or will he perhaps cajole the developer of Golf Gardens to take action by threatening to embarrass them for building such a shambles?

After long contemplation, he finally speaks. "*Al-hamdulillah,*" he says, giving solemn thanks to God. "I almost bought a villa in this neighborhood."

Austin's jaw falls open and Rhys clenches his fists. The procurement manager looks down at us, startled, as if he had forgotten we were there. He stammers, "Ah, yes, uh ... I will make some calls and see what we can do. Thank you gentlemen." With that, he ushers us unceremoniously from his office.

In the stairwell Austin asks, "Do you really think he's going to do anything?"

Rhys snorts. "The sad thing is, by now this surprises me not one bit."

Nineteen

End of the Road

Abu Dhabi was like a hotel. Everyone was in transit. Who seriously cares about the future of a hotel? One wants the service to hold up for the length of one's stay, and if it becomes intolerable, one checks out and moves on.—*Jonathan Raban,* Arabia: A Journey Through the Labyrinth

The crash came almost overnight. Even for those who had been expecting Abu Dhabi's boom to implode, it happened with stunning speed. For a half-dozen frantic years since Sheikh Zayed's death the emirate's developers had built with irrational exuberance. That had worked for a while, while Abu Dhabi still had plenty of pent-up demand left over from the Zayed years.

By the spring of 2011, however, Abu Dhabi's real estate shortage had become a glut, and everyone knew it. The housing crisis was abruptly reversed as the city's first mega-projects reached completion and flooded the market with thousands of new units. Property values plummeted. Many buyers in the new developments were either unwilling or unable to pay off the balances on sales contracts they had signed months or even years before when prices were still rising. For the first time in anyone's memory, rents across the city fell from the previous year.[1] *Plan 2030* had warned against the folly of unchecked growth: "When building a city of more than three million, there should be a carefully monitored balance between supply and demand of real estate. If the rate of development drastically outpaces the market there will be severely negative consequences."[2] Now that dire prediction was coming true.

Abu Dhabi's developers received a bruising wake-up call in the form of huge financial losses. In February 2011 Aldar, the largest developer, posted a whopping 12.6 *billion* dirham loss for the previous year. There would have been even more red ink had the government not bailed out the company with an emergency cash transfusion of more than 16 billion dirhams in exchange for ownership of Yas Island.[3] Aldar's CEO had presumably foreseen what was coming; he took a vacation abroad with his family shortly before the announcement and simply never returned. Sorouh, the second-largest developer, was left with a mess after a number of its Reem Island subdevelopers went belly-up, leaving their projects in various stages of partial completion. The most startling piece of bad news was the announcement that the new museums on Saadiyat Island, the crown jewels in Abu Dhabi's strategy to attraction international attention and visitors, had been put on indefinite hold. Every week the newspapers carried more and more bad news.

Rank and file speculators who had signed purchase agreements for new units weren't the only ones with buyer's remorse. As more of the emirate's myriad projects neared completion, word leaked out that the sheikhs were finally paying closer attention—and they weren't pleased with what they had received for their money. Lord Foster himself flew out from London for the opening of his vaunted Central Market to reassure the sheikhs that the project wasn't merely an expensive flop.[4]

Abu Dhabi's leaders had been forced to admit that the emirate's riches had a limit. The government had wildly overspent on everything from the new real estate and infrastructure projects to the subsidies lavished on state-owned enterprises like Etihad Airlines. The bill for this profligacy, when combined with the rising number of companies turning to the state for aid, caused the emirate to run a deficit that would eventually be reckoned at seventy billion dirhams.[5] That, at least, was the word on the street; the government had never published its official budget or annual results and was certainly not about to start now. What was undeniable was the wave of ascetic belt-tightening that followed. Agency budgets were slashed across the board. The UPC's allocation plunged from a half-billion dirhams in 2010 to thirty million the following year. The agency frantically shuffled staff around as it became clear that most of the work we normally contracted out to consultants would now have to be done in-house. The contracts axed by the management included Legendary Larry's lucrative retainer for his bimonthly mentoring visits.

In a way, the crash was a blessing in disguise. Many of the emirate's more outlandish projects were postponed or cancelled as part of the cutbacks. For example, the Executive Council finally vetoed the stalled plans for the Khaleej al Arabi tunnel and directed ADNEC to instead create a space for the IDEX arms exposition by simply shifting the highway fifty meters aside. Masdar, the vaunted carbon-neutral neighborhood, was forced to shave twenty-two billion dirhams from its budget by scrapping its plans for the futuristic personal transit system and solar panels on all its roofs.[6] The UPC's grandiose plans for the new Capital District were shelved. I actually found this last decision gratifying, as I had never understood the rationale behind constructing the new federal center on the mainland so far away from the natural asset of the waterfront.

At the same time, the triage also affected projects that were less dispensable. For instance, when the DOT unveiled its preliminary design for the integrated Metro and tram lines of the city's future transit system, the Executive Council balked at the seventy-five billion dirham price tag. They sent the DOT back to the drawing board to consider all the options, including dropping the trams entirely and replacing the Metro with additional buses. In my opinion, this was shortsighted. Even if Abu Dhabi hadn't added a single new resident from 2011 onward, the city still desperately needed alternative means of transport to relieve the pressure on its roads.

As if the emirate's economic chaos weren't already enough, Abu Dhabi's perfect storm was compounded by the Arab Spring, the revolutionary wave that swept across the Middle East in the early months of 2011. The unrest was sparked, quite literally, when a Tunisian street vendor set himself on fire to protest his country's repressive government.[7] His pyrrhic death unleashed a pan-Arab torrent of rage that had built up over decades under the misrule of the region's dictators. In a matter of weeks the citizens of Tunisia and Egypt had toppled their regimes, and Libya, Yemen, and Syria looked set to follow. In the Gulf, Bahrain's downtrodden Shi'a population took to the streets against their Sunni monarch. Abu Dhabi's sheikhs and the rulers of the other emirates joined the Saudis in sending troops up the coast to Bahrain to prop up their fellow autocrat. The chances of a similar uprising among Abu Dhabi's Emiratis were slim to none. The government gave its citizens everything they wanted and more—what did they have to protest? My housemates and I sat in our living room one afternoon watching televised images of smiling Emirati soldiers driving armored vehicles into Bahrain to help repress the protesters there. Rhys asked, "Could you imagine that happening here?" We all looked at each other, then broke down laughing.

Austin wiped tears from his eyes. "I can see the banners already: 'We demand justice! Three villas for every Emirati family!'"

"They'd probably just pay some Indians to do the rioting for them," I added. "It'd be the world's first outsourced revolution."

Nevertheless, Abu Dhabi's leaders didn't take any chances. The government ramped up its nanny-state entitlements even while it was slashing spending in every other sector. Emirati housing became the UPC's number one priority, not just planning the new neighborhoods, but getting them built as well. The agency's Capital District team, which had lost its name-sake and its purpose, was given the task of getting Emirati housing tracts built and delivered as fast as possible. The UPC was starting to look less like an innovative planning agency and more like a villa factory, not exactly the kind of work that had drawn my colleagues and me to Abu Dhabi.

Some of the other staff saw the writing on the wall and decided it was time to go. Elise left in haste with the parting comment that her greatest professional desire was for none of her projects to ever get built. Liz came to the conclusion that environmental protection would inevitably fall victim to the cost-cutting. She jumped ship to a consultancy that promised her the chance to travel around the region.

For my part, I felt at an impasse. The national railway project was still going strong, as the government fortunately still recognized its strategic importance. Yet I had done all I could to help finalize the railway's planning, and I had no desire to stick around for its construction. I had managed enough construction work in the past to know that it invariably caused more headaches than it was worth, as nothing ever went quite as planned.

More important, even if Abu Dhabi's downswing were to pass quickly and the action were to pick up again, the emirate's promises had begun to ring hollow. I had come to feel that all of my work at the UPC—indeed, all of Abu Dhabi's vaunted transformation—ultimately boiled down to one core purpose, and that purpose was to make a nation of wealthy people even richer. I couldn't fault the Emiratis' desire to preserve the fortune they had found in the sands beneath their feet, but I had also come to yearn for something more fulfilling.

I was thus quite thankful when another job offer came my way in February. It would require leaving Abu Dhabi, but that would be a welcome move. I had seen the changes that the emirate's decadent expat lifestyle was inflicting on my colleagues and me, and I didn't like the results. As the author Eric Weiner notes in his best-selling *The Geography of Bliss,* "adrift in a different place we give ourselves permission to be different people." I didn't particularly care for the different person I had given myself permission to become in Abu Dhabi. And besides, like my old friend Thesiger at the end of his Empty Quarter wanderings, "my mind was taut with the strain of living too long among Arabs."[8] I quietly accepted the new position and targeted early April for my departure, just past my two-year mark in the emirate.

The weekend before I intended to tender my resignation, Austin took his monthly house party on the road. I joined him and a dozen or so of the UPC's expats on Delma Island, another of the desert islands off the coast of Al Gharbia, where we made camp in every sense of the word and stayed up late around a bonfire worthy of *Lord of the Flies.* In the morning I saw that the hood on Austin's Jeep had dents the size of bowling balls. Austin emerged from his tent with his sunglasses askew on his nose. "What happened to your car?" I asked.

He cracked open a breakfast beer. "There may have been a dozen people dancing on it last night," he croaked. "I don't quite remember."

The Professor rode with me on the way back to the city. In the midst of our chitchat he asked nonchalantly, "So then, how long do you think you'll be staying in Abu Dhabi?"

The game was up. I must have done something in the previous week to alert him of my intended departure. Still, I tried playing it coy. "I don't know, a little longer yet. And you?"

"Well, to tell you the truth, it's not much fun here with the family back home." His wife and children had moved back to Australia several months before, having endured all they could of the emirate. "But someone has to pay the private school fees, so I guess I'll be here a while longer as well." We let the topic drop for the rest of the ride.

At the end of the following week, I sat down with the Professor and Alex late in the afternoon on Thursday, after most of our colleagues had already left for the weekend. I told them I was submitting my two weeks' notice. They seemed genuinely surprised.

"You didn't see this coming?" I said.

"No," said the Professor with a wry smile. "I guess you weren't quite letting on when we talked on the way back from Delma."

"Well, I did say I would be here a *little* while longer. You asked me a week too soon."

Alex asked where I planned to go, and I told them.

"Afghanistan!" the Professor exclaimed. "Haven't you people finished with that country yet?"

"After working here, I figure it's the one place that won't be an anticlimax."

Alex turned to the Professor and said, "Well, I guess that complicates things even more."

I did not have to wait long to discover what he meant. At the beginning of the following week, first thing on Sunday morning, the UPC's management convened an all-hands meeting of the staff. There the directors of all three of the agency's main departments—the Professor included—announced that they were leaving. They had evidently been planning this for some time and had worked out a deal with the general manager whereby they would return on a monthly basis for a week at a time to help ease the transition and mentor their replacements.

I caught up with the Professor after the meeting. "Looks like I wasn't the only one keeping mum," I said.

"Mmm ... right," he responded with his Cheshire-cat grin. "Great minds think alike."

The news went over like a bombshell, triggering a wave of additional resignations from the agency's expats throughout the following week. The move had erased any lingering doubts as to what was really going on. The rats were fleeing the ship. The UPC's Emiratis began to panic and tried to slap golden handcuffs on as many of their expat colleagues as they could manage. They offered Austin a manager's title and a trifling pay raise to stick with the Al Gharbia planning. He took the bait. My colleague Keith from Development Review, in contrast to his statement at the previous year's Cityscape about leaving town when the going got tough, bought into a similar offer.

In a short time the UPC's organizational chart looked quite different. There were many instances in which young Emiratis with just a few years' experience, none of it supervisory, were put in managerial roles overseeing expat staff who had until recently been their equals. Khalid, for example, was picked to head up the transport team after Alex moved into the Professor's vacated position. From what I could tell, the prospect of suddenly being in charge both excited and terrified my Emirati colleague. Although the idea had always been that the Emiratis would one day run the place, now it was sink or swim.

I admit that I was flattered when the management tried to get me to stay. Shortly after I submitted my resignation, Faisal, the human resources director, pulled me into his office for one last excruciating talk. "Ah, my Gatekeeper, I have heard the good news!" he began. "You have decided to stay with us."

Had someone actually told him this, or was it another example of his strange humor? "No, I'm still planning to leave," I said.

"Ah, but surely there is something we can do. Maybe you feel we do not pay you enough?"

For the next half-hour he offered me every incentive in his bag of tricks—a raise, a promotion, supervisory responsibilities, the opportunity to work on my own side projects, even a desk with a better view—but each time I politely declined. Refusing to take no for an answer, he finally allowed me to go. "I understand, you do not have to decide now," he said. "Take a few days to think it over and let me know." I agreed, but I knew my answer would be the same.

Khalid himself tried on several occasions to get me to change my mind. When he realized it was futile, he insisted that we get together after work on one of my last days at the office. We went to the bowling alley at Zayed Sports City, where the staff courteously but firmly refused to allow him to bowl because he was wearing his kandora. A more fitting Abu Dhabi irony could not be found: a local being banned from having fun for wearing his national uniform in his own city. I started to argue with the staff on Khalid's behalf, but he shrugged it off and suggested we play billiards instead.

Afterwards we moved on to the Shangri-La and gorged ourselves on dinner. Once more I tried to match Khalid's pace, but I gave up after his third return trip to the buffet. Over the meal he tried to dissuade me from leaving one last time. "Why you want to leave Abu Dhabi?" he said. "Look around. A man have everything he want here." I didn't know how to tell him that that was precisely the problem.

Khalid smiled when I mentioned my meeting with Faisal. "I know. Faisal asked me if I think you stay for more money. I tell him no. With you, I know it is not about money. You want to help those people. You want adventure."

I was floored. Khalid's thoughts were forever a mystery to me, and yet here he was, calmly and accurately assessing my motives. "Just promise you be safe," he continued. "You are more than just colleague, umkak? You like a brother." I didn't know what to say.

Khalid picked up another crab leg and I had to suppress my gag reflex. He waved it at me and said, "I give you one last piece of advice. You not need to go to Afghanistan for adventure." He took a bite and with his mouth half full of crabmeat he said, "You want adventure? Get married. Have some kids."

My last conversation with Mahra was more somber. She didn't try to persuade me to stay. "I always had a feeling you would move on to something else," she said. "I just didn't think it would be so soon."

I tried to change the subject by congratulating her on her recent success. She had just finished her master's degree and had been promoted to a manager in her section. "Aren't you excited? Your career path seems pretty bright," I said.

She smiled. "No," she said wistfully, "I'm not excited. No matter how much education I get, I will only go so far. I am nothing without a husband. I look around at the local men, and there are none I want to marry. They don't value a woman with a career and a mind of her own." She looked at me, her dark eyes shimmering. "I honestly don't have much hope for the future. I will not be someone's toy."

She had left me at a loss for words one final time. Here was this fascinating, intelligent young woman, held hostage by the culture of which she was so fiercely proud.

My housemates and I wrapped things up at the Qasr. Rhys took the last of his belongings and moved to Seren's apartment for good. His sleep improved dramatically without banging pipes to keep him awake all night. Austin signed a lease for a posh two-bedroom apartment for himself and Grace the cat, thereby prolonging his financial indenture in the emirate even further. I didn't want to deal with divvying up what the three of us had bought, so I told Austin that he could have it all after I left. We agreed to keep everything in the Qasr until April 1, the last day of our lease, when I would leave and Austin would move.

A little more than a week beforehand I left town for one last impromptu vacation, this time to spend a few days visiting a college friend in Syria. In view of the widening unrest of the Arab Spring, I realized I was cutting it close. Antigovernment riots broke out in Damascus the day after I flew back to Abu Dhabi.

I returned home and walked into the Qasr to find it completely empty. I called Austin in a panic. "If this is an early April Fools' joke, it's not funny," I said.

"What are you talking about?"

"Did you seriously already move?"

"Yeah. Why?"

"We had agreed that we were going to leave everything here until the end of the month!"

"Well, I just decided to move earlier."

"Did it ever cross your mind to ask? You took EVERYTHING. I don't even have forks to eat with."

"Oh ... yeah. I hadn't thought of that. What do you want me to do?"

"I want you to move it all back."

"Well that's not going to happen."

"No, obviously it's not."

"Look, what if I paid for—"

I cut him off. "You've really outdone yourself. I kept your cat alive whenever you went out of town. Now I go on vacation for four days, and you leave me homeless. This is pretty selfish, even for you." I hung up before he could respond.

Even in my anger, I was actually grateful to Austin for giving me one last reminder of why I had to get out. Had I been in his shoes, I might have done the very same thing. Such behavior was all too typical of the casual disregard for others that Abu Dhabi's expat culture bred.

Rhys and Seren took pity on me and invited me to stay in their guest bedroom for my final week in the city. I sold Big White, emptied my bank account, and shipped my modest inventory of books back home. I was a vagabond once more.

At the end of my final day at the office, I went out onto the top deck of the parking garage and looked out across the city. The late afternoon sun draped the ever-changing skyline in gilt, once more bringing to mind the image of the fabled City of Brass. In that tale from the *One Thousand and One Nights*, a party of explorers roaming through a trackless waste happen upon the immaculately preserved ruin of a once-great city. Inside its walls, the skeletal remains of its former inhabitants still sit in their shops and halls and palaces, sur-rounded by fabulous riches, their final inscriptions bearing silent witness to the futility of such treasures when calamity struck. Abu Dhabi's inhabitants would do well to heed the story's admonishing call:

> *Consider what thou beholdest, O man; and be on thy guard before thou departest;*
> *And prepare good provision, that thou mayest enjoy it; for every dweller in a house shall depart.*
> *Consider a people who decorated their abodes, and in the dust have become pledged for their actions.*
> *They built; but their buildings availed not: and treasured; but their wealth did not save them when*
> *the term had expired.*[9]

As I left Mamoura for the last time, I happened to glance over at the outdoor café tables that Jones the Grocer had set up in front of its entrance. I saw an Emirati couple with a handful of children get up from one of the tables and walk towards the adjoining private parking lot, which was restricted to VIPs visiting Mamoura's government offices. As the family got into a dazzlingly white brand-new Nissan Armada, I looked closer. Sure enough, it was the crown prince, presumably with his kin. He climbed into the driver's seat and the engine seemed to start of its own accord. As the vehicle left the parking lot, its windows electronically tinted themselves an opaque silver, obscuring the royal passengers inside. Many things can and will be said of the crown prince and his vision to transform Abu Dhabi. But among them, one must give credit to a man who is a de facto head of state and a billionaire many times over, valiantly attempting to chart a course for his people into an uncertain future, yet grounded enough to still cart around his kids in the family wagon.

My colleagues threw me a farewell dinner at Chamas, the same Brazilian steakhouse where I had met Mahra's brother Majid and his friends. Halfway through the meal I was asked to give a speech. I struggled to make myself heard over the din of the restaurant and the bossa nova band. I told my colleagues the truth, that we had been part of something remarkable in Abu Dhabi, an unprecedented endeavor that, for all its flaws, was still a landmark experiment in city-building, and it had been a privilege to witness.

After most of my colleagues had left, I sat in the restaurant's darkened bar with the Professor and Keith, smoking cigars and nursing overpriced glasses of wine. The Professor asked whether I planned to go straight to Afghanistan.

"No, I have to go back to the States for training first," I replied. "And that doesn't start for another month."

"What are you going to do in the meantime?"

"I don't know. Maybe I'll write a book about this place."

"Mmm ... yes," the Professor said. "Shouldn't we all?"

I asked them, "If you had to sum up Abu Dhabi in a single phrase, what would it be?"

Keith smiled, took a long pull on his cigar, and slowly blew it out. "The only thing certain about this place," he said, smoke trailing from the corners of his mouth, "is that it does not end well."

Epilogue

And I saw that all labor and all achievement spring from man's envy of his neighbor. This too is meaningless, a chasing after the wind. — *Ecclesiastes 4:4*

The story of Abu Dhabi's transformation does not end there. When the emirate's boom suddenly went bust in early 2011, it was a temporary setback, not a complete unraveling. Financially speaking, Abu Dhabi would be fine. The emirate's oil reserves would still be worth trillions of dollars as long as the world had need for the crude. It was certainly not as though Abu Dhabi stood in any danger of the fiscal insolvency that Dubai experienced during its own crash several years earlier.

In the years since, the dark cloud of the slowdown has already proven to have a silver lining. It gave breathing room to Abu Dhabi's leaders, government agencies, and developers, offering them a chance to regroup and reevaluate plans made in haste while the emirate was riding its wave of exuberant expansion. It forced the culling of wilder schemes and also provided an opportunity to refine sounder projects and initiatives. The reality check made Abu Dhabi's leaders bring their ambitious vision more in line with the laws of supply and demand, and may have led them to realize that even their reduced plans might take longer to implement than they had anticipated.

In that regard, Abu Dhabi has plenty of company. Nearly every significant effort in the history of city-building has been an exercise in delayed gratification. As the saying goes, Rome wasn't built in a day. Pierre L'Enfant's famous plan for what would become Washington, D.C., took nearly the entire century following its 1791 drafting to implement. Or look at the example of Brazil, whose citizens had considered moving their capital to a new location in the country's sparsely populated interior as far back as the late 1700s. It wasn't until the 1950s, however, that the mercurial Brazilian president Juscelino Kubitschek mustered the political and financial capital to build Brasilia, nearly bankrupting his country in the process.[1] Abu Dhabi could learn a thing or two from the Brazilian example, such as the importance of patience—and of restraint.

I returned to Abu Dhabi several times over the following two years while working in Afghanistan. At first, that city's mood was comparable to that of a funeral parlor. The newspapers were devoid of the formerly constant announcements of new, ever more awe-inspiring projects. Instead they carried stories intended to convey the message that everything was under control, like the Wizard of Oz saying "pay no attention to the man behind the curtain!" A number of high-profile project sites were left sitting conspicuously empty, including the spaces for the museums on Saadiyat. Meanwhile, other projects begun during the boom continued to come online, bloating the city's real estate glut even further. To help fill these scores of new buildings and stem the exodus of residents to low-rent Dubai, the government began requiring all employees at its public agencies and quasi-public companies to reside in Abu Dhabi. Amusingly enough, the official rationale given for this policy was "to avoid traffic and road accidents," an unintended acknowledgement that traffic was still as bad as ever.[2] Real estate consultants predicted that Abu Dhabi's market would remain suppressed for quite some time, possibly even a decade, while the oversupply slowly corrected itself.[3] The years of plenty were gone for the time being.

In the meantime, some of the emirate's projects continued trundling along, albeit with their scopes reduced. In January 2012 the Executive Council announced that the construction of the Saadiyat museums was back online, although it was still uncertain whether all five of the originally planned museums would be built.[4] Shortly thereafter the DOT unveiled its revised plans for the city's transit system, which were much smaller than those set forth in the original *Plan 2030*. The new network would feature two tram lines crisscrossing the downtown and a single Metro line running from the Mina Zayed port to the south end of the island near ADNEC.[5] Construction on the national railway began on schedule in mid-2011, with the Shah Line expected to be up and running by the end of 2013—although, disappointingly, the plans for the high-speed rail line between Abu Dhabi and Dubai were placed on indefinite hold.[6]

Although Abu Dhabi is hardly the first city in history to allow its dreams of grandeur to cross over into irrational exuberance and speculative excess, it had taken discrete steps to avoid such mistakes. Indeed, the very creation of *Plan 2030* and the UPC were intended to help the emirate grow in a measured, sustainable manner. What's more, Abu Dhabi's leaders had the added benefit of being able to watch and learn from the foibles of neighboring Dubai. So where did it all go wrong?

The answer probably has more to do with human nature than with anything exclusive to Abu Dhabi. Property seems to hold a unique place in the human psyche: "Buy land," Mark Twain said, "they're not making it anymore."[7] And real estate, by the very nature of its long project timelines and slow reaction to market forces, is given to cyclical extremes more than perhaps any other industry. Across the years and around the globe, people have bought into unsustainable real estate bubbles time and again despite the painful lessons of previous generations. New York City's decade-long boom in the 1920s, for example, spawned the construction of a host of skyscrapers, including the Chrysler Building, the Bank of Manhattan Trust Building, and the Empire State Building, all of which sat mostly empty throughout the subsequent years of the Great Depression. Indeed, financial analysts have noted an "unhealthy correlation" between skyscraper-building binges and subsequent financial crashes.[8] Even the richest city in the world is not immune to similar swings.

That being said, Abu Dhabi can certainly take steps to help avoid another bust in the future. The easiest of these would be to ensure that its plans and initiatives are grounded in economic reality—for example, by requiring every project to conduct a preliminary market study. And then, of course, the emirate's various entities should be made to stick to those plans, a prospect that is not so easy to accomplish in democratic societies but is entirely feasible under Abu Dhabi's autocratic system. The UPC, for instance, should be given the authority and resources to truly carry out its mandate as a government watchdog, forcing the developers in particular to work towards the public good and not just their own respective bottom lines.

In addition, Abu Dhabi's Emiratis must take a different approach to how their city is being built in a physical sense. Abu Dhabi's prolonged reliance on cheap South Asian labor for all of its construction work and its de facto policy of self-policing on building sites carry significant risks. There are, simply put, no shortcuts to quality. Perpetuating the status quo will only give the emirate exactly the kind of press coverage its leaders want to avoid, such as when construction was halted on New York University's fancy new Saadiyat campus in

December 2011 after a laborer was crushed by an improperly installed beam.[9] As it stands, it is likely only a matter of time before some building or bridge suffers an even more catastrophic failure.

In the professional sphere, the Emiratis must play a more active role in building their future. Currently they are neither numerous enough nor adequately educated and trained to do so without widespread reliance on foreigners. To be certain, Abu Dhabi's diversity is an asset, and the Emiratis should not (indeed, could not) jettison their foreign workforce entirely. But the present situation is untenable and is becoming more so. Many of the emirate's leaders and citizens already recognize this; now they must do something about it.

Abu Dhabi could also do much more to allow and even encourage open discussion about its plans for the future, something that manifestly does not take place at present. To be sure, transparency and public debate are Western values with little precedent in Emirati society. The Emiratis are fond of saying that they handle sensitive issues quietly amongst themselves rather than airing their dirty laundry in public. While this may be the case, and while it may have its advantages over the mudslinging that passes for civil discourse in certain Western nations, it also prevents Abu Dhabi's leaders and its rank-and-file citizens from hearing and dealing with hard realities. In a closed society it is all too easy to be carried away by delusional groupthink, as the spiraling "build it and they will come" mentality of the boom made clear. Yes, open discussion carries with it the risk of dissent, controversy, and even rancor, all of which the Emiratis shun. But a civilization that cannot criticize itself, much less accept others' criticisms, will not endure.

On that note, I realize that the parts of this book that look critically on certain aspects of modern Abu Dhabi may rub certain people the wrong way. My Emirati colleagues at the UPC, the rest of Abu Dhabi's citizens, and perhaps even the emirate's leaders—should any of them actually be reading this—may take umbrage at what I've said, as it contrasts with the perfect image they wish the world to see. To them I humbly reply, that's not what the world wants. When people seek out a place to live in, to work in, or even just to visit, they aren't looking for a stage-managed pseudo-utopia, a live-action version of *The Truman Show*. On the contrary, those cities that have had the greatest cultural and economic impact over the centuries—Babylon, Athens, Rome, Constantinople, Baghdad, London, New York, to say nothing of the great cities of the East—were all deeply flawed. And that's how I've attempted to portray Abu Dhabi: not terrible, but not perfect either.

Some Abu Dhabians may resent that this book's critiques come from an outsider, especially one who spent a mere two years in the emirate. All I can offer in response is that sometimes an external voice is needed to articulate that which cannot be expressed within a group. I've attempted to hold up a mirror to Emirati society, not out of scorn or spite, but out of genuine concern for a people who invited me into their young city-state and let me be a part of its formative years. For if the initial growth spurt of the 1960s and 1970s was Abu Dhabi's infancy, then the post-Zayed era has been its adolescence, a time to seek its own identity and place in the world. Teenage years are invariably full of mistakes and half-baked decisions. Every teenager can use a helping hand, an outside voice offering advice, whether he chooses to listen or not. To the extent my former hosts believe I have overstepped my bounds in doing so, I ask their understanding and forgiveness.

And it's not all bad news—far from it. Throughout this book I have attempted to include the positive along with the negative. There is plenty about Abu Dhabi that is worthy of admiration. In the brief span of a half-century its people have forged a modern metropolis in the middle of one of the world's least hospitable locations. One must at least applaud their resolve. And although Abu Dhabi is not the only rich Gulf state attempting to transform itself and diversify its economy, its leaders deserve credit for realizing that the emirate's present arrangement is unsustainable both economically and environmentally. If their vision has proven too ambitious for the time being, that is still certainly preferable to having done nothing. Theirs has been a deserving response to legendary planner Daniel Burnham's cry of "make no little plans, they have no magic to stir men's blood."[10]

The environmental aspects of Abu Dhabi's plans deserve particular commendation. The emirate has truly distinguished itself by trying to devise a more nature-friendly future. It is encouraging to see that these environmental initiatives have continued despite the slowdown. For example, in early 2013 Abu Dhabi launched the "Blue Carbon" project seeking to investigate how mangrove forests and other coastal biomes affect climate change and carbon mitigation.[11] Even the UPC's troubled Estidama program was eventually straightened out, more or less, and the agency began to require developers to follow its energy-efficiency guidelines. Of course, the boom also showed that Abu Dhabi's tree-hugging credentials are not inviolable; they can all too easily be suborned in the name of progress and profit. But at least the emirate's people have come to realize how important the issue is, and they have arrived at that realization much more quickly than did the West.

In its environmental aspects as in others, Abu Dhabi's present transformative juncture is rife with great rhetoric. What the emirate needs now is follow-through. It is relatively easy to cast grand visions and make sweeping plans. It is significantly harder to carry them through to fruition, especially in the face of unexpected setbacks. The Middle East of the modern era has been beset by leaders who made great promises about transforming their societies, only to fail, lose interest, or grow corrupt partway through. T.E. Lawrence (of *Lawrence of Arabia* fame) said of the region's peoples, "Arabs could be swung on an idea as on a cord.... Then the idea was gone and the work ended—in ruins.... They were a people of starts, for whom the abstract was the strongest motive, the process of infinite courage and variety, and the end nothing."[12] The challenge facing Abu Dhabi's citizens is to prove Lawrence wrong—to prove that they have staying power, that their city-sized experiment is not merely a flash in the pan.

The even greater challenge facing the people of Abu Dhabi is to not lose themselves in the process. Towards the end of my stay there, I reflected on my original thoughts regarding the emirate's transformation—of wondering whether Abu Dhabi could offer the world a lesson in balancing the modern with the traditional, as it claimed. In that regard, unfortunately, the experiment does not appear to be going well. The Emiratis' embrace of modernity and opulence has wreaked havoc on their cherished culture and traditions. Their society is wracked by unresolved tensions: the crisis in both their individual and public health, the breakdown of the family, dependence on the state's largesse, and the erosion of their customs and very identity. More than perhaps anything else, the Emiratis must use the present juncture to grapple with these problems.

For outsiders, it is perhaps all too easy to disdain the Emiratis as spoilt children who have lucked their way into their present prosperity and are fixated on acquiring even more wealth at the expense of everything else. Yet I wonder if the Europeans of the late eighteenth and nineteenth centuries felt similarly as they looked across the ocean at the upstart North American rabble just then emerging into prosperity. On Charles Dickens' inaugural trip to the United States, for example, he found Americans "overbearing, boastful, vulgar, uncivil, insensitive and above all acquisitive."[13] His fellow British writer Frances Trollope spent two years in Cincinnati during that city's own frontier-town boom in the 1830s, at the end of which she concluded that "every bee in the hive is actively employed in the search for honey.... Neither art, science, learning, nor pleasure can seduce them from their pursuit."[14]

From these sentiments we can perhaps conclude that the people of modern Abu Dhabi are not unique; throughout history, the obsession with gain has been so characteristic of rapidly growing cities that one might argue avarice and urbanization go hand in hand.

For my part, I can't help comparing Abu Dhabi to my hometown of Detroit, though at first glance they may seem to have little in common. Detroit enjoyed a meteoric rise that coincided with North America's industrial revolution of the late nineteenth and early twentieth centuries. By 1950 the city was the fifth largest in the United States, the heart of an American industrial empire that dominated the globe. Yet for all of Detroit's newfound greatness, its fortunes were hitched almost entirely to a single figurative wagon: the automotive industry. Over the following decades foreign competition and globalization sent that industry, and the city, into an economic tumble from which neither has yet to recover. Detroiters realized too late the perils of being a one-horse town.

The citizens of Abu Dhabi know this already. After all, the emirate's ongoing transformation has as its core purpose the diversification of the economy beyond its reliance on oil. If there is anything Abu Dhabians can learn from the example of Detroit, it is that they do not have forever to get it right; indeed, they have precisely as long as their oil lasts to find a new and better reason for Abu Dhabi's existence. This could be seventy years by some estimates; others put it closer to twenty-five or thirty in view of mounting demand from the developing countries of Asia. What is certain is that the reservoirs will one day run dry. The world may even come up with alternative fuels in the meantime. Either way, the clock is ticking. Time was one of the few things the Emiratis' Bedu forebears had in plenty; life in the desert was timeless. Now, amid all of Abu Dhabi's excess, time is the one luxury the emirate does not enjoy.

The Abu Dhabi of today has been called the richest city on Earth. Will it still be so in 2030? Or a hundred years after that? Herodotus, the ancient Greek historian, offers us a potent reminder that has held fast across the eons: "Most of those cities which were great once are small today; and those which used to be small were great in my own time.... Human prosperity never abides long in the same place."[15]

A Note About the Author

Michael Cameron Dempsey was born in Lansing, Michigan, in 1980. He graduated from the University of Michigan with a bachelor's degree in computer science in 2002 and a master's degree in urban planning in 2003. He was a recipient of the prestigious Bosch Foundation fellowship and spent 2003–2004 in Germany.

Michael saw firsthand the challenges of rebuilding and revitalizing America's cities while serving as an urban planner for the Detroit Economic Growth Corporation from 2004 to 2008. Michael had much to offer, and believed he had much to learn, so in 2008 became a civilian contractor in Iraq, working as senior governance advisor. From 2009 to 2011, he worked as senior associate planner for the Urban Planning Council of Abu Dhabi.

Michael spent the following two years as a senior field program officer for the U.S. Agency for International Development in Afghanistan, designing and overseeing projects to improve the everyday lives of Afghani citizens. In March 2013 he returned to the United States. In August 2013 his life was tragically abbreviated.

This book concerns Michael's experiences in Abu Dhabi. There is an Alice in Wonderland quality to the challenge of building a modern city in a society suddenly awash in prosperity—a dream for many urban planners.

With his experience in varying places as troubled as Detroit, Iraq, and Afghanistan, Michael learned the reality of urban planning outside the textbooks. Though he had reason to be cynical, he retained a core of idealism to his last day.

Let this book stand as a testament to Michael's life and work, and to the spirit of all those who spend their days striving to topple cultural barriers and to build a better world.

Chapter Notes

Introduction

1. Barney Gimbel, "The richest city in the world," *Fortune*, 12 March 2007.

Prologue

1. United Nations Department of Economic and Social Affairs (Population Division), *World Urbanization Prospects: The 2007 Revision* (New York: United Nations, 2008), 1.

2. "Detroit training helpful?" *Crain's Detroit Business*, 12 May 2008. The innocuous blurb prompted an angry letter to the editor that was printed in the 26 May 2008 issue of *Crain's*, in which the president of the urban development agency lamented "the real issue is that the amount of taxpayer money available to rebuild Iraq is so massive that a person can make more money rebuilding Baghdad than rebuilding an American city"—an absurdity with which I fully sympathized after witnessing firsthand the phenomenal waste of U.S. taxpayer resources in Iraq.

Chapter One

1. The quotes of Sheikh Zayed that introduce many of this book's chapters are taken from a listing published in Dubai's *Gulf News* newspaper nearly a year after Zayed's death. See "Shaikh Zayed in quotes," *Dubai Gulf News*, 31 October 2005, accessible at http://gulfnews.com/news/gulf/uae/general/shaikh-zayed-in-quotes-1.306268.

2. An online discussion about this topic can be viewed at http://boards.straightdope.com/sdmb/archive/index.php/t-559758.html, in which one commenter notes "it seems to be acceptable to the airlines to drop you into Dubai at 0230 but not into JFK at the same hour so flights to New York (for example) are scheduled for a good arrival time."

3. Two of those sources are Christopher Davidson, *Abu Dhabi: Oil and Beyond* (New York: Columbia University Press, 2009), which gives a well-researched political and cultural history of the emirate, and Mohammed Al Fahim, *From Rags to Riches: A Story of Abu Dhabi* (London: I.B. Tauris, 1998), a local's firsthand tale of living through Abu Dhabi's drastic changes during the second half of the twentieth cen-

tury. I do not wish to duplicate the superb accounts of these authors. The historical information in this chapter focuses on Abu Dhabi's development as a city and is intentionally brief. Another excellent source that outlines the history of Abu Dhabi's urban expansion is Yasser Elsheshtawy, "Cities of Sand and Fog: Abu Dhabi's Global Ambitions," in *The Evolving Arab City: Tradition, Modernity, and Urban Development*, ed. Yasser Elsheshtawy (London: Routledge, 2008), 258–304.

4. Frauke Heard-Bey, "The Tribal Society of the UAE and Its Traditional Economy," in *United Arab Emirates: A New Perspective*, ed. Ibrahim Al Abed and Peter Hellyer (London: Trident Press, 2001), 101.

5. Following Thesiger's convention, I use "Bedu" instead of the more common "Bedouin."

6. Heard-Bey, "The Tribal Society of the UAE and Its Traditional Economy," 102–109.

7. Elsheshtawy, "Cities of Sand and Fog," 262.

8. Yitzhak Oron, ed., *Middle East Record*, vol. 1, 1960 (Jerusalem: Weidenfeld & Nicolson, 1965), 407, notes that the Trucial States' population at the time was estimated at 80,000 (40,000 in Dubai alone) and also notes that Dubai was considered the administrative capital.

9. Al Fahim, *From Rags to Riches*, 113.

10. Ibid., 53.

11. See, e.g., Francis Owtram, *A Modern History of Oman: Formation of the State Since 1920* (London: I.B. Tauris, 2004), 71–72.

12. Jim Krane, *Dubai: The Story of the World's Fastest City* (London: Atlantic Books, 2010), 47.

13. Joel Kotkin, *The City: A Global History* (New York: Modern Library, 2005), 87.

14. Fred Halliday, *Arabia Without Sultans* (London: Penguin, 1974).

15. Davidson, *Abu Dhabi*, 70–71.

16. Elsheshtawy, "Cities of Sand and Fog," 270.

17. Henry David Thoreau, *Walden*, 150th anniversary edition (Princeton: Princeton University Press, 1971), 53.

18. Yasser Elsheshtawy, "Informal Encounters: Mapping Abu Dhabi's Public Spaces," *Built Environment* 37, no. 1 (2011): 95. Mr. Elsheshtawy provides a somewhat different history of Abu Dhabi's urban plans in this article than in his "Cities of Sand and

Fog," both of which also vary in places from what I encountered elsewhere in my research—perhaps not surprising for a city with so few written records.

19. Katsukiko Takahashi, "The Abu Dhabi Urbanization, 1967–1969," a presentation given to UPC staff on 12 December 2010.

20. Karen Attwood, "Building a City from the Sands," *Abu Dhabi National*, 11 September 2008. See also Fayza Hassan, "Abdel-Rahman Maklouf: A Passion for Order," *Al-Ahram Weekly Online*, issue 565, 20 December 2001, http://weekly.ahram.org.eg/2001/5 65/profile.htm, and Ann Wimsatt, "The houses that John built," *Abu Dhabi National*, 27 November 2010.

21. William H. Whyte, *City: Rediscovering the Center* (New York: Doubleday, 1988), 7.

22. Elsheshtawy, "Cities of Sand and Fog," 271.

23. Wimsatt, "The houses that John built."

24. Elsheshtawy, "Informal Encounters," 96.

Chapter Two

1. Jonathan Raban, *Arabia: A Journey Through the Labyrinth*, (London: Simon & Schuster, 1980), 40.

2. The rivalry between the two emirates precedes their respective existences, stretching back to when the Bani Yas tribe that would eventually found both settlements was still based in Liwa. The different subtribes that settled in Abu Dhabi and Dubai were frequently at odds with each other throughout the 18th and 19th centuries, periodically engaging in raids and skirmishes. In the modern era the competition has become one of stature. In the 1960s, Sheikh Shakhbut was so envious of the newly built bridge over Dubai's creek that he determined Abu Dhabi needed its own span—despite his opposition to almost every other kind of development in Abu Dhabi. The Maqta Bridge was duly erected at the southern end of Abu Dhabi, even though the creek it spanned was dry much of the time. See, e.g., D. Adams Schmidt, "Tiny Arab Sheikdom strives to outdo its neighbor," *New York Times*, 22 March 1969. The rivalry's ultimate stroke came in January 2010, when Dubai inaugurated the world's tallest tower—and announced it would be renamed from the Burj Dubai to the Burj Khalifa in honor of Abu Dhabi's ruler, acknowledging the ten billion dollars with which Abu Dhabi had helped Dubai stave off insolvency in the middle of its ongoing bust.

3. Economist Intelligence Unit, "Banks Express Concerns About Dubai's Property Market," *UAE Country Report*, August 2008.

4. David Conn, "Manchester City: a tale of love and money," http://theguardian.com/football/2012/ may/18/fall-and-rise-manchester-city 18 May 2012. The bounty played no small part in the club's 2012 Premiere League title, its first in forty-four years.

5. See also Richard Spencer, "Inside the world of the 'Kennedys of the Gulf,'" http://www.telegra ph.co.uk/news/worldnews/middleeast/unitedarabem irates/7549943/Inside-the-world-of-the-Kennedys-of-the-Gulf.html 4 April 2010, which notes that

such unclear lines between national and personal investments are common across the Gulf, "where families *are* the governments."

6. Viewable at http://media.abudhabi.ae/pdfdi rectview/en/147420/blaetterkatalog/blaetterkatalog/ pdf/complete.pdf.

7. Abu Dhabi Urban Planning Council, *Plan Abu Dhabi 2030: Urban Structure Framework Plan* (Abu Dhabi: Urban Planning Council, 2007), 6.

8. Ibid., 8, 31.

9. Ibid., 7.

10. The UPC was officially established by Emiri [Ruler's] Decree No. 23 for 2007.

11. *Plan Abu Dhabi 2030* formally defines the agency's mandate as follows: "The Abu Dhabi Urban Planning Council defines the shape of the Emirate, ensuring factors such as sustainability, infrastructure capacity, community planning and quality of life, by overseeing development across the city and the Emirate as a whole. The Abu Dhabi Urban Planning Council ensures best practice in planning for both new and existing urban areas…. By drawing on urban planning expertise locally, throughout the [Gulf Cooperation Council] and around the world, the UPC strives to be a global authority on the future of urban planning and design." See Urban Planning Council, *Plan Abu Dhabi 2030*, "Summary of Mandate," 1.

12. Urban Planning Council, *Plan Abu Dhabi 2030*, 7.

13. Emiratis still use falcons for sport hunting and pamper them like children. Abu Dhabi has a dedicated falcon hospital; falcons have their own passports and fly first class on Etihad Airlines.

14. Wuilfred Thesiger, *Arabian Sands* (New York: Dutton, 1959; republished 2006 by Motivate Publishing), 229–230. The notes in this book use page numbers from the 2006 edition.

15. Thesiger, *Arabian Sands*, 13.

16. Urban Planning Council, *Plan Abu Dhabi 2030*, 6.

Chapter Three

1. The utility companies argued that if their lines ran beneath the streets then they would need to tear up those streets in the event of maintenance or replacement, thereby necessitating the temporary closure of portions of the streets in question. That is, in fact, how it works everywhere else in the world: the utility company blocks off the street and reroutes traffic while they chop up the pavement and do their work. Abu Dhabi's utility companies did have a point to their argument in that the city's lack of frequent cross-streets made rerouting traffic more complicated and inefficient than in most other cities. However, the street design manual only contemplated running utility lines beneath a street's outermost lanes. With up to six lanes in each direction, most of Abu Dhabi's thoroughfares could afford losing a lane to a utility closure for a few weeks or months.

2. See, e.g., *Designing Roads That Guide Drivers to Choose Safer Speeds*, a 2009 study published by the Connecticut Department of Transportation, accessible at http://www.ct.gov/dot/LIB/dot/documents/dresearch/JHR_09–321_JH_04–6.pdf.

3. Abu Dhabi Urban Planning Council, *Plan Abu Dhabi 2030*, 39.

4. Essam Al Ghalib, "Tourist dies in Corniche hit and run," *Abu Dhabi National*, 11 May 2009.

5. The *Economist* was particularly infatuated with Vancouver, placing the city at the top of its annual survey of the world's most livable cities every year from 2002 to 2010.

6. This mantra of Larry's is repeated verbatim on page 10 of *Plan Abu Dhabi 2030*.

7. See http://gsec.abudhabi.ae/Sites/GSEC/Navigation/EN/MediaCentre/government-news, did=118724.html.

8. Jane Jacobs, *The Death and Life of Great American Cities* (New York: Random House, 1961). For example, in chapter 2, "The Uses of Sidewalks: Safety," Jacobs eloquently observes "under the seeming disorder of the old city, wherever the old city is working successfully, is a marvelous order for maintaining the safety of the streets and the freedom of the city. It is a complex order. Its essence is intricacy of sidewalk use, bringing with it a constant succession of eyes. This order is all composed of movement and change, and although it is life, not art, we may fancifully call it the art form of the city and liken it to the dance—not to a simpleminded precision dance with everyone kicking up at the same time, twirling in unison and bowing off en masse, but to an intricate ballet in which the individual dancers and ensembles all have distinctive parts which miraculously reinforce each other and compose an orderly whole. The ballet of the good city sidewalk never repeats itself from place to place, and in any one place is always replete with new improvisations."

9. Raban, *Arabia*, 102.

10. William Gibson, "Disneyland with the Death Penalty," *Wired* 1.04 (September/October 1993).

11. John Steinbeck, *Travels with Charley in Search of America* (New York: Viking, 1962, republished 2002 by Penguin), 70. Though Steinbeck is not on the required reading list of many (possibly any) graduate programs in architecture or planning, he should be. Consider another of his poignant urban observations on page 22: "American cities are like badger holes, ringed with trash—all of them—surrounded by piles of wrecked and rusting automobiles, and almost smothered with rubbish."

12. U.S. Department of State, *United Arab Emirates: Country Specific Information*, http://travel.state.gov/travel/cis_pa_tw/cis/cis_1050.html.

13. World Health Organization, *Global Status Report on Road Safety, 2009* (Geneva: WHO Department of Violence & Injury Prevention & Disability, 2009), 240–247.

14. Ryan Carter, "Gulf's region's road safety record 'appalling,'" *National*, 25 January 2011.

15. Krane, *Dubai*, 240.

16. Taken from Wikitravel's page on the UAE, http://wikitravel.org/en/United_Arab_Emirates, accessed 24 February 2013.

17. Manal Ismail, "Dangerous driving rooted in UAE culture, poll suggests," *National*, 30 July 2011.

18. Manal Ismail and Essam al Ghalib, "Three little girls who did not die in vain," *National*, 29 June 2011.

19. Commonly known in the built environment professions as the "Green Book," *A Policy on Geometric Design of Highways and Streets* has been published by AASHTO since the late 1930s; by 2011 its sixth edition had grown to more than one thousand pages. Despite its misleading name, the book was never intended to dictate a set of policies or standards and was rather meant to be a series of guidelines providing road designers with a range of options. Nevertheless, the Green Book has been held sacred by several generations of traffic engineers, to the detriment of cities across the United States and in other countries similarly deceived. Whenever you drive along a freeway trench that cuts like a festering wound through a formerly vibrant urban neighborhood, or when you orbit around the sodium-lit no-man's-lands encircled by a cloverleaf interchange, you have the Green Book to thank.

20. Thesiger, *Arabian Sands*, 231.

21. See, e.g., David Newland, *Vibration of the London Millennium Footbridge* (Cambridge: University of Cambridge Department of Engineering, 2006).

Chapter Four

1. See, e.g., William H. Whyte, *City*, 4, which contains a passage so lyrical it is worth repeating verbatim: "In the late sixties and early seventies the spectre of overcrowding was a popular worry. High density was under attack as a major social ill and so was the city itself ... Fifth Avenue through a telephoto lens: eight blocks of people, tense and unsmiling, squeezed into one; on the soundtrack, jackhammers, sirens, and a snatch of discordant Gershwin. This was the image of the city of the documentaries. Was there hope? Yes, a bright hope, says the narrator. A little child is shown running up a grassy hill in a new town. Back in the city, crews with hard hats and wrecking balls are shown demolishing old buildings. They are the good guys. As children look on, up go high, white towers, like Le Corbusier's radiant city. And they came to pass, these utopias, and with the best of intentions."

2. Thesiger, *Arabian Sands*, 184.

3. Besim Salim Hakim, *Arabic-Islamic Cities: Building and Planning Principles* (London: Kegan Paul, 1986), 33–39.

4. Thesiger, *Arabian Sands*, 78.

5. Thomas Barfield, *Afghanistan: A Cultural and Political History* (Princeton: Princeton University Press, 2010), 58. See also Thesiger, *Arabian Sands*, 245.

6. Thesiger, *Arabian Sands*, 66.

7. Al Fahim, *From Rags to Riches*, 113–116.

8. Davidson, *Abu Dhabi*, 28–30.

9. Gerhard Heck, *Abu Dhabi: Mit Al Ain und Dubai* (Stuttgart: DuMont Reiseverlag, 1996), 32.

10. Al Fahim, *From Rags to Riches*, 140.

11. Attwood, *Building a City From the Sands.*

12. Krane, *Dubai*, 267–269.

13. Davidson, *Abu Dhabi*, 110.

14. Ibn Khaldun, *The Muqaddimah: An Introduction to History*, vol. 2, trans. N.J. Dawood, Franz Rosenthal, and Bruce Lawrence (Princeton: Princeton University Press, 1969), 120.

15. Barfield, *Afghanistan*, 78.

16. Thesiger, *Arabian Sands*, 270.

17. See, e.g., "UAE 'coup plot' trial of 94 Islamist activists to begin," *BBC News*, 3 March 2013.

18. Economist Intelligence Unit, *Democracy Index 2010* (London: Economist Intelligence Unit, 2010), 7.

19. See, e.g., Spencer, "Inside the world of the 'Kennedys of the Gulf.'"

20. Kotkin, *The City*, 69.

21. *Constitution of the United Arab Emirates* (1971, as amended 1996), Article 9. Viewable at http://www.uaecabinet.ae/English/UAEGovernment/Pages/ConstitutionOfUAE.aspx.

22. *Constitution of the United Arab Emirates*, Article 2.

23. Christopher Davidson, "After Shaikh Zayed: The Politics of Succession in Abu Dhabi and the UAE," *Middle East Policy* 13, no. 1 (2006), 44.

24. See, for example, Bill Law, "Gulf states face hard economic truth about subsidies," *BBC News*, 18 December 2012, which states that "currently it is estimated that to meet their social contracts GCC countries need to take $80 out of the $110 they are paid for each barrel of oil."

25. Al Fahim, *From Rags to Riches*, 25.

26. Davidson, *Abu Dhabi*, 130–132.

27. For example, in the wake of the Arab Spring the government arrested ninety-four Emiratis and charged them with plotting a coup. See, e.g., "United Arab Emirates to try 94 accused of trying to seize power," http://www.cnn.com/2013/01/27/world/meast/uae-plot.

28. Thesiger, *Arabian Sands*, 84.

29. Ibid., 59.

30. Krane, *Dubai*, 268.

Chapter Five

1. Heard-Bey, "The Tribal Society of the UAE and Its Traditional Economy," 103–104.

2. Using the estimated world total of 100 million date palms given in A. Zaid, "The World Date Pro-duction: A Challenging Case Study," in *Proceedings of the Second International Conference on Date Palms* (United Arab Emirates University, 25–27 March 2001), 903. In its 20 August 2000 press release *Al Khaleej* 7763, WAM (the UAE's national news agency) gave the UAE's total date tree population as 40 million, of which 33 million are in the emirate of Abu Dhabi.

3. Malcolm Peck, *The United Arab Emirates: A Venture in Unity* (Boulder: Westview, 1986), 107–108.

4. Thesiger, *Arabian Sands*, 199.

5. Frauke Heard-Bey, *From Trucial States to United Arab Emirates: A Society in Transition*, 3rd ed. (Dubai: Motivate, 2005), 13.

6. The Czech automaker Skoda did actually produce a line of cars called the Felicia between 1994 and 2001—a boxy, utilitarian model that was far less exciting than Liz's ride.

7. William Gifford Palgrave, *Personal Narrative of a Year's Journey Through Central and Eastern Arabia* (London: Macmillan, 1866), 231. In this passage Palgrave was in fact describing the eastern coast of Qatar, which is fifty miles west of Sila'a. Having seen the shoreline in both places, I can attest that they are much the same.

8. Nadia Saleem, "UAE energy consumption beats global growth levels," *Gulf News*, 20 May 2008.

9. Himendra Mohan Kimar, "Abu Dhabi to construct 1,500 MW power plant," *Gulf News*, 17 October 2011.

10. Davidson, *Abu Dhabi*, 70–71.

11. Steven Stanek, "Nuclear deal 'model' for Arab states," *National*, 9 July 2009.

12. Hala Khalaf, "A cauldron of fumes and anxiety," *National*, 13 June 2009.

13. The entity was originally called Union Railway; it was formally changed to Etihad Rail in March 2011. For the sake of consistency, I have used the latter term throughout.

14. Thesiger, *Arabian Sands*, 231.

15. Khaldun, *Muqaddimah*, 178.

16. See, e.g., Edward William Lane, *Stories from the Thousand and One Nights*, vol. 16 (New York: P.F. Collier, 1909). The collection is more commonly known in English-speaking countries as *One Thousand and One Arabian Nights*, or simply as *Arabian Nights*.

17. Gloria Emerson, "Abu Dhabi, the unsociable baby boom town," *New York Times*, 10 March 1968.

Chapter Six

1. Abu Dhabi Urban Planning Council, *Plan Abu Dhabi 2030*, 10.

2. Krane, *Dubai*, 209.

3. India has the third-largest Muslim population in the world, with an estimated 177 million adherents—one-tenth of the world's Muslims (See, e.g., *The Future of the Global Muslim Population* by the Pew Research Center). However, India's Hindus

number over 800 million. This ratio is largely mirrored among the laborers who come to Abu Dhabi from the subcontinent, implying that the emirate's typical Indian laborer is, in all likelihood, Hindu.

4. Abdul-Ahad, Ghaith, "We need slaves to build monuments," *Guardian*, 7 October 2008.

5. Johann Hari, "The dark side of Dubai," http://www.independent.co.uk/voices/commentators /johann-hari/the-dark-side-of-dubai-1664368.html 7 April 2009. Although this article focuses on Dubai, the same labor practices it describes are widespread in Abu Dhabi—just not as widely reported.

6. See, e.g., Nesrine Malik, "Dubai's skyscrapers, stained by the blood of migrant workers," *Guardian*, 27 May 2011, in which Indian consular officials report that every week sees at least two Indian laborers in the UAE commit suicide.

7. Krane, *Dubai*, 207.

8. Suryatapa Bhattacharya, "Workers stranded without pay," *National*, 7 March 2011.

9. Suzanne Miers, *Slavery in the Twentieth Century: The Evolution of a New Global Pattern* (New York: Rowman & Littlefield, 2003), 345.

10. Nadim Kawach, "Abu Dhabi population growth picks up during oil boom," *Emirates 24/7 News*, 15 August 2010. See also Abdullah Rasheed, "Expat numbers rise rapidly as UAE population touches 6m," *Gulf News*, 7 October 2009.

11. Abdul-Ahad, "We need slaves to build monuments."

12. Thesiger, *Arabian Sands*, 44.

13. Samir Salama, "FNC aims for Emirati majority in demographic make-up by 2021," *Gulf News*, 26 January 2011.

14. Samir Salama, "Influx of foreigners spikes UAE population to 8.3m," *Gulf News*, 5 April 2011.

15. Thesiger, *Arabian Sands*, 199.

16. The slogan is repeated on page 17 of the bank's 2009 annual report, available at http://www.adcb. com/Images/AnnualReport_2009_En_tcm20-21097.pdf. On a more hubristic note, the report's introduction also boasts that ambition is "why people with money don't stop trying to make more money."

Chapter Seven

1. Gloria Emerson, "A mixture of goats and Cadillacs: Abu Dhabi is rolling in oil wealth," *New York Times*, 24 February 1968.

2. Afshan Ahmed, "Children spend too much time with nannies, study shows," *National*, 2 February 2011.

3. Bushra Hashemi and Larua Collins, "Expat teachers aren't the only ones leaving UAE schools," *National*, 14 May 2011.

4. Davidson, *Abu Dhabi*, 150–151.

5. Hashemi and Collins, "Expat teachers aren't the only ones leaving UAE schools."

6. Thesiger, *Arabian Sands*, 87.

7. Bana Qabbani, "UAE one of world's ten fattest countries," *National*, 2 February 2011.

8. Karen Leigh, "UAE spends $500m a year on diabetes 'epidemic'—experts," *Arabian Business*, 13 December 2010.

9. Faisal Masudi, "Insomnia epidemic grips city," *Gulf News*, 22 September 2011.

10. Abu Dhabi Urban Planning Council, *Plan Abu Dhabi 2030*, 37.

11. Rasha Elass, "Islamic family expert says high divorce rates are a disaster for Emirati society," *National*, 6 June 2009.

12. Maysam Ali, "Marriage in the UAE comes at a high price," *Gulf News*, 25 July 2008.

13. Thesiger, *Arabian Sands*, 231.

14. Ahmed, "Children spend too much time with nannies."

15. Krane, *Dubai*, 187.

16. *Constitution of the United Arab Emirates*, Article 7.

17. United States Department of State, "International Religious Freedom Report for 2011: United Arab Emirates," accessed 2 March 2013, http://www. state.gov/documents/organization/193123.pdf.

18. The pamphlet is distributed at the international airport and in hotels, and can be viewed at http://www.thenational.ae/deployedfiles/thenational/ Sound%20and%20Vision/PDFs%20and%20others/ proch.torsit.police1.jpg. Although kissing in public may happen often and could thus be seen as a legitimate concern, I never saw anyone cross-dress in Abu Dhabi, even at costume parties. Judging by the pamphlet's language, one would think the emirate was in imminent danger of being overrun by drag queens.

19. Bassama Al Jandaly, "Sharjah's decency law takes effect today," *Gulf News*, 26 September 2001.

20. See, e.g., Matthew Kalman, "Muslim family holds keys to sacred sepulchre," *San Francisco Chronicle*, 27 March 2005.

21. In reality, members of the Abu Dhabi royal family reportedly enjoy cozy relations with their high-level Israeli counterparts. For example, classified U.S. State Department cables released in the WikiLeaks fiasco claimed that Sheikh Abdullah, the UAE's foreign minister, enjoyed a "good personal relationship" with his Israeli counterpart, Tzipi Livni. Israel also supplies a significant portion of the UAE's military hardware through third-party channels. See, e.g., Barak Ravid, "WikiLeaks blows cover off Israel's covert Gulf states ties," *Haaretz*, 29 November 2010.

22. Thesiger, *Arabian Sands*, 231.

23. Jacob Riis, *How the Other Half Lives* (New York: Charles Scribner's Sons, 1890), 266.

Chapter Eight

1. Matt Kwong and John Henzell, "Corniche Beach to be reopened this month," *National*, 17 September 2009.

2. World Wildlife Federation, *Living Planet Report 2010*, 36; accessible at http://awsassets.panda. org/downloads/wwf_lpr2010_lr_en.pdf. The WWF's

Ecological Footprint measures a country's per-capita amounts of built-up land, cropland, fisheries, forests, grazing land, and carbon emissions.

3. Hari, "The dark side of Dubai."

4. Vesela Todorova, "Water price should go up, says scientist," *National*, 13 October 2008.

5. "Renewable internal freshwater resources per capita (cubic meters)," The World Bank, accessed 2 February 2013, http://data.worldbank.org/indicator/ER.H2O.INTR.PC.

6. Abu Dhabi Urban Planning Council, *Plan Abu Dhabi 2030*, 33.

7. Shuweihat actually consists of two plants, Shuweihat S1 and Shuweihat S2, with desalination capacities of 455,000 and 454,600 cubic meters per day respectively. See P.H. Gleick, *The World's Water, 2006–2007* (Washington: Island Press, 2006), 311.

8. "FAQ about desalination technology and use," Veolia Water, accessed 2 March 2013, http://www.sidem-desalination.com/en/Process/FAQ/.

9. Vesela Todorova, "Desalination threat to the growing Gulf," *National*, 31 August 2009.

10. The body of water between the Arabian Peninsula and the Iranian Plateau is more commonly called the Persian Gulf, a name whose usage stretches back at least as far as Greek and Roman historians in the first century of the Common Era. Many famous Arab scholars, including Ibn Khaldun and Ibn Battuta, used the same name in their own Arabic-language writings. The term "Arabian Gulf" arose with Arab nationalism in the 1950s and 1960s but has gained little traction outside of the Arab world. In the nations of the Arabian Peninsula, the body of water is invariably called the Arabian Gulf or just "the Gulf," and the Persian cognomen is strictly avoided. The continued wrangling by Arab countries and Iran over the name may seem like a petty spat, but it has real ramifications—for example, prompting the cancellation of the Islamic Solidarity Games in early 2010 (see "Islamic games axed over 'Persian Gulf,'" *Kuwait Times*, 18 January 2010).

11. Abu Dhabi Urban Planning Council, *Plan Abu Dhabi 2030*, 26.

12. S. Neelamani, K. Al-Salem, and K. Rakha, "Extreme Waves in the Arabian Gulf," *Journal of Coastal Research*, SI 50 (2007), 322.

13. An ecosystem and a natural wonder (containing one-fifth of the world's surface fresh water!) that my uncle has spent the better part of his adult life defending from a similar environmentally catastrophic fate as the Gulf. See Dave Dempsey, *On the Brink: The Great Lakes in the 21st Century* (East Lansing: Michigan State University Press, 2004) and *Great Lakes for Sale* (Ann Arbor: University of Michigan Press, 2008).

14. Coordinating Committee on Great Lakes Basic Hydraulic and Hydrologic Data, *Coordinated Great Lakes Physical Data, 1992*. See also Michigan Sea Grant College Program, *Extension Bulletins,*

1866–1870 (East Lansing: MSU Cooperative Extension Service, 1985)

15. Todorova, "Desalination threat to the growing Gulf."

16. Since the Dead Sea was already dead in an ecological sense long before humans arrived on the scene, a more appropriate comparison might be to the Aral Sea, the central Asian body of water that has been reduced to less than 10 percent of its original size by irrigation diversion and that has been rendered highly saline and polluted.

17. Erika Solomon, "Gulf corals adapt to warmer waters, still in peril," Reuters, 14 November 2010.

18. Todorova, "Desalination threat to the growing Gulf."

19. Vahid Sepehri, "Iran: spill, dolphin deaths spark alarm at Persian Gulf pollution," *Radio Free Europe*, 3 October 2007.

20. Thesiger, *Arabian Sands*, 79.

21. Jo Tatchell, *A Diamond in the Desert: Behind the Scenes in Abu Dhabi, the World's Richest City* (London: Grove Press, 2010), 132.

22. Mark Reisner, *Cadillac Desert: The American West and Its Disappearing Water* (New York: Penguin, 1986), 484.

23. Marc Gunther, "Building the world's cleanest city," *Fortune*, 7 March 2008.

24. John Vidal, "Desert state channels oil wealth into world's first sustainable city," *Guardian*, 20 January 2008.

25. Chris Stanton and Mahmoud Habboush, "UAE to house Irena headquarters," *National*, 30 June 2009.

26. Vesela Todorova, "Bu Tinah is given Dh28m push," *National*, 7 March 2010.

27. Abu Dhabi Urban Planning Council, *Plan Abu Dhabi 2030*, 26.

28. Jen Thomas, "Ancient secrets of Sir Bani Yas unveiled," *National*, 12 December 2010.

29. See, for example, Sharmila Dhal, "Pets in the UAE that nobody wants," *Gulf News*, 9 December 2010.

30. Hassan Hassan, "American gets suspended sentence on weapons charge," *National*, 13 December 2010.

31. Abu Dhabi Government, *Mangroves in the UAE: A Unique Ecosystem*, accessed 6 February 2012, https://www.abudhabi.ae/egovPoolPortal_WAR/app manager/ADeGP/Citizen?_nfpb=true&_pageLabel= p_citizen_homepage_hidenav&did=151944&lang=en.

Chapter Nine

1. In response to a lawsuit filed by displaced residents, the Michigan Supreme Court upheld the practice in its landmark 1982 *Poletown Neighborhood Council v. Detroit* decision. The United States Supreme Court reached a similar opinion on the use of eminent domain to promote economic development in the 2005 case of *Kelo v. City of New London*.

2. *Constitution of the United Arab Emirates*, Article 7.

3. Ibid., Article 39.

4. Zayed is rumored to have uttered this possibly apocryphal quote during a meeting with members of the Federal National Council on 5 April 1998.

5. Elsheshtawy, "Cities of Sand and Fog," 274–276.

6. Angela Giuffrida, Angela, "We only want to stay," *National*, 19 September 2009.

7. Mick O'Reilly, "The cost of bounced cheques," *Gulf News*, 12 July 2009.

8. Robert Worth, "Laid-Off Foreigners Flee as Dubai Spirals Down," *New York Times*, 11 February 2009.

9. Dina Aboul Hosn, "Violations, fines, and traffic points," *Gulf News*, 2010.

10. *Constitution of the United Arab Emirates*, Article 25.

11. Hassan Hassan, "Court rules on domestic discipline," *National*, 18 October 2010.

12. Thesiger, *Arabian Sands*, 245.

13. Al Fahim, *From Rags to Riches*, 152.

14. Abu Dhabi Urban Planning Council, *Plan Abu Dhabi 2030*, 7.

15. *Constitution of the United Arab Emirates*, Article 40.

16. Charlie Hamilton and Hiba Haddad, "Butchery counter closed after third hygiene breach," *National*, 13 July 2009.

17. Erin Conroy, "Store-bought salad leaves tainted with E. coli," *National*, 29 December 2010.

18. Elsheshtawy, "Informal Encounters," 92.

19. *Constitution of the United Arab Emirates*, Article 31.

20. Ibid., Article 30.

21. Tatchell, *A Diamond in the Desert*, 144.

Chapter Ten

1. Jon Muller, "Sheikh Zayed Bridge back on track," *Abu Dhabi Week*, 26 May 2010.

2. The emirates of Dubai and Sharjah learned this the hard way from a series of catastrophic tower fires, including one on Dubai's iconic Palm Island during its construction. See, e.g., "Safety concerns over building standards in UAE towers," *BBC News Online*, 22 December 2012, http://www.bbc.co.uk/news/world-middle-east-20823724.

3. Negar Azimi, "A Cultural Island: Abu Dhabi Imports Cultural Institutions to Build Upon Tradition," in *Al Manakh 2*, ed. Rem Koolhaas (Amsterdam: Archis, 2010), 229.

4. K. Daniel, "Bazaar buzz: The old world charm of Hamdan Souk in Abu Dhabi makes shopping a pleasure," *Gulf News*, 17 June 2002.

5. Elsheshtawy, "Cities of Sand and Fog."

6. Raban, *Arabia*, 128.

7. C. Sands, "End of an era: at midnight, Abu Dhabi's old souq will be history," *Gulf News*, 1 March 2005.

8. Rana Jimaa, "Aldar: Abu Dhabi's Trust Tower 70% complete,'" *ConstructionWeekOnline*.com, 6 July 2011.

9. The reader should not infer from this critique that I have a vendetta against Lord Foster. On the contrary, I am normally a fan of his work and that of his firm, and I believe that he is one of the few international starchitects who deserves his outsized reputation. That is precisely what made his Central Market project all the more disappointing—an unfortunate example of how the no-holds-barred avarice of Abu Dhabi's boom could bring out the worst in anyone.

10. *Huffington Post*, 8 June 2010. "Capital Gate Named World's Furthest Leaning Tower."

11. Robert Byron, *The Road to Oxiana* (London: Pimlico, 1937, republished 2004 by Macmillan), 378.

12. Rayeesa Absal, "Trapped workers rescued from Reem Island building blaze," *Gulf News*, 26 September 2009. The *National* did not report these details.

13. Praveen Menon and Rasha Elass, "Building collapses in Dubai," *National*, 17 August 2009.

Chapter Eleven

1. Abu Dhabi Urban Planning Council, *Plan Abu Dhabi 2030*, p.7

2. Nicolas Berube, "Real estate fever: leave Vancouver" (translated), *La Presse*, 15 October 2011.

3. Vancouver's inflated housing prices proved unsustainable; they began flattening out after 2009 and dropped 6.3 percent between November 2011 and November 2012. See Tracy Sherlock and Craig Wong, "Vancouver real estate slowdown helps sink national housing sales forecast," *Vancouver Sun*, 17 December 2012.

Chapter Twelve

1. William Kremer, "The pleasures and the perils of the open-plan office," *BBC News*, 27 March 2013.

Chapter Thirteen

1. Thesiger, *Arabian Sands*, 235.

2. This claim is made in a number of sources, including the obituary of Sheikh Zayed printed in *The Telegraph* on 4 November 2004, accessible at http://www.telegraph.co.uk/news/obituaries/1475775/Sheikh-Zayed-bin-Sultan-Al-Nahyan.html.

3. Thesiger, *Arabian Sands*, 239.

4. That being said, the exposition that follows has a number of parallels to Christopher Davidson's treatment of the Al Nahyans in his excellent *Abu Dhabi: Oil and Beyond*—enough to make me wonder whether Mr. Davidson came across the same clan-

destine family tree during his research. At any rate, the reader with an interest in Abu Dhabi's politics should run, not walk, to get Mr. Davidson's book.

5. This assessment came in a 31 August 2009 cable from the U.S. ambassador to the UAE, titled "Scenesetter for the President's meeting with Shaykh Mohammed bin Zayed," which characterized the relationship between Sheikh Khalifa and his younger brother Sheikh Mohammed as follows: "Shaykh Mohammed bin Zayed Al-Nahyan, or MbZ in USG [U.S. Government] speak, is the man who runs the United Arab Emirates. Officially he is the Crown Prince of the Emirate of Abu Dhabi (the most important principality of the seven emirate confederation) and his only federal title is Deputy Supreme Commander of the Armed Forces; in fact he is the key decision maker on national security issues. He will make deferential noises about his 'boss' (elder half-brother President Khalifa, a distant and uncharismatic personage), but we assess that he has authority in all matters except for final decisions on oil policy and major state expenditures." The disclosure of this rather indelicate communique in the Wikileaks scandal was one of the suspected reasons for the U.S. ambassador's hasty departure from Abu Dhabi in late 2010. Among the cable's other cheeky commentary, it quips "MbZ ... is seen as a particularly dynamic member of the generation succeeding the geriatric cases who have dominated the region for decades."

6. See, e.g., Davidson, "After Shaikh Zayed."

7. Rania Abouzeid, "Abu Dhabi death could spark dynastic struggle," *Time*, 30 March 2010.

8. Residents of the Seychelles were none too happy about Sheikh Khalifa's house. The island nation's government was accused of circumventing land ownership laws and environmental regulations to allow the seven-story palace to be built on the island's tallest hill, in exchange for millions of dirhams of foreign aid from the UAE. The palace's construction caused massive erosion and contaminated a water source used by thousands of locals, who were understandably furious. Some officials claimed that the contamination was the worst environmental disaster in the Seychelles' history. See, e.g., Margaret Copker, "Sheikh Abode a Sore Point in Seychelles," *Wall Street Journal*, 9 September 2010.

9. Heard-Bey, "The Tribal Society of the UAE and Its Traditional Economy," 115.

10. Thesiger, *Arabian Sands*, 252.

11. Further details on this episode are given on pages 137–139 of the *9/11 Commission Report*, in the section titled "The Desert Camp, February 1999." The report notes that the CIA and the Pentagon continued to track bin Laden's visits to the hunting camp after the aborted missile strike, evidently hoping to target him in a manner that would not result in the deaths of Abu Dhabi royals. However, the same antiterrorism czar who vetoed the missile strike then phoned his Emirati counterparts—allegedly

without the CIA's knowledge or approval—and let them know that the Americans were tracking bin Laden's visits. Within a week the camp had been hastily dismantled and the Emirati sheikhs were gone—as was bin Laden. The lead CIA official in the field and the CIA's bin Laden unit chief later identified this missed opportunity as the best chance to have eliminated bin Laden prior to the tragic events of 11 September 2001.

Chapter Fourteen

1. Ramona Ruiz, "Technical problem cancels Tiesto live concert in Abu Dhabi," *National*, 1 October 2010.

2. Otto Pohl, "What $3 Billion, More or Less, Buys: A Hotel Built for Kings," *New York Times*, 17 March 2005.

3. Gimbel, "The richest city in the world."

4. Aaron Cutler, "Abu Dhabi Film Festival 2010: An Interview with Executive Director Peter Scarlet," *Slant Magazine*, 29 October 2010.

5. Seaman, Anna, "New footage of classic film *Metropolis* unearthed," *National*, 22 October 2010.

Chapter Fifteen

1. Justin Thomas, "The biggest gender imbalance? It's not in China," *National*, 3 February 2010.

2. Charlie Hamilton, "Police act to dispel fears in rape cases," *National*, 13 December 2009.

3. Nin-Hai Tseng, "How China's lonely bachelors are helping its economy grow," *Fortune*, 15 February 2013.

4. Bill Loomis, "Drinking and dining in Old Detroit," *Detroit News*, 22 January 2012.

5. Elsheshtawy, "Cities of Sand and Fog," 298.

6. Augustine, *The City of God Against the Pagans*, trans. R.W. Dyson (New York: Cambridge, 1998), xix.24.

7. Lawrence Osborne, *Bangkok Days* (London: Vintage, 2010), 63.

8. Thesiger, *Arabian Sands*, 83.

9. Elass, "Islamic family expert says high divorce rates are a disaster for Emirati society."

10. United States Department of State, *Trafficking in Persons Report, 2010* (Washington: U.S. Department of State). See also Krane, *Dubai*, 215–218.

11. Haneen Dajani and Ola Salem, "Human trafficking cases rising, say officials," *National*, 9 March 2011.

12. Samir Salama, "Seven men get life terms for human trafficking in Abu Dhabi," *Gulf News*, 20 January 2010.

13. Such as Federal Law No. 51 of 2006.

14. Dajani and Salem, "Human trafficking cases rising, say officials."

Chapter Sixteen

1. Al Khalisi, "Gym hazards during Ramadan," *National,* 6 September 2009.

2. Simon Mills, "Invasion of the Bling-ion-aires," *Daily Mail,* 9 August 2010.

3. United Nations, "Yemen," in *World Statistics Pocketbook* (New York: United Nations, 2009).

4. Heard-Bey, "The Tribal Society of the UAE and its Traditional Economy," 101.

5. Mahmoud Habboush, "Abu Dhabi pledges 2.4bn to Yemen," *National,* 17 December 2009.

6. Raban, *Arabia,* 143

Chapter Seventeen

1. Salam Al Amir, "Lost passport leads to alcohol conviction," *National,* 25 February 2011.

2. Binsal Abdul Kader, "Drink driving: Survey reveals shocking truths," *Gulf News,* 10 June 2012.

3. Noorhan Barakat, "More drink driving incidents recorded in Dubai," *Gulf News,* 9 October 2012.

4. Lee Hoaglund, "Sheikh Zayed Bridge officially opens," *National,* 26 November 2010. The article conspicuously omits the details about the cost overruns and delays.

5. Hassan Hassan and Awad Mustafa, "Two fined for taking Yas Marina racetrack photos," *National,* 1 February 2011.

6. The reader curious as to the inspiration for this section may wish to consult Dante Alighieri, *The Inferno,* trans. Henry Wadsworth Longfellow (1867, republished 2003 by Modern Library), particularly the introduction to Canto I.

7. Thesiger, *Arabian Sands,* 112.

Chapter Eighteen

1. Further details on the study's results are reported in Ivan Gale, "Demand high for inter-emirate passenger rail: study," *National,* 10 November 2010.

2. Gordon Watts, "Focused development for communities in the capital," *National,* 21 December 2010

3. The UPC's ratified Urban Street Design Manual can be downloaded at http://www.upc.gov.ae/guidelines/urban-street-design-manual.aspx?lang=en-US.

4. Haneen Dajani, "Speed limits to rise in Abu Dhabi 'to make roads safer,'" *National,* 25 October 2010.

5. Abdulkhaleq Abdullah, "An ascendant Abu Dhabi sees its moment of history," *Gulf News,* 26 September 2010.

6. Rayeesa Absal, "Gridlock in Abu Dhabi as minor accidents, rush hour wreak havoc," *Gulf News,* 26 September 2010.

7. Awad Mustafa and Caline Malek, "Blackberry cuts make roads safer, police say," *National,* 15 October 2011.

8. Should any talent scouts happen to read this book, the station in question is on the west side of Muroor Road between 27th and 29th streets.

9. *Economist,* "Yemen's bad habit: You can't easily qat it out," 30 September 2010.

10. Samuel Hugh Moffett, *A History of Christianity in Asia* (New York: Orbis, 1998), 274.

11. Thesiger, *Arabian Sands,* 79.

12. Khaldun, *Muqaddimah,* 119.

Chapter Nineteen

1. Neeraj Gangal, "Abu Dhabi rents fall 8% in Q1, Asteco says," *Arabian Business,* 10 April 2011.

2. Abu Dhabi Urban Planning Council, *Plan Abu Dhabi 2030,* 8.

3. Bradley Hope, "Aldar seeks assistance from state after loss," *National,* 10 November 2010. See also Bradley Hope, "Aldar properties posts Dh12.65bn loss," *National,* 9 February 2011.

4. *Zawya Dow Jones,* "Lord Foster visits Central Market," 27 November 2010.

5. Martin Dokoupil, "UAE swings into $11bn fiscal surplus in 2011," Reuters, 10 June 2012.

6. Tamsin Carlisle, "Masdar City clips another $2.5bn from price tag," *National,* 1 December 2010. Doing away with the personal rapid transit system was perhaps just as well, as it had been dogged by persistent technical problems during its trials.

7. Lin Noueihed, "Peddler's martyrdom launched Tunisia revolution," Reuters, 19 January 2011.

8. Thesiger, *Arabian Sands,* 233.

9. Lane, *Stories from the One Thousand and One Nights,* 566–578.

Epilogue

1. James Holston, *The Modernist City: An Anthropological Critique of Brasilia* (Chicago: University of Chicago Press, 1989). See also Gary Duffy, "Brazil's 'new' capital set to celebrate 50 years," *BBC News,* 6 April 2010.

2. Parag Deulgaonkar, "Abu Dhabi government staff residence rule to have no immediate effect on rents," *Emirates 24/7,* 16 September 2012. See also Stanley Carvalho and Raissa Kasolowsky, "Abu Dhabi presses state employees to live there," Reuters, 13 September 2012.

3. Lucy Barnard, "UAE property market to remain a tale of two different cities," *National,* 19 December 2012.

4. Samia Badih, "Revival of Saadiyat museums 'energises Abu Dhabi tourism,'" *Gulf News,* 26 January 2012.

5. Samir Salama, "Abu Dhabi begins work on Metro and light-rail design," *Gulf News,* 28 March 2012. See also "Abu Dhabi reduces size of metro system," *Technical Review Middle East,* 28 March 2012, accessible at http://www.technicalreviewmiddleeast.com/logistics/rail/abu-dhabi-reduces-size-of-

metro-system.

6. Rym Ghazal, "National railway to begin construction in June," *National*, 3 April 2011. See also Ivan Gale, "Plans for passenger rail link between Abu Dhabi and Dubai shelved," *National*, 24 March 2011.

7. Of course, Mr. Twain didn't have the benefit of witnessing the island-making exploits of the Gulf's city-states.

8. See, e.g., "Skyscrapers 'linked with impending financial crashes,'" *BBC News*, 10 January 2012.

9. Jen Thomas, "Half-tonne pillar crushed labourer," *National*, 26 January 2012.

10. Charles Moore, "XXV Closing in 1911–1912," in *Daniel H. Burnham, Architect, Planner of Cities*, vol. 2 (Boston: Houghton Mifflin, 1921).

11. Caline Malek, "Eco-treasure hiding in Abu Dhabi mangroves," *National*, 18 March 2013.

12. Thomas Edward Lawrence, *Seven Pillars of Wisdom: A Triumph* (Oxford: private edition, 1922; republished 2001 by Wilder), chapter 3.

13. "When Charles Dickens fell out with America," *BBC News Magazine*, 13 February 2012.

14. Kotkin, *The City*, 92.

15. Herodotus, *The Histories*, trans. Aubrey de Selincourt (New York: Penguin, 1954, rev. 1996), 5.

Bibliography

Abu Dhabi Government. *Mangroves in the UAE: A Unique Ecosystem.* https://www.abudhabi.ae/egovPoolPortal_WAR/appmanager/ADeGP/Citizen?_nfpb=true&_pageLabel=p_citizen_homepage_hidenav&did=151944&lang=en (accessed 6 February 2012).

Abu Dhabi Urban Planning Council. *Plan Abu Dhabi 2030: Urban Structure Framework Plan.* Abu Dhabi: Abu Dhabi Urban Planning Council, 2007.

Al Fahim, Mohammed. *From Rags to Riches: A Story of Abu Dhabi.* London: I.B. Tauris, 1998.

Alighieri, Dante. *The Inferno,* translated by Henry Wadsworth Longfellow. 1867. Reprint, Modern Library, 2003.

Augustine. *The City of God Against the Pagans,* translated by R.W. Dyson. New York: Cambridge, 1998.

Azimi, Negar. "A Cultural Island: Abu Dhabi Imports Cultural Institutions to Build Upon Tradition." In *Al Manakh 2,* edited by Rem Koolhaas. Amsterdam: Archis, 2010.

Barfield, Thomas. *Afghanistan: A Cultural and Political History.* Princeton: Princeton University Press, 2010.

Byron, Robert. *The Road to Oxiana.* London: Pimlico, 1937. Reprint, Macmillan, 2004.

Constitution of the United Arab Emirates. 2 December 1971, as amended 1996.

Davidson, Christopher. "After Shaikh Zayed: The Politics of Succession in Abu Dhabi and the UAE." *Middle East Policy* 13, no. 1, pp. 42–59.

_____. *Abu Dhabi: Oil and Beyond.* New York: Columbia University Press, 2009.

Dempsey, Dave. *On the Brink: The Great Lakes in the 21st Century.* East Lansing: Michigan State University Press, 2004.

Economist Intelligence Unit. "Banks Express Concerns About Dubai's Property Market." In *UAE Country Report,* August 2008.

_____. *Democracy Index 2010.* London: Economist Intelligence Unit, 2010.

Elsheshtawy, Yasser. "Cities of Sand and Fog: Abu Dhabi's Global Ambitions." In *The Evolving Arab City: Tradition, Modernity, and Urban Development,* edited by Yasser Elsheshtawy. London: Routledge, 2008.

_____. "Informal Encounters: Mapping Abu Dhabi's Urban Public Spaces." *Built Environment* 37, no. 1 (2011): 92–113.

Gleick, P.H. *The World's Water, 2006–2007.* Washington: Island Press, 2006.

Hakim, Besim Salim. *Arabic-Islamic Cities: Building and Planning Principles.* London: Kegan Paul, 1986.

Halliday, Fred. *Arabia Without Sultans.* London: Penguin, 1974.

Heard-Bey, Frauke. *From Trucial States to United Arab Emirates: A Society in Transition.* 3rd ed. Dubai: Motivate, 2005.

_____. "The Tribal Society of the UAE and Its Traditional Economy." In *United Arab Emirates: A New Perspective,* edited by Ibrahim Al Abed and Peter Hellyer. London: Trident Press, 2001.

Heck, Gerhard. *Abu Dhabi: Mit Al Ain und Dubai.* Stuttgart: DuMont Reiseverlag, 1996.

Herodotus. *The Histories,* translated by Aubrey de Selincourt. New York: Penguin, 1954, rev. 1996.

Holston, James. *The Modernist City: An Anthropological Critique of Brasilia.* Chicago: University of Chicago Press, 1989.

Jacobs, Jane. *The Death and Life of Great American Cities.* New York: Random House, 1961.

Khaldun, Ibn. *The Muqaddimah: An Introduction to History,* translated by N.J. Dawood, Franz Rosenthal, and Bruce Lawrence. Vol. 2. Princeton: Princeton University Press, 2004.

Kotkin, Joel. *The City: A Global History.* New York: Modern Library, 2005.

Krane, Jim. *Dubai: The Story of the World's Fastest City.* London: Atlantic Books, 2009.

Lane, Edward William. *Stories from the Thousand and One Nights.* New York: P.F. Collier & Son, 1909.

Lawrence, Thomas Edward. *Seven Pillars of Wisdom: A Triumph.* Private ed. Oxford, 1922; republished 2001 by Wilder.

Michigan Sea Grant College Program. *Extension Bulletins, 1866–1870.* East Lansing: Michigan State University Cooperative Extension Service, 1985.

Miers, Suzanne. *Slavery in the Twentieth Century: The Evolution of a New Global Pattern.* New York: Rowman & Littlefield, 2003.

Moffett, Samuel Hugh. *A History of Christianity in Asia.* New York: Orbis Books, 1998.

Moore, Charles. "XXV Closing in 1911–1912." In *Daniel H. Burnham: Architect, Planner of Cities.* Vol. 2. Boston: Houghton Mifflin, 1921.

National Commission on Terrorist Attacks upon the United States. *The 9/11 Commission Report: Final Report of the National Commission on Terrorist Attacks upon the United States.* Washington: National Commission on Terrorist Attacks upon the United States, 2004.

Neelamani, S., K. Al-Salem, K. Rakha. "Extreme Waves in the Arabian Gulf." *Journal of Coastal Research* SI 50 (2007).

Newland, David. *Vibration of the London Millennium Footbridge.* Cambridge: University of Cambridge Department of Engineering, 2006.

Oron, Yitzhak, ed. *Middle East Record* 1 (1960). Jerusalem: Weidenfeld & Nicolson, 1965.

Osborne, Lawrence. *Bangkok Days.* London: Vintage, 2010.

Owtram, Francis. *A Modern History of Oman: Formation of the State Since 1920.* London: I.B. Tauris, 2004.

Palgrave, William Gifford. *Personal Narrative of a Year's Journey Through Central and Eastern Arabia.* London: Macmillan, 1866.

Peck, Malcolm. *The United Arab Emirates: A Venture in Unity.* Boulder: Westview, 1986.

Raban, Jonathan. *Arabia: A Journey Through the Labyrinth.* London: Simon & Schuster, 1980.

Reisner, Mark. *Cadillac Desert: The American West and Its Disappearing Water.* New York: Penguin, 1986.

Riis, Jacob. *How the Other Half Lives.* New York: Charles Scribner's Sons, 1890.

Steinbeck, John. *Travels with Charley in Search of America.* New York: Viking, 1962; republished 2002 by Penguin.

Takahashi, Katsukiko. *The Abu Dhabi Urbanization, 1967–1969.* A presentation given to UPC staff on 12 December 2010.

Tatchell, Jo. *A Diamond in the Desert: Behind the Scenes in Abu Dhabi, the World's Richest City.* London: Grove, 2010.

Thesiger, Wilfred. *Arabian Sands.* New York: Dutton, 1959; republished 2006 by Motivate.

Thoreau, Henry David. *Walden.* 150th anniversary edition. Princeton: Princeton University Press, 1971.

United Nations Department of Economic and Social Affairs, Population Division. *World Urbanization Prospects: The 2007 Revision.* New York: United Nations, 2008.

United Nations. "Yemen." In *World Statistics Pocketbook.* New York: United Nations, 2009.

United States Department of State. "International Religious Freedom Report for 2011: United Arab Emirates." http://www.state.gov/documents/organization/193123.pdf (accessed 2 March 2013).

_____. *Trafficking in Persons Report, 2010.* Washington: U.S. Department of State.

_____. *United Arab Emirates: Country Specific Information.* http://travel.state.gov/travel/cis_pa_tw/cis/cis_1050.html (accessed 1 March 2013).

Whyte, William H. *City: Rediscovering the Center.* New York: Doubleday, 1988.

World Health Organization. *Global Status Report on Road Safety, 2009.* Geneva: WHO Department of Violence and Injury Prevention and Disability, 2009.

World Wildlife Federation. *Living Planet Report, 2010.* http://awsassets.panda.org/downloads/wwf_lpr2010_lr_en.pdf (accessed 15 February 2013).

Zaid, A. "The World Date Production: A Challenging Case Study." In *Proceedings of the Second International Conference on Date Palms.* United Arab Emirates University, 25–27 March 2001.

Journals, Newspapers, and Magazines

Abu Dhabi National
Abu Dhabi Week
Arabian Business
BBC News
Built Environment
ConstructionWeekOnline.com
Crain's Detroit Business
Detroit News
Economist
Emirates 24/7 News
Fortune
Gulf News
Haaretz
Huffington Post
Journal of Coastal Research
London Daily Mail
London Guardian
London Independent
London Telegraph
Montreal La Presse
New York Times
Radio Free Europe
Reuters
San Francisco Chronicle

Slant Magazine
Technical Review Middle East
Time
Vancouver Sun

Wall Street Journal
Wired
Zawya Dow Jones

Index

Numbers in *bold italics* indicate pages with photographs.